MIMESIS
INTERNATIONAL

ASIAN PHILOSOPHICAL TEXTS
No. 1

G000080128

Book series edited by Roman Paşca (Kyoto University, Japan) and Takeshi Morisato (Sun Yat-Sen University, China)

Editorial Board

ASIAN PHILOSOPHICAL TEXTS

Exploring Hidden Sources

Edited by
Takeshi Morisato and Roman Paşca

MIMESIS
INTERNATIONAL

This book is published with the support of the Research Centre for East Asian Studies (EASt) at Université libre de Bruxelles (ULB), the Research Institute for Japanese Studies (RIJS) at Kanda University of International Studies, and the Graduate School of Letters at Kyoto University.

Isbn: 9788869772245
Book series: *Asian Philosophical Texts*, n. 1

CONTENTS

TRANSLATIONS

Takeshi Morisato (Sun Yat-Sen University)
Roman Pașca (Kyoto University)

INTRODUCTION

A small "opinions" corner in an evening news can occasionally thrust us into profound self-reflection, or at least help us to set forth a more dramatic self-interpretation of life in academia than many of the headline news. It was probably the *News Watch 9* at NHK in Japan (or perhaps one of the other similar programs from the commercial television companies in the Kanto area) that conducted such an interesting survey. The reporters from the show interviewed one hundred Chinese students enrolled at a private university in the suburb of Shanghai. At the same time, they managed to talk to another set of one hundred students at a private university in a suburb of Tokyo. They asked a single question to two hundred college students and it concerned something our students would usually be very good at answering: Who are the most famous people that you know? A twist in this questionnaire for the East Asian undergraduates was that they were only allowed to list the names that are supposedly famous in the other country.

The finding was quite shocking to those who lived in Japan. Chinese students listed not only so-called "celebrities" like Japanese actors, musicians, and J-pop idols, but also many of the leading authors that literary critics would categorize under the label of "contemporary Japanese literature." One of the famous names in the top twenty in the ranking (made by the Chinese students) received the Akutagawa Prize the year before the survey was conducted. This certainly highlighted the fact that his book was immediately translated into Chinese, which led to a series of guest lectures at several universities in Shanghai. (The NHK did another documentary about the Chinese reception of his book and his discussion with literature students was occasionally carried out in Japanese!) The list of Japanese celebrities that the Chinese students created was more or less what Japanese students of the same generation at another campus would create if they were asked to tell us about their own country. What was shocking about this survey to the Japanese viewers was the contrast. Japanese students failed to name any of the contemporary Chinese celebrities, artists, musicians, or writers, but as the news anchor remarked *en passant* with a bitter smile, "almost all of the top twenty in the list of the famous Chinese names come from China before the common era...." China and Japan have been neighboring countries for centuries and their historical development certainly enjoys a great degree of mutual influence. If one looks at any sentence written in these languages, one can immediately recognize their cultural and intellectual proximity. This is more obvious to those who can read classical Chinese and classical Japanese philosophical texts. However, this simple survey from a TV show in the twenty-first century, which was conducted at a very superficial level, is enough to demonstrate that there is a great discrepancy in our mutual, cross-cultural understanding of ourselves in East Asia today.

As specialists of comparative and Asian philosophy, the editors of this book cannot help but imagine the possible findings from conducting a similar survey in our own domain of philosophy. What would be the honest result if we ask contemporary philosophers in Europe, North America, and Asia: "Who are the famous thinkers in the history of humanity?" If we ask the same question to philosophy scholars in Asia and any other parts of the world that are currently (mis)labeled as representing "non-western" intellectual traditions, would their answers demonstrate a well-balanced, mutual understanding? We think that the results of these surveys would be far more devastating than the one given to two hundred students in China and Japan. If most philosophy scholars in Europe or North America were asked to name famous thinkers from China, their answers might not be any more different from the answers that the Japanese undergraduates gave to the news program about Chinese celebrities. In fact, we would be impressed if a philosophy scholar or student from anywhere in the world could name ancient Chinese names, such as Confucius, Laozi, Zhuangzi, Sunzi, Mencius, etc., in a proper chronological order. But what about a list of Chinese thinkers who developed philosophy in the common era? Are there any contemporary Chinese thinkers worthy of our critical engagement in relation to the ongoing philosophical discussions? Many of us may be inclined to say "No" to these questions, but our general ignorance about Asian philosophical traditions only generates a somewhat embarrassing silence.

We are not here, however, just to criticize the ways in which academic programs are set up across the field of philosophy (not only in Europe and North America, but also Asia). We do not think that the language of "institutional racism" is any longer effective to install a change in our life as academics.[1] What we would like to ask us in face of this catastrophic one-sidedness, the quantitative and informative discrepancy between our scholarship on the topic of western and non-western philosophies (which is simply unthinkable in other disciplines like history, anthropology, cultural studies, and religious studies), is to think about their differences in terms of the material and the efficient cause. What are, in other words, the ways in which we think of the list of European philosophers? Why is it easier for us to list them as being from ancient, medieval, modern, or contemporary historical periods with a relatively coherent narrative that clearly demarcates them as philosophers? What do we have here that is missing in our process of squeezing out Chinese or Japanese names from our Eurocentric brains? Our answer to these questions is simple: a number of monumental and yet accessible book series in western languages.

When we think about ancient and medieval philosophy in the European context, we can easily think about the "Loeb Classical Library" in their Christmas color coordination. As for Renaissance philosophy, the "Tatti library" stands out in any bookshelf with the glow of its stylish light blue exterior. "Cambridge Texts in the History of Philosophy," "Cambridge Editions of Kant," or affordable Hackett paperbacks would immediately come to mind when we talk about the primary sources that we often use for our courses in modern philosophy. Post-modern philosophy is, of course, expectedly a bit all over the place. However, there are many signature series for notable

---

1   Brian Van Norden, *Taking Back Philosophy: A Multicultural Manifesto* (Columbia University Press, 2017), xix. Jay L. Garfield makes this remark in his "Foreword" to this volume.

thinkers like Kierkegaard in "Kierkegaard's Writings" at Princeton University Press or recent publications of the Nietzschean corpus at "Oxford World Classics." It is not difficult to imagine that most of our readers may own a couple of copies from the "SUNY Series in Contemporary Continental Philosophy" or Polity's "Key Thinkers in Contemporary Philosophy." The thickness and the diversity of the layers in the publication infrastructure for European and North American philosophy, which can be seen as the material and the efficient cause of our intellectual discussions about ideas in these works is simply second to none.

To raise the status of Asian philosophical traditions to the level of the so-called "western philosophy" in academia, we certainly have to go through a structural change, where we can offer more courses on relevant topics for undergraduate and graduate students. However, this is only feasible when philosophy instructors (who probably lack the fluency requisite for working with primary sources in multiple Asian languages) have access to a number of reliable books that give a coherent narrative of the field of comparative and Asian philosophy. Our students, too, must have access to a great number of affordable and critical translations of these texts. What is required from specialists of Asian philosophies, then, is no longer to prove (to the Eurocentric part of our brains and to our colleagues) that there can be a philosophy outside the European and North American context, but rather to create a robust intellectual infrastructure in which we can produce scholarly representations of ideas and conceptual schemes available in these hitherto relatively unexplored traditions. Without creating more publication venues that match the quality and the productivity of those in western philosophy, most scholars and students cannot easily identify (or sensibly challenge) Asian philosophical texts as a part of the world philosophical narrative.

This is precisely our intention in launching this series, "Asian Philosophical Texts," at Mimesis International. Our goal is to provide a space in which we can explore a number of intellectual traditions originating from this vast continent of Asia, to introduce leitmotifs that are both historically and conceptually unique to them, and to steadily grow the library of primary sources in English translations. Our hope is that in a few decades (if not in centuries), philosophical readers can visualize our series as something like an Asian version of the Loeb Classical Library and recollect the spines of our books in their university or personal bookshelves as a way to answer the following question with more confidence: Who are the famous thinkers from China, India, Japan, Korea, Vietnam, and any other fertile intellectual soil from the Asian continent?

At the same time, we hope that the books published in this series will also contribute to the ongoing debate about what philosophy actually is. Do we understand philosophy to be solely the practice that was carried out under the banner of *philosophia* in the Greco-European tradition, or do we open up the definition to make it more accommodating for non-Western traditions? If the *enjeu* of philosophy is the search for truth, for the meaning of human existence, for the intricacies of the life and death debate, for ethic postulates or for aesthetic principles, then perhaps we can find clues to all these issues in the notions and concepts put forth by philosophers in the Asian traditions of thought. We believe that Dao, the Confucian *Analects*, or the whole plethora of comments to the Buddhist scriptures encapsulate numerous hints that might help us rethink our understanding of philosophy, of its practice and of its purpose.

This inaugural volume, as a starting point of this ambitious project, carries multiple blueprints of future monographs outlined by great scholars in the field of comparative and Asian philosophy. The volume is structured in two parts, with six original essays in the first part and three translations from original sources in the second part. All of the articles engage with philosophical texts, concepts, and notions from the Asian continent, from China and India to Japan and Vietnam.

In "'White Horse is Not [a] Horse': How the Translation Creates the Paradox," Yijing Zhang discusses the *White Horse Discourse* (*Bai ma lun*, 白马论) by Gongsun Long (公孙龙, 323–250 BCE), one of the most widely discussed Chinese philosophical texts in European and North American academia. After observing that in general there are two types of scholars who have commented on the text (Sinologists and logicians), Zhang attempts to problematize certain presuppositions that these scholars have been taking as starting points when approaching the text. The purpose of the article is to challenge and deconstruct these presuppositions by showing that they rest principally on misunderstandings motivated by the translation of the Chinese text; thus, the author clarifies her position as subscribing to the linguistic relativism of von Humboldt—where language is considered as conveying a worldview—and then moves on to identify and discuss in detail the three main problems that are responsible for the most widespread and serious misunderstandings of the white horse discourse. Zhang's conclusion is that, by ignoring the underlying linguistic and philosophical differences between the two intellectual traditions, scholars end up overlooking the authorial intent and that, in order to avoid misinterpretations, we need to properly understand the cultural and linguistic differences between the Chinese and European intellectual traditions.

In her article, "Philosophy for Children: Globalization and the Translation of a Neo-Confucian Text," Margaret Chu analyzes the *Yangzheng leibian* 養正類編, a text included in the *Zhengyi tang quanshu* 正誼堂全書 ("Collectanea of the Hall of Correctness and Principle") by Zhang Boxing 張伯行 (1652–1725), first published in the eighteenth-century. The text, which is meant for young children and ordinary folk, especially in remote or isolated areas in imperial China, covers a wide variety of topics, from pedagogical theories and children's rites to historical anecdotes of exemplary behavior and definitions of philosophical concepts. Starting from the observation that one of the features of Chinese philosophical discourse is the apparent absence of a formal argument, Chu provides detailed comments on all the sections of the text and then discusses some of the most problematic philosophical concepts, such as *qi* 氣 and *hun po* 魂魄. Asking rhetorically whether the text is indeed for children only, Chu concludes with several remarks on the role of translation in philosophy, suggesting that the inclusion of conceptualizations from an entirely different paradigm enriches the dialogue and broadens horizons.

In her article, "The Holism of Guanxue in the Song Dynasty," Na Song discusses the belief in holism in traditional Chinese thought by focusing on the local school of Guan (*Guanxue*, 關學), formed in Guanzhong around the second half of the eleventh century and centered on the work of Zhang Zai (張載, 1020–77). Song first describes holism as the cohesive whole that is believed to contain cosmic order, political legitimacy, as well as the moral order of society, and then discusses its two dimensions: the fact that it was considered to be a cosmic–political–ethical system/program serving as the root of morality, cultural identity, and political legitimacy; and the fact that it also refers to the wholeness of the human order (actual world) and of the cosmos (the world beyond). She presents the interactions between Guanxue and other Daoxue modes in the Song dynasty in an attempt to investigate how Guanxue holism was shaped by the local and national sociopolitical context. In her conclusion, Song suggests that exclusive emphasis on Zhang Zai's cosmology does not do justice to the whole image of the cosmology of Guanxue, and that this school is not merely a regional Neo-Confucian school, as its tenets are also relevant for mainstream Chinese thought; last but not least, she puts forth the idea that the issue of the modernization of China should perhaps be understood as a path to rethink modernity and to explore the multiple possibilities of world history.

In "Concerning Aesthetic Attitudes: Kant and Confucius on Emulation and Evaluation," Cody Staton examines Confucian and Kantian accounts of aesthetic experience. The aim of the article is to show that reading the one philosopher through the other allows us to approach contemporary intercultural issues: thus, Staton shows that, although Confucius is often regarded as a moral philosopher, he considers a meaningful life to be an ongoing aesthetic activity, an attitude that one pursues throughout the course of life. When discussing Kant, he adopts Makkreel's distinction between emulation and evaluation in an effort to demonstrate the Kantian point that one cannot defer to tradition. For Confucius, an aesthetic attitude likewise develops taste in all facets of life, but taste here is rather emulative. As Staton shows, however, far from advocating that one should blindly follow rules, the Confucian notion of emulation makes it clear that self-development is an outcome of aesthetic self-reflection. The key is to understand how, in the give and take of our relationships with others, emulation is about recognizing the appropriate response required in each context. For both Kant and Confucius, the enjoyment of both art and the beauty of nature teaches us how to develop emulative and evaluative aesthetic attitudes.

In "Contradiction and Recursion in Buddhist Philosophy: From *Catuṣkoṭi* to *Kōan*," Adrian Kreutz starts from three questions about the notion of *catuṣkoṭi* (i.e., the view that any claim can be true, false, both true and false, or neither true nor false): what is its role in Buddhist philosophy? What is its logical form? What is its historical position? He suggests that a fruitful treatment of the three questions (and, therefore, a fruitful philosophical analysis of the *catuṣkoṭi* itself) cannot be had by answering the questions in isolation (as the research literature suggests), but only in correlation. He argues that the *catuṣkoṭi* plays a distinctive soteriological role in practiced Buddhism and should be considered a schema for *upāya* (skillful means). To back this hypothesis, Kreutz extrapolates the *catuṣkoṭi* from the writings of Jízàng and consequently advocates the idea that the *Kōan* of the Zen tradition can be deemed an "abbreviated" *catuṣkoṭi*, playing the same (*upāya*) role as its historical precursors. The article thereby uncovers underexplored connections between South Asian and East Asian Buddhist texts. What ties the discussion together is the attempt to formalize the practitioner's path towards enlightenment (and beyond). The *catuṣkoṭi*, as it turns out, is of paramount importance in this endeavor.

In her article, Maitreyee Datta examines how classical Indian dialectics is used in order to refute the reality of temporal passage in two important texts: the *Mūlamadhyamakakārikā* by second-century Buddhist philosopher Nāgārjuna, and the *Khandanakhandakhādya* by twelfth-century neo-Advaitin philosopher Śrīharṣa. Datta's analysis is an attempt to shed some light on the contradictions and paradoxes that result from the logical and philosophical inquiries into the reality, perception, and experience of the passage of time, i.e., the move between the different tenses of past, present, and future. What both thinkers discussed here have in common is their critique of the realists' position concerning time, which leads them to conduct an examination of the concept and, eventually, to argue for its unreality. Datta shows that both philosophers refute the reality of the tenses by determining that no accurate account of them is actually possible: Nāgārjuna does so by interpreting *real* as *unconditional* and claiming that the past is conditioned, therefore unreal; Śrīharṣa, on the other hand, interprets *real* as *non-contradictory*, and suggests that all tenses involve circularity or contradiction and, as such, cannot be real.

The three texts in the last part are as follows: Đoàn Minh Huyên's *Esoteric Tradition of Venerable Master Buddha of Western Peace*, translated with commentary by Quảng Huyên; Kurata Hyakuzō's *Looking for One's Self in the Opposite Sex*, translated with commentary by Richard Stone; and Tanabe Hajime's *Requesting the Guidance of Professor Nishida*, translated by Richard Stone with Takeshi Morisato. These are all texts that have never been translated into English before, and as such we hope that they make a significant contribution to the corpus of Asian philosophy available in translation.

The first text belongs to Đoàn Minh Huyên (1807–56), known as "Master Buddha" to his followers, who lived on a "water frontier" between the northern and southern tributaries of the Mekong River in southern Vietnam; as such, he interprets Buddhist teachings in terms of water metaphors, speaking, for example, of the receding tide of dharma that leaves in its wake a "shallowed world." In the second text, Kurata (1891–1943) gives a very personal account of his meeting with Kyoto school philosopher Nishida Kitarō's philosophy and the spiritual and ethical benefits that it offered for him. To be more specific, Kurata outlines the way in which Nishida's philosophy helped him overcome his solipsistic tendencies that had come about during a highly stressful period of his high-school life. The third text represents an extensive and thorough commentary by Tanabe Hajime (1885–1962) of Nishida's *The Self-Aware System of Universals*, in which Tanabe, while expressing his admiration and respect for "Professor Nishida," discusses very rigorously his ideas and points out some of the shortcomings and inconsistencies that he finds in Nishida's writing.

Lastly, the compilation of this edited volume would not have been possible had we not been able to organize two international conferences under the title of "Asian Philosophical Texts" at the Research Centre for East Asian Studies (EASt) at Université libre de Bruxelles (ULB) in October 2018 in Belgium; and at the Research Institute for Japanese Studies (RIJS) at Kanda University of International Studies (KUIS) in September 2019 in Japan. We would like to thank Pierre Bonneels at ULB-EASt and Taisuke Ueno at KUIS-RIJS for providing us a place to share our research findings, translation projects, and the idea of this book series with a number of great scholars from around the world. Additionally, we would like to thank both EASt and RIJS for covering a significant portion of the publication subsidies for this project. We hope to continue organizing this APT conference as a way to introduce more scholars to our new series and, by supplying more books for discussion, to pursue the polyvocal depth of Asian philosophical traditions.

ESSAYS

YIJING ZHANG (SUN YAT-SEN UNIVERSITY)

"WHITE HORSE IS NOT [A] HORSE"
How the Translation Creates the Paradox

Introduction

The *White Horse Discourse* (*Bai ma lun*, 白马论) by Gongsun Long (公孙龙, 323–250 BCE) is one of the most discussed Chinese phil-osophical texts in European and North American academia. We can distinguish two types of scholars who have commented on this text: Sinologists, who work not only on Gongsun Long but also on other currents of Chinese thoughts; and logicians, for whom the problem of the white horse is one logical problem among many and who are interested exclusively in logical texts (which present problems that can be assimilated to those of western logic) within the corpus of classical Chinese thought. In practice, the two types of scholars represent two contrary positions. On the one hand, the Sinologists who are drawn to Gongsun Long generally believe that there is a fundamental difference between Chinese and western thought and maintain that this philo-sophical difference is due to linguistic differences.[1] On the other hand,

---

1   The writing of this article was supported by the research project "A Comparative study of Aristotle's *Categories* in Four Languages," funded by the China Post-doctoral Science Foundation Grant (No. 2019T120786) and the Fundamental Research Funds for the Central Universities (No. 18wkpy67). Just to recall the position of two well-known sinologists who commented Gongsun Long: (1) "Chinese thought before the introduction of Buddhism from India is the unique instance of a philosophical tradition which, as far as our information goes, is wholly independent of traditions developed in Indo-European languages." Angus Charles Graham, *Disputers of the Tao: philosophical argument in ancient China* (La Salle: Open Court, 1989), 389. (2) "It is quite conceivable that the nature of the Chinese language may have channeled Chinese thinking in certain ways that Indo-European languages have not channeled Indo-European thinking." Christoph Harbsmeier, "Marginalia sino-logica," in *Understanding the Chinese Mind:*

the logicians seek to reconstruct the argumentation of Gongsun Long by means of modern logic. This type of reconstruction is aimed more at proving the universality of western logic than uncovering Gongsun Long's thought.[2]

The objective of this article is not to furnish a new interpretation of the problem of the "white horse" but to problematize certain presuppositions that western commentators have been taking as their starting point when approaching Gongsun Long's text. These presuppositions rest principally on misunderstandings caused by the translation of the Chinese text, which is at least disconcerting if not erroneous. To some extent, it is the translation from Chinese into a European language that conditions the interpretation. The commentators often analyze the target language of the translation instead of the Chinese. Moreover, they share the practice of using so-called western concepts and theories to analyze the thought of Gongsun Long.

Gongsun Long is one of the Chinese thinkers who pay particular attention to questions of language and argumentation. For this reason, some aspects of his thought can be compared to western logic. Admittedly, some notions of western logic can shed light on a certain portion of Gongsun Long's treatise, but if we wish to prove the universality of western logic by using it to analyze "Chinese logic," we risk falling into a tautology: we presuppose that certain elements of western logic are universal in order to find their "equivalents" in other systems of thought. Such an approach suffers from the problem of decontextualization because it does not allow us to understand the worldview or the ways of reasoning behind them that characterize each system of thought.

In this article, I aim at understanding the *White Horse Discourse* by following Gongsun Long's own reasoning in relation to the characteristics of the Chinese language. I avoid reference to other texts of Gongsun Long, such as the *Ming shi lun* (名实论, *On Name and*

The Philosophical roots, ed. Robert E. Allinson (Oxford: Oxford University Press, 1990), 126.

2   Cf. Janusz Chmielewski, *Language and Logic in Ancient China. Collected Papers on the Chinese Language and Logic*, ed., M. Mejor (Warszawa: Polska Akademia Nauk, 2009). Thierry Lucas, "Yes, Western Logic applies to Gongsun Long and Mozi!," *Universitas*/與文化, Vol. 30, no.12 (2003): 25–38, http://dx.doi.org/10.7065/MRPC.200312.0025.

Reality), *Zhi wu lun* (指物论, *On Pointing at Things*), and *Jian bai lun* (坚白论, *On Hard and White*) because despite being related to the treatise under examination, there is also much controversy over interpretations of these texts, and an extensive reference to them could risk further clouding the problem in the *White Horse Discourse* especially for those of us who are not familiar with the questions posed by Gongsun Long or his method of philosophizing.

Since this article is in English, it inevitably employs some terms which make reference to western concepts, but unlike western commentators who use these concepts as analytical tools, my usage is critical. Stated otherwise, I will show the fundamental differences between the concepts of Gongsun Long and the western concepts which are seemingly close to them; and at the same time, I will highlight the points of comparison between them on the basis of knowledge of their differences. I am not necessarily opposed to the reading of Chinese texts through European or North American optics. On the contrary, I do think that this type of reading can be valuable insofar as it reveals the linguistic and philosophical differences between two traditions of thought. But it is not always easy to be conscious of these differences. Some western scholars present a contradiction: they insist on the distinctiveness of the Chinese language while applying western notions to it.

I subscribe to the linguistic relativism of Wilhelm von Humboldt where language is considered as conveying a worldview. To understand how the Chinese language influences Gongsun Long's framework of thinking, it is important to analyze the Chinese text itself, and not the translation of the Chinese text in any European language. I would also like to show in the following that on certain points where commentators believe that the Chinese text seems grammatically incompatible with Indo-European languages, Gongsun Long actually expresses—through Chinese grammar and vocabulary—logical relations that these commentators believe absent from his text.

There are at least three translation problems that are responsible for the most widespread and serious misunderstandings of the *White Horse Discourse*. The first is the translation of the phrase *bai ma fei ma* (白马非马) using the verb "to be." The second does not concern directly the translation of the Chinese text but the analysis of it using the linguistic or philosophical categories of the European intellectual tradition. The third is the translation of *ming jia* (名家) as "sophist," "logician" or "nominalist." These last two problems are linked to the first. We shall examine them in the following.

The Verb "To Be" and "A White Horse Is Not a Horse"

In the *Stanford Encyclopedia of Philosophy*, Chris Fraser summarizes the debate over Gongsun Long's *White Horse Discourse*:

> There is now a fairly broad consensus, at least among European and American scholars, that the text is unlikely to concern universals, since no ancient Chinese philosopher held a realist doctrine of universals.[3]

In order to solve the problematic relationship between the white horse and the horse, European and North American scholars have long discussed whether or not the concept of universals exists in ancient Chinese thought. This question seems important for them because, according to them, Gongsun Long can uphold the proposition, "White horse is not horse," only in denying the relationship of inclusion. This conclusion involves several presuppositions: (1) Gongsun Long tries to prove that "a white horse is not a horse." (2) With the phrase "white horse is not horse," Gongsun Long speaks mainly about the relationship between "white horse" and "horse." (3) When we say, "a white horse is a horse," we think that a white horse belongs to the class of horses. If a person maintains, "white horse is not horse," she cannot have in mind the concept of universals

---

3   Chris Fraser, "School of Names," The *Stanford Encyclopedia of Philosophy* (Spring 2017 Edition), ed., Edward N. Zalta, https://plato.stanford.edu/archives/spr2017/entries/school-names/. There is some confusion in this remark. It does not follow from the fact that "no ancient Chinese philosopher held a realist doctrine of universals" that "the text is unlikely to concern universals." The "realist doctrine of universals" is opposed to other doctrines of universals, not to universals themselves. This confusion undoubtedly stems from the opinion of some Sinologists that Gongsun Long is a nominalist. This would imply a contradiction: the nominalist doctrine is also a doctrine of universals. I will return to this in the second part.

or of class.[4] In other words, the absence of the concept of universals in Gongsun Long's works is the solution that European and North American commentators have provided for understanding the proposition "A white horse is not a horse."

There is at least one serious problem in each of these assumptions. First, Gongsun Long does not try to prove that "a white horse is not a horse." The phrase "white horse is not horse" can be understood as a trap to trick his interlocutor while playing with the ambiguity of Chinese language, or as a *captatio benevolentiae* for drawing attention from his audience. Second, the discussion in the *White Horse Discourse* is not centered on the relationship between white horse and horse. Third, in English, the affirmative phrase "a white horse is a horse" takes the form of predication. The verb "to be" expresses here the inclusion of a white horse within the class of horses. However, this linguistic structure does not apply to the negative phrase *bai ma fei ma* in Chinese. Moreover, Gongsun Long is certainly not interested in the truth value of a proposition, i.e., the relationship between a statement and the actual fact to which it corresponds. His theories of language consist in treating of the relationship between "name" and that which it designates. All these misunderstandings stem from the fact that the translation as "white horse is not horse" employs the verb "to be" and that western readers tend to understand the phrase of Gongsun Long through this term.

Fraser translates and interprets the phrase *bai ma fei ma* in the following way:

> To capture the flavor of the Chinese, we will render certain phrases in pidgin English, omitting articles and plurals. So we will translate the main thesis as "White horse is not horse," variously interpretable as "a white horse is not a horse," "white horses are not horses," "a white horse is not an exemplar of the kind horse," or "the kind white horse is not identical with the kind horse."[5]

The translations proposed by Fraser, just like the ones used by other western commentators on Gongsun Long, consistently use the verb

---

4   The two concepts, "universals" and "class," are different even though they are linked. Several commentators on Gongsun Long confuse them. See *infra* part 3.
5   Fraser, "School of Names."

"to be." These translations are certainly not wrong, but quite deceptive in the context of philosophy. In fact, it is quite difficult to avoid using the verb "to be" here if we want to convey its meaning in English (yet strictly speaking, there is no verb in the phrase *bai ma fei ma* and we can recognize the imposition of English grammar in translating this sentence). As a result, the commentators cannot help but take seriously the presence of the verb in the phrase "white horse is not horse" or, to be more precise, by the logical relationship that the verb is liable to establish between "white horse" and "horse." For this reason, they have devoted much time and energy to discussing this relationship. European and North American, as well as Chinese scholars who are trained in analytic philosophy, usually employ western concepts and theories developed in the field of logic, linguistics, or philosophy, to understand the proposition, "a white horse is not a horse."[6]

As far as the translation is concerned, I do not mean to say that since Gongsun Long did not use the copular—which did not exist in the Chinese at that time—we cannot use the verb "to be" to translate his text into English. As Aristotle argues, there is no difference between "the man is recovering" and "the man recovers."[7] This means that, for someone who thinks in a language that has the verb "to be," phrases using other verbs can be easily "translated" into those using the verb "to be" within the same language; and then we can still analyze them according to the structure of predication. The speaker of this language (that has a copular) probably tends to believe that the English translation of a Chinese sentence by using the verb "to be" means that the Chinese sentence has the same structure of predication. The usage of the symbols of modern logic by logicians who analyze Gongsun Long's text can also be seen as practicing a kind of translation and it does not change at all the fact that they are analyz-

---

6   Only some Sinologists try to employ a reading that allows to establish the internal coherence of the Chinese text itself, such as Christoph Harbsmeier, "Kungsun Lung and the White Horse Dialogue," in *Science and Civilisation in China*, Vol. 7, Part 1; *Language and Logic* (Cambridge: Cambridge University Press, 1998), 298–321. See also Bryan W. van Norden, "Gongsun Long," in *Introduction to Classical Chinese Philosophy* (Indianapolis/Cambridge: Hackett, 2011), 7: III.

7   Aristotle, *Metaphysics*, Δ7, 1017a 27–29, trans., David Ross, in *The Complete Works of Aristotle*, the Revised Oxford Translation, vol. 2, ed., Jonathan Barnes (Princeton: Princeton University Press, 1984), 68.

ing the structure of predication. This kind of analysis could give the impression that the structure of predication is independent from the verb "to be" and thus universal. In fact, the verb "to be" is so intuitive to its speakers with the structure of predication to such an extent that they no longer perceive its influence on their ways of expressing their thought or understanding the world. If the verb "to be" can replace other verbs or be replaced by mathematical signs for a speaker who thinks with this verb and with the notion of predication which it implies, then it seems to follow that the speaker of a language devoid of this verb such as Gongsun Long can still conceive the notion of predication from different types of sentence which, in his language, are not reducible to one and the same syntactical structure. However, this is a false assumption. The translation of a word and the conception of a notion are two different mental operations. When we read the *White Horse Discourse*, we should refrain from imposing the structure of predication that is available in Indo-European languages on the phrase *bai ma fei ma* (since *fei* is not even a verb).

According to Angus Charles Graham, all commentators of Gongsun Long (including himself) have mistakenly thought that Gongsun Long confuses identity and inclusion, while Gongsun Long is not interested in the problem of inclusion.[8] A number of commentators after Graham have interpreted *bai ma fei ma* as "white horse is not identical with horse." In other words, they hold that Gongsun Long denies only identity, not inclusion. However, the fact that Gongsun Long discusses the non-identity between the white horse and horse does not lead to a conclusion that he does not have any notion of inclusion or of universals. I will return to this point in the following paragraph. Here, I simply suggest the difficulty in believing that Gongsun Long makes an extensive effort to prove something so obvious as the non-identity between a white horse and a horse by developing an elaborate series of arguments. In fact, I argue that he focuses on something other than the relationship between white horse and horse.

---

8   Angus Charles Graham, "Kung-sun Lung's Discourse Re-read as Argument about Whole and Part," in *Studies in Chinese Philosophy and Philosophical Literature* (Albany: SUNY Press, 1990), 196.

Bai ma fei ma: "White horse is not horse." This phrase, which we can find at the very beginning of the treatise, functions something like a *captatio benevolentiae*. The phrase is designed to impress the reader by going against a common sense. In fact, the very aim of convening this strange phrase is quite ambiguous: one could understand that "a white horse is not a horse" or that "white horse" is not identical with "horse." "A white horse is not a horse" can also be a paradox, and for this reason, Gongsun Long has been considered as a "Chinese sophist" by a number of western scholars. But Gongsun Long does not formulate this paradox to construct a sophism in the pejorative sense of the term, i.e., to deceive the public with the ambiguity of natural language. On the contrary, by means of a provocative phrase, he aims at drawing our attention to the philosophical problem that he seeks to solve.

The same phrase also appears at the end of each argument. In this case, we are naturally led to believe that this is a kind of central thesis that Gongsun Long is trying to establish. It suffices to consider the first argument, which is the most concise and fundamental for understanding that Gongsun Long's main interest is not the question of knowing whether or not the proposition "a white horse is not a horse" is valid, but of clarifying what is designated by the terms *bai* (white) and *ma* (horse).

> "Horse" is that by means of which one names the shape. "White" is that by means of which one names the color. What names the color is not what names the shape. Hence, I say that a white horse is not a horse.[9]

In this argument, Gongsun Long explicitly discusses the "names." "White horse is not a horse" can be understood in this context as "the name *white horse* is not identical with the name *horse*," which means "white horse" and "horse" name different things. This argument is not complete, but it provides the basis for his following arguments. It consists in distinguishing two different types of "name," shape and color, in the instance of *ma* and *bai*. This distinction is fundamental for understanding the rest of the text. By "incomplete argument," I mean that at this stage of the analysis, the structure of the term *baima*

---

9   Bryan W. van Norden, *Readings in Classical Chinese Philosophy* (Indianapolis: Hackett, 2001), 363.

(white horse) has not yet been clarified. From the simple distinction between *bai* and *ma*, we do not immediately arrive at the conclusion "white horse is not horse."

In Chinese, *ma* (马, horse) and *bai* (白, white) are *ming* (名), "names." They are not substantives or adjectives—these grammatical categories did not exist in the language spoken by Gongsun Long. They have nothing to do with the notions of subject and predicate or of substance and accident as in Aristotelian logic. The notion of *ming* must be understood within the framework of the *ming jia* (名家, School of Names). The thinkers classified as part of this school were concerned with questions, such as "What are names?"; "What are the things that they name?"; "What is the relationship between names and things?" The fundamental difference between the Chinese theory of the "name" and western logic is that the former studies the relationship between names and things, whereas the latter focuses on the relationship between statements and facts.[10]

A statement consists of a noun and a verb. For Aristotle, a noun alone or a verb alone is neither true nor false. A statement can be true or false. It seems that most western commentators on Gongsun Long unconsciously share Aristotle's position: that is to say, by treating the Chinese thinker as a logician or sophist and his phrase "white horse is not horse" as a predication, they try to interpret the text in a way that makes the statement "white horse is not horse" true. However, it is not the truth of the statement that Gongsun Long discusses in his text. His reflection bears on the distinction between *bai*, *ma*, and *baima* insofar as they are names and not on white horses and horses as two classes (kinds), much less on the question of knowing whether *ma* (horse) is a predicate which can be appropriately attributed to *baima* (white horse). With regard to the problem of the white horse, the relationship between names

---

10   Reding notes that the *White Horse Discourse* focuses on the relationship between name and reference, without emphasizing that this is a fundamental feature of the Chinese language and the Chinese theory of language: "À noter que le débat est encore toujours mené en termes référentiels : 'cheval' ne désigne pas les mêmes objets que 'cheval blanc.'" Jean-Paul Reding, *Les fondements philosophiques de la rhétorique chez les sophistes grecs et chez les sophistes chinois* (Bern: Peter Lang, 1985), 407.

and things is examined in this way: on a linguistic level, how does "white" change when it is combined with "horse"?; on a real or extralinguistic level, what is in a white horse that makes it so different from a horse? In a word, what interests Gongsun Long is the problem of the relationship between white and the horse, or that of the role played by the name "white" in the term "white horse." Commentators, seeking to explain the relationship between white horse and horse in western languages, often pass over this actual problem because they are always thinking with the verb "to be."

Universals vs. Mass Nouns

The belief that Gongsun Long does not have a concept of universals is linked not only to the translation of the phrase "white horse is not horse" with the term "to be," but also to the tendency of scholars to apply western linguistic and philosophical categories to the Chinese text.[11] Insofar as these scholars think with these categories, their interpretation of the Chinese text gives a conceptual translation.

On the question of the absence of universals, I limit my discussion to the works of Chad Hansen. He is one of the first and the most influential figure in the European and American receptions of Gongsun Long.[12]

---

11   This section contains a translation of some parts of my article: "Les catégories d'Aristote à l'épreuve du 'sophiste' chinois Gongsun Long," *Revue Philosophique de Louvain* 117(2019).

12   For Hansen's influence in the Anglo-Saxon world, cf. Bryan W. van Norden, "Hansen on Hsun-tzu," *Journal of Chinese Philosophy* 20, no. 3 (Sep. 1993): 365–82. In French sinology, A. Cheng closely follows Hansen's interpretation. Cf. The chapter on Gongsun Long in Anne Cheng, *Histoire de la pensée chinoise* (Paris: Seuil, 1997). Hansen is also widely quoted by Chinese scholars, but in a critical manner. Cf. for example, Yuyu Liu and Yan Ren 刘玉宇 任远, "Chonglun Chad Hansen 'Zhiliao Mingci Jiashuo' yu Gongsun Long 'Baima lun' Jieshi," 重论陈汉生'质料名词假说' 与公孙龙'白马论' 解释 (Reflections on Hansen's Mass-Noun Hypothesis and the Interpretation of Gongsun Long's *White Horse Discourse*), *Zhongguo Zhexueshi* 中国哲学史 (History of Chinese Philosophy), no. 3 (Aug. 2018):122–129. I do not give here the list of bibliographical references in Chinese, which will be simply too long.

Hansen is strongly against the use of western terms or notions such as "universal, quality, property, concept, general idea, attribute, class, and meaning" in his process of interpreting Gongsun Long:

> All these alternatives share three characteristics: (1) they are abstract or ideal entities, that is, are not located in space-time; (2) they are relatively important notions in the development or elaboration of western logic, epistemology, ontology or semantics—that is, hard "respectable" philosophy; and (3) they are all concepts rarely or never found in other pre-Han Chinese thought.
>
> It is no objection that these are western ideas and therefore inappropriate to Chinese thought. ... Western analytic philosophy has given a wide range of semantic possibilities for understanding Chinese thought. Choosing one less central to western thought is more likely to help illuminate the disparity between the two cultural traditions.[13]

The important concepts in western philosophy are not appropriate for Chinese thought, and a less central concept from western thought can much more efficiently reveal the disparity between the cultural traditions. In this sense, he sets forth the concept of "mass noun."[14] I share Hansen's position on the disparity between two cultural traditions, but I cannot see why a less central concept of western thought is better suited to Chinese thought, and on what criteria he chooses this type of concept. I can understand Hansen's dilemma: he rightly perceives that the modes of Chinese thought are fundamentally different from the western frameworks of thinking. However, if we must avoid projecting the essential concepts of western culture over Chinese thought, for some of us whose way of thinking has been formed by the western sciences, what remains is nothing more than the most marginal concepts in the western intellectual tradition. After all, two statements that Chinese thought shares with the western counterpart the same central concepts and that Chinese thought does not possess these concepts seriously suffer from the single problematic perspective of Eurocentrism.

---

13   Chad D. Hansen, "Mass Nouns and 'a White Horse is not a Horse,'" *Philosophy East and West* 26, no. 2 (Apr. 1976): 190.

14   Fraser gave a detailed review of the criticisms of Hansen (at least from western scholars) and supported a modified version of Hansen's "mass-noun" theory to characterize ancient Chinese thought in general, without questioning the relevance of this theory in the case of Gongsun Long's white horse problem, as it is not the purpose of his article. Cf. Chris Fraser, "Language and Ontology in Early Chinese Thought," *Philosophy East and West* 57, no. 4 (Oct. 2007): 420–56.

Hansen's method seems somewhat arbitrary and contradictory in this regard. We can say that Hansen has taken Gongsun Long as a relatively "westernizable" Chinese thinker because his treatise can be more easily compared with analytic philosophy, but at the same time, the principal notions in analytic philosophy ought to be excluded from our interpretations of Chinese thought. The notion of "mass noun," therefore Hansen argues, is indispensable for understanding not only Gongsun Long's *White Horse Discourse* but also the nature of Chinese language in general.[15] This thesis derives from his conviction that the non-development of abstract thought is a main characteristic of Chinese thought.[16] But what is abstract thought? Unfortunately, Hansen has not provided us with any clear definition. In fact, we have an impression that it is somehow self-evident for him that only western philosophy can be qualified as abstract thought. The aptitude towards abstraction, I believe, is rather a necessary condition for the existence of all language. Certainly, the Chinese language has not invented a name for each horse. As soon as there is a general term for indicating all horses, the term is already an abstraction and implies a certain degree of universality. There is no language that only consists of proper nouns.

There is another extreme. Feng Youlan, for instance, maintains that the abstract concepts in Chinese thought are identical to the Platonic ideas: "[Gongsun Long] arrives at the same concept of Platonic ideas or universals that has been so conspicuous in western philosophy."[17] I am skeptical of this position as well. That is because, according to Plato, there is an ontological distinction between the idea of white and sensible white things; and a linguistic distinction between "white" (*leukos*) and "whiteness" (*leukotês*). None of these distinctions are found in Gongsun Long's texts. But this does not mean that the Chinese thinker makes no distinction between "white" that "names the color" and "white" in the term "white horse."

Feng's perspective must be re-examined both from a philosophical and a historical perspective. As to advocate Chinese philosophy as

---

15   Cf. Chad D. Hansen, *Language and Logic in Ancient China* (Ann Arbor: Michigan University Press, 1983).

16   Hansen, "Mass Nouns and 'a White Horse is not a Horse,'" 191.

17   Fung Yu-lan, *A Short History of Chinese Philosophy*, ed., Derk Bodde (New York/London: The Free Press, 1966), 87.

"philosophy" in the western sense of the term, he established the *rapprochement*, or rather equivalence, between Chinese and western concepts with the intention not of defending the universality of western philosophy but of proving that China enjoys the same philosophical richness as the West. This intention is certainly more strategic than scientific. Precisely for this reason, Hansen does not accept Feng's interpretation. However, we must recognize that Chinese scholars (or scholars who speak Chinese as their first language), even though many of them are trained in western philosophy and publishing their scholarly works in English, still continue to defend the position that Gongsun Long's names can be seen as some kind of universals.[18]

Hansen draws inspiration from the following modern commentary on Gongsun Long:

> Kung-sun Lung's (=Gongsun Long's) difficulty in proving this thesis (Platonism) is heightened by the nature of the Chinese written language, which because it is pictographic and ideographic, and at the same time non-inflected, can express the difference between singular and plural objects, the concrete and the abstract, etc., only with difficulty.[19]

The commentary also suggests that the ideographic and non-inflected nature of the Chinese languages make Chinese less capable than Greek in expressing abstract thought. Hansen adds at this point:

> This very account of the difficulties of the Chinese language provides the best argument against the abstract interpretations. The only evidence of what Kung-sun Lung (=Gongsun Long) thought is his writings in Archaic Chinese (written) style. If it is impossible for that language to express or distinguish abstractions, then it is impossible to provide crucial evidence that he was thinking about them.[20]

---

18 Examples of those who write in English: Chung-ying Cheng, "White Horse and Other Issues," *Philosophy East and West* 33, no. 4 (Oct. 1983): 341–54. Yiu-ming Fung, "A Logical Perspective on 'Discourse on White-horse,'" *Journal of Chinese Philosophy* 34, no. 4 (Dec. 2007): 515–36. Bo Mou, "A Double-Reference Account: Gongsun Long's 'White-Horse-Not-Horse' Thesis," *Journal of Chinese Philosophy* 34, no. 4 (Dec. 2007): 493–513.

19 Liou Kia-hway, "The Configuration of Chinese Reasoning," *Diogenes*, no. 49 (Spr. 1965): 68, cited in Hansen, "Mass Nouns and 'a White Horse is not a Horse,'" 193.

20 Hansen, "Mass Nouns and 'a White Horse is not a Horse,'" 193.

I still maintain that Gongsun Long is thinking about an abstract concept when he says that the term "white" names a color. However, Hansen seems to think that only when there is a word like "whiteness," which is distinguished from the word "white" by the addition of a suffix, and a word like "horse," which can be inflected in the singular and plural, there can be abstract thought.

Hansen's thesis on the absence of abstraction is more tied to the ideographic rather than non-inflected nature of the Chinese language. He argues in another place:

> We never need to import Platonism into Chinese graphs. Their reference is always concrete, always to stuffs or bits of stuffs in space-time. We are not forced to say a graph refers to a mathematical entity (a class), an abstract one (a universal), a mental one (an idea), or a semantic one (a meaning).[21]

In order to free us from this kind of western influence, can we simply imagine that the absence of inflection does not necessarily imply the absence of abstraction, but that abstraction can be expressed without inflection? It is one thing to argue that without inflection, Gongsun Long could not have made a morphological distinction between "whiteness" and "white" or between the horse in general and individual horses. But it is entirely another thing to say that the word "horse" is a general term which evokes an abstract concept. Hansen does not distinguish between the two sides.

This is what Hansen says about the Chinese word "horse":

> We could entertain the hypothesis that, in Long's conceptual scheme, the term means "horseness" or "the class horse" or "horse-flow" or "horse-stuff" or "horse-temporal-segments," etc.

> ... such terms as *ma* are analogous to English mass nouns. It is natural (though perhaps naive) to say semantically that each is a singular term which stands as the name of an object scattered in space-time.[22]

Hansen examines this hypothesis that the Chinese words are mass nouns in his process of interpreting Gongsun Long's text. But he does

---

21   Hansen, *Language and Logic in Ancient China*, 34.
22   Hansen, "Mass Nouns and 'a White Horse is not a Horse,'" 190, 193.

not clarify where this hypothesis comes from. Starting from what he says about the absence of a distinction between singular and plural in Chinese, I can only formulate his implicit reasoning: in English, countable nouns can be pluralized. This is not the case in Chinese. Therefore, there are no countable nouns in Chinese. In English, substantives are either countable or non-countable. The latter are also called mass nouns. In Chinese, therefore, there are only mass nouns.

If we start from the other side of the hypothesis that countable nouns do not exist in Chinese, we arrive at an absurd conclusion: the Chinese do not know how to count! In Chinese, one can put numbers in front of the word *ma* (horse) to indicate quantity. Regardless of whether it is "one horse" or "two horses," the word *ma* remains unchanged. This means that Chinese does not have the same grammatical means as English for indicating the plural, but not that Chinese nouns are not countable in the first place or that the Chinese do not know how to count the number of horses.

I cannot agree more with the criticism of Hansen provided by Christoph Harbsmeier:

> Before one can decide whether *ma* is a mass noun, one surely has to study closely the question of whether there is a distinction between count nouns, generic nouns, and mass nouns among classical Chinese common nouns.[23]

We can approach Gongsun Long's problem of the white horse without supposing that *ma* is a "mass noun." Harbsmeier has given many examples from different Chinese classical texts that refute Hansen's mass-noun and part-whole hypothesis.[24] These examples, however, are not drawn from the text of Gongsun Long. We can easily find examples directly in the *White Horse Discourse*. They serve as an evidence in favor of a concept of horse as implying a certain degree of generality and abstraction. Let us examine the following passage:

> If one wants a horse, that extends to a yellow or black horse. But if one wants a white horse, that does not extend to a yellow or black horse. Suppose that a white horse were a horse. Then what one wants [in the two cases] would be the

---

23   Harbsmeier, "Marginalia sino-logica," 157. See also Harbsmeier, *Language and Logic*, 312*sq.*

24   Harbsmeier, *Language and Logic*, 312–21.

same. If what one wants were the same, then a white [horse] would not differ from a horse. If what one wants does not differ, then how is it that a yellow or black horse is sometimes acceptable and sometimes unacceptable? It is clear that acceptable and unacceptable are mutually contrary. Hence, yellow and black horses are the same [in that, if there are yellow or black horses], one can respond that there are horses, but one cannot respond that there are white horses. Thus, it is evident that a white horse is not a horse.[25]

Gongsun Long definitely expresses the concept of inclusion in this passage by saying that to have a yellow or black horse is to have a horse, but to seek a horse is not the same as to seek a white horse. In a similar vein, in the *Mohist Canon* we can find the line, "A white horse is a horse; to ride a white horse is to ride a horse."[26] This phrase is probably a reply to Gongsun Long. For Graham, the *Mohist Canon* suggests that the phrase "white horse is horse" is the illustration of an irrefutable proposition, and that Gongsun Long attacks it precisely to produce a paradoxical effect. If this phrase is irrefutable for the Chinese, how can one deny that they possess the concept of inclusion?

For Hansen, since Gongsun Long never used a word which could be translated into English as "class" or "member," he did not have a corresponding notion in his thought.[27] The phrases such as "if one wants a horse, that extends to a yellow or black horse" and "to ride a white horse is to ride a horse" rightly demonstrate an attempt to express inclusion with a language which neither has a term corresponding to the notion of inclusion or the verb "to be."

There is another evidence for the abstract concept of whiteness:

"White" does not fix that which is white. It ignores that. The expression "white horse" fixes that which is white. That which fixes what is white is not white. "Horse" is indifferent to color. Hence, [if you were only looking for a horse,] a yellow or black horse would each be appropriate. "White horse" does select for color. So [if you were looking for a white horse,] a yellow or black horse would be rejected on account of its color. Hence, only a white horse alone would be appropriate. That which does not reject is not what does reject. Hence, I say that a white horse is not a horse.[28]

25   Van Norden, *Readings in Classical Chinese Philosophy*, 364.
26   Graham, "A First Reading of the 'White Horse,'" in *Studies*, 178.
27   Hansen, "Mass Nouns and 'a White Horse is not a Horse,'" 198.
28   Van Norden, *Readings in Classical Chinese Philosophy*, 367.

"*White* does not fix that which is white" is a Chinese way of saying "whiteness," an abstract concept. "The expression *white horse* fixes that which is white": this echoes a concrete "white" attributed to a horse. Therefore, in saying "that which fixes what is white is not white," Gongsun Long tries to distinguish "whiteness" and "white" with the lexical means of his language since he does not have the grammatical means to do it. Likewise, when he says, "*Horse* is indifferent to color," he speaks of an abstract concept of horse. This phrase can be compared with another argument where he says, "If there are white horses, one cannot say that there are no horses, because of what is called the 'separability of white.'" All this shows that Gongsun Long was trying to come up with the abstract concepts of horse and whiteness.

In some more recent articles, Hansen responds to critiques of his thesis that there are no abstract concepts in Chinese thought:

> Some critics ... construe me as saying Chinese has no sentences or no abstract terms. My argument, however, was a textual one. I argued that the Chinese theory of language did not postulate sentences or abstract objects.[29]

And on the mass-noun hypothesis:

> I did speculate about a linguistic matter that may have distracted readers. I noted that Pre-Han grammar was not a mass noun grammar because it directly modified nouns with numbers. ... My argument, however, was solely about reconstructing that background theory from the texts using Quine's Radical Translation argument form. The goal of the theory was explaining the White Horse dispute, not that speculative by-product.[30]

On each occasion, Hansen insists that his argument is based on the text. He also clearly defines what he understands as a "textual argument":

---

29   Chad D. Hansen, "Term-Belief in Action: Sentences and Terms in Early Chinese Philosophy," in *Epistemological Issues in Classical Chinese Philosophy*, eds., H. Lenk and G. Paul (Albany: SUNY Press, 1993), 46.

30   Chad D. Hansen, "Remembering Mass: Response to Yang Xiaomei," *Dao: A Journal of Comparative Philosophy* 10, no. 4 (Oct. 2011): 542.

I am not making a claim about what cannot be thought, but about what was not written.[31]

Moreover, Hansen advises his reader not to take English as a reference point:

> In our formulation we must avoid the fallacy that "English is the only real language."[32]

If we compare these justifications that Hansen provides for his position, we must ask whether or not they are in contradiction with each other. (1) On the textual principle, it is true that Gongsun Long never writes that "horse" is an abstract concept, but he does not speak any more about mass nouns nor about "horse-stuff." This is an interpretation introduced by Hansen in the translation process. (2) On the illusion that English is the only real language, in saying "horse-stuff," does not Hansen give the illusion that English (and not Chinese) is the subject of his analysis? In fact, Hansen draws the concept of mass noun from Quine to translate Gongsun Long's *ma* as "horse-stuff" or "horse-temporal-segments." But Quine's own usage of the concept of mass nouns could be subject of the same criticism against the illusion that English is the only real language. As Geoffrey Lloyd acutely puts, "[Quine's] account of mass nouns followed the standard practice among most linguists and philosophers of language of taking English as the prime target of analysis."[33]

"Sophist," "Logician," and "Nominalist"

"Sophist" and "logician" are the labels most commonly attributed to Gongsun Long by western scholars. Harbsmeier notes:

---

31   Hansen, "Remembering Mass: Response to Yang Xiaomei," 497.
32   Chad D. Hansen, "Chinese Language, Chinese Philosophy, and 'Truth,'" *The Journal of Asian Studies* 44, no. 3 (May 1985): 494.
33   Geoffrey Ernest Richard Lloyd, *Being, Humanity, and Understanding* (Oxford: Oxford University Press, 2012), 24.

Some scholars, notably Feng Yu-lan (= Feng Youlan) and Janusz Chmielewski, have read the dialogue as sustained serious logical discourse by a theoretician. Others, from earliest times onwards, have considered it a facetious piece of sophistry. I believe that the Dialogue is both these things.[34]

Thus, for Harbsmeier, Gongsun Long is both sophist and logician. This remark is not wrong, but it is irrelevant to our approach in the sense that the opposition between logic and sophistry did not exist in Chinese antiquity.

In ancient Greece, logic and sophistry have as their common basis, namely *logos*, which implies at once discourse and reason. A research on the history of Greek rhetoric shows that *logos* had a direct relationship with the city (*polis*) where public discourse played an essential role in political life.[35] Logic, then, was born from this sophistry:

Historically, rhetoric and sophistry, by analyzing the forms of discourse as the means of winning the contest in the assembly and the tribunal, opened the way for Aristotle's inquiries, which in turn defined the rules of proof along with the technique of persuasion, and thus laid down a logic of the verifiably true, a matter of the theoretical understanding, as opposed to the logic of the apparent or probable, which presided over the hazardous debates on practical questions.[36]

Therefore, at its origin, logic was defined in relation to sophistry. The opposition between logic and sophistry in ancient Greece signifies that each of the two opposing terms are only fully understood in their opposition to each other and in relation to both *logos* and *polis*. On the contrary, in ancient China, not only was the political structure radically different from that of the Greek city, but we do not find any form of discourse that would exactly correspond to *logos*.[37] From this point of view, by qualifying Gongsun Long as a "sophist" or "logician," we rather obscure than clarify the peculiarity of his

---

34   Harbsmeier, *Language and Logic*, 300.
35   Cf. Laurent Pernot, *La Rhétorique dans l'Antiquité* (Paris: Librairie Générale Française, 2000), 7.
36   Jean-Pierre Vernant, *The Origins of Greek Thought* (Ithaca: Cornell University Press, 1982), 50. *Les Origines de la pensée grecque* (Paris: PUF, 1962), 56–57.
37   For the conceptual and political differences between Greece and China around the problems of *logos* and sophistry, cf. Yijing Zhang, "La 'rhétorique' chinoise et la rhétorique aristotélicienne en Chine," *Revue internationale de philosophie* 286, no. 4 (Dec. 2018): 425–44.

questions and his mode of reasoning. Jean-Paul Reding was the first scholar to carry out a comprehensive comparison between Greek and Chinese sophistry based on a long critical review of the classical texts that are relevant to Greek and Chinese "sophists." His analysis, however, arrives at the unexpected conclusion that the assimilation of the Chinese "School of names" to the Greek sophists, which is very widespread in western Sinology, is a result of stereotypes and based on completely spurious judgements.[38]

Fraser proposes more precise translations of the Chinese appellation of the group of thinkers among whom Gongsun Long has been often classified while underlining the difficulties of this task:

> Before the Han dynasty, the social group of which these thinkers were a part was known as the *bian zhe*—"disputers" or "dialecticians"—because they spent much of their time in "disputation" (*bian*, also "discrimination" or "distinction drawing"), a form of dialectical persuasion and inquiry aimed fundamentally at "distinguishing" the proper semantic relations between names and the things or kinds of things to which they refer. "Disputers" is thus probably a more appropriate English label for Hui Shi, Gongsun Long, and the others than is the "School of Names," though it refers not specifically to these figures but to the broader class of scholars to which they belonged. ("Name-distinguishers" or "distinction-disputers" would be even more accurate, though these terms are too clumsy to adopt as English equivalents.)[39]

"Name-distinguishers" or "distinction-disputers" are the literal but clumsy translations while "logicians" or "sophists" are not translations but the projection of western concepts on a Chinese cultural phenomenon.

Graham similarly points out that while the construction of paradoxes is common to both the School of names and the Greek sophists, the Chinese school more closely resemble the Eleatics than the sophists.[40] I would like to insert my emphasis in this discussion by saying that even the construction of paradoxes is far from the aim

---

38   "Notre problème de départ reçoit ainsi une solution paradoxale : les seules similitudes qui, à notre avis, existent entre la sophistique grecque et la soi-disant sophistique chinoise n'ont pas été relevées et n'ont jamais pu servir à prouver l'existence de la 'sophistique' chinoise." Reding, *Les fondements philosophiques de la rhétorique*, 494.

39   Fraser, "School of Names."

40   Graham, *Disputers of the Tao*, 75.

of Gongsun Long (though perhaps it would characterize better the interests of Hui Shi, another famous "name-distinguisher"). As I have shown above, if the phrase "White horse is not horse" assumes a paradoxical or sophistic form, it is because western commentators have not been able to avoid thinking with the verb "to be" in understanding this phrase.

By calling Gongsun Long a logician or sophist, we are still suffering from an illusionary either/or: either that he seriously wants to prove that the proposition "white horse is not a horse" is true or that he deliberately formulates a paradox when his actual concern is to distinguish the names as "white" and "horse"—the task given by a "name-distinguisher." Another consequence of this misunderstanding is the devaluing of Chinese thought in the field of logic. We clearly find this point in Hansen's thesis of the non-development of abstract thought in China—a thesis which can be traced back to Marcel Granet.[41] Graham, taking the evolution of sophistry towards logic in Greek as a universal model of the evolution of the human spirit, concludes that Chinese thought has been underdeveloped.[42] For Anne Cheng, there is a *différence d'accent* between China and Greece.[43] All of these positions lead to the conclusion that Chinese thought is inferior to western philosophy, if we examine the former through the conceptual lens of the latter. Granet and Hansen clearly protest against this way of looking at Chinese philosophy, but their theoretical positions are not always consistent with their literal statements on Chinese thought.[44]

---

41 "La langue chinoise ne paraît point organisée pour exprimer des *concepts*. Aux signes abstraits qui peuvent aider à spécifier les idées, elle préfère des symboles riches de suggestions pratiques." Marcel Granet, *La Pensée chinoise* (Paris: Albin Michel, 1988 [1934]), 12.

42 "The first discovery of uninhibited reason is that it leads inevitably to absurd conclusions. So why go farther? The Greeks did get past this initial disorientation, the Chinese never did." Graham, *Disputers of the Tao*, 76.

43 Anne Cheng, *Histoire de la pensée chinoise* (Paris: Seuil, 1997), 136–137.

44 "La plupart des interprètes d'Occident voient cependant en elles [les notions cardinales de la pensée chinoise] les produits de telle ou telle pensée doctrinale. ... Ils commencent, en général, par leur chercher des équivalents dans la langue conceptuelle de nos philosophes. ... Elles leur paraissent témoigner du fait que la pensée chinoise ressortit à une mentalité qu'on peut (pour se servir d'expressions toutes faites et qui soient à la mode) qualifier de 'prélogique' ou de 'mythique'." Granet, *La Pensée chinoise*, 76. See also Hansen, *Language and Logic in Ancient China*, 23.

Now let us examine the label "nominalist" in the context of Chinese philosophy in light of what Hansen says about it:

> Early Chinese philosophy of language is nominalistic, in that it is not committed to recognizing any entities other than words, or "names" (*ming* 名), and the things that form their extensions. It does not appeal to universals, essences, concepts, meanings, Lockean ideas, or Platonic forms to explain the semantics of general terms or the relation between a particular thing and its kind.[45]

Hansen seems to use the term "nominalistic" as the equivalent of the Chinese "School of names." This practice belongs to "domesticated translation," which is opposed to "foreignizing translation." Generally speaking, however, the translation of philosophical ideas is not the right place for practicing "domesticated translation." The term "nominalist" has a specific meaning in the history of western philosophy. Nominalism consists in considering that universals do not have any extralinguistic existence. In other words, nouns are themselves the universals. As a result, Hansen is not properly using the term to describe the school of names: that is to say, he is claiming that the Chinese language is nominalist and yet it has no universals.[46]

---

45   Hansen, *Language and Logic in Ancient China*, 53.
46   The entry "Nominalism in Metaphysics" in the *Stanford Encyclopedia of Philosophy* claims that "the word 'Nominalism,' as used by contemporary philosophers in the Anglo-American tradition, is ambiguous. In one sense, its most traditional sense deriving from the Middle Ages, it implies the rejection of *universals*. In another, more modern but equally entrenched sense, it implies the rejection of *abstract objects*." As Hansen presupposes that there is neither universal nor abstract object in Chinese thought, it is natural for him to apply the term of nominalism to Gongsun Long in both of the senses that the term has in the Anglo-American tradition. In the same entry, we also find these words: "Nominalism, in both senses, is a kind of anti-realism. For one kind of Nominalism denies the existence, and therefore the reality, of universals and the other denies the existence, and therefore the reality, of abstract objects." (Gonzalo Rodriguez-Pereyra, "Nominalism in Metaphysics," *The Stanford Encyclopedia of Philosophy* (Summer 2019 Edition), ed., Edward N. Zalta, https://plato.stanford.edu/archives/sum2019/entries/nominalism-metaphysics/.) Compared with Fraser's words (in the same *Encyclopedia*) I quoted at the beginning, "There is now a fairly broad consensus, at least among European and American scholars, that the text is unlikely to concern universals, since no ancient Chinese philosopher held a realist doctrine of universals," the source of the confusion becomes clear: some Anglo-American philosophers or sinologists use "Nominalism" as synonym of "rejection of universals," while in the medieval context, where the term "Nominalism" came into being, what nominalists reject is the *reality* of

For Hansen, the fact that Chinese philosophy is nominalistic is a widely shared viewpoint. "Almost all attempts to characterize Chinese philosophy in general have stated, in one way or another, that the dominant character of Chinese thought is nominalistic."[47] Graham also confirms that many western Sinologists share the same perspective. Curiously, he signals its origin in European philosophy:

> Thinking with count nouns, western philosophy has searched for single entities denoted by particulars (Realism) or concepts shared by minds (Conceptualism). Thinking with mass nouns, the common name raises no problem other than how we recognize the rest when a part has been named, the simple answer to which is similarity; this explains why the early Chinese thinkers who theorize about common names ... take for granted the third of the classical western solutions, Nominalism.[48]

In full consonance with Graham, Cheng affirms that Gongsun Long is a nominalist by adding:

> Tout le débat qui a tant occupé la scolastique médiévale européenne sur l'existence ou la non-existence des universaux n'est pas seulement en l'occurrence dénué de sens, il peut constituer un obstacle majeur à la compréhension des débats chinois sur le langage dans leur spécificité.[49]

It is not clear what meaning Sinologists give to the term "nominalist" when they attribute it to Gongsun Long. Why should Gongsun Long, who never heard about the debate over universals, "take for granted" the nominalist position, one of the three positions which can only be understood in the context of this debate within European medieval philosophy? It seems that Sinologists, even those who are more favorable to the uniqueness of Chinese thought, often impose on it concepts which are only obvious for themselves. For the nominalists of the European Middle Ages, in particular there are *genera*

---

universals, but not the *concept* or the *term* of universal. Saying that universals are names is not the same thing as rejecting universals as such. Hansen seems to use the term "nominalist" to describe someone who simply has no idea of universal.

47   Hansen, "Mass Nouns and 'a White Horse is not a Horse,'" 191.
48   Graham, "Kung-sun Lung's Discourse re-read as argument about whole and part," 97.
49   Cheng, *Histoire de la pensée chinoise*, 140.

and *species* among the universals.[50] However, Hansen and Graham try to prove precisely the inability of conceiving the *genus* and *species* (or "class membership" and "inclusion" in their terminology) in their analysis of the *White Horse Discourse.*

Another contradiction in Hansen is to put together the mass-noun hypothesis, part-whole relationship, and nominalism on one hand, and to consider Platonic forms in opposition to Chinese nouns (which he supposes to be mass nouns) on the other, as if Platonic forms are incompatible with mass nouns and part-whole relationship. The relationship between forms and sensible things in Plato's theory of participation does not seem to be totally different from a part-whole relationship. Other scholars have also pointed out that Hansen confuses nominalism and part-whole relationship.[51]

While avoiding the term "nominalist" as a descriptor for Gongsun Long, I suggest that, within the European nominalist tradition, there is a principle known as "Ockham's razor," which could keep us from overinterpreting of Gongsun Long's text. This principle is expressed as follows:

> Plurality should not be posited without necessity. (*Pluralitas non est ponenda sine necessitate*).

To explain the combined word "white horse," Hansen further invents two concepts, "mass sum" and "mass product," by consulting other texts of Gongsun Long and the Mohist tradition. He finally concludes that "Gongsun Long's basic argument can be seen as a dilemma, either we interpret the compound *white house* as a mass sum or a mass product."[52] Even with these two additional concepts, Hansen does not succeed in clarifying the relationship between the horse and white, which is after all Gongsun Long's main problem.

---

50   Alain de Libera, *La Querelle des universaux* (Paris: Seuil, 1996), 166*sq*.
51   "Nor does thinking about masses and part-whole relations intuitively lead to nomi-nalism. Mereology is neutral between nominalism, conceptualism, and Platonism. Plato himself was a leading theorist of mereological relations." Fraser, "Language and Ontology in Early Chinese Thought," 434. See also Fung, "A Logical Perspec-tive on 'Discourse on White-horse,'" 515–16.
52   Hansen, "Mass Nouns and 'a White Horse is not a Horse,'" 208.

Conclusion

The problem of interpreting the *White Horse Discourse* in the western academia derives from the problems of translation and linguistic difference. Once translated into English with the verb "to be," the phrase "white horse is not horse" gives the impression that it is concerned with predication. Two consequences follow from this: firstly, we ignore that Gongsun Long is talking about the distinction of "names" and dedicate ourselves to the interpretation of the predication "a white horse is not a horse" while mobilizing various western concepts and theories to solve the relationship between "white horse" and "horse." However, Gongsun Long rather discusses the word "white" and its relationship with the word "horse." Secondly, there has been much debate over the question of whether Gongsun Long was a sophist, logician, or nominalist, without fully realizing that these terms presuppose a conception of language, which is radically different from the linguistic and cultural context in which the ancient Chinese thinker was asking his questions.

My intention in this article is to show how scholars overlook the authorial intent by ignoring the underlying linguistic and philosophical differences between the two intellectual traditions. If we ignore the linguistic structure of the ancient Chinese language, we cannot recognize the main thrust of Gongsun Long's argument. But if we miss the conceptual framework available in Chinese language by equating it with European philosophical concepts or radically differentiating them from each other, we end up reconstructing Chinese philosophy either as the same or the inferior version of the western counterpart. (We have also seen how important it is to properly understand the European philosophical concepts especially when we explain the Chinese philosophical texts with these terms.) Only by properly understanding the cultural and linguistic differences between Chinese and European intellectual traditions, we can avoid falling victim to these misinterpretations. Gongsun Long's *White Horse Discourse* is a clear case in which we must make this intercultural improvement.

References

Aristotle. "Metaphysics." In *The Complete Works of Aristotle*. Translated by David Ross and Edited by Jonathan Barnes. Princeton: PrincetonUniverstiy Press, 1984.

Cheng, Anne. *Histoire de la pensée chinoise*. Paris: Seuil, 1997.

Cheng, Chung-ying. "White Horse and Other Issues." *Philosophy East and West* 33, no. 4 (Oct. 1983): 341–354.

Chmielewski, Janusz, and Marek Mejor. *Language and Logic in Ancient China. Collected Papers on the Chinese Language and Logic*. Warszawa: Polska Akademia Nauk, 2009.

De Libera, Alain. *La Querelle des universaux*. Paris: Seuil, 1996.

Fraser, Chris. "Language and Ontology in Early Chinese Thought." *Philosophy East and West* 57, no. 4 (Oct. 2007): 420–456.

_____. "School of Names." The *Stanford Encyclopedia of Philosophy* (Spring 2017 Edition) Edited by Edward N. Zalta. https://plato.stanford.edu/archives/spr2017/entries/school-names/.

Fung, Yiu-ming. "A Logical Perspective on 'Discourse on White-horse.'" *Journal of Chinese Philosophy* 34, no. 4 (Dec. 2007): 515–536.

Fung, Yu-lan, and Derk Bodde. *A Short History of Chinese Philosophy*. New York/London: The Free Press,1966.

Graham, Angus C. *Disputers of the Tao: Philosophical Argument in Ancient China*. La Salle: Open Court, 1989.

_____. *Studies in Chinese Philosophy and Philosophical Literature*. Albany: SUNY Press, 1990.

Granet, Marcel. *La Pensée chinoise*. Paris: Albin Michel, 1988.

Hansen, Chad. "Mass Nouns and 'a White Horse is not a Horse'." *Philosophy East and West* 26, no. 2 (Apr. 1976): 189–209.

_____. *Language and Logic in Ancient China*. Ann Arbor: Michigan University Press, 1983.

_____. "Chinese Language, Chinese Philosophy, and 'Truth.'" *The Journal of Asian Studies* 44, no. 3 (May 1985): 491–519.

_____. "Term-Belief in Action: Sentences and Terms in Early Chinese Philosophy." In *Epistemological Issues in Classical Chinese Philosophy*. Edited by Hans Lenk and Gregor Paul, 45–68. Albany: SUNY Press, 1993.

_____. "Remembering Mass: Response to Yang Xiaomei." *Dao. A Journal of Comparative Philosophy* 10, no. 4 (Oct. 2011): 541–546.

Harbsmeier, Christoph. "Marginalia Sino-logica." In *Understanding the Chinese Mind: The Philosophical roots*. Edited by Robert E. Allinson, 59–83. Oxford: Oxford University Press, 1990.

_____. "Kungsun Lung and the White Horse Dialogue." In *Science and Civilisation in China*, Vol. 7, pt. 1, *Language and Logic*, 298–321. Cambridge: Cambridge University Press, 1998.

Liu, Yuyu, and Yan Ren 刘玉宇 任远, "Chonglun Chad Hansen 'Zhiliao Mingci Jiashuo' yu Gongsun Long 'Baima lun' Jieshi," 重论陈汉生'质料名词假说'与公孙龙'白马论'解释 (Reflections on Hansen's Mass-Noun Hypothesis and the Interpretation of Gongsun Long's *White Horse Discourse*). *Zhongguo Zhexueshi* 中国哲学史 (History of Chinese Philosophy), no. 3 (Aug. 2018): 122–129.

Lloyd, Geoffrey E. R. *Being, Humanity, and Understanding*. Oxford: Oxford University Press, 2012.

Lucas, Thierry. "Yes, Western Logic Applies to Gongsun Long and Mozi!" *Universitas*/哲學與文化, Vol. 30, no. 12 (2003): 25–38.

Mou, Bo. "A Double-Reference Account: Gongsun Long's 'White-Horse-Not-Horse' Thesis." *Journal of Chinese Philosophy* 34, no. 4 (Dec. 2007): 493–513.

Pernot, Laurent. *La Rhétorique dans l'Antiquité*. Paris: Librairie Générale Française, 2000.

Reding, Jean-Paul. *Les Fondements philosophiques de la rhétorique chez les sophistes grecs et chez les sophistes chinois*. Bern: Peter Lang, 1985.

Rodriguez-Pereyra, Gonzalo. "Nominalism in Metaphysics." *The Stanford Encyclopedia of Philosophy* (Summer 2019 Edition), edited by Edward N. Zalta. https://plato.stanford.edu/archives/sum2019/entries/nominalism-metaphysics/.

Van Norden, Bryan W. *Introduction to Classical Chinese Philosophy*. Indianapolis: Hackett, 2011.

_____. *Readings in Classical Chinese Philosophy*, Second Edition. Indianapolis: Hackett, 2001.

_____. "Hansen on Hsun-tzu." *Journal of Chinese Philosophy* 20, no. 3 (Sep. 1993): 365–382.

Vernant, Jean-Pierre. *Les Origines de la pensée grecque*. Paris: PUF, 1962.

_____. *The Origins of Greek Thought*. Ithaca: Cornell University Press, 1982.

Zhang, Yijing. "La 'rhétorique' chinoise et la rhétorique aristotélicienne en Chine." *Revue internationale de philosophie* 286, no. 4 (Dec. 2018): 425–440.

_____. "Les catégories d'Aristote à l'épreuve du 'sophiste' chinois Gongsun Long." *Revue Philosophique de Louvain* 117, no. 1 (Feb. 2019): 3–30.

MARGARET CHU

(THE ROYAL COMMONWEALTH SOCIETY IN HONG KONG)

PHILOSOPHY FOR CHILDREN

Globalization and the Translation of a Neo-Confucian Text, the *Yangzheng leibian* 養正類編

It is a common view of the educated global citizen or even experts on imperial China that the ordinary folk were illiterate, estranged from elite culture, with no channel of upward mobility and excluded from the civil service examinations. This general disconnect is assumed to have existed between high and low culture fortified by a political system that conferred arbitrary power on the local official and a social structure that licensed domination by the local gentry. Popular religions and Buddhist-Daoist practices characterized folk customs as distinct from Confucian rites and ceremonies. Linguistic demarcation between the refined, sophisticated speech of the literati-gentry, aristocracy and the imperial court on the one hand and, on the other, the rustic speech of the peasants who spoke local dialects and patois, testified to a top-down culture of political control that left the vast majority of the population out in the cold, alienated from the high culture of a very small minority.

Historical reality, however, offers a different narrative. Imperial China with its vast territory managed to stay united and lasted continuously for five millennia. It had a foundation stone laid in its written language, fortified by canonical texts woven together through the civil service examinations system that by the Song Dynasty (960–1259) was essentially open to all. The most essential content of these elite texts was disseminated to the little hamlet through more simplified works and primers. The sage king, Shun (舜) (3000 BCE) is lauded in Chinese history for his state sponsorship of village schools.[1] We know from an ancient text, the *Zhou li* (周禮), that official response was enthusiastic. Local officials down the ages had been known to have held periodic public lectures, especially on ethics and civic matters, in local schools. Elite values were shared, as were their history and identity. The interface of avant-garde intellectual notions and medical knowledge connected the fault plains of Sui 隋 (581–618), Tang 唐 (618–907) and Song 宋 (960–1279) China.[2] Numerous medical manuals were published alongside philosophical texts for the instruction and edification of medical practitioners, philosophers, the literate and the semi-literate. Philosophical insights on the osmotic relationship between the world external to the individual and the entire being of the person were picked up medically. The famous Tang doctor, Sun Simiao, and Chen Ziming[3] in the Song offered prescriptions for pregnant women which were included by Zhu Xi (朱熹) in his *Xiaoxue* (小學)[4] and, eight centuries later, by Zhang Boxing (張伯行), the author of the *Yangzheng leibian* (養正類編).

In the twenty-first century world of global languages, which include Chinese and English, the translation of a text from the one to the other may add to the international treasure trough of knowledge. With growing concern for youth empowerment and the dissociated, complexities compounded by a climate crisis, distributive injustice, predatory capitalism, instant accessibility to world-wide information without equivalent accessibility to employment opportunity, social mobility, economic and political security, there is a greater urgency for wisdom to be universally accessible, that life may be well-lived under any circumstance. The *Yangzheng leibian* offers a glimpse of a way the Chinese elite reached out to the nooks and corners of the country to connect with them, to make them feel they were a part of the historical entity and of the natural world, and to guide them to live wisely in it.

---

1   Zhang Boxing, "Theme of the Elementary Learning," *Xiaoxue jijie*, in *Zhengyi tang quanshu* [*The Collectanea of the Hall of Correctness and Principle*; hereafter *Collectanea*], reprinted by Zuo Zong-tong, vol. 30, no. 57 (Fujian, 1866–1870), 1a.

2   Chen Hancai, *Zhongguo gudai youer jiaoyu shi* (Guangdong: Guangdong gaodeng jiaoyu chubanshe, 1996), 185.

3   Chen Hancai, 185.

4   Zhang Boxing, "Establishing Teaching," in "Inner Chapters," *Xiaoxue jijie*, 1: 1b–2a.

The Text

The *Yangzheng leibian* is a text in a sixty-eight work collectanea, the *Zhengyi tang quanshu* 正誼堂全書 (*the Collectanea of the Hall of Correctness and Principle*) by Zhang Boxing (1652–1725).[5] The set was first published in the early eighteenth century, then reprinted by the famous late Qing general, Zuo Zongtang 左中棠, between 1866 and 1870.[6]

An eminent Cheng-Zhu schoolman in the Kangxi reign (1661 –1722), Zhang Boxing saw it his duty to revive and define the boundaries of Cheng-Zhu Neo-Confucianism after the political and philosophical turmoil of the late Ming and the disruption to society brought on first by the Ming collapse, then by the Manchu conquest. His *Collectanea* was such an effort. The *Yangzheng leibian*,[7] for its part, is a compilation of the education philosophy of the Cheng-Zhu School from the Song Dynasty down to his time, spanning half a millennium. The text is meant for young children and adult ordinary folk, especially in rustic areas or isolated hamlets.

A glance at its table of content reveals a host of authors with a medley of titles oriented around childhood learning. The text begins with the great Song Neo-Confucian, Zhu Xi's views on what young children should know, and ends with children's songs and axioms with a daily timetable of an entire month in the last chapter. In between are chapters on pedagogical theories (chapter 2), children's rites (chapter 3), conduct and curriculum (chapters 1, 3, and 5), rules and practices at a boarding school (chapter 7), the covenant of a charitable school (chapter 4), definition of philosophical concepts (chapter 6) and historical anecdotes of exemplary behavior in filiality (chapter 8), broth-

---

5   Zhang Boxing, literary name, Xiaoxian, official name, Jingan, was a native of Yifeng, in present-day Henan. A true representative of the Confucian literati, he combined scholarly pursuits with public service. His contributions to both is testified to the fact that, after his death in 1725, Zhang Boxing was conferred the title of Grand Guardian of the Heir Apparent by the Yongzheng Emperor and, a century-and-a-half later, in 1878, was enshrined as a worthy, *xian*, in the Confucian temple.

6   *Collectanea*, 68 works, 37 vols.

7   Zhang Boxing, *The Yangzheng leibian* (hereafter, *YZLB*), in *Collectanea*, vol. 32, no. 60.

erliness (chapter 9), clan harmony (chapter 10), good deeds (chapter 11) and diligence (chapter 12).

The nature of the content defines the various styles of speech and diction, from rustic patois to philosophical discourse, from philosophical verse to children's songs beyond the northern frontier. Characteristic of Confucian works on education, where the emphasis is on concrete learning and where childhood nurturing aims at watering and fertilizing this seed of natural goodness by means of such daily practice as sprinkling and sweeping, responding and replying, the *Yangzheng leibian* provides concrete prescriptions down to the minutest detail of how to cross one's hands and lively historical anecdotes featuring, for example, how a filial daughter-in-law served her unreasonable, widowed mother-in-law,[8] or the courage of a filial daughter in petitioning before the Han emperor, Wendi (文帝) (179–157), in behalf of her father while querying the inhumanity of the punishment.[9] The last chapter on children's songs and axioms reads a little like Aesop's *Fables* in the sense that it is closer to common sense morality and streetwise counsel targeting particular behavior. Chapter Six, the *Xingli zixun*, stands out for its verse form and its abstract philosophical content.

The Xingli zixun 性理字訓

The *Xingli zixun* is attributed to Cheng Ruoyong (1265–74, *jin shih*).[10] It is an expansion of a much shorter piece,[11] bearing the same

---

8   *YZLB*, chapter 8, 3a.
9   *YZLB*, 8: 3a.
10   Cheng Ruoyong (1265–74, *jin shi*), literary name Dayuan, courtesy name, Wuzhai, was a native of Xiuning, who studied Cheng-Zhu Neo-Confucianism under Raozhai.
11   Comparison of the two editions yields two identical texts but for seven characters, three of which make almost no difference in meaning. See Qing Shengzu, *Tingxun geyan* (Tianjin: Guangren tang, 1881), in *Qingding Siku quanshu zhungmu* (hereafter, *SKZM*). Compared with the version collected in *Siku quanmu congshu* (hereafter, *SKCS*), "Rujia lei," "Zi bu," no. 004, 744–98, there are seven places where the two versions are at variance, with three of them of any significance. Details are discussed in the notes below wherever relevant.

title, by Cheng Duan-meng (1143–91),[12] who was a student of Zhu Xi (1130–1200). This initial text, to a degree, imitates the work of another student of Zhu Xi, Chen Chun's (1159–1223) *Beixi ziyi* (北溪字義), although the former is much simpler with only thirty philosophical terms and is meant for young children. Chen Ruoyong expanded the piece to include a hundred and eighty-eight terms, each with a simple definition. The text is divided into six sections: (1) "Creation and Transformation"; (2) "The Feelings and the Nature"; (3) "Studying Efforts"; (4) "Good and Bad"; (5) "Completing Virtues"; (6) "The Way of Government."

An unusual feature of Chinese philosophical discourse is the apparent absence of a formal argument. *The Analects of Confucius* pales before any *Dialogue* of Plato. In the style of philosophical verse for country children, this text is written in independent lines of four characters per phrase or sentence, with usually four to six phrases/sentences per line. There is no positing of hypothesis, no dialectical or logical argument which ends in a conclusion. Each line can be read on its own for its independent message, or it can be understood jointly with any one or more relevant lines, or it can be comprehended with all the rest as a whole. For the reader foreign to this type of philosophical discourse and method of learning, she is more likely to find the English translation disconcertingly inadequate than helpful—the translation only serves to accentuate even more the foreignness of the language and mentality.

Perusal of the work yields an astounding list of philosophical terms for children's learning. Under Section One, "Creation and Transformation," twenty-seven terms on cosmology are included.[13] This section is translated in full further on, with discussion and annotations. An appreciation of the Confucian conception of the universe facilitates the understanding of its epistemology, ethics and metaphysics. It provides a window to Chinese mentality as a whole.

Section Two, "The Feelings and the Nature" comprises forty-eight terms, not so much on the affective as on the relation between meta-

---

12 Cheng Duan-meng (1143–91), literary name, Zhengsi, courtesy name, Mengzhai, was a student of Zhu Xi.

13 *Xingli zixun* (hereafter *XLZX*), in *YZLB*, 6: 1a–2b. A list of the philosophical terms of each section is included in the "Appendix."

physics and cosmology.[14] Here there is no mention of the seven emotions, *qiqing* (七情), and the six desires, *liuyu* (六欲), which one might have expected. Instead, it emphasizes a rational, systematic universe with its laws, logical sequence, standards and regulations. It explains meticulously the connection between the universe and the human world and what constitutes a human being. Often definitions are made in pairs to distinguish between, for example, the "way of heaven" and the "way of humans," with the former referring to a rational universe of principles while the latter, human relations, things and affairs.[15] While there is but "one principle," which is "goodness," and is universally bestowed on humans beings at birth, its manifestations are innumerable due to the "material force" we received at birth, which could be clear or muddy, hence the "substance" of a person could range from bright to murky, good to bad.[16] Herein lies the distinction between "heavenly mandate," which determines where we fall within the range of goodness to badness, and "human affairs," which are up to us to choose and decide on the action to take.[17] Without subscribing to the existence of a supernatural being, the Chinese tried to explain, by means of naturalistic philosophy, the question of freedom and determinism in human conduct.

What constitutes a human being is then defined as being the "heart-and-mind of heaven and earth," the meeting point of *gui* (鬼) and *shen* (神), the *ling* (靈) of all things which is capable of extending them for use.[18] All very mysterious since nowhere in the text is it illustrated what the heart-and-mind of heaven and earth are. Since the "principle of heaven" is all goodness and the "utmost principle" pervades the universe, it may be safe to assume that the heart-and-mind of heaven and earth are good, hence human beings are good. We know, moreover, that *gui shen* refer to the extension and contraction of the material force,[19] so somehow a human being is the meeting point of this extension and contraction. *Ling* is obviously some

---

14   *Xingli zixun*, 6: 2b–4b.
15   *XLZX*, 6: 2b.
16   *XLZX*, 6: 2b.
17   *XLZX*, 6: 2b–3a.
18   *XLZX*, 6: 3a.
19   *XLZX*, 6: 2a.

capability humans have which enables them to accomplish things. Juxtaposed with "things," which is a term referring to all living things, humans are more advanced because, constrained by the partiality of the "form of the material force" they are endowed with, things are unable to extend their capability the way humans can. A sort of primitive evolutionary theory is in place to explain a hierarchy of living things in nature.

A trio—the nature, the mind-and-heart, and the feelings—is elaborated to expound on the concept of Humans. While the nature is all good, being bestowed by heavenly principle, the mind-and-heart is commanded by one's self and unites the nature and the feelings.[20] The feelings, for their part, refer to responses to external things and have the capability to discern the good from the bad.[21] Feelings, therefore, are not irrational; in fact, they are rational, capable of making moral judgements. That is to say, the mind-and-heart is both good and rational. Thus, this self, which is equipped with innumerable goodness is capable prior to learning. How do we know what we know is answered by the view that all humans are born with principles and goodness, hence intellectual and moral knowledge. Ascertaining the concept of the self was important for preparing the learner to embark on the life-long journey of self-cultivation. Introducing the concept of the mind-and-heart opened the learner up to one of the mainstream philosophical dialogues spanning five centuries.

What is striking is the positive approach, deliberating on the creative, transformative but not the destructive or the bad. The term, *wu/e* (惡), badness, appears only twice, once in relation to material force being good or bad, the other when discussing the feelings, *qing* (情), which sense things and are capable of distinguishing good from bad.[22] "When the nurturing is vast, solid and upright, and is complemented by principles and righteousness, this is called the 'vast and correct material force.'"[23] Everyone, children and adults alike, are thus encouraged to work on transforming their material force.

---

20   *XLZX*, 6: 3a.
21   *XLZX*, 6: 3a.
22   *XLZX*, 6: 2b–3a.
23   *XLZX*, 6: 4a–b.

Section Three, "Studying Efforts," consists of thirty-two terms on epistemology and pedagogy,[24] which would be familiar to elite children. The piece also reads like a guideline for self-cultivation as groundwork for learning. Since human beings are endowed with heavenly principles and goodness, learning is a matter of nurturing oneself so that one can extend the mind-and-heart for the apprehension of knowledge.[25] Typically, a sequential approach is adopted. Having very briefly explained the meaning of teaching, learning and practice, the text goes on to establish the difference between elementary learning and great learning. Its significance lies in the content. While the former emphasizes sprinkling and sweeping, the Classic of Poetry, the Histories and the Six Arts for the purpose of disciplining the wanton mind-and-heart and nurturing the virtuous nature of children, the latter has the goal of training students to exhaust principles to the utmost, correct their mind-and-heart, cultivate their self and eventually govern the country well when they are in position.[26] The pedagogical method of rectification of things, that is to say, to exhaust principles inside and outside, to research, observe, deliberate and analyze everything, is to be combined with the extension of knowledge so that the mind-and-heart can perceive and understand to the utmost for future employ in society.[27] Apprehension, on this view, requires more than intellectual command. The self has to do its job. The person has to cultivate himself with "reverent seriousness," "oneness," "maintaining quiescence," "being circumspect when alone," "self-restraint with rites and propriety," "honoring the virtuous nature and nurturing the material force by being respectful," knowledgeable about righteousness, upright and fearless but without doing anything forcibly or unnaturally.[28] "Purity of the mind-and-heart" and a virtuous nature enable heavenly principle to flow freely within one. With such methodology of recitation, repetition and memorization, it renders it easier and more accessible for children to learn and remember.

---

24   *XLZX*, 6: 4b–5b.
25   *XLZX*, 6: 4b.
26   *XLZX*, 6: 4b.
27   *XLZX*, 6: 4b.
28   *XLZX*, 6: 5a–b.

In Section Four, "Good and Bad," there are thirty-three terms, where ethics is linked to metaphysics and cosmology.[29] In a culture which does not subscribe to a supernatural being complete with heaven and hell, afterlife, an immortal soul or reincarnation, ethical foundation is built on a good and rational cosmos which humans are an integral part of. This section begins by affirming that the mandate of heaven is called heavenly principle when it is endowed as goodness in humans.[30] As there is no "badness" per se that is endowed in us, no original sin, so to speak, this is a conception of human beings which views badness as deviation from, defiance or perversion of the Way due to some murky material force people happened to have received at birth, but which can be purified through self-cultivation and learning. The source of trouble comes from "selfish human desires," which are the result of the emotions and the senses having the tendency to degenerate into selfishness when being activated in response to things.[31] Thus, if we live by selfish human desires, we will degenerate every day, whereas if we return to heavenly principles, we will make progress every day towards the bright and lofty. Distinction is made between cognition which originates from the nature and the mandate, which is called the "mind-and-heart of the way," and cognition which originates from the "form of the material force," which is called the "mind-and-heart of humans."[32] Whether we comprehend via the former or the latter will impact our decision and action. Out of the thirty-three terms in this section, eleven are binary pairs at the opposite end of each other. Yet each pair has its positive lining up with the positive of another pair, as is the case with the negatives. Thus heavenly principle has its opposite, human desires; the mind-and-heart of the way, the mind-and-heart of humans; righteousness, advantage; impartiality, partiality; goodness, badness; tenacity, weakness; good fortune, calamity. Good fortune and calamity has nothing to do with luck as we know it; it is the consequence of whether principle is followed or violated and whether the material force is felicitous or perverse. Not unlike our natural endowments, the cir-

---

29   *XLZX*, 6: 5b–7a.
30   *XLZX*, 6: 5b.
31   *XLZX*, 6: 6a.
32   *XLZX*, 6: 6a.

cumstances of our lives are no less bound up with heavenly principle and material force. Within a certain confine, determinants, human choice and action define who and what we are, whether we are good or bad, courageous or timorous, brutal or parsimonious. The psychology of certain behavior is employed to illustrate the role of our choice and action: "Insisting that the Way is wrong and willfully rejecting it while plunging oneself into monstrous behavior, this is called 'self-brutalization.'"[33] Perhaps by way of caution, this section singles out more negative terms. Children growing up chanting them would have internalized the fine, moral distinctions of the positive and negative attributes of people, the characterization of different types of human conduct and the cosmology underlying it all. Crime and punishment, the exercise of laws and statutes in imperial China, perhaps no less today, may be more fruitfully appreciated through the lens of a very different view of humans, nature, and the universe.

Section Five, "Completing Virtues," is composed of twenty-six terms.[34] One of the more concrete schools of thought, Confucianism is hardly ever abstract. The orientation is human practice. Practice requires methods. There is no point deliberating on ideas which bear no relevance to Humans. What is sometimes overlooked in modern scholarship is the fact that this relevance to humans has relevance to the natural world, earth, and the cosmos, heaven. "Completing Virtues" inevitably means the attainment of sagehood. Putting knowledge we are born with into practice will do it. Spread throughout is a list of terms with concise explications which can be organized into several categories. The section begins by extolling intellectual attributes. "Extension of knowledge" depends on the vacuous essence of the mind-and-heart whose capability of apprehending principles is employed without hindrance for great achievement.[35] To be able to "abide in knowledge," it is necessary that the refined and subtle aspects of principle thoroughly light up the mind-and-heart so that the laws of each and every thing and affair are thereby understood.[36] When the exquisiteness in the exhaustion of principles and excellence in knowl-

---

33   *XLZX*, 6: 6a–b.
34   *XLZX*, 6: 7a–8a.
35   *XLZX*, 6: 7a.
36   *XLZX*, 6: 7a.

edge are reached, this is the virtue of the "exaltation of knowledge."[37] When one is genuine in following principle and fervent in putting it into practice, one is "yielding to rites and propriety."[38] Deportment and demeanor, which constitute the outward expressions of inner cultivation, are indeed adult attributes but the recognition of the genuine and the pretentious is no less important a perception for children for their self-protection. Dignified demeanor exhibits an utmost sincerity in the person which originates from the fulfilment of the nature.[39] This person possesses an Immovable mind-and-heart because the Way in him is bright and his virtues are established so he has neither suspicion nor fear.[40] He lives in accordance with the desires of the mind-and-heart, so he is naturally solid and correct, which is why he does "not transgress what is right."[41] With utmost sincerity all the time, he is one with heaven, hence he possesses "heavenly virtue."[42] That is to say, when one is sincere to the utmost without lapse, bright to the utmost without blemish and can cover the fine and the coarse of the inner and outer without missing a fine-tooth comb, then one is "fulfilling the nature."[43] When the person unites everything in him and he can function everywhere in full capacity without turning a hair, one is "fulfilling the mind-and-heart.[44] This state of being has to be accomplished by means of "sincerity of the intent," which manifests from thought and solicitude honestly and without recklessness.[45] Sincerity has to be complemented with a "correct mind-and-heart" whose cognition, when it reveals itself, is vacuously bright and impartial.[46] Other attributes are laid out for the learner to follow. In glaring contrast to the preceding section, not one single negative attribute is touched upon. This is the stage where the path to sagehood is paved. By now, the demons have been pretty

---

37   *XLZX*, 6: 7a.
38   *XLZX*, 6: 7a.
39   *XLZX*, 6: 7a.
40   *XLZX*, 6: 7b.
41   *XLZX*, 6: 7b.
42   *XLZX*, 6: 7b.
43   *XLZX*, 6: 7a.
44   *XLZX*, 6: 7a.
45   *XLZX*, 6: 7a.
46   *XLZX*, 6: 7a.

much dislodged if not subdued. The time has come for positive affirmation and constructive stimulus.

Section six, "The Way of Government," covers twenty-one terms.[47] Having given guidance to the attainment of sagehood, this section moves on to a lesson on the subject of governance. It is interesting that Confucians saw it their duty to educate country children at such a tender age on the meaning and content of governance and the distinction between good and bad ones. Egalitarian in their outlook on the privilege and duty of all sectors to engage in the business of serving society and country, the Confucians were eager to inculcate this sense of responsibility in all and sundry, not merely to inspire everyone to aspire to lofty goals in life but also to build as large a pool of talents to which they could resort. The Chinese empire being an extensive one even at its weakest, formal administrative units reached down only to prefectures. Beyond that, there were vast stretches of land and innumerable villages, hamlets, communities and clusters of groups and families which existed pretty much autonomously and self-reliantly despite an elaborate, sophisticated bureaucracy. Where official government was absent, people must still be taught how to govern themselves and understand what good leadership was, as much as what responsible members of a community entailed.

"Good governance," we are told, depends on an effective legal system with prohibitive rules and statutes as deterrents so as to correct the people when they are in the wrong.[48] But this should be preceded by, certainly complemented with, "good teaching," to transform people into pure individuals with humaneness, righteousness, rites and propriety, and music.[49] Rites and propriety are crucial for nurturing respectfulness, ethical and civilized conduct while music, with its tunes and melodies, songs and dance, played the role of nurturing the nature and the feelings by opening up blockages so that harmony is preserved in a person.[50] Since laws, systems and institutions depend on the human agent, while the duty of those in position is to "renew the people" by changing their bad habits and thereby transform-

---

47   *XLZX*, 6: 8a–9b.
48   *XLZX*, 6: 8a.
49   *XLZX*, 6: 8a.
50   *XLZX*, 6: 8a.

ing them, the duty of each individual is to "correct himself" with self-reflection but without putting the blame on others, with moral improvement and practical achievements.[51] An official was like a father and a mother to the people. Nurturing them is the motherly aspect; ensuring that there is equality, impartiality and judgement of others as human beings much like ourselves is the fatherly aspect known as being "equilateral."[52]

The world is constantly changing. Vis-à-vis all that goes on around us, it is often difficult to determine what to preserve and what to alter. As it applies to those entrusted with decision-making in office or in any position, so it applies to everyone in life. Timeliness is exercised in accordance with circumstances governed by righteousness so that each is proper and without being extreme or deficient.[53] The "warp" is the constant of the "substance of the way" complemented by the knowledge of heaven and earth and cannot be altered by future generations.[54] The "provisional exercise of power," for its part, refers to the necessity of altering the means of arriving at the Way due to the constraints of the times; but in terms of aiding the warp, it is far from it.[55] Thus, one learns about why sometimes changes are necessary and why certain things, including government measures, cannot be altered. Government cannot be without a head. "Ultimate regality" means that when the position which one holds is the most honorable, when one's virtues flourish and when one can propagate laws and regulations when abiding at home.[56] The son of heaven refers to one who has inherited the transmission from heaven, who is practicing the way of heaven, perpetuating the resolve and following the affairs of forebears.[57] But a distinction must be made between "kingship" and "hegemony." While kings guide the world with humaneness, righteousness, virtues, and rites and propriety, and the people follow suit, hegemons manage the world by means of advantages and profits

---

51 *XLZX*, 6: 8b.
52 *XLZX*, 6: 8b.
53 *XLZX*, 6: 8b.
54 *XLZX*, 6: 8a.
55 *XLZX*, 6: 8a.
56 *XLZX*, 6: 8b.
57 *XLZX*, 6: 8b.

with the people being fearful and submissive on those counts.[58] Even country children were taught how to gauge their emperors.

By the end of the piece, a child knows that we are a part of the universe, which is good and rational. It is possible to be good by exerting efforts to acquire intellectual knowledge with complementary endeavors to nurture the self. The source of badness is pointed out: the degree of badness in a person originates from the murky material force each receives at birth. Implicit, then, is a less rigid, more humane view of the undesirables. "Handicapped," one might say, they could exert both moral and intellectual efforts to make up for inadequacies. The fine lines of good to bad are drawn with descriptions to illustrate the differences and terms to define them. A child will grow up observing and distinguishing the conduct of herself and of those around her. Discernment without a goal can channel mental energies into being critical at best and condemnatory at worst. The attainment of sagehood could steer the trials and tribulations of moral endeavors as well as the stresses and strains of learning and living into a target-oriented conduit. A useful portrayal of the moral and intellectual attributes, desirable demeanor, state of mind and state of being is provided to enliven the discourse. Characteristic of Confucian concerns, the piece ends on governance. Country children, no less, were shown the methods of governing so that not only would they know what to expect of good governance but the ambitious, inspired or motivated would integrate their studies and self-cultivation with an awareness of political responsibility. They would also know who the king and who the hegemon was.

Almost two centuries after Zhang Boxing's inclusion of this little piece in his *Yangzheng leibian*, in 1881, it is collected into a volume along with other short works for young children and printed by Guangren tang. Its continuous inclusion and reprinting testifies to its importance in the Cheng-Zhu school. It illustrates how, in imperial China, the Confucians made express efforts to write and compile texts in simpler language, using local dialects and patois to educate the country folk, to share their cultural, intellectual and political her-

---

58   *XLZX*, 6: 8b–9a.

itage and to provide a reservoir of wisdom for the challenges con-
fronting human existence.

*Back to Basics: Translation of Neo-Confucian Conception of the
Universe in the* Xingli zixun 性理字訓 *(Definition of Terms on the
Philosophy of Nature and Principle)*

In the main, the province of classical Confucianism lies in the
anthropocentric domain. In rehabilitating the *Book of Changes*, Song
Neo-Confucians had advanced a rationalistic natural philosophy
based on cosmological speculations oriented around certain fundamental laws of the universe. The following is a translation of Section One, "Creation and Transformation." The target readership was
country children of five, six years old, and the scope and sophistication of the philosophical concepts speak for themselves.

Cheng Ruoyong, *Definition of Terms on the Philosophy of Nature
and Principle*

Section One, "Creation and Transformation"

The principle that is excellent pervades all. It is vacuous and noiseless, and is
never definite.[59] It is the axis of creation and transformation. It is the source of
all kinds of things. This is called the "great ultimate."
A material force that is indistinct fills the "great vacuity." Its activity and qui-
etude permeate everywhere. It develops and nurtures creation and transformation. This is called the "primordial material force."
When the material force is active, it is healthy. It is capable of causing the beginning of myriad things. It makes up the odd numbers. This is called "yang."
When the material force is quiet, it is compliant. It is capable of completing the
myriad things. It makes up the even numbers. This is called "yin."
That which receives the yang of the material force is light and clear, it takes on
forms and circulates outside the earth; it is huge and covers everything; it chiefly
produces things. This is called "heaven."

---

59   *XLZX,* 6:1a. The character used is *ding,* constant, definite. However, in the
     SKZM, 1a, and the *SKCS,* 1a, the character is *zhan,* meaning crack, a thin line of
     opening. In that case, the translation will be: "It is vacuous and noiseless, and there
     is no crack which it will not penetrate."

That which receives the yin of the material force is heavy and muddy, it takes shape and is contained in heaven; it is extensive and embraces everything; it chiefly completes things. This is called "earth."

It has the nature of yang, the virtues of heaven, is healthy and never rests; this is called *qian* (乾).

It has the nature of yin, the virtues of Earth, is compliant and constant; this is called *kun* (坤).

The material force circulates in heaven, it flows freely without borders.[60] In spring, it is wood; in summer, fire; in autumn, metal and in winter, water. Soil acts as the material force that gushes forth. The four seasons are entrusted to kings. This is called the "five agents."

Substance is born of the earth. It develops from the minute to the prominent. It fructifies the earth below and makes bounteous heaven above. Whether it should be crooked or straight, you follow the nature of the leather. The soil also contains it, and you can plough and harvest. This is called the "five elements."

The birth of the myriad things in the season of spring has young yang as its material force. This is the beginning of the way of heaven, which is called the "origin."

The growth of the myriad things during the season of summer has old yang as its material force. This is the penetration of the way of heaven, which is called "prosperity."

The progress of the myriad things in the season of autumn has young yin as its material force. This is the appropriateness of the way of heaven, which is called "benefit."

The completion of the myriad things during the season of winter has old yin as its material force. This is the correctness and firmness of the way of heaven, which is called "purity."

That which transcends form, and has neither sound nor smell, is called the Way.

That which has form, and has shape and substance, is called "implement."

The principle that is natural is called "heaven."

That which governs the myriad transformations is called the "lord."

To speak from the perspective of the two aspects of the material force, the yang essence is called *hun* (魂), the yin essence is called *po* (魄).

To speak from the perspective of the one material force, when the material force is there, it extends; when the material force has left, it contracts. Both are called *gui shen* (鬼神).

When the one material force circulates, it changes and penetrates without end. Its two aspects, yin and yang, stand at opposite poles to each other. They interact and interchange; this is called "change."

It is the result of gradual transformation that something slowly takes shape. It is the completion of change that something vanishes without a trace. This is called "change and transformation."

---

60 *SKZM*, 1a, yields *xing*, form, shape, while *YZLB*, 6:1a, gives *qi*, material force. The latter is undoubtedly the appropriate term here.

Yang is active while yin is quiet. Unpredictably, they unite as one. These two aspects of the material force grow and vanish; their execution and achievement are gradual. This is called "wondrous transformation."
The mandate of heaven is majestic. It has neither sound nor smell. It is called the "substance of the way."
The operation of yin and yang increases and decreases, begins and ends. It produces and reproduces without end. This is called "creation and transformation."
The original source of creation and transformation is extensive and minute. It is not easy for the beginner in learning to comprehend. If one is at a loss and unable to understand the general idea, one would still not be able to get it later despite diligence and hard work.
The terms are listed at the beginning of the chapter for students to study their definitions. If they can use them for the rest of their lives, it would be fabulous.

What is all this about?

In a matter of twenty-seven terms and less than three pages, a young child gets to know where and what we are in the universe. To know that, we have to know what the universe is in the first place, where it comes from (the great ultimate, *taiji* 太極, which is the term to describe the utmost principle, *zhili* 至理), what it is made of (the one material force, *yiqi* 一氣) and what all the natural phenomena are. Quickly we realize that change and transformation, *bian hua* (變化), is the characteristic of everything in heaven, earth and humans. Although the two aspects of the material force, *yin yang*, stand at opposite ends to each other, they interact and commingle. While things take shape as the result of gradual transformation, at the completion of change, things vanish without a trace. But it is a rational universe with its own regulatory system and order. For example, the birth, growth, progress and completion of the myriad things are linked to the "four seasons," with each of the different aspects (old and young *yang*, old and young *yin*) of the material force being connected with each of the four seasons, and the different stages (beginning, penetration, appropriateness, and correctness) of the way of heaven are correspondingly manifested in nature as origin, prosperity, benefit, and purity.[61] Humans play a role, for the four seasons are entrusted to kings.[62]

---

61 *XLZX*, 6: 1b–2a.
62 *XLZX*, 6: 2a.

A cursory reading would give one a sense of the origin of the universe, earth and humans, and their relationship with one another. It also helps one to understand the natural world with its climate change and seasons, and the interconnectedness between natural phenomenon and the human world. Above all, it provides rational understanding of the changes in the human world as part of the operation of the universe where there is no absolute and permanent bifurcation between good and bad but which the kings bear express responsibility in guarding the natural world. Thus, children growing up chanting such verses would be internalizing a cosmology which is the foundation of a metaphysical view that is the basis of human moral relationships from within the family to society and polity. It is a cosmology that is intimately knitted together with the earth and humans. More significantly, they would be assessing history past and present, as well as their own lives from such perspectives.

Translation and Romanization of Difficult Terms

I would like to begin with a familiar term, *qi* (氣). In *A Source Book in Chinese Philosophy*, published in 1963, Wing-tsit Chan translates it as "material force." In W. T. de Bary's *The Unfolding of Neo-Confucianism* (1970), and his subsequent works, the term is also translated as "material force." A student of both, I have been using this translation of *qi* consistently, though often feeling uncomfortable. In the context of this short piece at least, *qi* is never defined. Its condition, function and operations are given a cluster of terms, *yin yang*, *gui shen*, *hun po*, and *ling*, none of which can be appropriately translated into the English language. While *yin yang* are the two aspects of *qi*, differently termed because each describes a different condition of *qi* and each performs a different function, *gui shen* are terms used to describe *qi*'s operation, whether it is extending or contracting. Most scholarship follows W. T. Chan's translation of *gui shen* as "spiritual beings" or "spiritual forces";[63] and Chan has described them as "negative and positive spiritual forces";[64] "ghosts" is sometimes used by scholars to

---

63   W. T. Chan, *A Source Book in Chinese Philosophy* (Princeton: Princeton University Press, 1963), 504, 514, 547, 593, 690, 789, 822, 826.

64   Chan, "Appendix," 789–90.

refer to *gui* and "spirits" to *shen*. We have seen that *gui shen* comprises of a term to describe the activities of *qi*, with *yin yang* each describing its two opposite ends whose interaction is called change, but at which completion, things vanish without a trace. We are also told that *gui shen* do not refer to a separate being, thing or entity. Added to these various terms are *hun po* (魂魄), which is translated as "soul" by Chan.[65] In this children's piece, these two terms describe two aspects of *ling*, with the *yang ling* called *hun* and the *yin ling* called *po*. The term *ling* does not appear in the section on cosmology but in the next one, on "The Feelings and the Nature," where *ling* is defined as a condition of the heart-and-mind, *xin*, and of the body/self, *ti*, when they are vacuous and bright, capable of knowing and sensing. The Christian view of the soul as an everlasting, separate thing from the body is completely alien to the Confucian conception of *hun po*. Moreover, *hun po* are two different aspects, the *yang* and the *yin* aspects of *ling*. Woven into this conception of *qi* are *qian* and *kun*, which Chan translates as "heaven" and "earth."[66] Chen Ruoyong, however, defines them in relation to two aspects of the nature, with *qian* as the *yang* of the nature and *kun* as the *yin* of the nature; while the former is a term for referring to the virtues of heaven, the latter refers to the virtues of earth, as our children's piece states. Hence, *qian* and *kun* cannot be heaven and earth per se. The attributes of something are not that something itself. In short, surrounding the term *qi* is a group of words equally impossible to find comparable words in the English language which would render anything even in approximation.

While "material force" reads like a term in a science fiction or a figure in a film like Star Wars, it has no comparable usage in the English language; "ghosts" and "spiritual beings" are meaningful terms not only in the English language but also in Western civilization. For this reason, romanization is used to introduce foreign concepts from a different philosophical paradigm.

Gui shen are preferred to "ghost and spirit" in the preceding translation because, although "ghost" may be stretched for *gui*, "spirit" comes closer to the sense of the word in some context; there is,

---

65   Chan, 12.
66   Chan, 248.

however, no English word which can express the sense of seriousness and extension implied in the word, *shen*. Chan uses "spirit,"
"spiritual beings" and "spiritual forces" for both *gui shen* in different
contexts.[67] Probably uncomfortable with his choice in the English
translation of these two Chinese terms, he added an appendix in
which he explains at length.[68] Relying on Chen Chun's substantial
explanation of the terms in *Beixi ziyi* (北溪字義), Chan underscores
the four categories under which Chen Chun classifies them. The
first category of meaning is to be found in the Confucian classics,
by which the Song philosopher means the classics as understood
by the Neo-Confucians, who conceive of *gui shen* as negative and
positive forces behind events. On this view, expansion is *shen* while
contraction is *gui*. Chen Chun cautions that this naturalistic philosophical conception must be kept distinct from the meaning it carries in the other three categories, which regards *gui shen* as spiritual
beings. In ancient religious sacrifices, *shen* is often seen as heavenly
beings while *gui* refers to spirits of deceased human beings. Latter-
day religious sacrifices often take *gui shen* to be ancestors. In popular
religion, *shen* are perceived as gods, who are good and *gui* as demons,
some of whom are good while some others, not good. Although *gui
shen* may refer to all three categories by Neo-Confucian philosophers in certain contexts, they are generally regarded as the activity
of the material force. Quoting Zhang Zai (1020–77), "The negative
spirit (*kuei*) and positive spirit (*shen*) are the spontaneous activity of
the material force (yin yang)," Chan ascertains that this is the definition commonly accepted.[69] Our text for children, for its part, follows
more closely Chen Chun's definition by emphasizing the contraction and extension aspect of the one material force. By five to six
years old, a naturalistic, rational frame of mind of elite philosophy
had begun to be inculcated in rustic children against the possible
environment of cult and superstitious practices which they might
have found themselves in.

---

67   Chan, 495; also, see references in note 63.
68   Chan, 789–790. My account which follows is summarised from this section of the
      Appendix and Chen Chun's *Beixi ziyi*, https//zh.m.wikisource.org.
69   Chan, 789–90.

If *qian kun* cannot be rendered as "heaven and earth," what might they refer to in Chinese? *Qian kun* were first used by the Yin Yang School. The *Book of Changes* has this to say:

> Heaven is high, the earth is low, and thus *ch'ien [qian]* and *k'un* are fixed.... The way of *ch'ien* constitutes the male, while the way of *k'un* constitutes the female. *Ch'ien* knows the great beginning, and *k'un* acts to bring things to completion. *Ch'ien* knows the easy, and *k'un* accomplishes through the simple.[70]

> The Master (Confucius) said, "*Ch'ien* and *k'un* are indeed the gate of change! *Ch'ien* is yang and *k'un* is yin. When yin and yang are united in their character, the weak and strong attain their substance. In this way the products of Heaven and Earth are given substance and the character of spiritual intelligence can be penetrated."[71]

> *Ch'ien* is heaven. It is round, it is the ruler, the father, jade, metal, cold, ice, deep red, a good horse, an old horse, a lean horse, a piebald horse, tree fruit. *K'un* is the earth, the mother, cloth, kettle, frugality, the level, a young heifer, a large carriage, fiber, multitude, a handle, and black soil among the various kinds of soil....[72]

Playful substitute of the two Chinese terms with "heaven" and "earth" speaks volumes about their inappropriateness. To thus translate *qian kun* does injustice to the concepts in both the source text culture and the target language culture. Given the diverse meaning of the two Chinese terms, retaining them through romanization may arouse curiosity in the inquisitive, enables a deeper understanding of Chinese philosophy and may serve to enrich the target language and culture, as *yin yang* or *tai ji* have done. For the Chinese children and the country folk, *qian* "has the nature of yang, the virtues of heaven, is healthy and never rests" while *kun* "has the nature of yin, the virtues of earth, is compliant and constant."

---

70 Chan, 248, translated from "Appended Remarks," *Book of Changes*, part 1, chapter 1. To avoid confusion, I have here left out the words "Heaven" and "Earth" which are in parenthesis in Chan's translation.

71 Chan, 248–249, translated from "Appended Remarks," *Book of Changes*, part 2, chapter 1.

72 Chan, 249, translated from "Remarks on Certain Trigrams," *Book of Changes*, chapter 11.

Really for Children?

Perusal of the text reveals philosophical ideas which, in Western
discourse, could fall under such categories as cosmology, epistemology, ethics, metaphysics, ontology and pedagogy although, typically,
concepts outside of the Western philosophical discourse are numerous. Another familiar feature is the interconnectedness of the affective and the rational, the correlative way of thinking and the binary
categories, evident even in the titles of a few sections. Difficult though
many of such concepts are, the stated target were young children of
five to six years. How is that possible? The traditional Chinese language lends itself easily to recitation and memorization. The often-
used four-character phrase, clause or sentence allows for chanting by
children in a culture where recitation is part and parcel of learning.
The Confucian idea is that simple understanding is sufficient for
young children whereas once you have internalized the knowledge
through memorization, the understanding will come in time, with
life experience.[73]

---

73   The issue of the difficulty of the content of the text not only for young children but
      also for the author was discussed as early as the time of the completion of the origi-
      nal *Xingli zixun* by Cheng Duan-meng, Zhu Xi's student, in the Song Dynasty (W.
      T. Chan, *Zhu Zi xin xue an*, Taiwan: Xuesheng shuju, 1988, 421). The aim of the
      work was similar to that of another student of Zhu Xi, Chen Chun (1159–1223),
      who had just finished his *Beixi ziyi*, although the latter targets an older, more
      learned reader. Zhu Xi had initially commended the *Xingli zixun* for its brevity and
      even compared it to the *Er ya* Section of the *Classic of Poetry* (*Chang-zhou zhuru
      xue an*, in *Song Yuan xue an*, juan 69: 13b–14a, *Siku beiyao* edition); however, in
      his *Yulei*, Zhu Xi expresses query about some terms, remarking on the difficulty of
      composing this type of texts (*Zhu Zi yulei*, Zhonghua shuju, 1983, vol. 7, chap-
      ter 117: 421). Even with Cheng Ruoyong's expansion, the text had been received
      both positively and negatively into the late nineteenth century. Zhu Fenglin in
      the Song had found some of the terms and concepts too difficult for young chil-
      dren, expressing concern that inappropriate examples employed to explain these
      terms could be misleading because the origins of the terms for a proper under-
      standing were crucial. (*Shuangfeng xue an*, in *Song Yuan xue an*, juan 83: 6b–7a,
      Siku beiyao edition.) Half a millennium later, the *Siku chuanshu zongmu tiyao* is
      even more severe in its criticism: the content is a medley of disorganised terms
      with four-character sentence having no consistent rhyming scheme while there is
      no such genre in the tradition; probably unaware of Zhu XI's comments cited by
      W. T. Chan and recounted here, the editors go on to surmise that the author might
      well be an imposter from a village school (*SKZM*, 798). On the other side of the

The Confucian Paradigm

A quick read of the vocabulary brings to the fore the particular classification of terms under categories uncommon in the dialogue of Western philosophy. It also exposes an unfamiliarity with a wide swathe of intellectual territory among a huge sector of the world's non-Chinese-speaking population, especially those steeped in the Western paradigm of thinking. Until twentieth-century Western incursion in Asia, Chinese philosophy had been shared with its neighbors. Rich cultures such as Japan, Korea, and Vietnam had embraced, adapted and developed their own sophisticated schools of philosophy, each with characteristics unique to their people and heritage. These "Confucian" cultures share conceptions among themselves not dissimilar to the Greco-Roman, Judeo-Christian heritage shared by Western nations. It is neither the intent nor purpose of this study to engage in a comparative study save to accentuate possibilities of mentalities interchanged and intermingled between very different peoples with very different historical development, each living in their own cultural paradigm. The aim here is to inspire and encourage greater intellectual exchange through scholarly translation, following in the footsteps of the ancient cultures spanning the European Continent, the Middle East, and Asia.

---

spectrum, in the compilation, *Lishi, mingwu* by Fang Fengchen, et al, in the Song, Cheng Ruoyong's *Xingli zixun* is included (Fang Fengchen, et al., *Lishi, mingwu*, in *Gudai youxue chimeng jingdian*, no.4, Chi Lu shushe, 1998). In the early Qing, there is Zhang Boxing who included the piece in his *Yangzheng leibian*. More than a hundred years on, Wang Chengxian writes a Preface to *Xingli zixun* tracing the importance of the piece from the ancient *Er ya* to Chen Chun's *Beixi ziyi*, explaining that the latter expands on the former but is intended for serious studies and the exhaustion of principles, whereas *Xingli zixun* is designed for children to chant and memorise so that they would internalise the concept unconsciously. Furthermore, it could complement the *Xiaoxue*. Wang declares that Grand Historian Fang Taozi has also encouraged him to print it so that they could use it in the clan and village schools (Qing Shengzu, *Tingxun geyan*, 1a.). Thus, as late as 1881, the piece was still held as valuable for teaching young children that "they may understand it for themselves that the goal of heaven, people, the Nature and destiny, the origins of yin yang and *gui shen*, and the function of moral constants, statutes and rites are not divorced from the daily function of food and drink (Chan, 249).

Children's Songs and Maxims

Appreciating that wisdom and knowledge pervade everywhere, the Confucians never shied of reaching out to the common folk and spreading their contributions to all and sundry. Sophisticated ideas can be articulated no less in simple forms, through dialects and folk speech than with refined, literary language. The last chapter of the *Yangzheng leibian* comprises maxims for children of four-character, six-character or mixed-character phrases/clauses per line, a children's song, songs from the northern frontier and from beholding Jiangnan.[74] The *Xiao er yu* (小兒語, *Children's Songs*) were compiled by Lu De-sheng and the *Xu xiao er yu* (續小兒語) by his son Lu Xinwu (1536–1618).[75] The younger Lu is anthologized in Huang Zongxi's *Ming ru xue an* (*Anthology of Ming Philosophers*), and was famous for his integrity, honesty and righteousness. At his death, he was conferred the post-humous title of minister of the Board of Justice.[76] Thus, these were the intellectual and political elite of the Ming Dynasty who made it their duty to write for the edification of the simple folk and of their children. The late seventeenth-century mandarin, Zhang Boxing, no less eminent, who would prove to be more courageous in standing by the principles of governance at the risk of his life, explains in his introduction to this chapter that his purpose is to provide children of the common folk with edifying songs and ballads to sing while play-ing with each other in the alleyways. While elite children have their texts and curriculum, these simple people have been left to their own devices, picking up lewd and coarse jingle-jangles. By providing them with maxims which are useful in their everyday life, the goal, Zhang underscores, is to transform these rough and tumble youngsters gradu-ally through an unconscious process of internalization through playful singing into cultured, good and responsible people.[77]

Ming Dynasty vernacular writing style is generally simpler, free of the exuberance of the Han and the sophistication of the Tang and

---

74   *YZLB*, chapter 13.
75   *YZLB*, 13: 1a–4a, 4a–15a.
76   https://baike.baido.com. Lu Kun, *Lu Kun quanzi*, in *Lixue congshu* (Hong Kong :Zhong-hua shu ju, 2008).
77   *YZLB*, "Preface," 1–2a.

Song. It was as though the simple, direct style of speech of its founder had set the tone for greater simplicity in writing, more diffusion of high culture to society and increasing popularization of infrastructures for education and of their curriculum. The early Qing inherited this Ming trend, an unsurprising reason for the *Yangzheng leibian* to incorporate these songs. It was as though the foreign conquerors, the early Manchus, alien to Chinese culture and language, had preferred a simpler linguistic style of their conquered people. The foreign conquerors had to read the unfamiliar texts of the conquered in the conquered language. To end the text with a chapter of people's songs and maxims synchronizes with the taste of the Manchu Court and the ethos of Confucianism.

Chapter thirteen of the *Yangzheng leibian* reads like a little manual on common sense wisdom. It is filled with "dos and don'ts" for oneself and for one's interaction with others. Five hundred years have not diminished the wisdom it tries to convey. From the ordinary folk of Inner Mongolia to Tibet, Beijing to Hong Kong, Macau to Singapore, Taiwan to overseas Chinese communities, some would have been growing up with such maxims at home, others would have heard it from Chinese people from all walks of life. It is only a matter of extent and adaptation. It no longer requires the existence of a text for the perpetuation. It has a life of its own among the Chinese people. The global prevalence speaks to the resilience of folk wisdom which can withstand half a millennium of the most turbulent and revolutionary eras of Chinese history.

To get a flavor of what this may be, I shall begin with the translation of the entire four-character phrase/sentence per line of Lu Desheng's *Xiao er yu*. It is followed by the translation of a few selections picked out of all the songs and classified under a few categories to provide a sense of the scope.

Lu Desheng, Xiao er yu[78]

Four-character:

> Since you are a living human being, there are naturally principles for the art of living. If everyone is idle, who is going to feed and clothe you?

---

78   *YZLB*, 13: 1a–4a.

All your words and actions must be calm and relaxed. Nine out of ten errors are due to haste.

Be tranquil and composed. Speak with ease but don't be frivolous and mean. This will incur contempt and censure.

If you want to become a good person, you must select good people to be your friends. If you drink pure wine as though it was sour, where would you find sweet wine?

You bear burdens of the pole on your shoulders and you pushed the cart from behind; a poor fellow works for his living. Every day you see promotion and advancement, but do not get into conflict with others for that reason.

First learn how to be patient and how to make your temper subside quickly. The hot-tempered and the rash, their lives can never get anywhere.

With only a few ideas, you utter nonsense to everyone. The vast bell is soundless; a full bottle has no sound.

There is no need to conceal your mistakes; to do so, you would only be adding one more error to yourself.

What you forcefully grab and craftily acquire, you would never feel that you have enough. One day, catastrophe will hit you out of the blue, and you will have to endure it.

Unintended errors, once spoken, should be let go of. A misstep here and a wrong there, who in the world is above it?

You must at least acquire one life's skill; then, when poverty hits you, it will save you from disaster.

Whenever you talk to people, observe their facial expression. If your views conflict, you need not insist on yours.

If you fabricate stories and foment trouble, who would not be afraid of you? But beware! For there are laws of the land and heavenly principles.

You eat your fill and dress your best, flibbertigibbety you gossip-monger; in which case, you might as well be an ox or a horse.

If you point people out to their face, you can incur the greatest misfortune on yourself. Be it right or wrong, let people say what they want.

Animal Rights:

Bees and moths can no more endure hunger and cold than human beings. Ants, too, know pain. What person is not afraid of death and seeks survival? Don't kill living things and injure life.[79]

Women's Rights:

Do not force lofty human beings to look downwards. Do not turn women into despicable and worthless creatures.[80]

---

79   *YZLB*, 13: 2b.
80   *YZLB*, 13: 3a.

When you gaze at other people's women and daughters, you fill your eyes with delight. When other people gaze at your women and daughters, your heart is filled with anger. A bad name is difficult to erase while good repute is rare.[81]

Just mind the affairs of your own household; do not speak ill of another's daughter or wife. One who tittle-tattles about the women's quarters of others injures heaven and harms principles.[82]

Extol Frugality over Riches and Ambition:

It is possible to have sufficiency by being frugal; whereas if you want to have enough, when will you ever have enough? Pity those who bring destruction upon themselves; it is all because they engaged in accumulating things.[83]

When the heart is delighted upon seeing money and things, this is the source of becoming a thief.[84]

Those who thirst for wealth can never stop acquiring more unto their death. Wealth which is acquired immorally will be repaid with profligate sons.[85]

No Rage, Wine and Women:

Wine, women, riches and temper are four sources of ruin which you must shun.[86]

When the heart is clear and desires few, you will not be subdued by the four things. When you minimize issues and refrain from getting enraged, you need not submit to the four kings.[87]

Be Circumspect:

The mouth leaks all the secrets in the heart; the words of the heart must not be known by the mouth.[88]

Your thoughts and ideas are deep and silent; your words and expressions are calm and subtle. Although the challenge is overwhelming, you bear it all on your shoulders without noise or fuss.[89]

Observe people with a detached eye; listen to people with a disinterested ear; handle your emotions with dispassionate composure and deliberate on matters of principle with a tranquil mind-and-heart.[90]

---

81   *YZLB*, 13: 3b.
82   *YZLB*, 13: 7b.
83   *YZLB*, 13: 9b.
84   *YZLB*, 13: 11a.
85   *YZLB*, 13: 5b.
86   *YZLB*, 13: 11b.
87   *YZLB*, 13: 12a.
88   *YZLB*, 13: 13a.
89   *YZLB*, 13: 6b.
90   *YZLB*, 13: 6b.

Don't Let Your Tongue Fly:

In life, those who ruin their families and destroy their own lives, eighty percent do so through speaking ill of their own kind.[91]

You do not taste the bitterness or sweetness of what you swallow. Once you have spilled whatsoever that has come out of your mouth, you can no longer retrieve it. Pity that this eight-feet body has its life and death determined by the tongue.[92]

Magnanimity:

Let him take advantage as much as he wishes; what harm is there if I have less? All things external to me are mere extras. There is joy in yielding while strife doesn't make you shine.[93]

Treat others with magnanimity but yourself with abstinence. Admonish yourself with strictness but judge others with leniency.[94]

Your sorrows and anguish are best known to yourself; who would notice the pains and heartaches of another? When you deal with people, you must try to understand them by feeling for them; when you criticize people, you must never be harsh and severe.[95]

Don't Trample on the Vulnerable:

Despise not the lowly; deride not the elderly; debase not the poor; degrade not the insignificant.[96]

On Superstition and Adorning Statutes and Temples:

The family to the east does not believe in yin yang; the family to the west highly esteems *feng sui*. Good and ill-fortune similarly descend upon them; yet they do not regret all the money thus spent.[97]

The duke of heaven does not need to reside in a house; the way of the spirits does not require clothes to wear. If you insist on making statues, drawings and paintings of the Buddha, you might as well give charity to the poor and the suffering.[98]

---

91   *YZLB*, 13: 3a.
92   *YZLB*, 13: 7b.
93   *YZLB*, 13: 16b.
94   *YZLB*, 13: 6a.
95   *YZLB*, 13: 8a.
96   *YZLB*, 13: 13a.
97   *YZLB*, 13: 9a.
98   *YZLB*, 13: 7a.

How is the *junzi* like?

> From the mouth of a lofty man, you will not hear anything which violates the Way: he either talks about human relations or teachings of the world.[99]
> The lofty man's feet do not tread helter-skelter; he does so according to rules or standards.[100]
> In the breast of the lofty man is the "substance of constants": if it is not human feelings, it is heavenly principle.[101]

This is but a small sampling of a wide range of coverage. There are axioms of positive encouragement, including a whole song on goodness by the younger Lu. There is moreover a glimpse of philosophical terms employed in daily usage in dialects and patois. More interestingly for this study, some of the philosophical terms in the earlier piece are evident in these songs as part of their world view.

Globalization and the Yin Yang Approach

In the community of translators, two major schools exist in the West to define the art and practice of translation. The instrumentalists, who prefer a literal approach of equivalence, not necessarily word-for-word, but sense-for-sense reproduction of the source text which manages to preserve its invariant features in the translation, according to Lawrence Venuti, boast of such ancient practitioners as Cicero and the early Christian commentator, Jerome.[102] The hermeneutical approach, which favors a non-literal approach of creativity and interpretation, underscores the inevitability of seismic shifts between two linguistic and cultural entities, has among its ancient champions the great Roman poet, Horace.[103] The models are obviously more sophisticated and the dialogue, more sumptuous, relevant features of which are woven into this tapestry of discourse.

---

99   *YZLB*, 13: 12a.
100 *YZLB*, 13: 12a.
101 *YZLB*, 13: 12a.
102 Lawrence Venuti, *The Translation Studies Reader* (New York: Routledge, 2012), 13. This text serves as the major source of my discussion of the two models of translation.
103 Venuti, 14.

Earlier, the difficulty of a few philosophical terms, *qi, qian kun, gui shen, hun po* was highlighted as representatives of words whose comparable translation in the English language is not possible. Classicists who translate ancient Greek and Roman texts have expressed similar sentiments, especially when theirs are dead languages, similar to the situation with classical Chinese and *wen yan* (文言), the written language of pre-modern China. Crossing two paradigms of civilization makes it even more challenging, though exceedingly rewarding. The richness of the thinking in one is not found in the other, and vice versa. The translator is not only fascinated by the stark differences brought to light through an intimate engagement with the subtleties of mind, the intellectual inventiveness and the linguistic sophistication of the two civilizations she is confronted with, but she is also enriched by the contrast and complement offered to her treasure trough of knowledge and the end result which opens up even more insights and visions. In our era of computer technology, which is capable of translating on the spot from one language to another, the acquisition of knowledge and learning is made instantaneous; this pleasure of the mind—and heart—to learn through repetition and memorization passed on from one generation to another, has become, unwittingly, the luxury of the few.

Benefits and pleasure aside, under special circumstances where the gulf between civilizations cannot be bridged, there is always the option to retain some of the vocabulary from the source language through transliteration. Indeed, the translator is not to litter the target language with words and expressions from the source language. Where astute judgement is exercised, the inclusion would not only serve to expand the vocabulary of the practitioners of the target language but their mentality as well. Globalization has offered the world facile communication and exchange of information. Linguistic expansion necessarily opens up the mind and broadens one's horizons. Toleration, when reinforced by understanding of another's world view, lends more easily to peaceful co-existence. The function of translation goes beyond the text. Equally exciting is the opportunity for enriching the dialogue on translation with the inclusion of conceptualizations from an entirely different philosophical paradigm.

At the first appearance of activity, yang is produced. As activity reaches its limit, yin is produced. The interaction of yin yang gives full developments to the functions of Heaven. At the first appearance of tranquility, the element of weakness is produced. When weakness reaches its limit, the element of strength is produced. The interaction of these two elements gives full development to the functions of Earth.[104]

A chorus of Chinese children would chime in, "Yang is active while yin is quiet. Unpredictably they unite as one. These two aspects of the material force grow and vanish; their execution and achievement are gradual. This is called Wondrous Transformation. ... The operation of yin and yang increases and decreases, begins and ends. It produces and reproduces without end. This is called Creation and Transformation."[105]

This is also called Translation.

Appendix: Philosophical Terms Explained in Each Section of the Xing li zi xun

In Section One: "Creation and Transformation," they are the great ultimate, the primordial material force, yang, yin, heaven, earth, *qian*, *kun*, the five agents, the five elements, the origin, prosperity, benefit, purity, the Way, implement, heaven, the lord, *hun, po, gui, shen*, change, change and transformation, wondrous transformation, the substance of the way, creation and transformation.

In Section Two: "The Feelings and the Nature," they are the way of heaven, the way of humans, mandate, destiny, principle is one, manifestations are many, material force, substance, humans, things, the mandate of heaven, human affairs, the nature, the mind-and-heart, the feelings, innate good knowledge, innate good capability, *hun, po, ling*, talents, the will, intent, humaneness, rites and propriety, righteousness, intelligence, the Way, principle, virtue, achievement, sincerity, fidelity, centrality, harmony, big root, attaining the way, great virtue, small vir-

---

104 Chan, "The Numerical and Objective Tendencies in Shao Yung," in *Source Book*, 484. This passage is in Chan's translation of Shao Yung's *Huangji jingshi shu* (Supreme Principle Governing the World).
105 *XLZX*, 6:2a.

tue, substance, function, the root, letters, everlasting, constant, bright virtue, utmost goodness, vast and correct material force.

In Section Three: "Studying Efforts," they are teaching, learning, practice, elementary learning, great learning, rectification of things, extension of knowledge, diligently putting into practice, reverent seriousness, oneness, loyalty, empathy, filiality, brotherliness, maintaining quiescence, being circumspect while alone, correct nurturing, extending crookedness, broadening the culture of knowledge, self-restraint with rites and propriety, honoring the virtuous nature, seeking the unbridled mind-and-heart, understanding knowledge, nurturing the material force, uprightness, courage, preserving, nurturing, activation of the mind-and-heart, the nature that is content with inhumaneness, self-overcoming, reviving rites and propriety.

In Section Four: "Good and Bad," they are heavenly principle, human desires, the mind-and-heart of the way, the mind-and-heart of humans, righteousness, advantage, partiality, impartiality, reaching upwards, reaching downwards, goodness, badness, being wrong, vigorous goodness, vigorous badness, gentle goodness, gentle badness, self-brutalization, self-abandonment, arrogance, parsimony, fault, remorse, zeal, timorousness, tenacity, weakness, the small way, heterodoxy, good fortune, calamity, the incipient spring of the subtle, returning.

In Section Five: "Completing Virtues," they are extension of knowledge, abiding in knowledge, exaltation of knowledge, the yielding of propriety, fulfilling the nature, fulfilling the mind-and-heart, sincerity of the intent, the correct mind-and-heart, abiding, steadiness, the capacity of augmentation, perseverance, sufficiency, attainment, knowledge endowed at birth, practicing comfortably and naturally, sageliness, worthy, dignified demeanor at home, the ultimate mandate, immovable mind-and-heart, not transgressing what is right, transmission of the way, one thread, heavenly virtue, excellent prestige.

In Section Six: "The Way of Government," they are good governance, good teaching, rites and propriety, music, the classics, provisional exercise of power, canons, rules, laws, correcting oneself, renewing the people, timeliness, equilateral, beyond transformation, preserving *shen*, the ultimate of regality, the son of heaven, great prosperity, minor success, kingship, hegemony.

References

de Bary, William Theodore & John Chaffee, eds., *Neo-Confucian Education: The Formative Stage*. Berkeley: University of California Press, 1989.

Chan, Wing-tsit. *A Source Book in Chinese Philosophy*. Princeton: Princeton University Press, 1963.

Chan, Wing-tsit. *Zhu Zi xin xue an*. Taipei: Xuesheng shuju, 1988.

Chen, Hancai. *Zhong-guo gudai youer jiaoyu shi*. Guangdong: Guangdong gaodeng jiaoyu chupan she, 1996.

Cheng, Duan-meng. *Xingli zixun*, one chapter. Supplemented and edited by Cheng Ruojong. Xijing qinglu congshu edition. Printed between Tong-zhi reign and early Republican Period. Collected in *Siku quanmu congshu, zi bu*, no. 004, *rujia lei*. Shandong: Qi Lu shushe, 1995, 744–798.

Cheng, Ruoyong. *Xingli zixun*. In Zhang Boxing, *Yangzheng leibian*. Reprinted by Zuo Zong-tang, *Zhengyi tang quanshu*, vol. 32, no. 60, chapter 6. Fujian: 1866–1870.

Changzhou zhuru xue an. In *Song Yuan xue an*, juan 69. *Siku beiyao* edition.

Duan, Yucai. *Shuowen jiezi zhu*. Jingyun lu cangban. Shanghai: Shanghai guji chuban she, 1988 edition.

Fang, Fengchen. et al. *Li shi, Ming wu*. In *Gudai youxue chimeng jingdian*. Shandong: Qi Lu shushe, 1998.

Li, Jingde comp. *Zhu Zi yulei*, vol. 7, chapter 117. Hong Kong: Zhonghua shuju, 1983.

Lu, Kun. *Lu Kun quanzi*. In *Lixue congshu*. Hong Kong: Zhonghua shuju, 2008.

Qing Shengzu. *Tingxun geyan*, etc. Tianjin : Guangren tang, 1881. In *Qingding siku quanshu zongmu*. (In Rare Book Collection in the Central Library, HKSAR) *Shuangfeng xue an*, in *Song Yuan xue an*, juan 83, *Siku beiyao* edition.

Venuti, Lawrence. *The Translation Studies Reader*. Third edition, New York: Routledge, 2012, First ed. 2002.

Zhang Boxing. *Xiaoxue jijie*. Reprinted by Zuo Zongtang, *Zhengyi tang quanshu*, vol. 30, no. 57. Fujian: 1866–1870.

Zhang Boxing. *Yangzheng leibian*. In *Zhengyi tang quanshu*, vol. 32, no.60. Fujian:1866–1870.

Na Song (University of Göttingen)

THE HOLISM OF GUANXUE IN THE SONG DYNASTY

Introduction

When discussing the process of modernization in western culture, the belief in holism generally distinguishes (separates) the pre-modern and modern eras.[1] Holism in the pre-modern west refers to the meaning or the ultimate value that is immanent within the world, and thus, the world is both actual and transcendent. Similarly, we can also detect this belief in a cohesive whole (*Zheng Quan ti*, 整全體) in traditional Chinese thinking, as Qian Mu (錢穆, 1895–1900) points out that the Chinese people always thought of the cosmos (universe) as a whole that represents the ultimate value.[2] Holism refers to the way of thinking of the cosmos (universe) as a cohesive whole, or what Benjamin Schwartz calls the holistic character of Chinese thought. Historian Wu Chan-liang (吳展良) suggests that the holistic mode

---

1   For example, both György Lukács' critique that modernity created a loss of the feeling of totality and Martin Heidegger's theory that the essence of modernity dissolved pre-modern holism demonstrate how modernization rejected the value and belief in holism.

2   Mu Qian, "Zhongguo wen hua dui ren lei wei lai ke you de gong xian" (The Potential Contribution of Chinese culture to the future), *Zhongguo Wenhua*, no. 4 (1991.8). For a discussion of Qian Mu's ideas about holism, see Chan-liang Wu, "Cong zhengtixing yu Getixing de Ronghe lun Zhongguo Wenhua de Xiandaihua" (A Discussion of the Modernity of Chinese Culture from fusing holism and individualism), *Qian Mu Xiansheng Jinianguan Guankan*, no.3 (1995); Ying-shih Yu, *Lun tian ren zhi ji: zhongguo gu dai si xiang qi yuan shi tan* (Between the Heavenly and the Human: the Origin of Ancient Chinese Thought) (Taibei: Lian jing chu ban she, 2014).

of thinking is the fundamental characteristic of Chinese thought because every facet of the Chinese mentality is influenced by holism.[3]

The belief in the cohesive whole and the concept of holism have long been examined by historians, archaeologists, and theorists. Owing to their influential works, we have come to understand the complexity and significance of the value of the belief in the cohesive whole/holism in Chinese thought.[4] In the following, I shall give a brief introduction regarding the complexity of the cohesive whole/holism. Holism first appears in this way: the cohesive whole is believed to contain cosmic order, political legitimacy, as well as the moral order of society. This idea referred to a cosmic–political–ethical system/program, thereby serving as the root of morality, cultural identity, and political legitimacy.[5] For example, a leading archaeologist, Chang Kwang-chih (Zhang Guangzhi, 張光直), explains how, in ancient China, the cosmos was considered to combine politics and culture into a whole by employing the concept of correlative cosmology.[6]

The second dimension of this cohesive whole/holism refers to the wholeness of the human order (actual world) and the cosmos (the world beyond). This unity of the actual world and the world beyond is related to the first appearance of holism; namely, the cosmic–political–ethical system/program. Over the years, many outstanding scholars have discussed this issue in various ways, such as Joseph Need-

---

3   Chan-liang Wu, "Cong zheng ti xing yu ge ti xing de rong he lun zhong guo wen hua de xian dai hua" (A Discussion of the Modernity of Chinese Culture from fusing holism and indivualism), *Qian Mu Xiansheng Jinianguan Guankan*, no.3 (1995).

4   The cohesive whole and holism are two sides of one body. Thus, they do not require further distinctions in the following.

5   This way of defining it as "system/program" is because both "system" and "program" have been used by different scholars.

6   K. C. Chang, *Meishu Shenhua Jili* (Art, Myth, and Ritual), trans., Jing Guo (Beijing: Shenghuo, dushu, xinzhi san lian shudian, 2013). A correlative cosmology is an orderly system of correspondence among various domains of reality in the universe, correlating categories of the human world, such as the human body, behavior, morality, the sociopolitical order, and historical changes, with categories of the cosmos, including time, space, the heavenly bodies, seasonal movement, and natural phenomena. The concept of correlative cosmology originates from Claude Levi-Strauss' *The Savage Mind*. F. F. Mote, Benjamin Schwartz, and K. C. Chang all adopt Levi-Strauss's concept of correlative Cosmology in the Chinese context.

ham's theory of organic philosophy, the theory of heavenly principle by Wang Hui (汪暉), and the work of Ding Yun (丁耘) on the origin of ancient Chinese and Western civilizations.[7]

Aside from analyzing the dimensions of this cohesive whole/holism, intellectual historians have exposed how parts from the whole are thought to interconnect in a cohesive whole. Needham adopted one biological metaphor, the organism, to depict the total dependence on, and inseparability of, parts from the dynamic whole. Needham described Chinese holistic thought as one biological organism, while Schwartz discerned the hierarchical subordination of parts of the whole, thereby suggesting a familial metaphor or the metaphor of bureaucratic organization.[8]

As seen previously, current research has shown the different dimensions of the cohesive whole/holism concept and the ways in which the parts are said to incorporate with each other in a cohesive whole. All these concerns refer mainly to holism as it was applied during the Song dynasty. Scholars tend to believe that the typical characteristics of Chinese thought were mature by the time of the Song dynasty. For example, Needham argued that Zhu Xi (Chu Hsi 朱熹, 1130–1200) had undertaken this organic synthesis and organistic philosophy. Thus, it brought the organicist view to the forefront of Chinese culture and, consequently, it came to be seen by the world as representative of Chinese civili-

---

7   Joseph Needham, *Science and Civilisation in China* (Cambridge: Cambridge University Press, 1956). The organicist philosophy is a naturalist philosophy, a philosophy avoiding either the "theological vitalist idealism" or the "mechanical materialism" so common to Western thought. The organic philosophy refers to that universal harmony which comes about not by the celestial fiat of some King of Kings, but by the spontaneous cooperation of all beings in the universe brought about by their following the internal necessities of their own natures. Needham's Chinese organicist philosophy is based on postmodern scientific principles, he sees this organicist philosophy as a path to overcome Newtons' linear mechanics in postmodern science. Hui Wang, *Xiandai zhongguo sixiang de xingqi* (The Rise of Modern Chinese thought) (Beijing: Shenghuo, dushu, xinzhi san lian shu dian, 2008); Yun Ding, *Rujia yu qi meng: zhe xue hui tong shi ye xia de dang qian zhong guo si* (Confucianism and Enlightenment: Modern Chinese Thought from the Perspective of Philosophy) (Beijing: Shenghuo · dushu · xinzhi san lian chubanshe, 2011).

8   Needham, *Science and Civilisation in China*; Benjamin Schwartz, *The World of Thought in Ancient China* (Cambridge: Harvard University Press, 1985), 416–17.

zation.[9] Starting from traditional yin-yang cosmology, Wu Chan-liang shares some similarities with Needham's view as regards Zhu Xi's holistic worldview.

Despite the fact that the basic image of the cohesive whole and of holism is evident, the holism of the local schools is still poorly represented in the scholarship. Confucianism itself, as well as general ideas from traditional China, is multi-faceted and complex. An investigation of holism, in general, is not able to completely define the intricacy and different dimensions of Chinese thought, especially for the local schools that each endorse unique doctrines. This article intends to develop this discussion regarding holism by considering only one local school, the Guan school (*Guanxue*, 關學), formed in Guanzhong, Shaanxi, by the second half of the eleventh-century.[10] This intellectual school is centered on the work of Zhang Zai (張載, 1020–77), who was labeled by Zhu Xi as a co-founder of the Daoxue movement in the *Records on the Origin of the School of the Cheng Brothers* (*yiluo yuanyuan lu*, 伊洛淵源). According to Ong Chang Woei (王昌偉), since the late thirteenth-century, scholars retrospectively put Zhang Zai and his followers into a "school" named after the region: the Guan school.[11] Although Zhang Zai was a co-founder of the Daoxue movement in the Northern Song dynasty, he offered a very different response to the various pressing issues of his times. As a result, the holism of Guanxue shared some general features of holism with other

9   Aaron Grinter, "The Grand Tradition: Revisiting the work of Joseph Needham to Address Ethnocentrism in Contemporary Philosophy and Society," *Cosmology and History: The Journal of Natural and Social Philosophy* 14, no. 3 (2018): 310.

10   Here "Guanxue" is a historical concept. There is some discussion about the differences between the historical and philosophical definitions of Guanxue. See Lin Lechang and Lu Miaw-fen: Lin, "Liang dian hui ying: du Lu Miaw-fen Ming qing zhi ji de guan xue yu zhang zai si xiang de fu xing: di yu kua di yu yin su de sheng si" (The Guan school in the Ming-Qing period and the restoration of Zhang Zai's thought: a Discussion on regional and trans-regional aspects); Lu, "Ming qing zhi ji de guan xue yu zhang zai si xiang de fu xing: di yu kua di yu yin su de sheng si," "Hui ying lin le chang jiao shou de liang dian hui ying."

11   Ong Chang Woei, "Guan xue bian yu ming qing shan xi shi da fu de ji ti ji yi" (Cases of Guanzhong Learning and Guanzhong literati' collective memory in the Ming-Qing Period), in *Culture, Memory and Chinese Society*, ed., Guozhong He (Kuala Lumpur: Ma da Zhong guo yan jiu suo, 2008), 177.

regional Confucian schools, but also made some unique claims, such as the claim that the cosmos was centered on *qi* (氣).

In the following, I will examine whether or not Guanxue holism was identical with the concept of the cohesive whole and the theory of holism in general. I shall then present the interaction between Guanxue and other Daoxue modes in the Song dynasty. I will also investigate how Guanxue holism was shaped by the local and national sociopolitical context. When focusing on local history, this research endeavors to apply different methodologies—— that is, incorporating broader intellectual history into the discussion of a local history——to explore a new dimension of holism.

Holism in Chinese Thought

Wu Chan-liang once conducted a complete analysis of the sociological, economic, political, and religious sources of holism in traditional China: the Great Unity in politics; the agricultural economy; and the power deriving from the family-clan unit in China as the sociological source. He has argued that the sociological, economic, and political context of holism did not change until the end of the Imperial system.[12] However, the content of the two dimensions of the cohesive whole/holism changed over time. In what follows, I will examine how the concept of the cohesive whole/holism can be traced back to no later than the Shang-Zhou period (ca. 1600 to 221 BCE) and then reconstructed during the Song dynasty.

Chang Kwang-chih has described prehistoric China, that is, prior to the Shang-Zhou period, as having adopted a shamanistic civilization. In the primitive times, humans and deities were thought to intermingle. Every individual was a shaman, directly reaching toward the deity while the deity would reach down to every individual. Thus, the spheres of the divine and of the human were not separated. This is what we call primitive holism.

---

12 Wu, "Cong zheng ti xing yu ge ti xing de rong he lun zhong guo wen hua de xian dai hua."

Following the time of shamanistic civilization is the time of the "Separation of Heaven and Earth" (*Jue di tian tong*, 絕地天通), quoted from the *Book of Documents* (*Shang Shu*, 尚書). The "Separation of Heaven and Earth" is an ancient myth telling the story of the sage ruler Zhuanxu 顓頊 (traditionally dated to the twenty-fifth-century BCE), who rearranged the cosmic order by cutting communications between Heaven and Earth, thus separating humans from deities.[13] The phrase "Separation of heaven and earth" is used to express the period when the cosmological and human orders are divided, and also when the rites are completed. The move from primitive shamanistic civilization to the "Separation of Heaven and Earth" implies the transformation from the order of shaman deities to the order of universal kinship, which is the cosmic religious and political order. Only the king had access to Heaven (*tian* 天) via the shaman, and exclusively sacrificed to Heaven and Earth. Therefore, the King gained political legitimacy by making sacrifices to Heaven and Earth, as political legitimacy was drawn from the cosmos (universe). The human world as a whole was still united with Heaven. In addition, Ge Zhaoguang argues that the cosmos is within the order of a differentiated arrangement of Heaven-earth (*tian di cha xu*, 天地差序). Everything, including human beings and society in the human world, originates from the cosmos. The human world thereby must correspond to the order of the cosmos. The descent-line system is the projection of the order of the cosmos in the human world.[14] This unity of the cosmos, ethics, and politics during this period defines the prototype of the cohesive whole/holism concept.

With the demise of the Western Zhou dynasty came the breakdown of the ritual system of that dynasty. Confucius reinterpreted the ritual practice in order to restore harmony. "Rites and music" (*li yue*, 禮樂) became religious sacrifices to divinities and spirits invented by the shamans who governed the ritual tradition.[15] The most critical change

---

13   Ying-shih Yu, *Lun tian ren zhi ji: zhongguo gu dai si xiang qi yuan shi tan tan* (Between the Heavenly and the Human: the Origin of Ancient Chinese Thought) (Taibei: Lian jing chu ban she, 2014), 3.

14   Zhaoguang Ge, *Zhong Guo si xiang shi* (An Intellectual History of China) (Shanghai: Fudan daxue chubanshe, 2009), 50.

15   Yu, *Lun tian ren zhi ji*, 23–29 and 53–68.

of this time is the emergence of the idea of the Way of Heaven (*Dao*, 道), which refers to the socio-political order centered on the universal king, and gives the highest value to Heaven.[16] With the emergence of *Dao*, the primitive definition of Heaven changed accordingly. The Shaman-deity dimension of Heaven, what Ying-shih (余英時) called "personal god," vanished.[17] The concept of Heaven not only developed a cosmological dimension, but it was also interpreted in the sense of *Dao*. Heaven became the supreme moral order in the universe. With this new content, Heaven was given more value in Chinese thought. Therefore, the way of viewing Heaven as the supreme standard, the source of political legitimacy, and ethics was confirmed once again. The three entities of the cosmic–political–ethical whole were thereby developed into a new explanation with *Dao* at the center. Due to rapid changes during this period, many scholars have employed Karl Jaspers's theory of the Axial Age, which describes a kind of spiritual "breakthrough" in several high cultures during the first millennium BCE.[18]

From the breakthrough of the Axial Age to the emergence of yin-yang cosmology in the Han dynasty (202 BCE–220); to the metaphysics of the Wei-Jin period (220–589); to the threefold confrontation of Confucianism, Buddhism, and Daoism throughout the Sui-Tang (581–907) period; and finally, the cultural developments during the Song dynasty, the concept of the cohesive whole/holism developed new content centered on the notion of the principle (*li*, 理). Around this notion of the principle, Song Confucians reconstructed the holistic theory to encompass cosmology, ethics, and politics, or what Yu Ying-shih calls "the Confucian project."[19]

---

16   Schwartz, *The World of Thought in Ancient China*, 414–416; Wm Theodore de Bary, *The Trouble with Confucianism* (Cambridge, Mass: Harvard University Press, 1991), 11–12.

17   Yu, *Lun tian ren zhi ji*, 77.

18   The examples of discussion about the Axial Age in China are numerous, including accounts given by Benjamin Schwartz, Yu Yin-shi, Zhang Hao, Ge Zhaoguang, Xu Jilin, and others. *Twenty-first Century* (Hongkong: CUHK) published a special issue about the Axial Age in 2000. However, Ding Yun disagrees with Yu Ying-shih's theory of the breakthrough.

19   Yu Ying-shih, *Zhu xi de li shi shi jie: Song dai shi da fu zheng zhi wen hua de yan jiu* (The Historical World of Zhu Xi: A Study on the Political Culture of the Scholar-

The new content of this cohesive whole/holism was shaped by the historical context of the Song dynasty; the spread of Buddhist teachings and Daoism in conjunction with the Tang-Song transition.[20] For Song Confucian scholars, the challenge of Buddhism included the idea that the cosmos pertaining to the transcendent world is essentially empty (*kong*, 空), which posed a challenge to the established political–ethical order and questioned the rituals of everyday life. Facing the pervasive influence of Buddhism, Zhang Zai indicated that Confucius was no longer the most important philosopher for a thousand years after Buddhism had spread in China.[21] Therefore, for Zhang Zai and his companions, wiping out the influence of Buddhism became increasingly urgent in order to reestablish the authority of Confucianism.

The confrontation of ideologies opens at the cosmological level because Buddhism endorsed a metaphysical world, while Confucianism emphasized only the actual world of everyday life.[22] Prior to the Song dynasty, the eternal world beyond everyday life in Chinese thought was vague, unlike the eternal world in Buddhism. In order to completely erase the negative impact of Buddhism and Daoism, Confucians reconstructed its metaphysical basis, as exem-

---

Officials in the Song Times) (Beijing: Shenghuo · dushu · xinzhi san lian shu dian, 2011), 923.

20   The Tang-song transition points to the period from 750 to 1250. In 1910, Naitō Konan first proposed the "Tang-Song transition" idea, which brought continuous discussion from various angles. Now the "Tang-Song transition" is widely accepted. Over the course of this period, the rice economy of the Yangzi River developed and this area thus became the Chinese economy's center of commerce; the population shifted from north to south, and the empire's population reached 100 million. Meanwhile, the extraordinary sweep of economic change during the Tang-Song transition bespoke fundamental institutional transformations: private ownership of land became the rule, Chinese imperial examinations became widely utilized as the major path to office. These two facets together gave rise to the gentry class of scholar-bureaucrats and declined noble families; a central government came into existence, while the gentry class began to carry the responsibilities of governance.

21   Guozhong Liu, Zhenping Huang ed., *Zhong guo si xiang shi can kao zi liao ji: sui tang zhi qing juan* (Referencing documents of Chinese Intellectual History: From Suitang to Qing) (Beijing: Qing hua da xue chu ban she, 2004), 139.

22   Wang Fan-sen, *Quan li de mao xi yue guan Zhong yong: qing dai de si xiang, xue shu yu xin tai* (Capillary Power: Thought, Academy, Mind in the Qing Dynasty) (Beijing: Beijing daxue chubanshe, 2015), 2.

plified in the works of Zhang Zai and the Cheng Brothers.[23] Xiong Shili (熊十力, 1885–1968) shared similar views by suggesting that the most important task for Song Confucians is to "be metaphysical" when establishing Neo-Confucianism in the Northern Song dynasty.[24] Song Confucians regarded the cosmos as the source of political order and ethic. The debate at the cosmological level thereby intertwined with ethical doctrines and political order.

The concept of the principle (*li*) is the answer Song Confucians delivered, as Zhu Xi argued for the common and fundamental principle of all beings. Song Confucians attempted to discover one fundamental transcendent principle, which could also serve as the ultimate coherent explanation of the order of the human world and the cosmos, the principle of mind and human nature (*xin xing*, 心性). Thus, *li* is the inner principle of nature, yin-yang and all beings, and at the same it appears everywhere in the universe. Wang Hui sees Heaven as the innate order of the cosmos (universe) and *li* as the appearance of this order.[25]

Principle is interrelated with the Great Ultimate, referred to in different Confucian schools by different names, such as *Taiji* (太極), *Taixu* (太虛), or heavenly principle (*Tianli* 天理).[26] The Great Ultimate is the Way of heaven and earth, as it is the principle of all beings in the universe. However, the Great Ultimate itself cannot properly be defined as being because it has no physical form, but consists of the principle of its totality. The Great Ultimate also includes material force. *Li* is incorporeal, one, eternal, unchanging, uniform, constituting the essence of things, and always good, but it does not contain a dichotomy of good and evil nor does it create things.[27] For Zhu Xi, principle gives being its substance form while material force gives physical form

23   Lihua Yang, *Qi ben yu shen hua: Zhang Zai zhe xue shu lun* (Qi root and Spiritual Transformation: A Discussion of the Philosophy of Zhang Zai) (Beijing: Bei jing da xue chu ban she, 2008), 16.

24   Wang, *Quan li de mao xi yue guan Zhong yong*, 2.

25   Wang, *Xiandai zhongguo sixiang de xingqi*, 47–71, 258.

26   The Great Ultimate normally points to *Taiji*. Here we mean the highest standard, deity, the Heavenly way. In Zhang Zai's philosophy, it is *Taixu*; in Cheng brothers' and Zhu Xi' philosophies, it is *Tianli*.

27   Wing-tsit Chan, *A Source Book in Chinese philosophy* (Princeton: Princeton University Press, 1969), 572, 590–1.

to being. Compared with substantial form, the physical form is transitory, changeable, unequal in things, constituting both good and evil. Principle is the inherent nature and destiny of everything; in other words, it is the ontological root of everything. The principle of a thing or a man is his very nature, which is real and concrete. Accordingly, the nature of all beings is not emptiness, the view that Buddhism endorses.

More important is the metaphysical dimension of principle. Scholars conventionally employed the terminology of the metaphysical and transcendent, which derived from Western philosophy, to describe the realm beyond according to Neo-Confucianism. As the innate order of the cosmos (universe), principle is also transcendent and metaphysical. With the invention of principle, Heaven becomes more abstract. Based on the metaphysical dimension of principle, Song Confucians constructed an account of the metaphysical world by systematizing *li*. Wang Fan-sen (王汎森) argued there were two reasons for Song Confucians to develop an account of the metaphysical world. One is to fight against the threat of the concept of the metaphysical world engineered by Buddhists. The other reason is that Song Confucians, in a time of chaos and violence, argued for a metaphysical world as the ultimate standard and final purpose of ethics, society, and politics of the actual world.[28] Put differently, Song Confucians could not link institutions of the present system to Heaven, thus constructed the eternal metaphysical world. The world beyond is abstract, eternal, not influenced by the physical form, and thus always good. Moreover, as Wang suggested, the metaphysical world is the destination and basis of all human existences and human morality. Prior to the Song dynasty, the realm of beyond in Confucianism was not directed to the realm of the worldly.

Therefore, Song Confucian accounts of an ideal world held that the actual world should be incorporated with the world beyond. This means that an ideal human world necessarily implies accomplishing principle and, therefore, the human world can fuse into the transcendent world. The source and basis of the actual world in traditional holism shifted from heaven, deities, and *Dao* to heavenly principle. Through the confirmation of the notion of principle, the counterposi-

---

28 Wang, *Quan li de mao xi yue guan Zhong yong*, 2.

tion between the cosmological order and the order of the human world is no longer in the picture of holism. Instead, the order of universe, that is, principle, is the innate principle of human beings. This is the first dimension of the cohesive whole/holism of Song Confucianism.

Wu Chan-liang's study of Zhu Xi provides another interpretation of the unity of the actual world and the world beyond. According to Wu, in Zhu Xi's view of the world, the ideal human world is part of the universe. The order of the human world is supposed to be in accord with the way of Heaven. Hence, the order of the human world should be interlinked with the way of Heaven. Political and social practice for an ideal human world is also for the way of Heaven, thus it has a cosmological dimension. In this sense, the human world is not separated from the transcendent world, the cosmos, ethics, society and politics being intertwined with each other. [29] This points to the second facet of holism in the Song dynasty, the cosmic–political–ethical system/program.

When Song intellectuals envisioned the human world and the world beyond as a whole, the order of the human world was considered to necessarily correspond to cosmological order, which includes both political and ethical order. Principle as well as the metaphysical world are the source and origin of morality and all beings in the actual world. Therefore, morality (ethics) must be in accordance with principle; the ideal ethical order is the appearance of principle. At the same time, the principle has a political dimension, too. According to Yu, among Song Confucians the mainstream was devoted to political reformation with the hope of reviving the harmony of the Three dynasties—Xia, Shang, and Zhou (1700 to 221 BCE)—in the Song dynasty. He calls this trend the "post-Wang Anshi era" (後王安石時代). [30] Despite the different views regarding Yu's post-Wang Anshi era argument, scholars achieved some consensus about Song Confucian politics: in the ideal system/program, Song Confucians designed the political to be in accordance with the cosmological order, which is evident in their account of the principle.

---

29   Chan-liang Wu, "Zhu zi de shi jie zhi xu guan zhi gou cheng fang *shi*" (The Organizational Principle of Zhu Xi's View of World Order), in *Dongya jin shi shi jie guan de xing*, ed., Chan-liang Wu (Taibei: Taida chu ban zhong xin, 2007), 300.

30   Yu, *Zhu xi de li shi shi jie*.

The third building block of this cohesive whole is the "unity of Heaven and man" (*tian ren he yi*, 天人合一), one of the most monumental topics in the study of Confucianism and Chinese intellectual history.[31] For example, Yu Ying-shih's article, "Between the Heavenly and the Human," raised rather influential issues on this topic.[32] Principle is the nature internal to humankind, all beings, and the cosmos. Feng Youlan (馮友蘭) states in his *Short History of Chinese Philosophy* that the moral principles of man are also metaphysical principles of the universe, and the nature of man is an exemplification of these principles.[33] Human nature is identical with the (Heavenly) principle (*xing ji li*, 性即理), thus showing the unity of Heaven and man.

Despite Heidegger's view that there were no *Subjectum* and *Objectum* in pre-modern times, the example of holism during the Song Dynasty is not an exception. Insofar as principle is internal to humankind, man itself is constituted by this whole without there being a subject and an object. Hence, there is no way of conceiving how man could be external to the cosmos and to thereby to become a *Subjectum*, nor can we objectify the world (universe) apart from man.[34] Thus, epistemologically, a dichotomy between subject and object is unknowable.

Guanxue Holism in the Northern Song Dynasty

The rise of the Guan school is part of the Daoxue movement in the Song dynasty. Guanxue is only one of the four regional Neo-Confucian schools, but it gained national influence. According to Ong, from the late thirteenth-century onwards, the Guan school of Zhang Zai has been part of the "four schools."[35] The other three include the Lian School of Zhou Dunyi (周敦頤, 1017–73), the Luo school of the Cheng brothers (程頤, 1033–1107; 程顥, 1032–85), and the Min

---

31   A few examples: Ying-shih Yu, Shuxian Liu, Guorong Yang, Chunfeng Jing, etc.

32   Yu, *Lun tian ren zhi ji*.

33   Youlan Feng, *Zhongguo Zhexue Jianshi* (*A Short History of Chinese Philosophy*), trans., Fusan Zhao (Tian Jin: Tianjin shehui kexueyuan chubanshe, 2005). 71.

34   Ge, *Zhong guo si xiang shi*, 123.

35   Chang Woei Ong, *Men of Letters: Within the Passes* (Cambridge: Harvard University, 2008), 106; Chang Woei Ong, "Guan xue bian yu ming qing shan xi shi da

school of Yang Shi (楊時, 1053–1135) and Zhu Xi. In the eyes of Li Zhou (李澤厚), it is Guanxue that broached the rudimentary principles and questions of Song Daoxue and thus laid the foundation of Neo-Confucianism. Zhang Zai's *Zheng Meng* (正蒙) best represents the cosmology and ethical system of Neo-Confucianism.[36]

One of the greatest Guanzhong scholars, Feng Congwu (馮從吾, 1557–1627) in the Ming dynasty (1368–1644), once summarized the features of the Guan school in his genealogical record of Guanxue. In his *Cases of Guanzhong Learning* (*Guanxue bian* 關學編), Feng claimed that Zhang Zai's philosophy followed *yi* (易), took the form of *Zhongyong* (中庸), aimed at achieving the *Rites of Zhou* (周禮), followed doctrines from Confucius and Mencius (孔孟), united Heaven and man, and denounced heresy.[37] Feng's summarization points out to several basic doctrines of the Guan school: Zhang Zai's philosophy is based on the *Book of Changes*, especially the cosmology; Guanzhong scholars endeavored to counteract Buddhism in the actual world, to rediscover *Dao* which had been lost after Mencius, to unite Heaven and man, and to restore the system of antiquity to transform the world.

These doctrines served as the new system *Guanzhong* scholars implemented, which combined moral philosophy, sociopolitical management, and cosmology. These doctrines shared some common featurues with other Daoxue modes in the Northern Song dynasty while endorsing uniqueness. The holism of Guanxue also indicates its common points with other Daoxue modes.

As a critic of Buddhism, Zhang Zai's theory is heavily cosmological. Peter Bol has pointed out that Zhang Zai developed a coherent understanding of the cosmic process in terms of the circulation of *qi*, the matter and energy that makes up all things.[38] Indeed, Zhang Zai's cosmology is centered on the concept of *qi* and the Great Void. The Great Void

fu de ji ti ji yi," in *Culture, Memory and Chinese Society*, ed., Guozhong He (Kuala Lumpur: Ma da Zhong guo yan jiu suo, 2008), 177.

36   Zehou Li, *Zhong guo gu dai si xiang shi lun* (History of Thought in Ancient China) (Beijing: Shenghuo, dushu, xinzhi san lian shu dian, 2008), 234.

37   Congwu Feng, Junmin Chen ed., Xinghai Xu Dianxiao, *Guanxue bian (fu xu bian)* (Cases of Guanzhong Learning) (Beijing: Zhong hua shu ju, 1987), 2–3.

38   Peter Bol, *Neo Confucianism in History* (Cambridge: Harvard University Asia Center, 2008), 87.

serves as the source of value for everything. All things under heaven are made up of the same *qi*, including the Great Void. Therefore, all things naturally share in the inherent goodness that characterizes the Great Void.[39] As Huang Siu-chi suggested, this unique cosmology explains how all beings are connected in a whole. He thinks that there existed a concept of organic process in which all things are related to each other in terms of the function of "*Chi (qi)*" in Zhang Zai's philosophical system.[40] This is the first unique dimension of Guanxue holism. At the same time, by explaining the structure of existence through *qi* and the Great Void, Guanxue demonstrated the existence of matter and the existence of the cosmos, thus responding to the challenge posed by the doctrine of emptiness in Buddhism and Daoism.[41]

Second, among all the theories of the actual world and the transcendent world in Song Neo-Confucianism, Guanxue's design is slightly different from other regional modes of Daoxue. For Guanxue, the physical world is directly designed by the cosmic order, namely, the hierarchical order. Zhang Zai believes that the cosmos is hierarchical, while human society reflects the hierarchical order of the cosmos. For him, the famous *Western Inscription* (*Xi Ming*, 西銘) is the best example of this hierarchical image: "Heaven (*Qian*, 乾) is my father, and Earth (*Kun*, 坤) is my mother and even such a small creature as I find an intimate place in their midst.... The Great ruler [the emperor] is the eldest son (*zongzi*, 宗子) of my parents [Heaven and Earth], and the great ministers are his stewards."[42] Zhang Zai envisioned the whole cosmos as a family with everyone being interconnected by means of his/her own role and duty. Put differently, human society with naturally bonded members had a natural hierarchy preordained by Heaven and Earth. Furthermore, philosopher Yang Guorong (楊國榮) claims that the *Western Inscription* extends the family relation-

39   Ong, *Men of Letters: Within the Passes*, 52.

40   Siu-chi Huang, "Chang Tsai's Concept of Ch'i," *Philosophy East and West* 18: 4 (1968): 258.

41   Guorong Yang, "Guanxue de Zhexue yi han—ji yu Zhang Zai Sixiang de kao cha" (The Philosophical Implication of the School of Guan: An Examination Based on Zhang Zai's thought), *Journal of East China Normal University*, no. 1 (2017): 22.

42   Zai Zhang, Xichen Zhang xiao, *Zhang Zai Ji* (Collected Works of Zhang Zai) (Beijing: Zhong hua shu ju, 2012), 62; cf. Chan, *A Sourcebook in Chinese philosophy*, 497.

ship to the whole cosmos. It, therefore, demonstrates that the ethics of the actual world is present in the transcendent world, thus showing the interplay between the social order in human society and the cosmological order in the world beyond.[43]

In this hierarchical order, Chow Kai-Wing argues that Zhang's writing places greater emphasis on the social distinction that separates the class of scholar-officials from the common people and that the existence of such a hierarchy is also a manifestation of the basic principle of natural order. According to Chow, Zhang Zai emphasized this hierarchy between scholar-officials and the common people because he perceived Buddhism to be a significant threat to the leadership role of the scholar-officials. This emphasis is his effort to "revive" the ancient rituals and was thus an attempt to build a Confucian society that acknowledged the elite status and privilege of such families.[44] Ong Chang Woei also mentions Zhang Zai's concern regarding the declining leadership of scholar-officials.[45]

Nevertheless, Zhang's ultimate motive was to build not only a society that recognized hierarchy, but also one in which everyone—monarch, scholar-officials, and common people—had an active role.[46] As far as I am concerned, Ong's opinion is more convincing not only because of the family metaphor of the *Western Inscription* regarding everyone's interconnectivity through roles, but also because *Guanzhong* scholars attempted to build a local community as described in the *Western Inscription*. For them, the *Western Inscription* indicates the ideal institution, and the ultimate goal of learning is to create such a society. For example, the Lü brothers' famous *Lüshi XiangYue* (呂氏鄉約) drew on the same family metaphor in their vision of constructing a local community. The Lü brothers' ideal community is the community where *dao* is present from antiquity onwards, as outlined in the Rites of Zhou.[47] This directs us to the third attribute of Guanxue

43   Yang, "Guan xue de zhe xue yi han," 23.
44   Kai-wing Chow, "Ritual, Cosmology, and Ontology: Chang Tsai's Moral Philosophy and Neo-Confucian Ethics," *Philosophy East and West* 43: 2 (1993): 218–221.
45   Ong, *Men of Letters: Within the Passes*, 55.
46   Ong, 56.
47   The capitalized Dao refers to the Way of Heaven, the Way; the small dao refers to the dao of sages, the understanding of Dao, and so forth.

holism in the Northern Song dynasty: the interconnectedness of *dao* and the traces (*ji*) that Ong Chang Woei previously discussed.[48]

In the Northern Song dynasty, among all the critics of Wang Anshi's *New Policies* (王安石新政), Zhang Zai and his students were the only group who not only criticized such policies, but also devised institutional alternatives, such as the restoration of the system of antiquity in the Rites of Zhou. As Anne D. Birdwhistell points out, Guanxue was composed of patterns of both thought and practice.[49] Guanzhong scholars planned the ritual system as institutional alternatives for the New Policies as they believed that the sophisticated ritual system as described in the Three Dynasties was the most viable account of how Dao could truly manifest itself. Ong argues that Zhang Zai believed that the sages built the sophisticated ritual system: "*Ji* is the genuine manifestation of the *dao* of the sages, and this *dao* is none other than the *dao* of Heaven and Earth."[50] In other words, the belief in the traces, the ritual system of the Three Dynasties, refers to the belief in the oneness of *dao* and *ji*. This attribute of Guanxue holism is also unique in the Northern Song dynasty.

Song Confucians did creatively draw on the ideal of the system of the Three Dynasties to criticize both the tendency of the Song state to centralize power and the rising inequalities linked to the emergence of a market economy. However, based on Wang Hui's observation, Song Confucians did not aim to bring the Three Dynasty system back; rather, they inscribed their own ideals into their image of the Three Dynasties and then often spoke of infusing the prefectural system of the Song dynasty with the ideals of *fengjian* (封建) and the well-field system (*jing tian*, 井田). Comparatively, Guanzhong scholars aimed to achieve what the Three Dynasties had achieved through the concept of the traces—that is, the sophisticated ritual system, which includes three integral components: descent line, *fengjian*, and the well-field system. Because of their faith in the interconnection of *dao* and *ji*, Guangzhong scholars believed that the only way to harmonize the way of Heaven is to put all descent lines, *fengjian*, and the well-

---

48   Ong, *Men of Letters: Within the Passes*, 47–68.
49   Anne D. Birdwhistell, *Li Yong (1627–1705) and Epistemological Dimensions of Confucian Philosophy* (California: Stanford University Press, 1996), 37.
50   Ong, *Men of Letters: Within the Passes*, 51.

field systems into practice. Their insistence on the ritual system and *fengjian* was also uncommon in the Northern Song dynasty. Wang Hui has reminded us that, due to the historical context of the prefectural system and the market economy, Song Confucians argued that the ideal of the rituals and music of the Three dynasties, and even the idea of *fengjian*, no longer legitimized a particular political system.

Understanding this unique theory of the interconnection of *dao* and the traces requires some context. Along with the New Policies initiated by Wang Anshi came the fact that the state was attempting to penetrate local society, a policy that Zhang Zai did not approve of, as the central government was interfering in local affairs. According to Ong Chang Woei, Zhang Zai argued that the literati (*shi*, 士) were experts in government, and that they should be entrusted with the task of running local society without direct intervention from the court.[51] In this respect, as I see it, the *fengjian* system is more appropriate for such an ideal system than the prefectural system in reality. Moreover, the belief in the ritual system makes *fengjian* indispensable to Guanzhong scholars' plan of institutional alternatives for Wang Anshi's New Policies.

The strong interest in rituals, which is also different from their contemporaries, was regarded as one main characteristic of Guanxue. Rituals were linked to Heaven. The rituals and music of the Three Dynasties fully embodied the political ideals of Heaven/nature. However, as Wang Hui argued, the rituals and music of the Three Dynasties no longer legitimized a particular political system in the Northern Song dynasty. Based on our previous discussion of *dao* and *ji*, I think that constructing an account of the world that manifests the same principle governing the universe is the aim of Zhang Zai's emphasis on the meaning of rituals and the practice of rituals. At the same time, this emphasis also intended to show the unification of Heaven and man, which is the final layer of Guanxue holism.

Guanxue's claim regarding the unity of Heaven and man is the same as in the other Neo-Confucian schools. Zhang Zai is the first one who proposed the connection between Heaven and man. Only through practicing self-cultivation can man comprehend the eternal

---

51   Ong, *Men of Letters: Within the Passes*, 51.

Dao, the way of Heaven. This emphasis on self-cultivation is common among Song Confucians. However, Zhang sees the formulation, implementation, and learning of rituals from antiquity as essential components of self-cultivation, while the Cheng brothers regard morality as the most important facet of self-cultivation. The other point touches on Zhang Zai's cosmology that is centered on *qi* and the Great Void. All things are produced by the same source and share the same physical constitution, including Heaven and human beings. The unity of Heaven and man is the fourth aspect of Guanxue holism.

The final aspect of the cohesive whole/holism is documented by Ong Chang Woei's research: the threading together of the state, the literati, and society forming a coherent whole. From the Northern Song dynasty, Zhang Zai and his students tried to construct an ideal socio-political order in which the state, society, and elites could be integrated into a coherent whole. They believed the well-being of state and society were interlinked, while literati were merely the unofficial agents of the state who organized the local community.[52] *Lüshi Xiangyue* is one evidence of their attempt to construct such an order. According to Guanzhong scholars' alternative institutional plan, the realm of the worldly is also a whole. This interconnection from the socio-historical perspective can be seen as a counterpart in northern China to the rise of elite localism occurring in southern China since the twelfth-century.

Indeed, as presented above, Zhang Zai and his students designed a coherent program interrelating cosmology, ethics, and politics. This system, on account of the cosmology centered on *qi* and the Great Void, implies the following facets: the unity of Heaven and man; the world is both actual and transcendent owing to the rituals of antiquity; the interconnectedness of *dao* and *ji*. I would conclude that Guanxue holism is mainly about the actual world and the world beyond fused into one, the connection of *dao* and *ji*, that Heaven and man are the ways in which the realms of beyond and the worldly become connected into one, and that the interconnected state, the literati, and society depict the cohesive whole.

---

52   Ong, *Men of Letters: Within the Passes*, 61.

Within the "four schools" format, a linear transmission is traced from Zhou Dunyi to the Cheng brothers and then through Yang Shi to Zhu Xi. This line of transmission came to be the orthodox ideology of the state. As such, Zhang Zai became the odd man out.[53] Although Zhang Zai did not fit nicely into the line of transmission above, the unique doctrines of Guanxue have been the intellectual source for later generations, e.g., the emphasis of Gu Yanwu (顧炎武, 1613–1682) on ritualism during the Ming dynasty. More importantly, the cohesive whole/holism in the Song dynasty laid the foundation for Guanxue holism in the Qing dynasty, which is also unique. Guanzhong scholars still held the belief in holism in the late Qing dynasty while the whole country had abandoned the idea of holism, as well as the notion of the metaphysical world, and had become more concerned with the actual world, with statecraft learning, and had thus turned towards evidential scholarship from the late Ming dynasty onwards. The integration of holism into Chinese thought began in the period before modernization, perhaps earlier than the seventeenth-century. In this sense, Guanzhong scholars' insistence on holism could be read as a counteraction to the mainstream.

Conclusion

Focusing on the concept of holism, my attempt has been to broaden the scholarship on Guanxue. Some previous studies have treated Guanxue as just another Neo-Confucian school. These studies strongly emphasize three characteristics of Guanxue: cosmology centered on *qi*, moral education through ritual practice (*yi li wei jiao*, 以禮爲教) and the combination of essence (*ti*, 體) and application (*yong*, 用). They ignored this "practical" aspect and focused on philosophy exclusively. At the same time, some studies treated the institutional pursuit as an entity divorced from the "philosophical" aspect.

In the investigation of Guanxue holism, I would like to suggest that exclusive emphasis on Zhang Zai's cosmology does not do justice to the whole image of the cosmology of Guanxue. We cannot under-

---

53   Ong, *Men of Letters: Within the Passes*, 133.

stand the Guanxue cosmology without situating it in the historical context of the construction of the metaphysical world of the Song Daoxue movement that emphasized this cosmic–political–ethical whole. At the same time, the concept of "moral education through ritual practice" is not only a moral philosophical doctrine. It indeed refers to Zhang Zai's unique doctrine of learning rituals to realize one's essential nature, which will result in the manifestation of *dao*. However, their stress on rituals also has a practical aspect, which is to restore the ritual system in the actual world. This may help explain why Zhu Xi followed the Lü brothers' effort in constructing the local community with ritualism, and why Liang Shuming (梁漱溟) later devoted himself to the ritual reconstruction experiment in modern China. With regard to the contribution of Guanxue holism, I think the Guan school is not merely a regional Neo-Confucian school as many scholars have argued. This study of Guanxue holism also attempts to respond to Chen Lai (陳來)'s claim that we should combine Zhang Zai with the Daoxue movement, place them in a broader context and highlight Guanxue's contribution to the mainstream of Chinese thought, namely, the universal significance of Guanxue.[54] In the end, I hope to have responded to Chen Lai's theory regarding the universality and regionality of Confucianism.[55] Guanxue holism exhibits Guanxue's universal significance and its regional character.

Second, I would like to renew the knowledge of the holistic character of Chinese thought. As presented above, the most well-known theory about Chinese holism is Needham's organicist philosophy, which was developed under the influence of Alfred North Whitehead. Needham's theory is indeed controversial. I think it seems that Needham held a normative position of Chinese science and organicist philosophy. Through the study of Guanxue holism, I attempt to reinforce Schwartz's question of Needham's insistence that there is no trace of "world souls" or heavenly rulers in this holistic order. Schwartz argues that the "mind of Heaven" or the concept of Heaven as ruler never departs from the ordered regularities of nature in the

---

54   Lai Chen, "Guanxue de jingshen" (The Spirit of the Guan School), *Journal of Shaanxi Normal University*, no.3 (2016): 8.

55   Lai Chen, "Ruxue de pubianxing yu diyuxing" (The universality and Locality of Confucianism), *Tianjin shehui kexue*, no. 3 (2005): 4–10.

dominant strains of Chinese thought.[56] Nevertheless, Schwartz did not give too much effort when discussing the holistic character of Chinese thought. Through the investigation of holism in Chinese thought above, we could conclude that the concept of ruler in Chinese thought has always existed, from shamanist civilization to the Song dynasty. In primitive time, the "ruler" was a deity, and then it was Heaven within *Dao* in the Axial Age, and the Great Ultimate/heavenly principle in the Song dynasty. Therefore, the belief in the cohesive whole/holism is unlike a natural organic, and therefore, the biological metaphor—organicist philosophy—may not be the right name for the holistic character of Chinese thought.

In the end, my concern with holism in the Song Dynasty is anchored in a comparative perspective. The belief in holism generally distinguishes between the pre-modern and modern eras, similarly to the process of modernization distinguishing between periods of western culture. In the western context, holism started to disintegrate with the rise of modernity. By contrast, the disintegration of belief in holism in Chinese thought may have begun before the First Opium war (1839–42), when China first encountered the modern West. Most likely, this belief began to erode because of the developments in Chinese philosophy in the Ming-Qing periods (1368-1911). However, as Wu Fei suggested, the restoration of ritualism in late Qing somehow implies the restoration of holism in modern China.[57] With regard to this, how shall we understand China's modernity?

My focus on the Song dynasty is motivated by this well-acknowledged belief that the basic paradigm of Chinese thought was established by Song Confucians and continued its influence long after, during the later dynasties. Another important reason is the Kyoto school theory of seeing the Song dynasty as being pre-modern. In the context of modernity in East Asia, philosophers of the Kyoto school suggested that the Song dynasty was pre-modern because society was organized around a centralized government, market economy, long distance trade, proto-nationalism, individualism, and so on. However, Wang Hui argues that the political and social content of Confu-

---

56   Schwartz, *The World of Thought in Ancient China*, 417–8.
57   Fei Wu, "Cong xiangyue dao xiang cun jian shen" (From Xiangyue to Rural Building Movement), *Sixiang yu xiandai she hui: jiaoyu yu xiandai shehui*, 07 (2009).

cianism at that time shows elements of a so-called "early modernity."[58] Viren Murthy criticizes Wang Hui for focusing on a supposed clear distinction between what exists (*shiran*, 實然), any historical system past or present, and what ought to be (*yingran*, 應然), an ideal system. We can see a similar pattern in Western Enlightenment thinkers, such as Immanuel Kant, who did not base morality on empirical facts or objects, but on a transcendental faculty of reason.[59] The case of Guanxue holism also informs us of the distinction between present system and ideal system, but also of the Guanzhong scholars' effort to bring the ideal system to existence. To respond to Wang Hui's critical theory of the modernity of China is not in my intention here. However, with the history of Guanxue holism, I think Murthy's interpretation of Wang's work, as pitting modernity against modernity, is more convincing. Also, I would like to ask whether it is possible, as Ding Yun suggests, to consider the issue of the modernization of China as no longer being a peculiar case of the localization of modernity. Instead, it is a path to rethink modernity, to rethink political philosophy and its universe, and to explore the multiple possibilities of world history. Therefore, reconsideration of the history of modern China is also a contribution to world history.[60]

References

Bol, Peter K. *Neo-Confucianism in history*. Cambridge: Harvard University Asia Center, 2008.

Chan, Wing-tsit 陳榮捷. *A Source Book in Chinese Philosophy*. Princeton: Princeton University Press, 1969.

Chang, Kwang-chih 張光直. *Meishu, Shenhua, Jili*. Translated by Jing Guo. Beijing: Shenghuo, dushu, xinzhi san lian shu dian, 2013.

Chen, Lai 陳來. "Guanxue de jingshen" 關學的精神 (The Spirit of the Guan School).

---

58   Wang, *Xiandai zhongguo sixiang de xingqi*.

59   Viren Murthy, "Modernity against Modernity: Wang Hui's Critical History of Chinese Thought," *Modern Intellectual History* 3, 1 (2006): 137–165.

60   Yun Ding, *Zhong Dao zhi guo: zheng zhi zhe xue lun ji* (The Way of the Mean of the country: Essays on Political Philosophy) (Fuzhou: Fujian jiaoyu chubanshe, 2015), 11–14.

Journal of Shaanxi Normal University, no.3 (2016): 7–9.

_____. "Ru xue de pu bian xing yu di yu xing" 儒學的普遍性與地域性 (The Universality and Locality of Confucianism). *Tianjin shehui kexue*, no. 3 (2005): 4–10.

Chow, Kai-wing. "Ritual, Cosmology, and Ontology: Chang Tsai's Moral Philosophy and Neo-Confucian Ethics." *Philosophy East and West* 43, no.2 (1993): 201–228.

Ding, Yun 丁耘. *Ru jia yu qi meng: zhe xue hui tong shi ye xia de dang qian zhong guo si xiang* 儒家與啓蒙：哲學會通視野下的當前中國思想 (The Way of the Mean of the country: Essays on Political Philosophy). Beijing: Shenghuo·dushu·xinzhi sanlian chubanshe, 2011.

Feng, Congwu 馮從吾, Junmin Chen ed., Xinghai Xu dianxiao. *Guanxue bian (fu xu bian)* 關學編 (附續編) (Cases of Guanzhong Learning). Beijing: Zhonghua shuju, 1987.

Ge, Zhaoguang 葛兆光. *Zhong guo si xiang shi* 中國思想史 (An Intellectual History of China). Shanghai: Fudan daxue chubanshe, 2009.

Grinter, Aaron. "The Gran Tradition: Revisiting the work of Joseph Needham to Address Ethnocentrism in Contemporary Philosophy and Society." *Cosmology and History: The Journal of Natural and Social Philosophy*, vol. 14, no. 3 (2018): 297–320.

Heidegger, Martin and Grene, Marjorie. "The Age of the World View." *Martin Heidegger and Literature*, Vol. 4, no. 2 (Winter, 1976): 340–355.

Huang, Junjie 黃俊傑, ed., *Zhongguo ren de yu zhou guan* 中國人的宇宙觀 (Chinese View of Universe). Hefei: Huangshan shushe, 2012.

Kasoff, Ira E. *The Thought of Chang Tsai (1020–1077)*, Cambridge: Cambridge University Press, 1984.

Lukács, György. *Li xing de hui mie* 理性的毀滅 (Destruction of Rationality). Translated by Jiuxing Wang, Zhimin Cheng, Dikun Xie, et. al. Nanjing: Jiangsu jiaoyu chubanshe, 2005.

Miyazaki, Ichisada. *Dongyang de jinshi* 東洋的近世 (The Early Modern Period of Tōyō). Translated by Xuefeng Zhang. Shanghai: Shanghai guji chubanshe, 2018.

Mote, F. F. *Intellectual Foundations of China*. New York: A.A. Knopf, 1971.

Murthy, Viren. "Modernity against Modernity: Wang Hui's Critical History of Chinese Thought." *Modern Intellectual History*, 3, 1 (2006): 137–165.

Ong, Chang Woei 王昌偉. "Guan xue bian yu mingqing shaanxi shidafu de jiti jiyi" 關學編與明清陝士大夫的集體記憶 (Cases of Guanzhong Learning and Guanzhong literati'collective memory in the Ming-Qing Period). In *Cultural Memory and Chinese Society*, edited by Guozhong He, 166–177. Kuala Lumpur: Institute of China studies, University of Malaya (2008).

_____ *Men of Letters: Within the Passes: Guanzhong Literati from the Tenth to Eighteenth Centuries*. Cambridge: Harvard University Asia Center, 2008.

Schwartz, Benjamin. *The World of Thought in Ancient China*, Cambridge: Harvard University Press, 1985.

Wang, Fansen 王汎森. *Quan li de mao xi yue guan Zhong yong: qing dai de si xiang, xue shu yu xin tai* 權力的毛細血管作用: 清代的思想、學術於心態 (Capillary Power: Thought, Academy, Mind in the Qing Dynasty). Beijing: Beijing daxue chubanshe, 2015.

Wang, Hui 汪暉. *Xiandai Zhongguo sixiang de xingqi* 現代中國思想的興起 (The Rise of Modern Chinese thought). Beijing: Shenghuo · dushu · xinzhi san lian shudian, 2008.

Wu, Chan-liang 吳展良. "Cong zheng ti xing yu ge ti xing de rong he lun zhong guo wen hua de xian dai hua" (A Discussion of the Modernity of Chinese Culture from fusing holism and individualism). *Qian Mu Xiansheng Jinianguan Guankan*, no.3 (1995).

Wu, Fei 吳飛. "Cong xiangyue dao xiang cun jian shen" 從鄉約到鄉村建設 (From Xiangyue to Rural Building Movement). *Sixiang yu xiandai she hui: jiaoyu yu xiandai shehui*, 07 (2009).

Yang, Guorong 楊國榮. "Guan xue de zhe xue yi han—ji yu zhang zai si xiang de kao cha" 關學的哲學意涵—基於張載思想的考察 (The Philosophical Implication of the School of Guan: An Examination Based on Zhang Zai's thought). *Journal of East China Normal University*, no.1 (2017): 21–25.

Yang, Lihua 楊立華. *Qi ben yu shen hua: Zhang Zai zhe xue shu lun* 氣本與神化: 張載哲學述論 (Qi root and Spiritual Transformation: A Discussion of the Philosophy of Zhang Zai). Beijing: Beijing daxue chubanshe, 2008.

Yu, Ying-shih 余英時. *Songming l xue yu zhengzhiwen hua* 宋明理學與政治文化 (Song-Ming Neo-Confucianism and Political Culture). Taibei: Yunchen wenhua, 2004.

———— *Lun tianren zhiji: zhongguo gu dai si xiang qi yuan shi tan* 論天人之際: 中國古代思想起源試探 (Between the Heavenly and the Human: the Origin of Ancient Chinese Thought). Taibei: Lianjing chubanshe. 2014.

Zhang, Zai 張載, Zhang, Xichen xiao. *Zhang Zai Ji* 張載集 (Collected Works of Zhang Zai). Beijing: Zhonghua shu ju, 2012.

Cody Staton (Sun Yat-Sen University)
CONCERNING AESTHETIC ATTITUDES
Kant and Confucius on Emulation and Evaluation

Introduction

It could easily be argued that Kant and Confucius are the most iconic thinkers of their respective philosophical traditions. Numerous commentators have drawn comparisons between the two thinkers, mostly by identifying ways in which their moral theories are compatible.[1] But in terms of form and style, there could hardly be two drastically different thinkers for comparison. The one rigorously critiqued the idea of a total system of philosophy that would catalogue all scientific knowledge, the other conveyed his philosophy almost exclusively in conversation with students. Surprisingly, however, both Kant and Confucius find accord with regard to their aesthetic theories. Both hold that it is not just about the fine arts, but that it also refers to a kind of joyful experience that develops moral character. Some commentators in recent years have even claimed that Confucianism is best understood as an "aesthetic turn" in classical Ruism.[2] Similarly, it has been argued that appreciating Kant's moral philosophy requires a thorough understanding of his aesthetics. While some commentators have provided thoughtful discussions of Kantian and Confucian accounts of aesthetics, they have generally limited their

---

1   Cf. Ching, "Chinese Ethics and Kant," and the edited volume compiled by Palmquist, *Cultivating Personhood: Kant and Asian Philosophy*, which contains numerous articles comparing Kant and Confucius.

2   See Peimin Ni, *Confucius: The Man and the Way of Gongfu*, who argues that Confucianism is best understood as *gongfu* (功夫/工夫), the art for life. Also, cf. Weiming, *Confucian Thought: Selfhood as Creative Transformation*, for arguments regarding Confucian notions of self-development (51–66).

examinations to narrow topics (e.g., the sublime and beauty). In this paper, I will investigate how, according to Kant and Confucius, aesthetic experience yields self-development.[3] For Confucius, this is a matter of *emulating* traditional models of virtue or excellence (*de*, 德), whereas, for Kant, such a development of the person requires aesthetic *evaluation*, which does not defer to tradition.[4]

The Confucian approach to self-development has been widely commented on, not just as an outline for social order, but also as a holistic approach to the practice of life.[5] Although he does not provide a detailed theory of aesthetic doctrines, Confucius often describes how the performance of social rituals (*li*, 禮) is like playing music.[6] Observing social rituals with propriety requires more than "gifts of jade and silk" in the same way that performing music is not reducible to ringing bells and banging drums.[7] What must be sought in both instances is the achievement of harmony (*he*, 和). For the Confucian, harmony is not gained by canceling differences and equalizing all members of society, such that they all perform their roles in the same way. Just as a chef combines various ingredients proportionately in order to attain the right flavor in a dish, the person of exemplary character (*junzi*, 君

---

3   Perhaps the most developed accounts of these include Nelson, "China, Nature, and the Sublime in Kant," and also Wenzel, "Beauty in Kant and Confucius: A First Step," who compares Kant and Confucius with regard to beauty. However, I disagree with the latter's assumption that Kant's theory of beauty in the third *Critique* is constrained within the limits of transcendental philosophy as outlined in the first *Critique*. Wenzel has questioned whether or not such an aesthetic attitude indeed obtains in Confucius, for while Kant considers objects of sensible intuition to be the objects that we find beautiful, Confucius rather focuses on acts, behavior, customs, and so on (97). My view, however, is that the Kant and Confucius focus on different sensible *objects* as outcomes of aesthetic experience. Moreover, I disagree with Wenzel's assessment that aesthetic judgment plays no part in moral development (cf. Kant, KU, §59 of the third *Critique* titled "Beauty as the Symbol of Morality," where Kant argues that natural beauty teaches us how to be moral).

4   Confucius, *Analects*, 17.8. All references to the *Analects* are cited in Ames and Rosemont, *The Confucian Analects: A Philosophical Translation*.

5   General discussions of Confucian education abound and are too numerous to mention here. For an insightful commentary on the Confucian account of the central role that recognition plays in "dismantling" negative relations with others, see Nelson, "Recognition and Resentment in the Confucian Analects."

6   Cf. Confucius, *Analects*, 8.8, 16.5, and 17.21.

7   Confucius, *Analects*, 17.11.

子) recognizes the reciprocity (*shu*, 恕) needed between individuals to achieve harmony.[8]

What makes this activity aesthetic is that such endeavors are taken to be self-generating achievements that emerge from our encounters with others in the social sphere.[9] To separate the normative aims described in the *Analects*, as though they are merely theoretical (moral) principles, from the aesthetic social sphere out of which such norms are constituted would entirely misconstrue the context of the Confucian perspective. Put simply, genuine self-development requires that we appreciate beauty and reflect on how it promotes our overall progress as participants in society. A person (*ren*, 仁) in the Confucian sense that does not observe ritual propriety (*li*) cannot be called a person, let alone would such a person lacking in propriety have anything to do with art.[10] This can be interpreted in two ways: that art and the aesthetic way of living lead one down the path of *li* and goodness and also that living a life devoted to *li* is the only means by which one can live an aesthetic life.[11]

Self-development always involves the reciprocal broadening of oneself and others. What I aim to show is that this broadening of one's learning is an aesthetic attitude, whereby the ability (*shan*, 善) to grow develops on the basis of encounters with art and with others.[12] The capacity to appreciate the reciprocity (*shu*) between individuals as always being flexible and indeterminate yields a harmonious social landscape.[13]

In contrast to the Confucian emphasis on reciprocity, Kant has been widely criticized for supposedly reducing aesthetic reflection to mere *subjective* concerns. From Schiller onwards, readers have pre-

---

8   Confucius, *Analects*, 13.23; cf. 5.12, 12.2, and 15.24.

9   I follow Ames and Hall, *Thinking Through Confucius*, when rendering the Confucian account of society as being essentially aesthetic. Also, cf. Ames and Rosemont, *The Confucian Analects: A Philosophical Translation*, 58, and Ni, *Confucius: The Man and the Way of Gongfu*.

10   Confucius, *Analects*, 3.3.

11   This seems to be the interpretation that Zhu Xi offers. See Gardner, *Zhu Xi's Reading of the Analects: Canon, Commentary, and the Classical Tradition*, 87–88, 190.

12   The term *aesthetic attitude* has been much debated in the Analytic tradition of aesthetics. Most agree that the aesthetic attitude involves disinterestedness.

13   Confucius, 15.24; cf. 5.12 and 12.2.

sented Kant's doctrine of taste and beauty as though it had nothing to say about the beautiful apart from mere subjective judgments. After all, Kant, in the opening paragraph of the third *Critique*, does argue that an aesthetic judgment *"cannot be other* than *subjective."*[14] But to argue that aesthetic judgments are not *about* objects is an unfortunate misunderstanding, given that Kant's use of the term *subjective* was intended to reject Baumgarten's claim that aesthetics could become an objective science.[15] Nor is it the case that Kant's theory of taste endorses a bourgeois ideology, as if the so-called pure taste is only a product of historical domination, as Pierre Bourdieu has claimed.[16] When describing judgments of the beautiful, Kant argues that they are "public," a matter of "common sense," and that they are universally valid for everyone.[17] Aesthetic judgments of the beautiful are always carried out by means of the harmony (*Zusammenstimmung*) or concord (*Einstimmung*) of our representational powers (imagination and understanding).[18] Kant presents the harmony as the free play of the imagination and/with the understanding such that the beautiful releases us from always seeking determinacy, which often ends in overdeterminacy.[19] Judgment (*Beurteilung*) of the beautiful is not reductive, but leaves open the possibility that my feelings toward the beautiful can mature. This indicates a departure from mere imitation, which relies on prejudices and non-reflective views.

According to Rudolf Makkreel, Kant, much like Confucius, does not think that all prejudices should be dismissed.[20] Established tradi-

---

14   Kant, *Critique of Judgment*, §1, 203. All citations from the *Critique of Judgment* are from Pluhar, *Immanuel Kant: Critique of Pure Reason*. Hereafter abbreviated as KU.

15   Kant also stresses the subjectivity of aesthetic judgment to make it clear that the principle of purposiveness without a purpose in no way governs our determination of objects themselves, but only regulates our feeling of pleasure in judgments of the beautiful.

16   Bourdieu, *Distinction: A Social Critique of the Judgment of Taste*.

17   Kant, KU, §8, 214–16. Also, see Makkreel, 103–04.

18   Kant, KU, §9, 216; cf. 190 and 219.

19   Zuckert has an insightful analysis of the three modes in which Kant presents the imagination in relation to the understanding. I cannot go into further detail here. See Zuckert, *Beauty and Biology in Kant: An Interpretation of the Critique of Judgment*, 279–320.

20   Makkreel, *Orientation and Judgment in Hermeneutics*, 49.

tional views give our prejudicial understanding the stamp of authority. But unlike Confucius's nuanced account of emulation, Kant often characterizes deference to tradition as tasteless imitation. Encountering opposing views from other cultures, for instance, requires the ability to overcome prejudicial views of taste deriving from one's tradition. Kant recognizes this demand in the third *Critique*, where he argues that, while all human beings have the capacity to judge the beautiful, the object of our taste will vary according to our cultural backgrounds and openness to different kinds of taste.[21] The dialogical method of subsuming opposing judgments will only render confusion.[22] My view is that aesthetic *Beurteilung* as Kant describes it cannot proceed exclusively from emulation. Aesthetic *Beurteilung* is an evaluation that develops the capacity of taste by allowing for an appreciation of expressions of the beautiful from various different platforms that are not limited by traditional (monocultural) views.

In the first part of this paper, I discuss the Confucian notion of self-development, arguing then that this is an aesthetic activity. From there, I take up Kant's account of aesthetic judgment (*Beurteilung*) before assessing his notions of prejudice and aesthetic evaluation. Although Kant is generally thought to exclude consideration of the community in his account of reflective judgment, I aim to show that aesthetic *Beurteilung* is developed out of culture.

Confucian Self-Development

It is difficult to narrowly define the cornerstone concept of the *Analects*, but the notion of the person (*ren*, 仁), I suppose, is the best place to start. Some of the most well-known contemporary commentators of Confucian philosophy have argued that Confucius advocates a role-based system for participants in society.[23] Taking

---

21   Cf. Kant, KU, §17, 234.

22   See Makkreel, *Orientation and Judgment in Hermeneutics*, especially the second chapter on the shortcomings of the dialogical method of Gadamer in this regard and how reflective hermeneutics can resolve these problems.

23   Cf. Ames, *Confucian Role Ethics: A Vocabulary*, and Ames and Rosemont, *Confucian Role Ethics: A Moral Vision for the 21ˢᵗ Century?*

ownership of our actions requires us to carry out acts with authority, thus properly speaking, a person only acquires personality in the
company of others. This is not to say that personhood is some kind
of herd identity acquired by following others, as *ren* is self-reflexive.[24]
Thus, "it is the presence of the authoritative person (*ren*, 仁) that is
the greatest attraction. How can anyone be called wise who, in having the choice, does not seek to dwell among authoritative people?"[25]
The magnetizing attraction that authoritative persons invite certainly
separates the wheat from the chaff: "In going astray, people fall into
groups. In observing these divergencies, the degree to which they are
authoritative (*ren*, 仁) can be known."[26]

    Ren persons attract others who are also authoritative in their
actions because, among other reasons, they recognize the way that
reciprocity (*shu*, 恕) functions. When "Zhonggong inquired about
authoritative conduct (*ren*, 仁)," for instance, Confucius replied
that our dealings with others are simple: "Do not impose upon others what you yourself do not want, and you will not incur personal
or political ill will."[27] *Shu* is not about presupposing what others
need, nor does it reduce those needs to scripted or blasé responses.
Zilu and Ranyou once asked Confucius the same question, to which
he replied with different answers.[28] Here, the lesson given serves
Confucius as much as the lessons acquired benefit his students, as
"authoritative persons establish others in seeking to establish themselves.... Correlating one's conduct with those near at hand can be
said to be the method of becoming an authoritative person."[29] The
authoritative heart-mind (*xin*, 心) gives shape to the manifold of
experience with others, thus rendering self-reflexivity possible.[30]

---

24   On selfhood being self-reflexive, see Shun, "Conception of the Person in Early
      Confucian Thought."
25   Confucius, *Analects*, 4.1.
26   Confucius, *Analects*, 4.7.
27   Confucius, *Analects*, 12.2.
28   Confucius, *Analects*, 11.22. It is not insignificant that the question asked by both
      Zilu and Ranyou concerns the relationship between learning and acting upon what
      is learned. Confucius replied that the model provided by their father and brothers
      should already have given them the answer.
29   Confucius, *Analects*, 6.30.
30   Confucius, *Analects*, 6.7.

Becoming *ren* is near to hand always, as to think about how to act already indicates the opportunity to realize *ren* for oneself.[31] The question that we have to ask is how much of the process of becoming *ren* derives from tradition and how much of our authoritative conduct emerges from within ourselves. The two are not mutually exclusive.

We have already seen that *xin* guides the observance of *shu*, making possible the self-reflexivity that promotes self-development. This strongly suggests that self-development unfolds *in situ*. Yet passages in the *Analects* adamantly endorse following tradition. For instance, self-development appears imitative whenever Confucius tells his students to look to a Yao or a Shun as models for cultivating character.[32] He also argues that his method proceeds in the same way: "Following the proper way, I do not forge new paths; with confidence I cherish the ancients—in these respects I am comparable to our venerable Old Peng."[33] Just how serious we should take this comment is debatable; Confucius was an innovator, to be sure. But Confucius also describes how knowledge (*zhi*, 知) is more valuable when acquired from studying the ancients.[34] I take it that the so-called "proper way" has less to do with preestablished norms than it has to do with the organic way in which self-reflexivity emerges, namely, by way of *tian* (天).

As a whole, the proper model for self-cultivation is *tian* (天), which cannot be reduced to any particular concept of the celestial or divine, but is instead limitless and "expansive."[35] As *Mencius* argues, above all, *tian* reveres *ren*.[36] The unfolding progress of *tian* lives in the culture of a people from which *tian* emerges: "With King Wen (文) long dead, does not our cultural heritage reside here in us? If *tian* (天) were going to destroy this legacy, we latecomers would not have had access to it."[37] The *Shu Jing* (書經) indicates that "*tian* hears and sees

---

31 Compare Confucius, *Analects*, 7.30 and 9.31.
32 Confucius, *Analects*, 8.18.
33 Confucius, *Analects*, 7.1; cf. 3.14.
34 Confucius, *Analects*, 7.20, cf. 16.9.
35 Confucius, *Analects*, 8.19.
36 *Mencius*, 公孫丑上, Gong Sun Chou, 2A7. Cited in Ames and Rosemont, *The Confucian Analects: A Philosophical Translation*, 236n62.
37 Confucius, *Analects*, 9.5; cf.19.22

as our people hear and see."[38] *Tian* is neither reducible to the transcendent nor to the immanent spheres; it is both the condition for the possibility of the emergence of *ren* and also the outcome of meaningful human endeavors. Thus, *tian* preserves the legacy of a culture, but only insofar as its participants practice the *li* (禮), which is, as David Jones indicates, genuinely "divine."[39]

The intergenerational harmony secured by the practice of *li* is rooted in the divinity of the family, the model *par excellence* for social engagement.[40] Zizhang desiring to know what culture will be like in ten generations from now is, according to Confucius, a pedestrian curiosity: all previous generations "adapted the observances of ritual propriety (*li*, 禮)."[41] The Confucian recognizes that life is only ever ready to be lived when one carries out the practice of *li* that passes through generations.[42] Individuals emerge from the sphere of culture inasmuch as that culture arises from the collective participation of individuals working in harmony. But "harmony just for its own sake without regulating the situation through observing ritual propriety (*li*, 禮) will not work."[43] *Li* is an ongoing pursuit that one must practice continually with others.

What we then emulate is the way in which *li* emerges naturally in the culture. But "learning without due reflection (*si*, 思) leads to perplexity; reflection without learning leads to perilous circumstances."[44] It is not enough to follow blindly in the ways of the ancients; *li* must be thoughtfully put into practice. Emulating the model of *ren* persons is not a practice of following whatever comes along the way in experience or of finding mere agreement (*tong* 同) with just anyone.[45] The

---

38 Cited in Legge, *The Chinese Classics*, translation modified. For related passages on *tian* in the *Analects*, see 9.6, 11.9, and 14.35.

39 Jones, "Walking the Way In-Between with Confucius: *Tianwen* and Emerging Patterns of Human Nature," 21.

40 Cf. Confucius, *Analects*, 1.11, 4.20, and 9.20.

41 Confucius, *Analects*, 2.23.

42 Or as Confucius puts it to Zilu: "Not yet understanding life, how could you understand death?" (11.12). After all: "If at dawn you learn of and tread the way (*dao* 道), you can face death at dusk" (4.8).

43 Confucius, *Analects*, 1.12.

44 Confucius, *Analects*, 2.15.

45 Confucius, *Analects*, 13.23. On this, see Jones, "Walking the Way In-Between with Confucius: *Tianwen* and Emerging Patterns of Human Nature," 30–31.

Confucian differentiates between education and cultivation in the same way that imitation and utility are nowhere near the sphere of emulation and personality, the latter always requiring the exercise of the reflective heart-mind (*xin*).[46] As Tu Weiming has argued, the significant philosophical distinction that the Confucian *Analects* makes is not between self and society, between the inner impulses driven by selfish desires and the constraints of cultural values. The real tension that Confucius elucidates is between the authentic self that strives to live according to the *li* and the petty, inauthentic self that views value as always being reducible to economic interests.[47] Even the most fundamental Confucian virtue of filial piety (*xiao*, 孝) distinguishes between proper care and attention to others and merely following orders.[48] Confucius clearly instructs his students that, when "striving to be authoritative (*ren*) in your conduct, do not even yield to your teacher."[49] Emulating one's parents and teachers is a process of self-generating reflection.

I suggest that *li* is carried out according to the practice of *shu* that is emulative.[50] The Han Dynasty Confucian Zheng Xuan (鄭泫) emphasizes this point as follows: "脩，治也。治而廣之，人放傚之，是曰教 (脩 *xiu*, to repair, broaden, adorn, or cultivate, is also to govern *zhi* 治. In governing and broadening, whereby others emulate, is called *jiao* 教 teaching)."[51] The reciprocity established between Confucius and his students is not merely about the teacher implanting knowledge into the minds of students; the reciprocal flow of development between oneself and others always requires the aesthetic sphere out of which such broadening cultivation becomes possible. This is what I take *shu* to mean, namely, that there must be an individual effort to broaden oneself whereby others come to emulate such self-development.[52] And *ren* persons are not worried "about not being acknowledged by others," as they "worry about failing to acknowl-

---

46   Confucius, *Analects*, 2.12 and 17.22.
47   Weiming, *Humanity and Self-Cultivation: Essays in Confucian Thought*, 17–34.
48   See Ames and Rosemont, *The Confucian Analects: A Philosophical Translation*, 264n278.
49   Confucius, *Analects*, 15.36.
50   Confucius, *Analects*, 6.30.
51   Johnston and Ping, *Daxue and Zhongyong*, 215, translation modified.
52   See Confucius, *Analects*, 11.22.

edge" others.[53] I take it that Confucius considers this activity to be essentially aesthetic.

The Confucian Aesthetic Attitude

In what follows, I will argue that cultivating personhood is an aesthetic achievement, as Confucius prescribes that one should "set your sights on the way (*dao*, 道), sustain yourself with excellence (*de*, 德), lean upon authoritative conduct (*ren*, 仁), and sojourn (*you*, 游) in the arts."[54] Here, I will touch on the Confucian aesthetic attitude by focusing on the interrelation of art, especially music (*yue*, 樂), and *li*, ritual propriety. The *Analects* are punctuated with reflections on these two activities, which are often coupled in Confucius's reflections.

Peimin Ni points out that 樂 has two meanings depending on pronunciation; as *yue*, it refers to art, but when pronounced as *le*, it refers to enjoyment or happiness.[55] The relationship between music and enjoyment is reciprocal in the same way that a writer shares a relation with her readers; without the audience, the poetry that the artist produces has no meaning, while the art itself serves to reward the audience with pleasure. Music, especially, engenders the reciprocal progress of enjoyment between artist and participant: "Much can be realized with music if one begins by playing in unison, and then goes on to improvise with purity and distinctness of flow, thereby bringing all to completion."[56] Insofar as the ritual performance of music achieves a beautiful sound, it serves as a model for the establishment of harmony in society as a whole.[57]

Since the "first to come to observing ritual propriety (*li*, 禮) and to playing music (*yue*, 樂) were the simple folk," Confucius suggests that the interdependence of ritual, music, and enjoyment arises naturally.[58] Indeed, the "enjoyment found in attuning oneself to the rhythms

---

53   Confucius, *Analects*, 1.16.
54   Confucius, *Analects*, 7.6.
55   Ni, *Confucius: The Man and the Way of Gongfu*, 56–57.
56   Confucius, *Analects*, 3.23.
57   Ni, *Confucius: The Man and the Way of Gongfu*, 57.
58   Confucius, *Analects*. 11.1.

of natural propriety (*li*, 禮) and music (*yue*, 樂)" are expressions of one and the same aesthetic attitude.[59] For Confucius, one finds "inspiration by intoning the songs," learns "where to stand from observing ritual propriety (*li*, 禮)," and finds "fulfillment in playing music."[60] The activities of art and social engagement are mutually inclusive and informative of one another. Of course, sloppy music is as injurious to taste as the company of petty people is to *li*.[61] "*Shao* music," for Confucius, is superior to all others because it is both beautiful (*mei*, 美) and adept (*shan*, 善), whereas *wu* music is beautiful, but not adept.[62] The *Analects* describe Confucius as not even desiring the taste of meat after having enjoyed the beautiful *Shao* music.[63] Well-performed pieces of music render life joyful, which promotes thoughtful action because art and ritual arise naturally together, thereby producing harmony, while harmony is at the same time the necessary condition for the enjoyment of art and ritual.[64] These facets of our relationship to aesthetic experience require a lifetime of development.

For instance, when reflecting on his life's journey, which is perhaps one of the most iconic passages in the *Analects*, Confucius remarks as follows:

> From fifteen, my heart-and-mind was set upon learning;
> from thirty I took my stance;
> from forty I was no longer doubtful;
> from fifty I realized the propensities of *tian* (*tianming*, 天命);
> from sixty my ear was attuned;
> from seventy I could give my heart-and-mind free reign without overstepping the boundaries.[65]

Educating oneself is as much about educating the senses to the unfolding myriad of life's opportunities as it is about learning through books and lessons. Here, Confucius provides both a phenomenological and physiological description of how he develops his attitude

---

59   Confucius, *Analects*, 16.5.
60   Confucius, *Analects*, 8.8.
61   Cf. Confucius, *Analects*, 9.25 and 11.26.
62   Confucius, *Analects*, 3.25.
63   Confucius, *Analects*, 7.14.
64   Confucius, *Analects*, 3.3.
65   Confucius, *Analects*, 2.4.

throughout his life. The focus on the heart-and-mind seeking out learning—the way a river charts a course by finding a groove in the landscape—on the body taking its stance, and on the awareness of the emerging forms of the natural world all suggest that developing one's ability to learn more is an aesthetic achievement.

It is not as if mere participation will render an excellent performance of music, however. Zilu's zither offended Confucius greatly because the style of playing was rather poor.[66] Becoming virtuous or excellent in character is an ongoing performance, where harmony (*he*, 和) is progressive and the result of the asymmetrical reciprocity among participants, rather than being a mere equalizing of all things.[67] Even in the thickest of sporting competitions, exemplary persons (*junzi*, 君子) express excellence aesthetically.[68]

Likewise, Kant discusses harmony as an outcome of or contributing factor to aesthetic enjoyment. For both Kant and Confucius, neither human happiness nor pleasure in the beautiful are the goal or purpose of aesthetic experience nor of life in general, but they are nonetheless the rewarding fruit of cultivated life experiences.

Kant's Account of Aesthetic Judgment (Beurteilung)

Kant's requirement for aesthetic judgment (*Beurteilung*) is that taste declares something to be beautiful for all of us. And yet, aesthetic *Beurteilung*, in contrast to cognitive judgment (*Urteilung*), determines objects without any kind of *conceptual* (determinative) judgment of the object itself.[69] According to Kant, it is not the object itself that gives judgments of taste all license to judge beauty, and to hence feel pleasure, but it is rather on account of the way in which the imagination and the understanding enter into a free harmony prior to any conceptual determination of the object. In a rather long passage, Kant writes:

---

66   Confucius, *Analects*, 11.15. On this, see Ames and Hall, *The Confucian Analects: A Philosophical Translation*, 247n177.
67   Confucius, *Analects*, 7.32.
68   Confucius, *Analects*, 3.7.
69   Cf. Kant, KU, 5: 169 and 20: 211, where he seems to distinguish these two terms.

The pleasure in the beautiful is neither a pleasure of enjoyment, nor of a lawful activity, and not even of a contemplation involving subtle reasoning in accordance with ideas, but of mere reflection (*Reflexion*). Without having any purpose or fundamental principle for a guide, this pleasure accompanies the common apprehension of an object by the imagination, as a faculty of intuition, in relation to the understanding, as a faculty of concepts, by means of a procedure of the power of judgment, which it must also exercise for the sake of the most common experience: only in the latter case it is compelled to do so for the sake of an empirical objective concept, while in the former case (in the aesthetic judging (*Beurteilung*)) it is merely for the sake of perceiving the suitability of the representation for the harmonious (subjectively purposive) occupation of both cognitive faculties in their freedom, i.e., in order to feel (*empfinden*) the representational state with pleasure.[70]

I feel pleasure in the judgment that an object is beautiful, which is merely in my representation, because of the universal communicability of the imagination and the understanding in their freedom.[71] The free play of the imagination with/and the understanding promotes the ability of aesthetic judgment to produce reflection.[72] Unlike mere satisfaction, which is private and in no way sustains our mind's attention, reflection enhances our ability to feel pleasure. Aesthetic reflection does not reduce a representation of the beautiful to any particular concept, but rather holds it up in comparison with other representations.[73] Moreover, the aesthetic *sensus communis* in which imagination and understanding participate is in no way "private," but is rather a "communal feeling" regarding the beautiful.[74]

---

70 Kant, KU, §39, 292.
71 Kant, KU, §9, 217.
72 On Kant's varying descriptions of the free play of the faculties, see Zuckert, *Beauty and Biology in Kant: An Interpretation of the Critique of Judgment*, 279–320. While I take it that the harmonious free play of the faculties is the *act* responsible for promoting judgments of the beautiful, which thereby give rise to aesthetic pleasure, subjective purposiveness without a purpose is, as Zuckert rightly points out, the principle that governs the aesthetic pleasure that emerges from our judgments of the beautiful. The free play of the faculties *and* the principle of purposiveness are what make possible the feeling of the beautiful and aesthetic pleasure (cf. 277–78).
73 Kant, KU, First Introduction, 20: 211.
74 Kant, KU, §21, 5: 239. See Makkreel, *Orientation and Judgment in Hermeneutics*, 59.

The pervasive misunderstanding regarding Kant's notion of the *subjective* aspect of aesthetic judgment is thus peculiar, given his argument concerning the universal communicability of the beautiful carried out by the free play of the cognitive powers. Of course, Kant concedes that it seems counterintuitive to demand that a "taste of reflection, with its claim that its judgment (about the beautiful) is universally valid for everyone," especially when we judge something to be beautiful without soliciting the views of others. That I consider a landscape to be beautiful assumes that my aesthetic judgments express a "general validity (*Gemeingültigkeit*)" for everyone.[75] Yet Kant goes further and claims that the harmony of the cognitive powers provides a kind of aesthetic universal validity (*Allgemeingültigkeit*) in a judgment of the beautiful that "extends that predicate [of the beautiful] over the entire sphere *of judging persons*."[76] Moreover, Kant refers to this universal validity as disinterestedness, for although we take pleasure and reflect on our feelings, we make no rational (conceptual, objective, and so on) claim about the object itself. An attitude of disinterest regarding the object does not achieve a universally valid judgment by means of mere description (*Urteilung*) about the object, but only because of the universal communicability of the harmonious cognitive powers (imagination and understanding) in their free play. Put differently, aesthetic judgments are universally valid not because they are agreed upon by everyone in that moment, but rather they are valid because we all have a harmonious disposition between imagination and understanding.

Kant addresses this argument in §40, where he claims that, in the same way that "we speak of a sense of truth, a sense of decency, of justice, etc.," we also speak of a shared *sense* of taste deriving from culture.[77] Aesthetic *sensus communis* then refers to "the idea of a sense *shared* [by all of us], i.e., a power to judge that in reflecting takes account (a priori), in our thought, of everyone else's way of representing [something], in order *as it were* to compare our own judg-

---

75   Kant, KU, §8, 214.
76   Kant, KU, §8, 215.
77   Kant, KU, §40, 293.

ment with human reason in general."[78] This allows us to avoid the prejudice that our judgments are objective and apply to everyone. Instead, aesthetic judgment makes possible the reflection (*Reflexion*) regarding the "limitations" of our judgment by comparing them to the reflections of others. Comparing reflections of taste is not about imitating the reflections of others. Comparison serves to scrutinize all matters of taste. Aesthetic *Beurteilung* is communal and in no way reduces the beautiful to mere agreeableness or private interests. Nor does the communal sense of taste rely on empirical principles derived from conventions; though, culture does indeed allow us to presuppose universal assent regarding the beautiful.[79] How deeply saturated prejudices are in one's culture and how far aesthetic judging rids harmful prejudices—not only for oneself, but also for culture as a whole—is, however, questionable.

Kant on Prejudice and Aesthetic Evaluation

The aesthetic sensus communis produces the conditions necessary for reflection. Although Kant writes that aesthetic judgment proceeds without a concept of the object's purpose, this activity is all the more purposive for our cognitive powers in general.[80] Rudolf Makkreel has argued that, for Kant, we look to the past for imitative models to configure judgments of taste, but taste is cultivated further by turning outward to exemplars of good taste.[81] One cannot always rely on traditional models when cultivating good taste, as tradition often preserves prejudices that need to be examined for oneself. Rather, what is required is an aesthetic evaluation (*Beurteilung*) that discards indigenous prejudices that emulation preserves. In what follows, I will connect Kant's notions of prejudice and good taste in

---

78　Kant, §40, 293, translation modified. See Makkreel, *Orientation and Judgment in Hermeneutics*, 101–03.

79　Cf. Kant, KU, §40, 293 and §41, 296. In the latter, Kant specifies that only in society can we find an empirical interest in the beautiful; also, cf. Makkreel, *Orientation and Judgment in Hermeneutics*, 101–03.

80　Kant, KU, §9, 218–19.

81　Makkreel, *Orientation and Judgment in Hermeneutics*, 93–98; 103–04.

an effort to shed light on the function of aesthetic evaluation. This requires us to distinguish between imitation, emulation, and evaluation—thereby elucidating how prejudice operates at these different levels of judgment.

Imitation is the source of prejudice in art and in life. Following tradition will invariably involve some form of imitative judgment. In the Bloomberg Logic, Kant is said to argue as follows:

> Taste is quite ruined by imitation, a fertile source of all prejudices, since one borrows everything, thinks nothing of a beauty that one might be able to invent and come up with oneself, as [compared to] what others have already thought up and have previously cognized, and what is considered beauty by these people.[82]

But prejudices are not so easily corrected, as if a mere second glance at something will render a judgment of taste free of all prejudice. Even among the fine arts, where the geniuses thrive, there "are various kinds of prejudices," as, for example, "in music, in poetry, in painting, in statuary, etc., Everywhere!, in every taste[,] prejudices always prevail, even, indeed, in moral taste."[83] So, while imitation is the enemy of genius, taste nonetheless preserves prejudices for the judgment of fine art. The prejudice toward admiring certain styles of art surely has something to do with originality and the feel for authenticity, which is a hallmark for all artistic geniuses.[84]

The most important facet of this original work of genius is that it becomes *exemplary*, not imitative, that is, a model for other artists (and spectators) to follow—even though exact replication of the work is not possible. One might consider the emulation (*Nachfolge*) of a genius to be a stepping-stone on the path toward producing an authentic capacity of taste. Kant writes:

> *Emulation* (*Nachfolge*) by reference to a precedent, rather than by imitation (*Nachahmung*), is the right term for any influence that products of an exemplary author have on others; and this means no more than drawing on the same

---

82   Kant, *Lectures on Logic*, 24: 173.
83   Kant, *Lectures on Logic*, 24: 173.
84   Kant, KU, §46, 307–8.

sources from which the predecessor himself drew, and learning from him only how to go about doing so.[85]

Makkreel indicates the normativity of Kant's argument here, as orienting oneself according to exemplary artists is both rationally and aesthetically developmental. That being said, judgments of taste also require a kind of *negative* model of emulation: "If each subject always had to start from nothing but the crude predisposition given him by nature, [many] of his attempts would fail, if other people before him had not failed in theirs."[86]

The Kantian cannot presume that past models suffice to develop taste authentically. This is not to say that the Confucian naively imitates popular opinions, or fashions her views after her teachers––that is, not without both cultural and self-criticism. The Confucian rather has the burden of weighing personal taste on cultural scales, a task that does not so easily allow for the development of taste free of cultural prejudices, as does Kant's account of aesthetic judgment, or so it would seem.

It may be true, for example, that at times, having only a crude impression of a certain variety of wine at dinner, we go along with what others say about it, because we are too embarrassed to reveal a lack of knowledge. But Kant argues that the "fact that others have liked something can never serve [us] as a basis for aesthetic judgment."[87] So, the dinner guests decide on a peppery wine while I prefer something lighter, but their opinions are a mere "empirical *basis of proof*," and can never impel my judgment of taste to be so modified. Thus, while some aesthetic judgments can be empirical and contingent according to the person, judgments of taste are always pure and universal.[88] Moreover, that peers can cite the wisdom of lauded critics, who prescribe a priori rules as principles for judging beauty does not provide me with a legitimate basis of proof against my taste. Kant's contention is not that taste cannot mature by emulating others. Quite to the contrary,

---

85   Kant, KU, §32, 283, translation modified.
86   Kant, KU, §32, 283.
87   Kant, KU, §33, 284.
88   Kant, KU, §13, 223. Cf. Makkreel, *Orientation and Judgment in Hermeneutics*, 100.

we need emulative models for taste. Rather, he rejects the rationalist view that one's taste should conform to specific given rules by means of which my judgment follows suit.[89] This is not to say that our judgments of taste are free of prejudices.

As the *Bloomberg Logic* indicates, age, social rank, clothing, manner of speech, and reciprocal approval contribute to the aesthetic prejudices of every culture. According to Kant, nowhere is imitative prejudice more pervasive than in the multitude of society.[90] Because praise from the multitude is often shallow, we should be wary of prescriptive rules for taste. Instead of providing determinate rules for judging, different cultures give *exemplary* models that should not be imitated completely.

Kant points out how Africans, Europeans, and Chinese will indeed draw on empirical examples from their culture to judge standard ideas of beauty regarding certain human features (e.g., the size and look of the face and body), all of whom disagree as regards what constitutes a beautiful face. But no single culture can provide the imagination with the adequate intuition necessary to exhibit (schematize) the ideal of beauty as such.[91] Thus, for Kant, culture is indeed instructive for taste. Yet it is up to the individual to develop her capacity of taste, irrespective of local contexts. This development is then a kind of normative aesthetic evaluation both of oneself and interculturally.[92] As Kant writes: "taste must be an ability one has oneself; and although someone who imitates a model may manifest skill insofar as he succeeds in this, he manifests taste only insofar as he can judge that model himself."[93]

Of course, for Kant, this model can never be empirically given, but must only be an ideal point of reference, produced by the imagination, that is self-prescribed. This is not to say, however, that the imagination's ideal of beauty has no determinate rational basis. Flowers, beautiful gardens, a mountainous landscape, cascading waterfalls, a

---

89   Kant's charge is against Georg Friedrich Meier, who defined aesthetics as the "science of rules" (1754, §3, 6). On this, see McQuillan, 2017.
90   Kant, *Lectures on Logic*, 24: 175.
91   Kant, KU, §17, 234.
92   See Makkreel, *Orientation and Judgment in Hermeneutics*, 113–14.
93   Kant, KU, §17, 232.

picturesque countryside cabin—all of these suspend our imagination and reward us with pleasure in their beauty, thereby allowing us to exhibit aesthetic ideas. But when judging them to be beautiful, we cannot fix a determinate concept of their purposiveness, precisely because we judge them to be free. When I feel pleasure from judging the red Japanese maples circling the placid pond in Autumn to be beautiful, I only reflect on my feelings toward their beauty and take no interest in their purposiveness. Thus, only humanity, the individual herself, can serve as the ideal of beauty.[94] Aesthetic evaluation provides our taste with more ability to think for oneself about the demands regarding culture.

Our approach to global problems regarding climate change, for instance, cannot defer to traditional models for emulation. We have never faced a problem like this before; intercultural dialogue on this issue requires aesthetic evaluation, where participants in all societies make judgments that assess imbued prejudices set against or in view of other cultural values. Moreover, I think that the kind of *imaginative resistance* needed for intercultural discussion concerns a desire for the indeterminate, which, instead of positing a surplus of cultural determinations, makes way for hitherto unimagined possibilities.

There are some intercultural values that may never find resolution among different societies, nor should we attempt to overcome all differences. Westerners are unlikely to concede that the surest way for all participants in society to achieve equality is by any other means than by liberal democratic values. The Chinese, however, contend that a role-based society demonstrates how participants change roles according to context and that freedom is accomplished by means of the harmonious efforts of all members working together. I think that Makkreel is right to say, along with Kant, that dismissing all prejudices is not the answer, nor even possible. However, neither Kant nor Confucius can give a definite answer to our problem. What we must do, along with Kant and Confucius, is to consider the ways in which aesthetic emulation and evaluation can complement one another when assessing intercultural demands. Instead of beginning from the perspective of prescribed moral doctrines derived from a particular cul-

---

94   Kant, KU, §17, 233.

ture, we ought to consider the ways in which aesthetic reflection promotes and develops our moral judgments globally considered. *Li* and *Reflexion* are neither prosaic, nor abstract, nor even rigid functions, but ongoing activities of realizing one's humanity as both an outcome and process of aestheticizing life. Openness to the infinite variety of nature's beauty, to the multifarious forms of art that every culture produces, and to our capacity to aesthetically respond to problems will only serve to disabuse us of ingrained and harmful prejudices and to thereby enlarge our capacity to evaluate the way forward.

References

Ames, Roger. *Confucian Role Ethics: A Vocabulary.* Hong Kong: Chinese University of Hong Press, 2011.

Ames, Roger T. and Hall, David L. *Thinking Through Confucius.* Albany: SUNY Press, 1987.

Ames, Roger and Rosemont, Henry. *The Confucian Analects: A Philosophical Translation.* New York: Ballantine Books, 1998.

_____. *Confucian Role Ethics: A Moral Vision for the 21ˢᵗ Century?* Göttingen: V&R Unipress, 2016.

Bourdieu, Pierre. *Distinction: A Social Critique of the Judgment of Taste.* Cambridge: Harvard University Press, 1984.

Ching, Julia. "Chinese Ethics and Kant," *Philosophy East and West*, 28, no.2, (1978): 161–72.

Gardner, Daniel K. *Zhu Xi's Reading of the Analects: Canon, Commentary, and the Classical Tradition.* New York: Columbia University Press, 2003.

Johnston, Ian and Ping, Wang *Daxue an.d Zhongyong.* Bilingual Edition. Hong Kong: The Chinese University Press, 2012.

Jones, David. "Walking the Way In-Between with Confucius: *Tianwen* and Emerging Patterns of Human Nature" in *Confucius Now: Contemporary Encounters with the Analects*, edited by David Jones. Peru, Illinois: Open Court Publishing, 2008.

Kant, Immanuel. *Kritik der Urteilskraft* in *Kants gesammelte Schriften*, herausgegeben von der Deutschen Akademie der Wissenschaften, vol. 5. Berlin, Walter De Gruyter, 1902– .

_____. Kant, I. *Lectures on Logic.* Translated and Edited by Michael J. Young. Cambridge: Cambridge University Press, 1992.

Legge, James. *The Chinese Classics*, volume 3. Hong Kong: London Missionary Society, 1876.

Makkreel, Rudolf. *Orientation and Judgment in Hermeneutics*. Chicago: University of Chicago Press, 2015.

Meier, Georg Friedrich. *Anfangsgründe aller schönen Wissenschaften*. Halle: Hemmerde, 1754.

McQuillan, "Kant, The Science of Aesthetics, and The Critique of Taste," *Kant Yearbook* 9 (2017): 113–132.

Nelson, Eric. "China, Nature, and the Sublime in Kant" in *Cultivating Personhood: Kant and Asian Philosophy*, edited by Stephen Palmquist. Berlin, New York: De Gruyter, 2010.

_____. "Recognition and Resentment in the Confucian Analects," *Journal of Chinese Philosophy* 40, no.2 (2013): 287–306.

Ni, Peimin *Confucius: The Man and the Way of Gongfu*. London: Rowman & Littlefield, 2016.

Palmquist, Stephen, ed. *Cultivating Personhood: Kant and Asian Philosophy*. Berlin, New York: De Gruyter, 2010.

Pluhar, Werner, ed. and trans. *Immanuel Kant: Critique of Pure Reason*. Indianapolis: Hackett Publishing Company, 1996.

Shun, Kwang-loi. "Conception of the Person in Early Confucian Thought" in Shun, KL and Wong, David B., *Confucian Ethics: A Comparative Study of Self, Autonomy and Community*, 183–99. Cambridge, UK: Cambridge University Press, 2004.

Weiming, Tu. *Confucian Thought: Selfhood as Creative Transformation*. New York: SUNY Press, 1985.

_____. *Humanity and Self-Cultivation: Essays in Confucian Thought*. Boston: Cheng & Tsui Company, 1998.

Wenzel, Christian Helmut. "Beauty in Kant and Confucius: A First Step," *Journal of Chinese Philosophy* 33, no.1 (2006): 95–107.

Zuckert, Rachel (2007), *Beauty and Biology in Kant: An Interpretation of the Critique of Judgment*. Cambridge, UK: Cambridge University Press.

ADRIAN KREUTZ (UNIVERSITY OF AMSTERDAM)

CONTRADICTION AND RECURSION IN BUDDHIST PHILOSOPHY: FROM *CATUṢKOṬI* TO *KŌAN*

Introduction

Everything is real and is not real,
Both real and not real,
Neither real nor not real.
This is Lord Buddha's teaching.
MMK (18:8)

A Monk asked:
"What is Buddha?"
The Zen Teacher answered:
"Three pounds of flax"
Wúmén Guān: (18)

Prima facie, MMK (18:8) on the left, and Wúmén Guān (18) (Ch. 無門關) on the right don't have a lot in common—but they do.[1] Both are, and this is the main hypothesis of this essay, a schema for *upāya* (Skt. उपाय): skilful means of teaching the path to enlightenment.

Wúmén Guān: (18) is a *Kōan* (Ch. 公案), which features predominantly in the Chinese Chan and the Japanese Zen tradition. The focus of §4 will be on the *Kōan*.

The subsequent section, §2, will be concerned with the argument from MMK (18:8) above which goes under the name *catuṣkoṭi* (Skt. चतुष्कोटि), which literally means "four corners." In its simplest from, the *catuṣkoṭi* is the view that any claim can be *true, false, both true and false* or *neither true nor false*. Those are, metaphorically, the four corners (*koṭis*). The origins of the *catuṣkoṭi* and the origin of Buddhism are concomitant. In fact, as Ruegg (1977) holds, we recognize (parts of the *catuṣkoṭi*) in the earliest sutras, in the intellectual circles of the historical Buddha Gautama, as in the *Māluṅkyaputta Sutta*, for instance.

---

1   I am indebted to the audience at the *Asian Philosophical Texts* conference at the Centre for East Asian Studies (EASt), Université Libre de Bruxelles in November 2018. Furthermore, I would like to express my gratitude for helpful comments by two anonymous referees which have improved the quality of this essay and also to Jan Westerhoff for a translational remark.

As this teaching has its origin in Brahmanism (or the rejection thereof), it is only sensible to anticipate the earliest manifestations of the *catuṣkoṭi* in Brahmanical texts. Yet, although the fourth koti features in the *Bṛhadāraṇyaka Upaniṣad* and the third koti can be found in the *Samavayanga Sutra*, they have never been endorsed together. So, the *catuṣkoṭi* seems to be a genuinely Buddhist concept. Clearly, it has found its most prominent use in the Madhyamaka school of Buddhism and the writings of Nāgārjuna,[2] and his *Mūlamadhyamakakārikā* (henceforth: MMK) and commentaries thereon. I shall focus the discussion on Nāgārjuna's *catuṣkoṭi*.

Taking the Buddhist worldview into perspective, it is not surprising that metaphysical, epistemological and logical notions (such as the two instances above) have a practical import. At least for the practicing Buddhist, any philosophical concept should be tried in practice to decide whether it is (or not) an expedient means towards enlightenment—i.e. *upāya*.[3]

Here, again, is my main hypothesis: *catuṣkoṭi* and *Kōan* have the same function in Buddhist philosophy, Madhyamaka and Zen respectively, and share a systematic structure. Both are to be considered a schema for *upāya*—means towards the soteriological "end-goal," which is enlightenment.

Nāgārjuna's Catuṣkoṭi

A lot of ink has been spilled on the *catuṣkoṭi* in the philosophical academic literature, compared to its (in)-significance to the Euro- and Anglo centrism of Western academic philosophy of the last centuries. David Ruegg (1977) once said: "The doctrine (the *catuṣkoṭi*) has been described as nihilism, monism, irrationalism, misology, agnosticism, scepticism, criticism, dialectic, mysticism, acosmism, absolutism, relativism, nominalism, and linguistic analysis with therapeutic value." And we can add *deconstructivism*, and what we will be concerned with, *dialetheism* and *ontological non-foundationalism*, to the list. It is

---

2   See Jan Westerhoff, *Nāgārjuna's Madhyamaka. A Philosophical Introduction.* Oxford: Oxford University Press, 2009.

3   As described in the Lotus Sutra.

the aim of this essay to contribute to the ongoing endeavour to make sense of this seemingly mysterious logical schema. Whether it adds just another interpretation, and the mystery remains, I cannot judge. Also, this essay will seriously question whether it, at all, makes sense to make sense of the *catuṣkoṭi*. This, however, is a vexed question: isn't judging something not to make sense, in the end, making sense of it? I shall not attempt to grapple with the overarching question here, although I shall allow myself a standpoint on whether there is sense to be found in the *catuṣkoṭi* in the conclusion.

A Set of Open Questions on the Catuṣkoṭi

Although a lot has been said about the *catuṣkoṭi*, there is as yet no comprehensive answer to the following questions:

(1) What is the *catuṣkoṭi*, and what role does it play in Buddhist philosophy?
(2) What (if there is one) is the logical from of the *catuṣkoṭi*?
(3) What is the *catuṣkoṭi's* historical position in the wider history of Buddhist philosophy?

In fact, I believe myself to have discovered a possible source for the controversy around the *catuṣkoṭi* in Western commentarial literature. The constant nullification of efforts in making sense of the *catuṣkoṭi* was to be anticipated for two reasons (other than the usual suspicion of Eastern thoughts being mystical, incoherent and unsystematic):[4]

(i) Questions 1–3, if they have been addressed at all, have been addressed in (nearly complete) isolation. Furthermore, Western academic research has primarily been concerned with the second question. Hence, we see a "logic-first" approach in the research literature on the *catuṣkoṭi*. It is, then, no surprise that the *catuṣkoṭi* has been considered perplexing, mysterious and incoherent—it does not fare well with Classical Logic, as the remainder of this section is set to demonstrate. Not only in Buddhist philosophy, but in philosophy *tout*

---

4   For this reason, it is important to show with the tools of contemporary formalisms that those Eastern thoughts perfectly stand to reason. We can thereby contribute to an alleviation of those misconceptions.

court, it is the metaphysics which plays significantly into the logic. Therefore, avoiding the metaphysics and purely focusing on the logic is dangerous. The *catuṣkoṭi*, for unknown reasons, as for the most part been detached from its metaphysical surrounding and has been considered and treated as exclusively a piece a logic—Priest/Garfield (2010) might be an exception here.

(ii) The recent literature almost exclusively focuses on Nāgārjuna's Madhyamaka, and the use of the *catuṣkoṭi* therein. Sure, I do too, but merely to take Nāgārjuna as the starting point. The *catuṣkoṭi* didn't suddenly appear in Buddhist philosophy with Nāgārjuna, just to disappear again. My hypothesis is that the *catuṣkoṭi* appears in various forms throughout Buddhist thought and not solely in Madhyamaka. I propose that we widen our horizons and look beyond Nāgārjuna.

To give you an (albeit old, but relevant) example of what the research literature is addressing, one of the most influential papers on the subject[5] states the following:

> It is thus important to examine (1) how it was that Nāgārjuna came to make such extensive use of the *catuṣkoṭi*; (2) the logical form of Nāgārjuna's *catuṣkoṭi*; and (3) with that purpose and in what manner this "logical apparatus" was handled by Nāgārjuna in exposition of his philosophy.[6]

In the same paper, we find—and this, for many reasons, is astonishing—two further positions on how to see the *catuṣkoṭi* which the author considers necessary to get "the overall picture."

> (D) The *catuṣkoṭi* was used by him (AK: Nāgārjuna) as a dialectic which progressively leads one to truth. (E). The *catuṣkoṭi* was used as an instrument of meditation. It is clear that these positions need not be mutually exclusive. Limitations of space prevent any consideration of (D) and (E) here, although I think that both of these are possible interpretations of Nāgārjuna's use of *catuṣkoṭi* and the consideration of them is necessary to get the overall picture of Nāgārjuna's effort in the (MMK).[7]

---

5   Although the philosophical environment in which the *catuṣkoṭi* came up is mentioned in question (3), it has not been taken into account when answering question (2)—this is characteristic of the "logic-first" approach to the *catuṣkoṭi*: a misguided approach.

6   Ranil Dion Gunaratne, "The Logical Form of the Catuṣkoṭi: A New Solution," *Philosophy East & West* (1980): 214.

7   Ranil Dion Gunaratne, 215.

It is exactly positions (D) and (E) that I want to advocate in this essay. I find it peculiar how Gunaratne came up with these positions, as there is, as far as I am aware, no trace of it in Nāgārjuna's corpus. It is even more surprising why the author, being unsatisfied with the (hitherto) noncomprehensive treatments of the *catuṣkoṭi* did not continue research on those two possibilities, already guessing them to be indispensable for the attaining of a cohesive concept. The decision to disregard the ontological, soteriological, and historical framework has (unsurprisingly) led to an unrewarding treatment of the *catuṣkoṭi*, detached from its philosophical context.[8] This essay is supposed to take up Gunaratne's legacy.

It is, perhaps for those two reasons given above, that Tillemans (1999,189) held that "within Buddhist thought, the structure of argumentation that seems most resistant to our attempts at a formalization is undoubtedly the *catuṣkoṭi*"—a thought which stretches back to Poussin's (1917) paper (probably the earliest philosophical treatment of the *catuṣkoṭi* in the West) and manifested its position as the "*Buddhist dilemma*."

Why a dilemma? In fact, if at all, the *catuṣkoṭi* is a tetralemma as it has four positions as opposed to two. Why the *catuṣkoṭi* is posing a tetralemma becomes apparent through logical formalization. This is what I shall turn to now.

The Logic of the Catuṣkoṭi

The reason why the *catuṣkoṭi* is considered resistant to formalization is the following: in Western orthodoxy,[9] we encounter the principle of *tertium non datur*: everything is either true, or false—*c'est tout*. The *catuṣkoṭi* inflates (while denying) this principle to a *quintum non datur*: It states four exhaustive and mutually exclusive possibilities for any proposition: (1) either it holds, (2) it does not hold, (3)

---

8   As a metaphysical example, try examining the natural behaviour of a dolphin in a swimming pool where it is not surprising that the results of the study will not be true to the studied object (we cannot expect the dolphin to behave naturally in captivity). We need to put the dolphin back to the ocean to study its natural behavior.

9   As well as classical Indian Nyāya thought, by the way.

it both holds and does not hold, (4) it neither holds nor does not hold—those are the four *kotis* (corners). It seems (but it is not) easy to spell out the basic schema of the *catuṣkoṭi* in classical Boolean terms. Here is a first (bad) try. Let "everything" from our example in MMK (18: 8) be expressed by "A." The four corners of the *catuṣkoṭi* become visible before our eyes:

Positive *catuṣkoṭi*

(1) A
(2) ¬A
(3) A∧¬A
(4) ¬(A∨¬A)

A (formal) model for the *catuṣkoṭi* has to maintain the *mutual exclusivity* and *exhaustive nature* of the kotis. The reason for the exhaustivity, other than wanting to be charitable to the coherence and logical abilities of the authors who have employed the *catuṣkoṭi*, lies in the way the (negative) *catuṣkoṭi*,

Negative *catuṣkoṭi*

(1) ¬A
(2) ¬¬A
(3) ¬(A∧¬A)
(4) ¬¬(A∨¬A)

which denies all four possibilities, is commonly employed as an argument that is supposed to undermine all possible ways a predicate can be attributed to something—a kind of *reductio* argument to reveal the deficiency of the concept in question. Mādhyamikas have called this method *prasaṅga*. The concepts the MMK is dealing with are causation, motion, self, identity and others. In MMK (18: 8), specifically, the thesis is that *everything* is *real*. The four kotis are supposed to exhaust all of the logical space and to mention every possible way "reality" can be attributed to the object which is "everything." Hence, the argument sees the anti-thesis that 'everything' is not real, the conjunction of thesis and anti-thesis, and the disjunction of thesis and anti-thesis. A denial (as in the negative *catuṣkoṭi*) of every possible way in which "realness" can be attributed to "everything" is then a *prasaṅga*-argument against the possibility of ascribing "realness" to "everything."

The conclusion the Mādhyamikas drew from this is that nothing is "real." While this alone might sound mystic to the Western philosopher, it should become comprehensible as a philosophical argument once the metaphysical fundament on which it is based is made explicit. Consider Priest (2010) here:

> The central concern of the MMK is to establish that everything is empty of self-existence (*svabhāva*), and the ramifications of this fact. The main part of the work consists of a series of chapters which aim to establish, of all the things which one might plausibly take to have svabhāva (causes, the self, suffering, etc.), that they do not do so.[10]

To do what Priest describes, every possible way something can *be* has to be ruled out eventually, to illuminate its emptiness of self-existence (lack of *svabhāva*)—this is what is meant by saying that something is not "real" in a Buddhist context: it lacks self-existence. The quadruple-wise exclusivity, i.e., that none of the kotis expresses something that one of the other kotis already expresses, comes as a natural consequence of wanting to establish the exhaustivity of the kotis. Only if none of the kotis is equivalent to any of the other kotis; and only if each koti establishes a distinct possibility, can the logical space be exhausted, and the *catuṣkoṭi* used as a *prasaṅga*-argument.

Evaluation of the Proposed Formalization

That the *catuṣkoṭi*, as formulated above, does not go hand in hand with classical logic is no surprise. In fact, it collapses in a classical framework: (4) is equivalent to (3) by De Morgan, and (3) entails both (2) and (1). Priest (2010) convincingly refutes a number of influential attempts to capture the spirit of the *catuṣkoṭi* in a bivalent framework and puts forward his formalization of the *catuṣkoṭi* in (plurivalent) First-Degree-Entailment which allows for things to be *both true and false*, and *neither true not false*—just what *koti* three

---

10   Graham Priest, "The Logic of the Catuṣkoṭi," *Comparative Philosophy* (2010): 12.

and *koti* four are saying. This is not the point to go into the logic, but it is (nearly) undeniable that once the *Law of Non-Contradiction* and *Explosion* are given up, the mutually exclusive and exhaustive nature on the *kotis* can be preserved.[11]

One formality which is going to be crucial for a thorough understanding of the subsequent discussion is the notion of a status-predicate, which is a meta-linguistic tool to express the alethic status of a truth carrier.

In the search for an adequate model for the (Nāgārjuna's) *catuṣkoṭi* Priest (2010) expresses the four kotis with the following set of status-predicates: S={T, F, B, N}. Let T be the truth-predicate "is true," F is "is false," B is "both true and false," N is "neither true nor false." T(A) is the proposition "A is true," where (A) is a name for A To define B, N Priest first defines F as F(A)= T(¬A). Here is how we define the four kotis.

(1) $T(A) = T(A) \wedge \neg F(A)$
(2) $F(A) = \neg T(A) \wedge F(A)$
(3) $B(A) = T(A) \wedge F(A)$
(4) $N(A) = \neg T(A) \wedge \neg F(A)$

Bear in mind that koti three and koti four are genuine possibilities in the logic Priest is using, although they surely appear paradoxical, they are not—in fact, what (partly) motivated the development of those logics was the quest to deal with paradoxes, such as the liar paradox. The *catuṣkoṭi* can now be expressed in the following way:

---

11 Unfortunately, the framework has a problem on its own, which, in the modern debate on non-classical logic, is known as the *Recapture Problem*. The paraconsistent logic in which the *catuṣkoṭi* is formulated makes classical principles such as modus ponens invalid, but in certain situations those classical inferences are taken to be valid. (this is the classical *Recapture Problem*). The MMK might be such a situation, where Nāgārjuna, on the one hand, is using the *catuṣkoṭi* in the paraconsistent and paracomplete framework, but is on the other hand using classical inferences such as modus ponens, hence, Nāgārjuna is facing a *Recapture Problem*. For a detailed analysis of the logic and a proposed solution to the problem, see Adrian Kreutz, "Recapture, Transparency, Negation and a Logic for the catuṣkoṭi," *Comparative Philosophy* (2019): 8.

Catuṣkoṭi: T(A)∨F(A)∨B(A)∨N(A)

Can I, at this point, already motivate my main hypothesis, that the *catuṣkoṭi* is an instance of *upāya?*[12] There are clear indications in both Nāgārjuna and Candrakīrti which prompt the suspicion that both were seeing a connection between the study of reality from several perspectives (perhaps the *catuṣkoṭi*) and a change in attitude of soteriological/psychological importance (perhaps enlightenment). Consider the final verse of the MMK (27.30), for example, which claims that the purpose of Buddhist teaching is the abandonment of all views—which is what the negative *catuṣkoṭi* announces. Also, there is Candrakīrit's metaphor of a *purgative drug* in his commentary on MMK (13.8), where emptiness is compared to a drug that purges other things before purging itself as well. Also, we find the point that a *prasaṅga* argument is always in a dialectical context in opposition to another view (it is *upāya* applied to philosophical argumentation as it were). Are these considerations decisive? I am not sure. I shall therefore leave the realms of Indo-Tibetan Buddhism and follow the development of the *catuṣkoṭi* further to the East. Things will become clearer there, yet also somewhat cryptic.

Going Beyond Nāgārjuna

We have familiarized ourselves with Nāgārjuna and shall skip the epoch of his commentator's and arrive in China (500AD), where Madhyamaka Buddhism and Daoism merged into one.[13] It is here that the role of the *catuṣkoṭi* as *upāya* becomes perspicuous. The school of *Sānlùn* (Ch. 三論宗), which translates as "Three Treatises,"[14] absorbed Madhyamaka philosophy and with it the *catuṣkoṭi*. In Jízàng's (Ch. 吉

---

12   Thanks go out to an anonymous referee for making me aware of this.

13   See Wing-Tsit Chan, *A Sourcebook in Chinese Philosophy* (Princeton NJ: Princeton University, 1963), 360.

14   The "three treatises" from which the Chinese version of Madhyamaka took its name are: Mūlamādhyamakakārikā—Zhōnglùn (Ch. 中論), Nāgārjuna's Dvādaśanikāya-śāstra—Shíèrménlùn (Ch. 十二門論) and Āryadeva's Śatakaśāstra—Bǎilùn (Ch. 百論). It later came to Japan under the name Sanron, but disappeared during the Nara period, or was most probably absorbed into Shingon.

藏) *Erdi Zhang* (Ch. 二諦章) we can rediscover the *catuṣkoṭi*, albeit in a modified form.[15]

The Erdi Zhang

With this framework at hand, let us now turn to the role of the *catuṣkoṭi* in Jízàng's "*Erdi Zhang*" (Ch. 二諦章; Eng. "Essay on the Two Levels of Truth"), which commences with:

> The three kinds of "Two Levels of Truth" all represent the principle of gradual rejection, like building a framework from the ground. Why? Ordinary people say that dharmas, as a matter of true record, possess being, without realizing that they possess nothing. Therefore, the Buddha propounded to them the doctrine that dharmas are ultimately empty and void.[16]

What Jízàng describes in this opening paragraph of his most influential text is a hierarchy of truth-levels, built from the "ordinary people's" idea that dharmas possess being (i.e., in Madhyamaka vocabulary, that things have *svabhāva*). In line with Madhyamaka thought he holds instead that no dharma (i.e., no phenomenon, may it be physical or psychological) possesses being (i.e., everything is devoid of *svabhāva*), and only emptiness (i.e., *sunyata*) is to be ascribed to all dharmas—*nothing has (intrinsic) self-being, everything is empty*. We can read the "ordinary people's" view that dharmas have self-being, taking the status-predicates into account, as $T(B)$, and so we have the first koti. Its negation, therefore, is the Buddha's doctrine that dharmas are ultimately empty and void—$\neg T(B)$[17]—which is our second koti.

Jízàng's following analysis then, sustaining the thought that what is described here are the corners of the *catuṣkoṭi*, supports the hypoth-

---

15 Shortly after this paper has been given at the APT Conference, Priest (2018, 7) also published on the hierarchy of truth-values and expressed it with a recursive model. He is not, however, drawing the same conclusions from it as I do, as will be explicit in §3.3 and §3.4.

16 Ibid. 360.

17 Which is equivalent to $F(B)$, i.e., the ultimate falsehood that B (that dharmas have self-being). Which is equivalent to the ultimate truth $T(\neg B)$, i.e., that ultimate truth that dharmas have no self-being. As we will see later, formulating the ideas of Jízàng with the status-predicate T (and its negation) only avoids confusion.

esis that the *catuṣkoṭi's* position in Buddhist philosophy is *upāya* (skilful means).

> When it is said that dharmas possess being, it is ordinary people who say so. This is worldly truth, the truth of ordinary people. Saints and sages, however, truly know that dharmas are empty of nature. This is absolute truth, the truth of sages. *The principle is taught in order to enable people to advance from the worldly to the absolute,* and to renounce the truth of ordinary people and to accept that of sages. This is the reason for clarifying the first level of twofold truth.[18]

We can interpret Jízàng as saying that it is an ordinary truth that dharmas have being—$T(B)$—but it's the absolute truth that they don't (i.e. a falsehood that they do), i.e., $\neg T(B)$. Still being on the first level of twofold-truth (there are many more to follow), let me construct a diagram that depicts the metaphysical hierarchy of levels of truth.[19]

1st Level of Truth $T(B)$ $\neg T(B)$

                       Ordinary Truth   Absolute Truth

The highlighted part in the quote above is, I guess obviously, referring to *upāya*, which, in this case, consist in the negation of ordinary belief. The negation of the ordinary belief that dharma's have being, we can stipulate, is the first step on the path towards enlightenment. Jízàng's essay continues:

> Next comes the second stage, which explains that both being and non-being belong to worldly truth, whereas non-duality (neither being nor non-being) belongs to absolute truth. It shows that being and non-being are two extremes, being the one and non-being the other. From these to permanence and non-permanence, and the cycle of life and death and Nirvana are both two extremes, they therefore constitute worldly truth, and because neither-the- absolute-nor-the-worldly, and neither-the-cycle-of-life-and-death, nor Nirvana are the Middle Path without duality, they constitute the highest truth.[20]

---

18   Ibid. 360, *emphasis added.*
19   In Nāgārjuna's words, Jízàng describes *"a truth of mundane conventions (saṁvṛti-satya) and a truth of the ultimate (paramārtha-satya)"* as in Westerhoff, *Nāgārjuna's Madhyamaka,* 2.
20   Ibid. 360

We are being told that $T(B)$ and $\neg T(B)$ are merely worldly truth, this is, something that "ordinary people" would hold—which is no surprise, as both propositions are expressed in language, and language is usually considered to be an aspect of the ordinary realm. Speaking of realms here; whence the compartmentalization of reality into different realms? Madhyamaka Buddhism distinguishes between conventional (ordinary) reality, which is the realm of language, thought, and the (from the ultimate perspective) erroneous view that things have own-being, and ultimate reality in which nothing has own-being and language and thought lack their descriptive power. Ordinary truth, then, are truth about the conventional reality, whereas ultimate truths are truths about ultimate reality.

To hold both $T(B)$ and $\neg T(B)$ is being grounded in duality, which has to be overcome on the way to enlightenment. But we have to be aware that, for Jízàng, $T(B)$ and $\neg T(B)$ is not a metaphysical duality, as they both correspond to different metaphysical realms. This would come down to saying that "car A is red" and "car B is blue" is a duality, where it is clearly not. The conjunction of both, thus, is a worldly truth, as thought and language (in which this duality is formulated in) is part of only one realm, the conventional realm. It is thus *dualistic thinking* that is conventionally false, and ultimately not-false. This dualistic thinking, as part of the Buddhist practice, has to be overcome. The gist of Jízàng's treaties, then, is that overcoming dualities is seeking enlightenment, and enlightenment is the state of non-duality.[21] In other words: the duality does not rest in the world, but in the (cognitive) apprehension of it. It is Jízàng who hints at it, and Zen Buddhism (with which we will later be concerned with) that makes it explicit.

From a semantic point of view, since we are now evaluating the status of the statements on the first level of truth, we are working on a "second" and higher level of truth (i.e., in a meta-meta-language), and so I shall introduce a second-level status predicate "$\underline{T}$" which semantically works just like T but ranges over the first level status-predicates instead of propositions. The worldly truth on the second level— $\underline{T}(T(B) \wedge \neg T(B))$—is koti (3), which, since ordinary and errone-

---

21   The problem with language, again, is that non-duality itself refers to a duality in that the "non" provokes an opposite concept from which non-duality is demarcated, which is duality. It is therefore better to refer to emptiness, rather than non-duality.

ous can be overcome, just like $T(B)$ can be overcome by negating the duality. We establish koti (4), which in Jízàng's framework reads, by negating the worldly duality, as follows: $\neg T(T(B) \land \neg T(B))$.

2nd Level of Truth	$T(T(B) \land \neg T(B))$	$\neg T((T(B) \land \neg T(B)))$
1st Level of Truth	$T(B)$	$\neg T(B)$
	Ordinary Truth	Absolute Truth

The Sānlùn catuṣkoṭi

Moving this schema into a vertical position, we see the four corners of the *catuṣkoṭi* before us:

The Sānlùn catuṣkoṭi

(1) $T(B)$
(2) $\neg T(B)$
(3) $T(T(B) \land \neg T(B))$
(4) $\neg T((T(B) \land \neg T(B)))$

Each *koti* is established by a recursive method of conjoining ordinary and absolute truth on the nearest lower level to yield the ordinary truth on the higher level and negating the ordinary truth in the same level to yield the absolute truth.

Yet again, the systematic thinker will recognize that $T(T(B) \land \neg T(B))$ and $\neg T(T(B) \land \neg T(B))$ are dualities, which, so says the Buddhist doctrine, shall be overcome. Jízàng noticed this himself and opts for an again higher level, intended to overcome the duality between duality and non-duality. But does that help? At every level of truth, we return to a higher-level duality which contradicts the Buddhist doctrine of non-duality, and so on *ad infinitum*.... The production of new levels of truth will never come to a halt.

Let the following be a schematic model of the recursion,[22] where C^x stands for conventional truth, U^x for ultimate truth, the x for the

---

22   Not a mathematical model of the recursion, of course.

respective truth-level,>for the step from one conventional to ultimate truth "horizontally" on one level to the other via negation, and » for the "vertical" transgression to the next higher truth-level. I call this a truth-transfer (TT).

$$TT: C^0 > U^0 \gg C^1 > U^1 \gg ...C^n > U^n \gg ...$$

It is interesting to see that TT, without being explicit on its potentially infinite nature, can already be found in the MMK, also in verse 18: 8, where Nāgārjuna affirms all four alternatives: "All is so, or all is not so, both so and not so, neither so nor not so. This is the Buddha's teaching."

As Westerhoff points out, the commentarial literature on this verse, especially Candrakirti, interprets this verse as referring to the graded nature of the Buddha's teachings (*anusasana*).[23] Candrakirti's comments reflect the idea that "all is so" is taught to ordinary disciples, "all is not so" to those while informing then about the doctrines of momentariness and impermanence, and so on.

Returning to the main threat of the analysis of Jizang: what shall we make of this now, knowing that the four corners of the *catuṣkoṭi* are just the beginning of an infinite and never terminating process of overcoming non-duality? In Garfield (2015) and Fox (1995) we find some noteworthy comments on Jízàng's levels of truth, and the observation that genuine non-duality can never be found:

> This is why I claim that either of your two truths, i.e., interdependent nature and discriminative nature; or two truth that is not two, or firmly-establish truth on the one hand, and "Non-two and Non-non-two"; i.e., three non-nature or non-firmly-established truth on the other hand, is merely my conventional truth, whereas "Forgetfulness of words and annihilation of thoughts" is really ultimate truth.[24]

Yet, there is also Fox elaborating on Jízàng, establishing that, apparently on the fourth level,

23   Jan Westerhoff, *Nāgārjuna's Madhyamaka*. 89.
24   Jay Garfield, *Engaging Buddhism: Why It Matters to Philosophy* (Oxford: Oxford University Press, 2015), 257.

... all of these distinctions (on the lower three truth levels) are deemed conventional, and the authentic discourse regards that any point of view cannot be said to be ultimately true, and is useful only so far as it is corrective in the above sense.[25]

A sudden stop of the recursion at *whatever* level, however, seems arbitrary, and unsupported by the other texts of Jízàng, so, let us not take the third or fourth level to have any significant role. Let us call genuine non-duality (*forgetfulness of words and annihilation of thoughts*), or rather the experience or insight into it; N.[26] Jízàng, as the sources above suggest, gives no precise answer as to when insight into is achieved (i.e., how many levels of truth have to be crossed)— sometimes it is three, and sometimes four—but let us assume that after n-progressions through higher and higher truth-levels, insight into can be achieved. We can add it to our model in the following way:

n^{th} Level of Truth	N	N
...	...	...
2nd Level of Truth	$T(T(B) \& \neg T(B))$	$\neg T((T(B) \& \neg T(B)))$
1st Level of Truth	$T(B)$	$\neg T(B)$
	Ordinary Truth	Absolute Truth

$$TT(N): C^0 > U^0 \gg C^1 > U^1 \gg ... C^n > U^n \gg ... N$$

The Bóxiè Xiànzhēn

In a way, then, the recursion's cul-de-sac, the soteriological "end-goal" is external to the *catuṣkoṭi*, as there is no bridge of logical necessity between the recursion (everything that happens before N and "N" itself. This supports the argument that the *catuṣkoṭi* is more than a merely argumentative framework to refute philosophical enemies

---

25   Allen Fox, *Jizang* (New York: Harper Collins, 1995), 87.
26   Based on the Sanskrit *śūnya* (Sanskrit: शून्यता), Chinese wú (無), or kong (空), all loosely translated as "emptiness" or "nothing-(ness)."

but a schema of the (Bodhisattva's, or Arhat's) path to the soteriological "end-goal," while it is also coherent with the idea that the *catuṣkoṭi* does not defend any position on its own. One could say that what the (positive) *catuṣkoṭi* is (implicitly) defending is the Buddhist doctrine of non-duality, although the defence never fully terminates: each level of truth, then, is upāya for the nearest upper level of truth, which again is upāya for the nearest upper level of truth—genuine non-duality, via this process, can never be achieved. So, the *catuṣkoṭi* does not defend a position on its own. It is, if we believe Rogacz (2015), Jízàng who disagrees:

> This pragmatical approach (the levels of truth) provides us to the central concept of "refutation of erroneous views as the illumination of right views," *bóxiè xiànzhēn* (驳谢现真), which was enunciated in the "Profound Meaning of the three Treatises." As we remember, Prāsaṅgikas claimed that Mādhyamaka is only a negative method of refuting views, but Svātantrikas believed that it has also its own, undoubted view. Although Jízàng cannot have been a witness of this dispute, he subverted the salience of this argument: *refutation of erroneous views is always the illumination of right views, and vice versa*. All beliefs are empty because they depend on their rejections. Two opposite beliefs (statements) share the same premises and the horizon of possible continuations. Tetralemma is transcending these artificial oppositions, such as nothingness/absolute, false/truth, samsara/nirvana, and so on. ... In this perspective, the doctrine of emptiness seems to be the reinterpretation of the doctrine of expedient (skr. *upāya*, ch. *fāngbiàn*, 方便) means.[27]

We have now discovered that the role of the *catuṣkoṭi* in Buddhist philosophy exceeds its usage as a purely argumentative tool. We have also witnessed how the *catuṣkoṭi* has lost its distinctive four-valued form. We do not find the distinction into positive and negative *catuṣkoṭi* in Jízàng anymore. In a sense, they have melted into one. We also do not call it the *catuṣkoṭi* anymore, but *bóxiè xiànzhēn:* the concept of the "*refutation of erroneous views as the illumination of right views,*" (Ch. 驳谢现真, Eng. Refute the Truth). What is not clear now, however, is whether the *bóxiè xiànzhēn* (i.e., the *catuṣkoṭi*) is defending a position on its own, or not.

---

27   Dawin Rogacz, "Knowledge and Truth in the Thought of Jizang," *The Polish Journal of the Arts and Culture* (2015): 232.

On the one hand, we have the formalization which strongly suggests that the *bóxiè xiànzhēn* does not, in fact cannot, defend a position on its own. On the other hand, we have Rogacz's interpretation of Jízàng, according to which Jízàng's takes the *bóxiè xiànzhēn* to defend a position on its own. I shall put forward a different interpretation of Jízàng's comments and argue against Rogacz.

For Jízàng, as the title of his essay suggests, the *bóxiè xiànzhēn* is not only intended to refute other philosophical positions, but also for an illumination of the right view. For Rogacz's interpretation of Jízàng, the recursion (i.e., the refutation of all possibilities) is equivalent to "N" (i.e., "the right view"). Hence, not defending any possibility *is* defending "N." But how can this be right as there is no logical inference from the first position "T(B)" to "N," *at all*? If the logical apparatus is right, the *bóxiè xiànzhēn* does not defend a position on its own, as there is no logical connection between the kotis and "N," *whatsoever*. We are desperately searching for an argument in either direction in Jízàng's work. We can approach this problem with considerations on *upāya*.

The *bóxiè xiànzhēn* understood as *upāya* alleviates the problem. The idea is simple: a means must not ultimately terminate in a goal, and might only be *but one* of many means necessary to reach a goal. In other words: a means doesn't have to be *on its own* sufficient to reach a goal, and so the recursion that is the "refutation of erroneous views" might be necessary, but doesn't have to be, on its own, sufficient for "the illumination of right views." From the viewpoint of *upāya*, for "N" (i.e., "the illumination of right views) to be brought about, the "refutation of erroneous views" has to be brought about, yet the "refutation of erroneous views" is *on its own* not enough to bring about "N." It is then wrong to think of the "*as*" in the "refutation of erroneous views *as* the illumination of right views" in terms of logical equivalence. Rogacz's use of the term "vice versa" is clearly misleading. It is the "illumination of right views" which is always the "refutation of erroneous views," but not vice versa. Hence, the *bóxiè xiànzhēn* does not defend a position on its own, neither did its predecessor, the *catuṣkoṭi*.

The Paradox

The problems do not end here. The right view for Jízàng is that of the middle way between dualities, inherited from Nāgārjuna, which we express with. He also writes that attachment to the doctrine of emptiness is misguided, hence it should be overcome.

> It is like water able to extinguish the fire, if the water itself could ignite, what would be used to extinguish it? Nihilism and eternalism are like fire and emptiness can extinguish them. But if someone insists on adherence to emptiness, there is no cure which could help him.[28]

This comment is paradoxical only if we were thinking that the *bóxiè xiànzhēn* terminates in "N," and does not go on, as expressed in TT(N). What the comment suggests, though, is that "N," although it represents some kind of qualitative change, does not force the *bóxiè xiànzhēn* to a halt, as ascribing to all things is one-sided and doctrinal, and thus needs to be overcome.[29] One could argue in the following way: "N" is the soteriological end-goal of Buddhist practice with which *upāya* (i.e., an ongoing refutation of erroneous views), *prima facie*, seems to become redundant—most means to reach a goal seem to be useless, once the goal is reached. The existence of a car, for examples, loses its immediate significance once the destination is reached. Thinking about having to find a parking place, we see that a means can even become obstructive. As soon as it has satisfied its immediate purposes, it loses its value.

So here is a problem: "N" both does, and does not bring the *bóxiè xiànzhēn* to a halt. We either have,

$$TT(N): C^0 > U^0 \gg C^1 > U^1 \gg \ldots C^n > U^n \gg \ldots N$$

where brings the recursion to a halt. Or we have,

---

28 Huseh-Li Cheng, *Empty Logic: Madhyamaka Buddhism from Chinese Sources* (Motilal Banarsidass, 1991), 49.

29 The relates to footnote (14). Yet, the argument here is slightly different: Whereas the linguistics of non-duality provokes a duality, ascribing emptiness (and only this) to a phenomenon is one-sided, regardless of whether there is a dual or not. This one-sidedness is doctrinal and therefore to be rejected.

$$TT(N)^*: C^0 > U^0 \gg C^1 > U^1 \gg N \gg \ldots \ C^n > U^n \gg \ldots$$

where the recursion does not halt. According to Jízàng (he has no stance on that), either is a viable option. To dissolve this looming paradox, let us now follow the development of Buddhism (and with it the *catuṣkoṭi*) further to the East.

Towards Kaku-an Shi-en

Jízàng is at the same time the greatest and the last philosopher of the *Sānlùn* school. Yet, the development of Mahayana Buddhism did not stop, and with it, the development of the *catuṣkoṭi* did not either. I shall put forward the idea that what is known as a *Kōan* in the Chan/Zen tradition bears so many similarities to the *catuṣkoṭi* that it is hard not to recognize a systematic connection. The situation in which Jízàng has left us is, from the perspective of Zen, no longer paradoxical, as I shall attempt to illustrate.

The Kōan

A monk asks:
"Does a dog have Buddha-nature?"
The Zen Teacher says:
"Mu"
Wúmén Guān: (1)

We now find ourselves in the teachings of Chan/Zen Buddhism. What to make of this little dialog is difficult to say. The answer is baffling, and, at first sight, sense cannot be made of it. The Zen Teacher's answer is "Mu" (Jap. 無), which translates as "nothing-(ness)."[30] The answer turns into something intelligible, only if we think a little more carefully about question. The question, in fact, goes wrong in two ways.

First, it is the *Nirvanasutra* that explicitly states that all sentient beings have Buddha-nature, it is their fundamental nature, so a dog

---

30   Chao-chou Ts'ung-shen (Jap. Joshu) is the teacher referred to.

has Buddha-nature, too. The monk, we can guess, should have known
this. It is the question, now, that seems to be ill-posed and based on
an inadequate concept of being. But this is not the reason for the
teacher's enigmatic answer. So, what is the answer supposed to tell us?
The question, as it is posed, is supposed to be answered with an affir-
mation-negation linguistic device, i.e. simply with "yes" or "no." But
the latter presupposes that the question is well-formed, which, taking
into account the metaphysics of being in Mahayana Buddhism—of
which Zen, in which context the question is posed, is a branch—it
is not. But how then, does the answer refer to the ill-posed nature of
the question?

Let me try a different approach: The above, Wúmén Guān: (1),
is known as "Joshu's Dog" (Ch. 趙州狗子), and often ridiculed in
popular culture. Just like Wúmén Guān: (18), it is a *Kōan* (Jp. 公案).
Kōans feature heavily in the teaching and practice of Zen Buddhism.
The aim of grappling with, and meditating over a *Kōan* is to overcome *conceptual thinking*—exactly the thinking that has instigated
the monk's question. Therefore, it is not the monk's ignorance of the
fact that, according to Mahayana tradition, every sentient being has
Buddha-nature, but his conceptual thinking which manifests itself in
a yes/no-dichotomy, in which a concept either applies or does not
apply. The *Kōan* practice (grappling with Joshu's Dog for example)
is intended to overcome conceptual thinking, not to teach doctrines,
such as that of Buddha-nature. Now, I argue, it is the dichotomy in
conceptual thinking that the Zen teacher's answer is pointing at, as a
hint for the monk to question his thought process (not necessarily his
knowledge of the sutras).

Abbreviated Catuṣkoṭis

A possible answer to "Joshu's Dog" could be stated as a negative
catuṣkoṭi. The act of denying all kotis comes down to denying all possible ways a dog could or could not have Buddha nature. As the case
of Buddha-nature is certainly an exceptional case, let us rethink the
Kōan in a Nāgārjunian manner.

In the context of the MMK, the *Kōan* would have been stated as:
"does a dog have *svabhāva*?" The Nāgārjunian answer, which we are

already familiar with, is a denial qua negative *catuṣkoṭi* of all the possible ways a dog could have *svabhāva*. Ultimately, the dog's nature is *śūnyata*(emptiness), Nāgārjuna would say. It is not a big conceptual leap from "emptiness" (*śūnya,* Skt. शून्यता) to "nothing-*ness*" (Mu, Ch. 無). In effect, both Nāgārjuna's and Joshu's answer to the monk's question are, conceptually, equivalent.[31] It is only that Nāgārjuna gives a profound logical apparatus with which all the possible ways a dog could have own-being, i.e., *svabhāva*, is denied. It is this logico-ontological apparatus in the background that has vanished from the Zen tradition, but given the historical connection, we can assume that it still resonates somewhere among other implicit principles that have been inherited from India. I shall, therefore, put forward the thesis that the *Kōan* is an abbreviated *catuṣkoṭi.*

Identifying the *Kōan* with *upāya* is not as reckless as my initial thesis that the *catuṣkoṭi* should be considered *upāya*, as it is widely agreed that the *Kōan's* role in Chan/Zen is that of a meditational object. We have the Rinzai school of Zen which focusses heavily on the *Kōan* as a means to gain enlightenment (Jap. *satori*). Zen, furthermore, makes a distinction regarding how enlightenment occurs. According to the Sōtō school, enlightenment comes gradually, sometimes glossed at as "silent enlightenment," as it is seen as a process of discovery through *Zazen* (sitting meditation). On the other hand, we have the Rinzai school which advocates "sudden enlightenment." The *Kōan* and *Zazen*, both are a *means* of reaching satori. Hence, satori is for Zen what we have, so far, referred to as "N."

We have now gone the full circle to support the main hypothesis of this essay: *Catuṣkoṭi* and *Kōan* play the same role in Buddhist philosophy and share a systematic structure. Both are to be considered a

---

31   I have to mitigate this parallelism: whereas the Indian Buddhist's an-atman (no own being) and Nāgārjuna's sunyata (emptiness) are *epistemological concepts*—referring to the fact that things are only forms (as superimpositions), "Asian nothingness" (*tōyōteki mu*), referring to the Kyoto School's concept of nothingness through satori (and therefore the intellectualisation of Zen), refers to a lived experience of reality as a way arising naturally out of nothingness, and should therefore rather be considered a *pragmatic concept.*

schema for *upāya*—means to the soteriological "end-goal," which is enlightenment.

Although I cannot claim that the verification of my hypothesis is airtight (it lacks a lot of historical exegesis), I still hope that it makes sense on the grounds of the material provided. The similarities and practical use of concepts (*Kōan* and *catuṣkoṭi*) is *too apparent* not to draw this connection.

That *Kōan* and *catuṣkoṭi* share a systematic structure still needs to be elicited. We have left Jízàng with the paradox that both terminates and does not terminate the *upāya*, and I have promised a dissolving of this paradox in the Zen tradition, so the next section shall model the remainder of the *catuṣkoṭi*, once it reached Japan. For this, I shall consult another staple of the Zen tradition: the *jūgyūzu*. It is here that the schematic structure which is missing in the *Kōan* is made overt.

The Zen catuṣkoṭi *(aka. the* Jūgyūzu*)*

In fact, what is left over of the *catuṣkoṭi* in the Zen tradition is perhaps too sparse for it to still be an instance of the *catuṣkoṭi*. In any case, it is drastically abbreviated. It is merely the very scaffold of the *bóxiè xiànzhēn* that has found its way into Zen literature in the form of ten pictures of a man and an ox and their corresponding verses: the *jūgyūzu* (Jp. 十牛図, Eng. Ten Ox Herding Pictures).

The pictures and verses of the *jūgyūzu* above, as it is widely conceded recognized, are similes of the path to enlightenment, with the ox as a symbol for meditation (*Kōan* or *Zazen*) practice.

The ox is actually ubiquitous in Buddhist literature. It features in texts as early as the *Maha Gopalaka Sutra* as a symbol for meditation (perhaps because wrestling with one's mind is as strenuous as wrestling with an ox), and is one of the many iconographics that has survived the Mahayana's journey from India to the East. According to D. T. Suzuki (unpublished), the Oxherding pictures and verse made their first appearance in China around the twelfth century. The most well-known version of the *jūgyūzu* is the one by the Chinese Chan

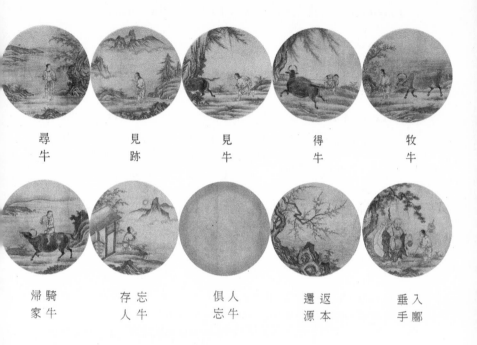

尋　　見　　見　　得　　牧
牛　　跡　　牛　　牛　　牛

帰騎　　存忘　　俱人　　還返　　垂入
家牛　　人牛　　忘牛　　源本　　手鄽

"Ten Bulls" by Tokuriki Tomikichiro

master Kaku-an Shi-en (Ch. 廓庵師遠), who was also the first to con-tribute verse to the pictures as well as an introduction.

It is also with Kaku-an Shi-en that the Ox Herding becomes a *jūgyūzu* (*jū*, Jp. 十, Eng. ten), instead of a *hachigyūzu* (*hachi*, Jp. 八; Eng. eight). It is the blank space at which the *hachi*gyūzu halts, whereas the *jūgyūzu* incorporates two further pictures. This detail is of outmost significance for our ongoing discussion. To see the rela-tions and the similarities between *bóxiè xiànzhēn* and *jūgyūzu*, we need to know the meaning behind the pictures, and we need to refer back to the recursive schema (TT), which is the scaffold of the *bóxiè xiànzhēn*.

To remind you, the reader, of (TT), here is the schema again:

n^{th} Level of Truth	N	N
...	...	...
2nd Level of Truth	$T(T(B) \& \neg T(B))$	$\neg T((T(B) \& \neg T(B)))$
1st Level of Truth	$T(B)$	$\neg T(B)$
	Ordinary Truth	Absolute Truth

$$TT(N): C^0 > U^0 \gg C^1 > U^1 \gg ... C^n > U^n \gg ... N$$

Also, we haven't settled whether (TT) is the correct analysis, or whether (TT*) is what the *bóxiè xiànzhēn* expresses.

$$TT(N)^*: C^0 > U^0 \gg C^1 > U^1 \gg N \gg ... C^n > U^n \gg ...$$

The *jūgyūzu* depicts a character, a boy in the case above, and his search and taming of an ox as a metaphor for on his path to, and through, enlightenment. So, it already suggests that there is a post-enlightenment state, such as $TT(N)^*$ describes it.

In the first picture, we meet him alone in the wilderness, lost and confused, but searching. He knows about the conventional truths and is unsatisfied with them, it is interpreted. Let this conventional belief be $T(B)$, and his stage on the way towards enlightenment be represented by C^0.

The boy goes on and finds the traces of the ox in picture three and four, which serve as a metaphor for finding the sutras and inquiring into the Buddhist doctrines. He then learns about the erroneous nature of conventional truth and, for the first time, has a glimpse of the ultimate truth, $\neg T(B)$. Let this stage be represented by U^0. Here we have the first two kotis, and the first level of Jízàng's truth-hierarchy complete.

However, the boy is unable to distinguish conventional from ultimate truth, and his mind is still confused as to truth and falsehood, and so the boy believes in both $T(B) \& \neg T(B)$, and is yet not ready to discriminate them—this is the third koti. This stage, C^1, depicts the boy catching and taming the ox in the fourth and fifth picture.

Picture six shows the boy riding the ox. He has successfully tamed the beast and is able to let loose the line. He has realised that the duality of truth and falsehood needs to be overcome. This is stage U^1 of Jízàng's hierarchy and the fourth and final koti $\neg T((T(B)$ & $\neg T(B)))$. As the series continues, the ox has disappeared, and the boy is back at home.

The next picture is an empty circle, which I shall represent as "N." It's the manifestation of an ineffable reality which is beyond the dualities of language and thought. This is where, for the boy, the illusion of self has vanished, and he experiences non-duality. Hence not only ox, as it is now useless (as the discussion on what it means to be a means as already revealed; meditation is a means and not in itself sufficient, yet necessary for enlightenment[32]), but also the boy, is gone. This represents enlightenment. This is where the *hachi*gyūzu ends. The boy has found enlightenment, and the ox, which is a metaphor for the boy's *upāya*, like Wittgenstein's ladder, has become redundant. Let the *hachi*gyūzu (OX_8) be represented by this schema, which shall remind us of the *bóxiè xiànzhēn* in its $TT(N)$-reading:

$$OX_8: C^0 \gg U^0 \gg C^1 \gg U^1 \gg N$$

This has been the first option of two readings of the *bóxiè xiànzhēn*, which has led us to a paradox in Jízàng for which we couldn't find a solution within his own canon. If the *hachi*gyūzu is a successor of the *bóxiè xiànzhēn*, the process is supposed to terminate with reaching enlightenment, and the recursion has become obsolete. However, the *jūgyūzu* above includes two further pictures after the enlightenment. What to make of those?

The ninth picture shows a serene landscape with the boy still gone. We can interpret it as a return to the ordinary world, which, although the boy has found enlightenment, has not vanished. The boy, too, has not vanished either. He returns to the world in the last picture of the *jūgyūzu*. It hence appears as though the journey continues, and as with Jízàng's hierarchy, has not brought the process to a halt.

---

32   Some traditions of Zen would even reject that. Formal Meditation, such as *zazen*, might not be necessary, enlightenment can come unexpected. But even if formal meditation is not required, some kind of quasi-meditative process is involved.

The *jūgyūzu* and the *hachigyūzu* seem to contradict themselves in that in the latter "N" is the end of the series, whereas in the former it is not. But to think in this way is to overlook a significant detail in the iconography: the ox is still missing, and *upāya* has become pointless after enlightenment. Although the boy has returned to the ordinary, he has not returned to a pre-enlightened state which would again necessitate and overcoming of dualistic thinking and thereby, analogously, keep the recursion going. For the boy, the illusion of a self and that of a world with *svabhāva* (to serve the Nargarjunian term) has vanished, and conventional reality is seen as what it is—a conceptual superimposition on ultimate reality. The *jūgyūzu* (OX_{10}) shall hence be represented in the following way, where the superscript ^{C} represents the post-enlightened perspective on conventional reality, knowing that the states-of-affairs in C are merely conceptual impositions on ultimate reality N:

$$OX_{10}: C^0 \gg U^0 \gg C^1 \gg U^1 \gg N \gg C^N$$

It is important to note that the process does not stop with C^N, but it is the post-enlightened state C^N in which the boy will remain throughout his post-enlightened life.[33] What a lucky boy.

Solving Jízàng's Paradox

Jízàng's paradox can now be resolved if we take the distinction into pre- and post-enlightened states into account. In both cases of the *bóxiè xiànzhēn* ($TT(N)$ and $TT(N)^*$) the recursion stops, it is only in the latter that the post-enlightened state is added. With this in the background, we now know how to interpret Jízàng's comment that a dogmatic belief in "N" is erroneous and has to be overcome. Not by applying the recursive method of the *bóxiè xiànzhēn* to "N," but by returning to the starting point with a post-enlightened perspective. A famous Chan/Zen saying articulates this thought:

---

33   In fact, several comments of Hakuin suggest that experiences of enlightenment can be had over and over again, and only through ongoing practice, the post-enlightened state could be maintained and cultivated. This would question the complete repudiation of *upāya*. Still, one could guess that post-enlightened *upāya* is different from pre-enlightened *upāya*, which in consequence would not question the account given above.

Thirty years ago, before I practiced Chan, I saw that mountains are mountains and rivers are rivers. However, after having achieved intimate knowledge and having gotten a way in, I saw that mountains are not mountains and rivers are not rivers. But now that I have found rest, as before, I see mountains are mountains and rivers are rivers.[34]

Here, talk of the mind being still and at peace in Nāgārjuna (MMK dedication and 25.24) is also worth mentioning.[35] For Nāgārjuna, compulsive philosophical questioning (such as asking questions in form of the four corners) would be stopped when the mind stops grasping at philosophical theories and simply accepts those as conventional. Nāgārjuna calls this *prapañca upaśama* (Eng, "pacification (*upaśama*) of mental proliferations (*prapañca*)"[36]). Hence, the idea of quietening the mind of philosophical questioning is integrated in Madhyamaka thought. Candrakīrti commented on it in the Prasannapadā, saying that

For the Nobles when they see dependent-arising as it really is, that very dependent-arising is called "the calming of manifoldness (*prapañca upaśama*)—in the sense that there is the calming of instances of manifoldness in it. And because it is entirely without the misfortunes of birth, old age, death and so forth owing to the ceasing of (any) dealing with (the dichotomies): cognition and cognizables in view (of the fact) that mind and mental factors do not arise in it, it is (ultimate) welfare.[37]

The leap from Nāgārjuna to Candrakīrti to Zen is a minute one.

Conclusion

In seeking a comprehensive account of the *catuṣkoṭi*, this paper has been working on logical, ontological, historical, and soteriological aspects *in unison*. The fact that the logical aspects of the *catuṣkoṭi* have

---

34 Urs App, *Master Yunmen: From the Record of the Chan Teacher Gate of the Clouds* (New York: Kodansha International Press, 1994).

35 Thanks to an anonymous referee for making me aware that we can return to Nāgārjuna at this point.

36 Thanks go to Jan Westerhoff for this translation.

37 Compare, Anne McDonald, *In Clear Words: The Prasannapada, Chapter One, Volume Two* (Österreichischen Akademie der Wissenschaften, 2015).

been unhinged from their ontological fundament has prevented any fruitful modelling and obstructed further insight into the historical development of this fascinating piece of Buddhist philosophy. I hope that with this study of the development of Madhyamaka thought and with the help of the formal modelling applied thought the paper it is now clearer what the *catuṣkoṭi* is, and how it functions in the Buddhist canon. As the confluence of the last chapters suggests, we should not consider the *catuṣkoṭi* as exclusively a phenomenon of Madhyamaka thought, but think of the Madhyamaka's *catuṣkoṭi* as an instance of a much broader category, which is a schema of, and for, *upāya*, which includes the *bóxiè xiànzhe* and the *jūgyūzu* (and perhaps many, yet unexplored others).

References

App, Urs. *Master Yunmen: From the Record of the Chan Teacher Gate of the Clouds.* New York, NY: Kodansha International Press, 1994.

Chan, Wing-Tsit. *A Sourcebook in Chinese Philosophy.* Princeton NJ: Princeton University Press, 1963.

Cheng, Huseh-Li. *Empty Logic: Madhyamaka Buddhism from Chinese Sources.* Dehli: Motilal Banarsidass, 1991.

Chi, R. *Buddhist Formal Logic.* London: Luzac and Co., 1969.

Fox, Allen. "Jizang." In *Great Thinkers of the Eastern World.* Edited by Ian McGreal, 84–88. New York: Harper Collins, 1995.

Garfield, Jay. *Engaging Buddhism. Why It Matters to Philosophy.* Oxford: University Press, 2015.

Gunaratne, Ranil Dion. "The logical form of the catuṣkoṭi: A new solution." *Philosophy East & West* Vol. 30, No.2 (1980):211–238.

_____. "Understanding Nagarjuna's Catuskoti," *Philosophy East & West* Vol. 36, No.3 (1986): 213–234.

Kreutz, Adrian."Recapture, Transparency, Negation and a Logic for the *catuṣkoṭi.*" *Comparative Philosophy* Vol. 10, No.1 (2019): 56–81.

McDonald, Anne. *In Clear Words: The Prasannapada, Chapter One, Volume Two.* Wien: Österreichischen Akademie der Wissenschaften, 2015.

Murti, Tirupatur. *Central Philosophy of Buddhism: A Study of Madhyamaka System.* Barnsely: George and Unwin, 1955.

Poussin, Louis. *The Way of Nirvana.* Cambridge: Cambridge University Press,

1917.

Priest, Graham. *Introduction to Non-Classical Logic*. Cambrdige: Cambridge University Press, 2001.

_____. "The Logic of the catuṣkoṭi." *Comparative Philosophy* Vol, 1. No.2 (2010): 24–54.

_____. *The Fifth Corner of Four*. Oxford: Oxford University Press, 2018.

Robinson, Richard. *Early Madhyamaka in India and China*. Madison: University of Wisconsin Press, 1967.

Rogacz, Dawid. "Knowledge and Truth in the Thought of Jizang (549–623)." *The Polish Journal of the Arts and Culture*, Vol. 16, No. 4 (2015): 125–137.

Ruegg, David. "The Use of the Four Positions of the *Catuṣkoṭi* and the Problem of the Description of Reality in Mahayana Buddhism." *Journal of Indian Philosophy* Vol.5, No.1 (1977): 1–171.

Staal, Frits. *Exploring Mysticism*. New York: Penguin, 1975.

Tillemans, Tom. *Scripture, Logic, Language: Essays on Dharmakirti and His Tibetan Successors*. Sommervile MA: Wisdom, 1999.

Westerhoff, Jan. *Nāgārjuna's Madhyamaka: A Philosophical Introduction*. Oxford: Oxford University Press, 2009.

MAITREYEE DATTA (JADAVPUR UNIVERSITY, INDIA)

CLASSICAL INDIAN DIALECTICS

Refuting the Reality of Temporal Passage
in *Mūlamadhyamakakārikā* and
Khandanakhandakhādya

1.

The enigma of *temporal passage* enthralled the philosophers of classical India as well as of the West of the contemporary period. Though our everyday experience appears to be temporal to us, yet this temporal character is not immune to philosophical scrutiny. It is found from time immemorial that philosophers sought to pursue logical analysis of our experience of *temporal passage* and such analysis resulted into certain paradoxes and contradictions. Such endeavors have made the philosophers doubt the reality of *temporal passage*.

In classical Indian philosophical systems, the second-century *Mādhyamaka* Buddhist philosopher, Nāgārjuna and the twelfth-century neo-Advaitin philosopher, Śrīharṣa have used certain methods to probe into the nature of *temporal passage*. In the present paper an effort will be made to discuss these methods in detail with reference to the issue whether *temporal passage* is real or not. This will be a text based study in which all the arguments will be studied at length with reference to two important texts, namely, *Mūlamadhyamakakārikā* of Nāgārjuna, and *Khandanakhandakhādya* of Śrīharṣa respectively. According to many scholars in *Mūlamadhyamakakārikā* the *Mādhyamaka* scholar of second-century AD Nāgārjuna sought to examine different notions like causality, motion, sense-organ, time etc., admitted by different realist schools of Buddhism. Being an anti-realist, after examining the realist notions of causality etc, Nāgārjuna refuted the alleged reality of these. For him these notions, do not have any intrinsic nature. Thus, they cannot be real.

In the nineteenth chapter ("Kālaparīkṣā") of *Mūlamadhyamaka kārikā*, he employed arguments to refute the reality of *time*, which involves *temporal passage*. In other realist schools of Buddhism like Vaibhāṣika etc. the reality of *temporal passage* has been acknowledged. Nāgārjuna used his method of dialectics to analyze the notion of *time* upheld by his opponents and has proved the *temporal passage* and *time* to be unreal.

In the *Khandanakhandakhādya*, on the other hand, the neo-Vedānta philosopher of twelfth century CE Śrīharṣa has also critiqued the reality of *tenses* and *temporal passage*. Here he has taken *Naiyāyika* and *Vaiśeṣikas* as the opponents who advocated the reality of *time* and *temporal passage*.

In the context of the definition of causality, Śrīharṣa started analyzing the definition of cause advocated by the *Naiyāyikas*. While analyzing the definition of cause, he started analyzing the notion of *priority* which the definition of cause contains within. The analysis of "priority" demanded a need for analyzing the notions of *past*, etc. Thus, Śrīharṣa's examination of a realist account of *tense* and thereby *temporal passage* is a result of his critical assessment of *Naiyāyika's* assessment of "cause."

In the present paper the arguments offered by the two classical Indian anti-realists, namely, Nāgārjuna and Śrīharṣa to prove the unreality of *tense* and *temporal passage* will be discussed at length with reference to the above-mentioned texts. This discussion will give us an opportunity to compare their different methods of critiquing the realists' positions and will help us to determine how in classical India different forms of dialectics have developed.

2.

Before going to discuss different arguments offered by Nāgārjuna and Śrīharṣa to refute the reality of the alleged *temporal passage*, there is a need to discuss the relationship between three different tenses, *past*, *present* and *future* on the one hand and *temporal passage* on the other. Our experience of *temporal passage* is the result of our experiencing an event or a moment as *past*, *present* and *future* successively. In other words, we experience an event or a moment as *past*, *present* and *future* successively which is regarded as our experience of *tempo-*

ral passage. Now according to some philosophers our experience of *temporal passage* is veridical and it is real. They held that the tensed sentences in our language and the experience of an event as past, present and future are due to the presence of real *temporal passage.*

3.

Nāgārjuna, the great Buddhist philosopher of second-century AD refutes the reality of temporal determinations like *past, present,* and *future* by showing that none of these is proved without reference to the others. So as their existence is conditional, these cannot be taken to be real. The conditional existence of something makes it *svabhāvaśunya,* i.e., devoid of intrinsic nature. Thus, for Nāgārjuna an ultimate real is always unconditional. On the other hand, Śrīharṣa being an *advaitin* took *non-contradiction (avādhitattva)* as criterion of reality. According to the advocates of *Advaita Vedānta* that which is never contradicted in any time, namely, past, present, and future can only be considered as real in the true sense of the term. Thus, for them *non-contradiction* is the criterion of reality. In this sense there is only one reality, i.e., *Brahman* who cannot be contradicted at any time. Apart from him each and everything is contradicted at least in some or the other time. So all alleged real things are ultimately unreal.

In the book called *Mūlamadhyamakakārikā,* Nāgārjuna composes a full chapter to refute the reality of *past, present,* and *future* time. As these temporal determinations are results of our experience of *temporal passage,* the refutation of these tantamount to the denial of the *passage of time.* In order to understand Nāgārjuna's arguments for refuting the reality of *temporal passage,* we have to know in which context he offers his arguments. In the nineteenth chapter (*Kālaparikṣā*) of *Mūlamadhyamakakārikā,* he examines a particular view of *temporal passage* advocated by some other Buddhist philosophers by means of his dialectical method and finally refutes it.

The human personality is analysed into five aggregates or sometimes into six elements by Buddha. All these aggregates as well as elements are objects of experience. With the advent of scholasticism in Buddhism after the demise of lord Buddha, the analytical approach is carried to its logical conclusion and as a consequence the theory of atom as well as the theory of moments is generated in Buddhist philosophy.

In Buddhaghoṣa's commentary on the *Vibhanga*, the second book of the *Abhidhamma Pitaka*, it is said that the theory of *moments* is a doctrine found in the *Abhidhamma* and not found in the *Suttānta*. According to the *Suttānta*, *rūpa* (matter or form) is classified as *past, future* or *present* and this division is made on the basis of *becoming*. However, in *Abhidhamma* the division is made on the basis of *moments* (*khṣaṇena paricchinna*).

The *past*, *present* and *future* moments as real were admitted in a Vaibhāṣika school, namely, *Sarvāstivāda*. The *Sarvāstivādin* philosophers advocating such a position have tried to provide an adequate account of time in terms of these three *temporal determinations*.

According to some interpreters of Nāgārjuna the above realist position of *Sarvāstivādins* has been challenged by Nāgārjuna in his *Mūlamadhyamakākarikā*. Here he employs a dialectical method, namely, *prasanga* for examining this position. *Prasanga* is a reduction method by virtue of which at first the position to be refuted has been accepted for the time being. Later on, it is proved that as the position admitted initially leads to some kind of contradiction, it cannot be accepted.

According to a particular variety of *Sarvāstivādin* positions the presence of *kāritra* or causal efficacy determines an entity as *present* whereas when *kāritra* is destroyed in an entity it is regarded as *past* and when it is not yet generated in the entity it is *future*. This variety has been advocated by Vasumitra, the Sarvāstivādin. *Past, present* and *future* are determined in the above way.

Nāgārjuna's criticism is directed towards the above *Sarvāstivādin* position in which time is understood in terms of *temporal determinations* like *past, present* and *future*. There is another interpretation of Nāgārjuna's *Mūlamadhyamakakārikā* according to which *Sarvāstivādins* are not the opponents here. Whatever be the case, here we come across the critical examination of the linguistic counterparts or tenses like *past, present*, and *future*.

Nāgārjuna has employed his method to understand *time* through determinations like *past, present* and *future*. Then he argues that none of these is said to exist intrinsically (by virtue of its *svabhāva*). In other words, the existences of these are dependent existences. In interpreting Nāgārjuna the contemporary Buddhist scholar Garfield holds that Nāgārjuna implicitly assumes a dilemma of the following form: the *present* and the *future* either *depend upon* the *past* or they do not. In the first verse of "Kāla Parīkṣā" of *Mūlamadhyamakakārikā* Nāgārjuna states one horn of the dilemma, i.e., present and future do depend upon the past.[1] In presenting this alternative, he seeks to clarify the meaning of "depend upon." If present and future *depend upon* the past in any sense, then that could plausibly negate their inherent existence. In other words, they must emerge from the *past* as a basis. Thus, they must have existed in the *past*. According to Nāgārjuna if *present* and *future* were to be admitted as existent depending upon *past*, then the *present* and the *future* time would be inherent in the *past*. This statement expresses an internal relation which holds among *past*, *present*, and *future*. Accordingly, if something does not exist in a particular thing, then the former cannot depend upon the latter, that is, cannot be contingent upon the latter.[2] Now, if the dependence of *present* and *future* upon the *past* implies that these two exist in the *past* then there will be the following difficulties. Being existent in the *past*, *present* and *future* are said to have the same nature like the *past*. Thus, these also become *past*.[3]

According to Nāgārjuna if we consider the other horn of the above-mentioned dilemma, then it has to be admitted that *present* and *future* do not depend upon the *past*. But this position cannot be accepted because then *present* and *future* cannot exist.[4]

In such circumstances there cannot be any *past* also. *Past* is defined as that state, which emerges after the cessation of the *present*. As it is already proved that *present* and *future* are impossible, *past* also cannot

---

1   *Pratyutpannonāgatas ca yady atitam apeksya hi; pratyutpannonāgatas ca kālotite bhavisyatah*, MS.XIX, I, ed., Raghunath Pandey (1989), 80.

2   *Yasmāt, yasya hi yatrāsatvam, tat tena nāpeksyate.*

3   *Tadatra yadyatīte kāle vartamānānāgato kālāviṣyeteopekṣasidhyarthamevam satyatīte kāle vidya mānatvad atītakālātmavattayorapyatitvam syāt.*

4   *Anapekṣya punah siddhhirnātītam vidyate tayoh/Pratyupannonāgataśca tasmātkālo na vidyate//*, MS: XIX, III, ed., Raghunath Pandey (1989), 8.

exist because *past* is also defined in terms of *present* or *future*. Thus, *past* does not exist.

Present and *future* lose their individuality by existing in the *past*. Thus, there would be neither *present* nor *future* if these exist in the *past*. But under such a circumstance *past* also cannot exist, because it is regarded as *past* with respect to *present* and *future* only. As there is neither *present* nor *future*, *past* also cannot be there.

In the first chapter of *Mūlamadhyamakakārikā*, Nāgārjuna critiqued some of the philosophical views regarding "causal relation." According to one such view it has been held that the effect exists in the cause prior to its emergence. Thus, an effect which is dependent upon the cause must exist in the cause. If we admit this view, then *being dependent upon* the *past*, *present* and *future* are said to be existent in the *past* and that implies the *past* existence of *present* and *future*. Thus, *present* and *future* cannot hold their distinct existences.

Nāgārjuna through the above analysis shows that as none of the *temporal determinants* like *past*, *present* and *future* "*exists independently*," none of these can be taken to be *real* in the true sense of the term. In other words, the *interdependence* of *past*, *present* and *future* which constitutes their very being results in denial of their candidature as real.

Nāgārjuna initiates his philosophical analysis from our experience of *temporal passage* and thereby our everyday understanding of *temporal determinants* and proceeds to make a logical analysis of these concepts of *temporal determinations*, he becomes successful in showing the inconsistencies involved in our experience of *temporal passage*.

From Nāgārjuna's above analysis of time through determinations like *past*, *present* and *future* some problems crop up. Nāgārjuna has tried to determine *present* and *future* by making these dependent upon *past*. This particular analysis has led him to prove that time is unreal. Nāgārjuna's interpretation of "dependence upon" is a specific one but not the only one. Here the semantic dependence of *present* and *future* upon *past* has been extended to ontological dependence. One can raise a question regarding the legitimacy of such extension of meaning of "dependence upon." This remains as an open question against Nāgārjuna's claim that time is unreal. This phenomenological account of time through *temporal passage* which Nāgārjuna has critiqued is not the only account of time. Thus, it cannot be said that Nāgārjuna was successful in refuting the reality of time.

4.

There is another anti-realist philosopher of classical India who is a post Advaita-Vedāntin. In this paper I am also going to discuss his method of refuting the reality of temporal determinants and thereby *temporal passage*. His name is Śrīharṣa. Śrīharṣa (second half of the twelfth century), the great dialectician of *Advaita-Vedānta* (a classical Indian philosophical system) has attacked the reality of different categories admitted in *Nyāya-Vaiśeṣika* system.

The fundamental tenet of *Advaita-Vedānta* as advocated by Śankarācārya is that the *ultimate reality* is absolutely non-dual and its nature consists of pure Consciousness. In order to retain this principle of *Advaita-Vedānta*, Śrīharṣa adopted a method of dialectics by virtue of which he refuted the *ultimate reality* of worldly phenomena. It is important to note that *Advaitins* maintain a distinction between *phenomenal reality* and *transcendent* or *ultimate reality* which helps them to explain our experience as well as enables them to uphold the *ultimate reality* which remains free from all kinds of contradiction by which the *phenomenal reality* is often contaminated. Thus, for them the criterion of *ultimate reality* (*pāramārthika sat*) is *non-contradiction*. In Śrīharṣa's deliberations we come across the application of this criterion to prove that *temporal passage* is ultimately unreal. In this connection, it would be pertinent to mention that the gnosos of the *Advaita* system explicates and holds that the *phenomenal reality* emerges out of and dissolves back into *ultimate reality*, in somewhat but not totally identical manner as dream emerges out of the mind in the state of relative ignorance that is the sleeping state, and dissolves back into the mind in the stage of phenomenal wakefulness. As such, *ultimate reality* is held to be the fundamental reality.

The basic thesis of Śrīharṣa is that no *phenomenal entity* can be explained. In other words, no adequate explanation can be given about these things. Therefore, in the absence of any adequate explanation of anything, each and every thing of this world becomes unreal.

Here we come across the application of Śrīharṣa's criterion of reality, namely, *explicability* which is a necessary corollary of *non-contradiction*. The main opponents of Śrīharṣa in his endeavor are the votaries of *Nyāya-Vaiśeṣika* who seek to provide an adequate explanation of our experiences by admitting the reality of the objects of experience.

By his method of dialectics Śrīharṣa attacked the views of *Nyāya-Vaiśeṣikas*, who were realist philosophers of classical India, regarding the reality of different entities to go on to prove ultimately that the explanations provided by *Nyāya-Vaiśeṣika*[5] were inadequate. Thus, resultantly, in the absence of any adequate explanation of the entities of the world, the reality of these could not be accepted.

In the present section, we propose to discuss a critique made by Śrīharṣa, the neo-Advaitin regarding the Nyāya view of *past* etc. In the fourth chapter of the book called *Khandanakhandakhādya*, Śrīharṣa sought to critique the Nyāya lakṣaṇa of *kāraṇatva*. In this lakṣaṇa, the Naiyāyikas defined *kāraṇatvam* (causality) in terms of invariable prior absence (*niyata prāgabhāvitva*). Here, the lakṣaṇa of *kāraṇatva* is provided in terms of *prior time* where the term prior (*prāk*) denotes this *prior time*.

As Naiyāyikas and Vaiśeṣikas often provide *lakṣaṇa* along with *pramāna* (sources of knowledge) to prove the reality of an entity, Śrīharṣa in order to refute the reality of an entity attacks its *lakṣaṇa*. He refutes the reality of the entity by showing the *lakṣaṇa* to be inadequate.

In the section Vartamānatvādilakṣaṇakhandanam of *Khandana khandakhādya*, Śrīharṣa in order to explain the usage and meaning of prior occurring in the lakṣaṇa of *kāraṇatva*, held that the determination of such a lakṣaṇa of *kāraṇatva* requires the determination of *present* as well as *future* time which are to be determined as distinct from prior which refers to *past* time. Thus, the determination of the lakṣaṇa of *kāraṇatva* and the determination of the meaning of "prior" occurring in the lakṣaṇa would be possible provided the three above

---

5   *Nyāya* and *Vaiśeṣika* as separate philosophical systems have evolved in classical India with the aphorisms of Gautama and Kaṇāda respectively during first century CE (approx.) Later during tenth and eleventh CE these two systems were often regarded conjoinedly as system of *Nyāya-Vaiśeṣika* due to their allegiance to some common presuppositions and principles.

mentioned temporal determinations could be established. But he held that such determination could not be possible.

The defenders of the reality of time and temporal determinations were not ready to accept the denial of the reality of temporal determinations like *past* etc. so easily. Śrīharṣa presented the defense of the Naiyāyikas for the reality of temporal determinations by providing their lakṣaṇas of present, future and past time. Naiyāyikas defined present-hood (*vartamānatva*) as that which is the object of the notion "to exist." Future-hood (*bhavisyatva*) is that which is the object of the notion "will exist" and past-hood (*atitatva*) is that which is the object of the notion "has existed." Thus, present, future and past times are proved by their notions which are used in everyday discourse.

But Śrīharṣa is not ready to accept such a position due to the following reason. According to Śrīharṣa, there are only two alternatives which can explain the above-mentioned distinct times. Either the "differences" are something natural or these are adventitious.[6] The "differences" cannot be natural because, he argues, as the defenders of the reality of *past, present* and *future* themselves admit time to be one, the alleged differences cannot be natural. If time is one, then there cannot be different times. In response to the above argument it can be said that as the single Time is actually characterized by the threefold character of *past, present* and *future*, the differences are inherent in Time.

But, Sriharsa's position is that such a way of characterizing *time* cannot be accepted. Firstly, since the diversity of characters should cause diversity in the object itself, if *time* is characterized by the threefold character, then it has to be regarded as three and not one. Secondly, if *time* is characterized by the threefold character of *past, present and future*, then at the very time when we have the idea that a certain thing "exists," we could also have the idea that it "existed" or that "it will exist." In other words, the threefold nature of *Time* would make the use of tenses meaningless.

Therefore, as it is found that the "difference" of time cannot be natural, the "difference" of time has to be taken as adventitious. But

---

6   Kālasya viśeṣah svābhāvik oupādhikī vā? *Khandanakhandakhādye* Caturtha Paricchede "Vartamānatvādilakṣaṇakhaṇḍam," 726.

if the "difference" is adventitious, then the limiting adjunct (*upādhi*) due to which the adventitious difference is generated has to be specified. According to *Nyāya-Vaiśeṣika* the adventitious difference in *time* is due to the diversity of connection with the movements of the sun and such other objects.[7]

Śrīharṣa refutes the above position in the following manner. Since the same day being connected with movements of the sun is cognized as *present* and it is also cognized as *past* or *future* due to the connection of movements of the sun, this connection being common to all divisions of *time*, it cannot be admitted as the limiting adjunct (*upādhi*) which can explain the various divisions of *time*.

In response to Śrīharṣa's above criticism, the *Nyāya-Vaiśeṣikas* argued as follows. Though they accepted the difficulty as mentioned above by Śrīharṣa in explaining the difference in *time* by virtue of the limiting adjunct—connection with the movements of the sun—they sought to circumvent the difficulty by seeking to explain the notions of "present," "past" and "future" in the following way. According to them when the connection with the Sun's movement actually exists in time, that time is regarded as "present." When that connection is destroyed, that time is regarded as "past." When the connection is yet to come, that time is regarded as "future."

Still, the abovementioned way of explaining the notions of "present," "past" and "future" was not immune to criticism. According to Śrīharṣa the above way of explaining the notions like past, present and future involved the fallacy of vicious circle or infinite regress. *Present tense* is a linguistic expression which signifies the *occurrence of a particular event*. In the above case "present" is determined by the *occurrence of an event* called sun's movement. So the meaning of "present" is determined by the *occurrence of an event*. Thus, the *Nyāya-Vaiśeṣikas* are found to try to explain the idea of "present" in terms of the *occurrence of an event* and vice versa. Thus, there is the fallacy of vicious circle. Also, the method of explaining the notion of "present" by virtue of another idea of "present" leads to the fallacy of infinite regress. Similarly, in the example of 'movement of the sun' the

---

7   Sūryādikriyāsambandhavedaḥ ... *Khandanakhandakhādye* Caturtha Paricchede "Vartamānatvādilakṣaṇakhaṇḍam," 726

tensed verbs "destroyed" and "yet to come" are only synonymous with "past" and "future" (tenses) respectively. Thus, the *Nyāya-Vaiśeṣikas* are found to have chosen one synonym from a number of synonyms and attempted to explain it by virtue of another synonym. This effort is faulty and useless.

The effort of explaining the notions of *past, present* and *future* in the above way proving to be unfruitful, the *Nyāya-Vaiśeṣikas* seek to explain the notions in a different way again. They held that the time which is characterized by action is the *"present."*[8] The time which is characterized by prior negation of action, is the *"past."*[9] The time which is characterised by the destruction or absolute absence of action, is the *"future."*[10] Here only at the backdrop of this Advaitin attack it becomes clear why *Naiyāyikas* kept changing their formulations of *past* etc.

Śrīharṣa provides more than one criticism against the above explanations of "past," "present" and "future" offered by *Nyāya-Vaiśeṣikas*. Firstly, according to Śrīharṣa, even when we experience "past" and "future," we continue to have the conception of the time which is characterised by action. Therefore, according to the latest formulation of "present" as provided above by the *Nyāya-Vaiśeṣikas*, "past" and "future" would also have to be cognised as "present" which makes their effort untenable. It follows that the characterisation of time by action also cannot explain the difference in time which they seek to hold as real. It thus follows that *time*, which to start with is seen not characterizable by action, can never be characterized by "previous negation" or "destruction" of action since in order to be characterized by the "previous negation" or the "destruction" of an action, time has first to be amenable to characterization by action itself. As per Sriharsa's reasoning presented above, this is not possible.

Further, unless and until the meaning of *"previous"* be determined, one cannot understand the meaning of *"previous negation."* Thus, it would also not be possible to understand the meaning of *"previous*

---

8   Kriyāvacchinnah kālo vartamānah ... *Khandanakhandakhādye* Caturtha Paricchede "Vartamānatvādilakṣaṇakhaṇḍam," 727

9   Tatprāgabhāvāvacchinno bhūtah, 727,

10   Tatpradhvamsāvacchinno bhaviṣyanniti, 727.

negation of action." As a result, the meaning of "*past*" would remain unexplained.

In his effort at critiquing and refuting comprehensively the *Nyāya-Vaiśeṣika* thesis of the reality of *past, present* and *future,* Śrīharṣa argues to negate the latter's premises as well as the manner of depiction of such premises from all possible angles leaving no aspect or description of their averments untreated. Thus, he goes on to insist that it would not be possible to discriminate between *Nyāya-Vaiśeṣika* formulations of *past* and *future* since it would be impossible to distinguish between "previous negation" (*prāgabhāva*) and "destruction" (*dhvamsābhāva*). Against this view of Śrīharṣa, one might say that the distinction between "previous negation" and "destruction" is possible because "previous negation" has an end[11] while "destruction" has a beginning.[12] Śrīharṣa proceeds to invalidate this alleged criticism in the way discussed below.

According to Śrīharṣa, the above-mentioned distinction is untenable, because if one analyses the meaning of "having an end" (*vināśī*), then one would find that "destruction" like "previous negation" also has an end. The "previous negation" is said to have an end, because as soon as its counter-entity (*pratiyogi*) emerges, say for example when the counter-entity of "negation of a jar," namely "a jar" itself emerges, the "previous negation" comes to an end. But, since "destruction" also has a counter-entity, in similar manner it should also come to an end. Thus, as both "previous negation" and "destruction" have their respective ends, these two cannot be distinguished by the property of "having an end."

Again, when "destruction" is determined above as the negation which has a beginning, the meaning of "having a beginning" has to be determined. If an entity is assumed to have a beginning, the non-existence (absence) of that entity has to be admitted till the beginning. Destruction is determined as having a beginning. So destruction which is an absence is said to have a non-existence. It amounts to a positive existence which makes destruction (a type of non-existence) meaningless.

---

11   Abhāvo vināśī prāgabhāvah ... *Khandanakhandakhādye* Caturtha Paricchede "Vartamānatvādilakṣaṇakhaṇḍam," 728

12   Utpattimān pradhvamsa, 728.

"Beginning" cannot be predefined as the "*sattvā*," by declaring it (*sattvā*) as the coming into existence of what was previously non-existent, because the meanings of the terms like "previously," "now" and "subsequently" are not determined till now. Since as yet the meanings of "before" and "after" are not determined, no adequate explanation of *cause* is possible. Thus, the definition of "beginning" as "existence determined by *cause*" cannot also be admitted. In the absence of any adequate definition of "beginning" it is not possible to distinguish "destruction" from "previous negation." Therefore, the definition of "*past*" and "*future*" cannot be given in terms of "previous negation" and "destruction" of action respectively.

Śrīharṣa further asserts that if the *Nyāya-Vaiśeṣikas* would base the distinctions of time upon differences by limiting adjuncts like the movements of the sun, then it can well be argued that time, which they hold to be one only, would become many because the limiting adjuncts (*upādhi*) determining circumstances are innumerable. It would be also impracticable for them to choose one circumstance among many as the determinant for the alleged divisions of time.

From the above discussion of the arguments as well as counter-arguments regarding the possibility of *past*, *present* and *future* time it follows that *Nyāya-Vaiśeṣikas*, the proponents of the reality of *past*, *present* and *future* try to justify their claim by providing alternative interpretations of terms like *past* etc. But Śrīharṣa unceasingly makes effort to refute their arguments by providing counterarguments and ultimately proves that in the absence of any adequate interpretation of "past," "present" and "future" as distinct from each other, the impossibility of these *temporal determinations* stands proved. So these are also proved to be unreal. Since *past*, *present*, and *future—temporal determinations* are proved to be unreal, the *temporal passage* which we experience also is proved to be illusory.

5.

Both Nāgārjuna and Śrīharṣa attacked the realist positions in which temporal determinants like *past*, etc., were admitted to be real. These two renowned dialecticians of classical India employed their

methods of dialectics to refute the reality of *past*, etc., by showing
that no adequate account of these would be possible. In this particular context, Nāgārjuna interprets real as *unconditional*, whereas
Śrīharṣa interprets it as *non-contradictory*. In the above discussion we
have found how Nāgārjuna refuted the reality of *past*, etc., by considering these as conditioned. Śrīharṣa has refuted the reality of *past*,
etc., by showing that either of these involved circularity or contradiction in some way or the other. Thus, for both of them our experience
of *temporal passage* is illusory which we consider to be real during
our everyday experience. Still the question remains as to do these critiques by virtue of logic actually succeed in refuting the phenomenal
reality of temporal passage which constitutes an important part of
our everyday experience? Further study will be helpful to resolve this
apparent conflict between philosophical analysis of *temporal passage*
and its phenomenal reality.

References

Garfield, J. L. *The Fundamental Wisdom of the Middle Way*. Oxford: Oxford University Press, 1995

Nāgārjuna, *Madhyamakaśāstram*. Edited by Raghunath Pandey. Delhi: Motilal
Banarsidass, 1989

Śrīharṣakrta *Khandanakhandakhādya*, Ānandapūrṇamunikrta *Khandanaphakkikā
bhibhājan*, Jogindranath Svami (ed), Varanasi: Ṣadarśan prakashan Pratisthan,
Udāsīn Sanskrita Vidyālaya, 1979

TRANSLATIONS

QUẢNG HUYỀN (CORNELL UNIVERSITY)

ESOTERIC TRADITION OF VENERABLE MASTER BUDDHA OF WESTERN PEACE

A Shallowed World

Hồ Cứ Islet no longer exists. There, towards the right bank of the Tiền River, the northern branch of the Mekong River in southern Vietnam, was the location where Master Buddha said he "stepped over" (1)[1] to deliver his *Esoteric Tradition* in circa 1842. But Hồ Cứ Islet has since eroded away into the Mekong. The nearby islet where the teacher's home village of Tòng Sơn lay has also been largely lost to the river.[2]

According to local legends, a geomancer was instrumental in this transformation. On behalf of villagers on the left bank of the Tiền River, he captured a gander and his mate. At night, in the cover of darkness, the geomancer tethered the female goose to a pole on the Tiền River's left bank. He then rowed to the other side of the river and, after attaching talismans to the gander, released the bird to seek out his mate. For three consecutive nights the geomancer plied his trade so that the gander bearing his talismans would spirit away the geomantic properties of the Hồ Cứ–Tòng Sơn islets to the left river-bank. Sure enough, come the dry season, the islets near the right bank had been devastated by the river's corrosion, and its rich alluvial soils

---

1   Parenthetical numbers indicate corresponding line numbers in the translation and transliteration. See translation note below.

2   Nguyễn Văn Hầu, *Sấm truyền Đức Phật Thầy Tây An* (Tòng Sơn: Ban Quản tự Tòng Sơn cổ tự, Ban Chẩn tế Giáo hội Phật giáo Hòa Hảo, 1973, 1990), 15–16. The former Hồ Cứ Islet was commemorated by renaming a riverside downstream on the left bank of the Tiền River the Hồ Cứ Area (miệt Hồ Cứ), which is in Cao Lãnh District's Mỹ Xương Hamlet in Đồng Tháp Province.

emerged as islets towards the left bank that nearby villages eagerly claimed.[3]

It is amidst such an unsettled riverscape that Đoàn Minh Huyên's (段明暄, 1807–1856) *Esoteric Tradition* must be understood. Huyên, who is known to the Vietnamese and his followers as *Phật Thầy* or "Master Buddha," lived in a fluid, changeable, and uncertain "water frontier" along the Tiền and Bassac Rivers, the northern and southern distributaries of the Mekong River in southern Vietnam.[4] To people of the delta like Huyên, the world seemed to be coming apart before their eyes. Observing scenes such as the seemingly imminent erasure of his native Hồ Cứ–Tòng Sơn islets, Huyên spoke in *Esoteric Tradition* of a world "teetering on the vast sea, falling away on the banks of a pond" (46) as "mountains split and land crumbles, drifting into the offing" (12). Đoàn Minh Huyên associated the transforming landscape of the delta and its attendant calamities with Buddhist prophecies about the fading *dharma*, the Buddhist teachings. In Huyên's waterborne vision, the tide of *dharma* was receding, leaving in its wake a "shallowed world" (*cạn đời*). But eventually the tides would shift, for Buddhist lore also spoke of Maitreya Buddha (*Phật Di Lặc*), who would descend from the Tuṣita strata of the heavens to inaugurate a new *dharma* dispensation.

According to several *sūtra* dedicated to this prophecy, Maitreya would achieve enlightenment beneath a "dragon flower tree," and so his coming congregation was known as *hội Long Hoa* or Dragon Flower Assembly.[5] This congregation would consist of those who had culled

---

3   Ibid., 17–18.

4   Li Tana, "The Water Frontier: An Introduction," in *Water Frontier: Commerce and the Chinese in the Lower Mekong Region, 1750–1880*, ed., Nola Cooke and Li Tana (New York: Rowman and Littlefield, 2004), 1–17.

5   *Sūtra Spoken by Buddha about Maitreya's Descent to Be Born and Achieve Buddhahood* 佛說彌勒下生成佛經 (T.454.14.424b23–26). Cf., 大乘本生心地觀經 (T.159.3.306a5–7), 彌勒來時經 (T.457.14.434c16–19), and 三彌勒經疏 (T.1774.38.316a17–18). The dragon flower tree is said to be 40–50 *li* tall (roughly 15km high). For comparison with the Pāli tradition, in which Mettayya (Maitreya) inaugurates his *dharma* dispensation at "a blossoming *nāga* (dragon) grove," see Upatissa, *The Stream of Deathless Nectar: The Short Recension of the Amatarasadhārā of the Elder Upatissa: A Commentary on the Chronicle of the Future Buddha Metteyya, with a Historical Introduction*, translated by Daniel M. Stuart (Bangkok, Thailand: Fragile Palm Leaves Foundation, 2017), 213.

"karma of goodness" (*thiện duyên*, 善緣). In prophecies endemic to the Mekong Delta, the gathering of Maitreya's congregation would be foretold by the appearance of highly advanced *dharma* practitioners, so-called *bodhisattva*, such as the Jade Buddha (*Ngọc Phật*, 玉佛), who would task themselves with finding those with "karma of goodness" and sequestering them from the dangers and evils of an imploding world.[6] Đoàn Minh Huyên dedicated his life to this mission. But rescuing the good was a precarious affair before what Huyên described as "reeling sights" (45) of "scenes of natural disaster" (36). People's native landscape—indeed, the entire perceived world—was turning against itself. Not only did the land and waters seem bent on annihilation, but as the geomancer in the legend about the erosion of Huyên's native land suggests, spiritual leaders, religious clergy, thaumaturges, and all sorts of adepts with extraordinary abilities participated in internecine struggle, thereby interweaving their practices into the earth's self-destruction. Even ghosts and spirits appeared set on total ruination.

A look at a vernacular Vietnamese apocryphal *sūtra* about the Dragon Flower prophecy offers insight into Đoàn Minh Huyên's dystopian vision. The extant text, a xylographic reprint from 1944, reveals not only how the vision that Huyên helped spread continued to impact later generations during the Second World War, but it also intimates how believers in the prophecy may have beheld the nuclear tragedies that would soon ensue in the Pacific and the decades-long mutilation of the earth by war machines and defoliants in Vietnam as well as how such believers may envision future disasters associated with dramatic environmental and climatic transformations[7]:

6　*Di Lặc chơn kinh diễn am* 彌勒真經演音 (Vernacular Exposition of the True Sūtra about Maitreya), xylographic text, Hanoi, National Library of Vietnam, accession no. R.1800.

7　With eerie semblance to the Dragon Flower prophecy, recent studies of rising tidal waters in the Mekong Delta project that virtually all of the Vietnamese south will be submerged at high tide by 2050. S. A. Kulp and B. H. Strauss, "New Elevation Data Triple Estimates of Global Vulnerability to Sea-level Rise and Coastal Flooding," *Nature Communications* 10, no. 4844 (2019); Dennis Lu and Christopher Flavelle, "Rising Seas Will Erase More Cities by 2050, New Research Shows" *New York Times*, October 29, 2019, *https://www.nytimes.com/interactive/2019/10/29/climate/coastal-cities-underwater.html.*

You will see species of numinous ghosts and monsters, who occupy large and small shrines and temples, obstruct the wind and rain, causing calamities of great drought that ruin rice crops and inflict pain and suffering on ten-thousands of people. Moreover, species of demons and monsters beneath the water like dragons, snakes, turtles, otters, whales, water serpents, frogs, crabs, eels, and fish along with oyster, eel fry, clam, snail, mussel, and arca demons will constantly transform their powers to draw in the water to make great rain clouds and flood rains that will cause the rivers and streams to inundate with flood water, destroying dykes and flooding rice crops and fruits of the earth.[8]

What message did Đoàn Minh Huyên derive from this imagining of the world's transformation? Huyên's teachings about the prophecy reveal a conceptual double movement at once outward and inward. Towards the former, the centrifugal thrust of Huyên's teachings called for people with "karma of goodness" to abscond to the remote periphery. He exhorted his followers to "towards the west, trek straight out in search" (50). There, in the Seven Mountains of the frontier west, an unsettled no-man's-land between the Khmer and Vietnamese polities, Huyên sought to cloister his followers from nature's precipitous destruction and weather her storms of restitution.[9]

Đoàn Minh Huyên described the travails of this journey:

Heaven renders a hundred beings to waste,
    Such that ferrying across is arduous with unspeakable toil.
Mountaintops float on water, and earth builds up,
    Dragons lurk at the bottom of the sea as rivers constantly catch the dew.
    (69–70)

At the same time, Huyên saw the physical trek to the Seven Mountains as a spiritual flight:

As this moment comes, divine dragons descend;

---

8   *Di Lặc chơn kinh diễn am*, 40a–b. For a synopsis of the *sūtra*, which bears the alternative titles *Di Lặc độ thế chơn kinh, Kinh Đức Phật Di Lặc xuống đời*, and *Kinh quý trọng của Đức Di Lặc*, see Ho-Tai Hue-Tam, *Millenarianism and Peasant Politics in Vietnam* (Cambridge, MA: Harvard University Press, 1983), 31; "Perfect World and Perfect Time: Maitreya in Vietnam," in *Maitreya, the Future Buddha*, ed., Alan Sponberg and Helen Hardacre (Cambridge: Cambridge University Press, 1988), 164–6.

9   For the locations and identities of the Seven Mountains, see Recluse (Trần Văn Nhựt) and Nguyễn Văn Hầu, *Thất Sơn mầu nhiệm* (s.l.: NXB Từ Tâm, 1955, 1972), 15–21.

> We are as if on a little boat buffeted by the wind on the rivers and lakes.
> "Amitābha," with the six words "Nam Mô,"
>   One transmigrates to be born in the Pure Land, coming and going at ease.
> Once you escape the sea of suffering, you cross over,
>   To take shelter from the cycle of mundane dust and avoid the realm of life
>   and death. (93–95)

In the hearts of many from the delta, the Seven Mountains conjured the horizons of the imagination; for teachers like Huyên, they posed "the ultimate environment for self-cultivation."[10] The very earth of the Seven Mountains like the adepts who alighted there were potent with numen. The geomancy of the Seven Mountains was primed for the Dragon Flower Assembly. Whereas *thượng nguơn* or "Fountainhead" (literally "Upper Spring") of Śākyamuni Buddha's dispensation began in the heights of the Himalayas[11] at the Mekong River's source, *hạ nguơn* or "Receding Spring" (lit. "Lower Spring") at the time of the *dharma's* fading would transpire in the Mekong Delta, where the river's waters, its geomantic energies, and the potency of *dharma* vanished as they flowed out towards the offing.[12]

At the same time, the salvific journey that Đoàn Minh Huyên envisioned during the "Receding Spring" was directed inward. In contrast to apocalyptic visions of an astrological, celestial, nuclear, or extraterrestrial nature, the exigencies of the Dragon Flower prophecy were not initiated from without but rather accelerated from within.[13] The inward movement of the Dragon Flower prophecy, in which delta inhabitants' native landscape turned on itself, implied introspection

---

10 Đỗ Thiện, *Vietnamese Supernaturalism: Views from the Southern Region* (London: Routledge Curzon, 2003), 177–178.

11 That Śākyamuni has been associated with the Himalayan Mountains in Vietnamese Buddhist imagination since at least the seventeenth century is evidenced by devotional statues from that time that depict Buddha in the Himalayas. Nguyễn Bá Thanh Long, *Cổ Vật Hải Phòng* (Hải Phòng: Hội cổ vật Hải Phòng, 2009), 109.

12 Recluse (Trần Văn Nhụt) and Nguyễn Văn Hầu, *Thất Sơn mầu nhiệm*, 43–49. For analysis of the temporality of the Upper, Intermediate, and Lower Springs, see Vương Kim (Phạm Bá Cẩm), *Đời hạ nguơn* (Sài Gòn: NXB Long Hoa, 1960), 11–56; cf., Jan Nattier, *Once upon a Future Time: Studies in a Buddhist Prophecy of Decline* (Berkeley, CA: Asian Humanities Press, 1991), 27–64.

13 For scriptural sources, variations, and comparison of Buddhist apocalypses, see Jan Nattier, *Once upon a Future Time: Studies in a Buddhist Prophecy of Decline*, 119–32.

and thus drew beholders' vision toward their interior karmic land-scapes. Huyên led his followers to see in their inner moral configura-tion the mirror image of the land's physical chaos and, conversely, in the deterioration of the land, their own moral degeneration. Because people's inner and outer worlds were intrinsically intertwined, Huyên saw in his world's devolution the concomitant retribution of human misdeeds.[14]

But Đoàn Minh Huyên's message ultimately inspired hope. By the same karmic logic of the world's decline, moral reparation could restore. Alluding to the depletion of the *dharma* that paralleled the Mekong River's descent from its Himalayan wellspring to the delta during the "Receding Spring," Huyên taught, "Today's world has already shallowed, to open, transform, and establish the Fountain-head era" (62). Huyên believed that if people with "karma of good-ness" would *tu* (修)—a term that applies both to moral cultivation and material reconstruction—then the world would be restored to peace. Thus, even amidst the misery of traversing through the "Receding Spring," Huyên inspired hope, "Amidst calamity, with luck a fish from a spring may come across a lotus lake" (42).

Therefore, imbedded in the inward and outward journey inherent in Đoàn Minh Huyên's teaching about the Dragon Flower prophecy was a promise. Just as Śākyamuni's story over incalculable lifetimes is also *our* story,[15] Maitreya's anticipated achievement of Buddhahood beneath the dragon flower tree would be the collective fruit of indi-viduals' participation in cultivation as well as the realization of salva-tion for ourselves and our world.

---

14   Ho-Tai Hue-Tam, "Perfect World and Perfect Time: Maitreya in Vietnam," in
      Maitreya, the Future Buddha, ed., Alan Sponberg and Helen Hardacre (Cam-
      bridge: Cambridge University Press, 1988), 164.

15   John S. Strong, "A Family Quest: The Buddha, Yaśodhara, and Rāhula in the
      Mūlasarvāstivāda Vinaya," in *Sacred Biography in the Buddhist Traditions of South
      and Southeast Asia*, ed., Juliane Schober (Honolulu: University of Hawai'i Press,
      1997), 113–28; *The Buddha: A Short Biography* (Oxford: Oneworld Publications,
      2001), 14; Jonathan S. Walters, "Story, Stūpa, and Empire: Construction of the
      Buddha Biography in Early Post-Aśokan India," in *Sacred Biography in the Bud-
      dhist Traditions of South and Southeast Asia*, ed., Juliane Schober (Honolulu: Uni-
      versity of Hawai'i Press, 1997), 160–92.

Master Buddha

> Sitting ruefully, I recall the teacher's words;
>> In the year of the Earthen Cock, east and west were in throngs.
> As an epidemic seized thousands upon thousands,
>> All beneath the skies panicked, villages frightened out of their wits.
> The skies halted the waters suddenly;
>> Teacher, seeing this, was moved and resolved to deliver us to peace.
> To rescue the hundred clans who faced calamity,
>> At that time, teacher descended to Tòng Sơn village... [16]

Thus begins a vernacular hagiography of Master Buddha of unknown authorship(s). This opening passage offers us a moment to consider the challenges of narrating the teacher's life story. The narrator begins by speaking in plaintive nostalgic verse. He summons Master Buddha by memory, and so his telling of the teacher's story is an act of recollection. However, as the storyteller progresses, he draws our remembrance of Master Buddha to the present by exhorting us to uphold his teachings. The narrator reiterates the former master's teachings for immediate practice. Then, by avowing the veracity of Master Buddha's message about the world's immanent restitution beneath the dragon flower tree, the narrator speaks to the future. Thus, the temporality of "Master Buddha" reverberated through past, present, and future and redounded cyclically. As the storyteller concludes, "Master Buddha" and his embodiment in memory, teachings, practice, and, perhaps, unknowable mystery[17] echoes throughout "affairs of the world like rhythms of a wooden fish."[18] Therefore, "Master Buddha" is at once an individual, a body of teachings, and a figure of worship. We must remain mindful of this in the discussion to follow.

In 1807, the historical Đoàn Minh Huyên was born in Tòng Sơn Village on an eponymous islet near the right bank of the Tiền River.[19]

---

16 "Giảng xưa về Phật Thầy," in Vương Kim (Phạm Bá Cẩm) and Đào Hưng, *Đức Phật Thầy Tây An*, second edition (Sài Gòn: NXB Long Hoa, 1954), 158.

17 The likening of the body of Buddhist teachings (V. *pháp thân* 法身, S. *dharmakāya*) to the pervasive rhythms of a sonic *dharma* calls to mind the "three bodies" (V. *tam thân*, S. *trikāya*) theory of Mantrayāna (Esoteric Incantation) Buddhism.

18 Ibid., 166.

19 Today, a village by the name of Tòng Sơn is located in Mỹ An Hưng Hamlet, Lấp Vò Discrict, Đồng Tháp Province, Vietnam. Tòng Sơn Pagoda and other structures

A contemporary gazetteer described his native islet, "All four sides are lapped by undulating waves. Gazing upon it [from a distance], the islet seems like drifting duckweed. The sunlight shimmers on river dolphins, and the wind stirs the water's cranes."[20] Huyên became accustomed to the unmoored life of his riverine homeland early in his youth. Stories that mention Huyên's childhood tell us that once his father died, he and his mother coursed the rivers and canals by boat, selling betel and areca. The extent of their travels is unknown, but Huyên's mother was buried along the Cái Tàu Thượng waterway about three kilometers by boat from Tòng Sơn.[21]

When Đoàn Minh Huyên's mother died is unclear, but after her passing, Huyên continued to wander. According to oral tradition, he drifted throughout the waterways of the Mekong Delta, clinging to just a culm of bamboo.[22] By his thirties, Huyên seems to have mastered an array of cultivation arts, including embodied practices such as breath work, swift traveling, and martial yoga as well as uncanny abilities in healing, geomancy, talismans, presaging, thunderbolt-cultivation, and vanishing.[23] He also achieved fluency in Sinographic

commemorative of Đoàn Minh Huyên are found there.

20   「四面波濤， 望之如水上浮萍，日閃江豚，風翻水鶴」。Trịnh Hoài Đức 鄭
      懷德 (1765-1825), *Gia Định thành thông chí* 嘉定城通志 (*c.*1820), Sinographic
      text in *Gia Định thành thống chí*, ed. Đào Duy Anh, trans. Đỗ Mộng Khương
      and Nguyễn Ngọc Tinh (Tp. Hồ Chí Minh: NXB Giáo dục, 1999), 75b/162.
      The river dolphin was probably a species of finless porpoise. *Đại Nam nhất thống
      chí*, another contemporary gazetteer, likened the islet to a raft drifting in the river.
      Quốc sử quán triều Nguyễn, *Đại Nam nhất thống chí*, ed., Đào Duy Anh, trans.,
      Phạm Trọng Điểm (Viện Sử học, NXB Thuận Hóa–Huế, 2006), vol. 5, 214.

21   Vương Kim (Phạm Bá Cẩm) and Đào Hưng, *Đức Phật Thầy Tây An*, second edi-
      tion (Sài Gòn: NXB Long Hoa, 1954), 16–17.

22   His travels at this time are said to have included Mỏ Cày, Bến Tre, Cần Chông, Sóc
      Trăng, Bạc Liêu, Cà Mau, Rạch Giá, and the Seven Mountains. Nguyễn Văn Hầu,
      Sấm truyền Đức Phật Thầy Tây An, 30. Swimming through the delta's waterways
      was quite hazardous considering the crocodiles, snakes, and pirates who populated
      them. Nevertheless, accounts from twentieth century memoirs reveal that some
      did succeed in coursing the waters by clinging to bamboo. Nguyễn Văn Quảng and
      Marjorie Pivar, *Fourth Uncle in the Mountain: A Memoir of a Barefoot Doctor in
      Vietnam* (New York: St. Martin's Press, 2004), 43–46.

23   These are my provisional translation for *khí công* (breath work), *khinh công* (swift
      traveling), *võ* (martial yoga), *phù thủy/thuốc nước* (healing), *phong thủy* (geo-
      mancy), *bùa* (talismans), *tiên tri* (prognostication), *điển* (thunderbolt-cultivation,
      vajra), and *tàng hình* (vanishing). Some of these practices are described in Thích

writing and Buddhist *sūtra* literature.[24] Huyên never attributed his training to any particular lineage(s) or teacher(s). However, present day accounts of adepts' training the sundry assortment of skills and practices associated with a spiritual teacher like Huyên suggest that he studied sporadically with multiple masters of various affiliations (and lack thereof) during the course of this travels.[25]

By 1842, Đoàn Minh Huyên felt compelled to preach. Internal clues in *Esoteric Tradition* reveal that Huyên alighted at Hồ Cứ Islet that year, warning of the calamities soon to befall a "shallowed world."[26] The previous year, a Khmer monk had led his followers to arms, disrupting life throughout the delta from the coastal east to the Seven Mountains.[27] Amidst such chaos, Huyên alluded to the Vietnamese zodiac to project the miseries to come during the three years to follow (1843–45) and implore the delta's people to seek shelter in the mountains of the west, "The cat's cry resounds! The cat's cry resounds! Scaring snake and dragon to flee into the mountains and hide" (39). He appears to have drifted up and down the Mekong River spreading his message, and, by 1844, he preached another esoteric litany at Gò Công in the eastern delta.[28]

Quảng Huyên, *Dharma Mountain Buddhism and Martial Yoga*, temple publication (Frederick, MD: Chùa Xá Lợi, 2007).

24   Ho-Tai Hue-Tam, *Millenarianism and Peasant Politics in Vietnam*, 4, 11.

25   Nguyễn Văn Quảng and Marjorie Pivar, *Fourth Uncle in the Mountain: A Memoir of a Barefoot Doctor in Vietnam*.

26   *Esoteric Tradition of Venerable Master Buddha of Western Peace*, 1. In *Esoteric Tradition*, Đoàn Minh Huyên begins with the words "upon [the year] Nhâm." Nhâm (壬), one of the ten heavenly stems of the 60-year calendrical cycle, most likely referred to the year 1842. A decade earlier in 1832 seems too early, and by a decade later in 1852, Đoàn Minh Huyên was restricted to the Seven Mountains area well-west of Hồ Cứ. References to the zodiac in *Esoteric Tradition* also point to the year 1842 as the beginning of a chain of events (39). Moreover, oral tradition tells us that, after leaving Tòng Sơn in 1849, Huyên was averse to returning to his native islets. Even though he is said to have visited his cloister in Kiến Thạnh–Xẻo Môn for three months, he appears never to have ventured further east and largely remained in the Seven Mountains area after 1850.

27   The monk was known in Vietnamese as Sãi Kế and Lâm Sâm. Ho-Tai Hue-Tam, *Millenarianism and Peasant Politics in Vietnam*, 7.

28   Gò Công ("Peacock Hill"), which was formerly its own province, is now part of Tiền Giang Province. Nguyễn Văn Hầu, *Sấm truyền Đức Phật Thầy Tây An*, 30.

During these years early in his career, few seem to have heeded Đoàn Minh Huyên's exhortations. In the *Esoteric Tradition*, he lamented, "Pity the world of dust! —I keep teaching, but none listen" (26). Still, moved by the precipitating sufferings that he perceived, he felt compelled to speak out, "Seeing this, I feel sorry for myself. To speak of it is terrible, but to stay silent only compounds my sadness" (103). Huyên's activities for the next four years after Gò Công are unknown, but by 1849, he felt consigned to return to his home village on Tòng Sơn Islet, where he lived in relative obscurity behind the village *đình* or community hall. He drew notice only for his habit of speaking in undiscernible (esoteric?) whispers, trancelike comportment, and burning foliage for a lantern at night, which caused some alarm as a fire hazard.[29] However, Huyên would soon garner attention. The episode through which Huyên began to be taken seriously not only reveals the circumstances of his emergence as a religious leader, but it also reveals early indications of his inward-directed reflection on people's sufferings—that they were the baleful fruits of human waywardness.

Later in 1849, the "year of the Earthen Cock" mentioned in the above poem about recollecting Master Buddha, a cholera epidemic broke out in the delta, which, due to the creation of new, more urban settlements in the frontier waterscape as well as its frequent movement of peoples and products, was prone to such outbreaks.[30] In response, Đoàn Minh Huyên's villagers devised to perform a ritual that would "cast off the wind" (*tống gió*), since they believed that pestilence was caused by external demonic winds. Huyên, whom none of the villagers recognized as a village native and instead regarded as an eccentric vagabond, stood up to object, saying "If you yourself dislike the wind, then to whom will you send it off?"[31] With these words, Huyên entreated

---

29 Nguyễn Văn Hầu, *Sấm truyền Đức Phật Thầy Tây An*, 31.

30 From the seventeenth through nineteenth centuries, typhoons, trade, state rice transportation, migration, pilgrimage, mining, prostitution, war, and piracy contributed to the outbreak and spread of disease. Li Tana, "Epidemics in Late Premodern Vietnam and Their Links with Her Neighbours," conference paper presented at "Imperial China and Its Southern Neighbours," Institute of Southeast Asian Studies, Singapore, 28–29 June, 2012.

31 Nguyễn Long Thành Nam, *Phật giáo Hòa Hảo trong dòng lịch sử dân tộc* (Sante Fe Springs, CA: Tập san Đuốc Từ Bi, 1991), 112; Nguyễn Văn Hầu, *Sấm truyền Đức*

his fellow villagers to look within to see the roots of the terrible disease in their own karmic demerits rather than treat the epidemic as a bane that had befallen them from outside. Moreover, Huyên implored, passing the baleful winds off to others would only compound their misdeeds and, ultimately, their suffering. Nevertheless, the village elders would not be swayed, and they banished the vagabond. As he departed, Huyên revealed himself to his surviving kin, who had not recognized him before.[32] Huyên would never return.

Thereupon, Đoàn Minh Huyên again clutched his bamboo culm and swam along the Cái Tàu Thượng waterway around to Xẻo Môn Canal.[33] As he coursed the waterways, he encountered numerous "ghost rafts" from all the villages that performed "casting off the wind" sacrifices. The scene of drifting rafts, coffins, and corpses as well as the ghostly moans of afflicted people and cries of startled animals must have felt exceedingly eerie.[34] To Huyên, it must have seemed like he presaged seven years earlier, "The scene is severe! The scene is severe...! I now watch as suddenly in the world, endless ghosts lead themselves along—who could shelter us? Here in the morning, lost by night in a life of hardships, like a flash of lightning whose brilliance cannot endure" (37, 52–53). Huyên stayed for a time at Trà Bư Village, where he unveiled his uncanny healing powers. Although he made no such claims, rumors spread that he was a living Buddha.[35] Eventually, as his reputation grew, he traveled up Xẻo Môn Canal to where it met Tiền River. There, at the waterways' intersection at Kiến Thạnh, Huyên treated the sick, who came by boat in throngs.[36] At this river crossway, Huyên's followers would establish their first cloister.[37]

Phật Thầy Tây An, 32.

32 Nguyễn Văn Hầu, *Sấm truyền Đức Phật Thầy Tây An*, 32.

33 Vương Kim (Phạm Bá Cầm) and Đào Hưng, *Đức Phật Thầy Tây An*, 17.

34 Nguyễn Văn Hầu, *Sấm truyền Đức Phật Thầy Tây An*, 34.

35 Nguyễn Long Thành Nam, *Phật giáo Hòa Hảo trong dòng lịch sử dân tộc*, 112; Nguyễn Văn Hầu, *Sấm truyền Đức Phật Thầy Tây An*, 42. By contrast, in Hòa Hảo hagiography, Master Buddha, called "Venerable Buddha," is the first in a series of Buddha incarnations leading up to Huỳnh Phú Sổ or "Venerable Teacher."

36 Trà Bư is now in Hội An Hamlet, and Kiến Thạnh (Long Kiến) is in Long Giang Hamlet; both are part of Chợ Mới District, An Giang Province. Nguyễn Văn Hầu, *Sấm truyền Đức Phật Thầy Tây An*, 34–36.

37 After Đoàn Minh Huyên's death, the cloister was named "Old Pagoda of Western Peace" to distinguish it from Western Peace Pagoda at Sam Mountain. It was origi-

Within a year, the commotion that accompanied Đoàn Minh Huyên's healing activities (and the resulting overburdened waterways) drew the attention of Nguyễn Dynasty authorities as well. A provincial governor, who suspected the teacher's intentions, detained him in 1850. After determining the self-avowed layman was an essentially harmless, albeit eccentric "monk," the governor sent Huyên to be formerly ordained in the Lâm Tế Buddhist order at Western Peace Pagoda (Chùa Tây An).[38] Aside from evoking the blissful western realm of Amitābha Buddha,[39] the name of the temple, "Western Peace" (Tây An, 西安), conveyed settlers' recent pacification of a multiethnic frontier as the pagoda, which was built just three years earlier in 1847, lay at the foot of Sam Mountain in the Seven Mountains region at the western fringe of Vietnamese dynastic authority.[40] Once relocated in the loosely controlled periphery, Đoàn Minh Huyên was left relatively free to heal, teach, and even leave the pagoda as he wished.[41] In keeping with the faintest echoes of *dharma* that Huyên believed the "shallowed world" could still recall of Buddhism's receding teachings, Huyên taught a minimalist practice, the so-called Intangible Way or *đạo vô vi* (道無爲). He instructed his followers to perform observances before a blank red cloth (*trần điều*) in lieu of votive images and make

---

nally the makeshift hermitage of a certain Adept (Đạo) Kiến.

38 Ho-Tai Hue-Tam, *Millenarianism and Peasant Politics in Vietnam*, 11. Ostensibly, Đoàn Minh Huyên thus became a "disciple" of the temple's abbot, Nguyễn Nhứt Thừa. Nguyễn Long Thành Nam, *Phật giáo Hòa Hảo trong dòng lịch sử dân tộc*, 115.

39 In its Buddhist context, Tây An (西安) or "Western Peace" is an abbreviation of *Tây Phương An Lạc Tịnh Thổ* (西方安樂淨土) or "Western Blissful Pure Land" of Amitābha Buddha. *An lạc* (安樂) was one of the Sinographic translations of *sukha* or "bliss" in *Sukhāvatī*, the Sanskrit name of Amitābha's Pure Land.

40 Quốc sử quán triều Nguyễn, *Đại Nam nhất thống chí*, vol. 5, 226. Although employed (and often conscripted) by the Vietnamese Nguyễn state, these settlers included peoples of Chinese, Khmer, Cham, and Malay ethnicities in addition to Vietnamese. Vũ Đức Liêm, "Rama III, Minh Mạng and Power Paradigm in Early Nineteenth Century Mekong Valley," *Rian Thai: International Journal of Thai Studies* 5 (2012) 308–309; "Vietnam at the Khmer Frontier: Boundary Politics, 1802–1847," *Cross-Currents: East Asian History and Culture Review* 5, no. 2 (2016): 550; Nicolas Weber, "Securing and Developing the Southwestern Region: The Role of the Cham and Malay Colonies in Vietnam (18th–19th Centuries)," *Journal of the Economic and Social History of the Orient* 54, no. 5 (2011): 739–72.

41 Ho-Tai Hue-Tam, *Millenarianism and Peasant Politics in Vietnam*, 12.

offerings of water, incense, and flowers. To demarcate votive spaces, he practiced geomancy by merely having his followers plant five solid-colored tantric flags for the Buddhas of the five directions.[42] His healing art, too, was remarkably simple. He prescribed talismanic rainwater—sometimes mixed with the ash of paper or cloth prayers—and moral rectification.[43] Finally, for the transmission of the *dharma*, he vernacularized his teachings into *sấm* or orally transmitted esoteric verses, thus doing away with physical *sūtra*.[44]

Within a year, the "layman of Western Peace" as Đoàn Minh Huyên referred to himself,[45] had conveyed his message to numerous followers, twelve of whom he seems to have chosen to establish "fields" (*trại ruộng*) as religious farming communities. These lay and clerical adepts, who called themselves "people of the way" (*đạo*), set up agrarian camps throughout the delta. Most reclaimed land in the frontier jungles of the Seven Mountains area, but others spread as far east as Biên Hòa and west as the lands of present-day Cambodia.[46]

Since Đoàn Minh Huyên's practices were so artless and bare, and his prophetic message was so diffuse, the array of "fields" that sprouted

---

42 The flags or banners were called *thẻ năm ông*. The creation of *mandala* with five Buddhas for each direction (cardinal directions and center) suggests Tantric Vajrayāna influence, but the color scheme shows that they were influenced by Sinographic convention (and, perhaps, "Daoism") as well.

43 Ho-Tai Hue-Tam, *Millenarianism and Peasant Politics in Vietnam*, 37; Nguyễn Long Thành Nam, *Phật giáo Hòa Hảo trong dòng lịch sử dân tộc*, 112–113; Nguyễn Văn Hầu, *Sấm truyền Đức Phật Thầy Tây An*, 49; Vương Kim (Phạm Bá Cầm) and Đào Hưng, *Đức Phật Thầy Tây An*, 23.

44 Ho-Tai Hue-Tam, *Millenarianism and Peasant Politics in Vietnam*, 24; Vương Kim (Phạm Bá Cầm) and Đào Hưng, *Đức Phật Thầy Tây An*, 19.

45 Nguyễn Văn Hầu, *Sấm truyền Đức Phật Thầy Tây An*, 79.

46 Ibid., 43–46; Recluse (Trần Văn Nhựt) and Nguyễn Văn Hầu, *Thất Sơn mầu nhiệm*, 113–164. Although much is said of Master Buddha's twelve disciples in oral literature and Hòa Hảo hagiography, there is no uniform list of their identities. Nguyễn Long Thành Nam suggests: Trần Văn Thành (d. 1873), "Monk Bùi" (d. 1907), Bùi Văn Tây (1802–90), Nguyễn Văn Xuyến (1834–1914), Đặng Văn Ngoạn (1820–90), Phạm Thái Chung (d. 1877), "Adept (Đạo) Lãnh" (?–1856?), Trần Văn Nhu (1847–1914), Nguyễn Văn Thới (1866–1927), "Adept (Đạo) Sang," "Adept (Đạo) Thạch," and "Adept (Đạo) Lãnh of Gò Sát." Nguyễn Long Thành Nam, *Phật giáo Hòa Hảo trong dòng lịch sử dân tộc*, 123–4. That some of these adepts postdate Master Buddha shows that "disciple" (*đệ tử*) in the hagiographies was used quite loosely to connect an otherwise fragmentary and decentralized layout of "fields."

up throughout the delta was fragmentary and decentralized.[47] In addition, the challenges of communication and travel in the delta isolated the "fields," which were already by conception meant to be cloistered from the outside world. Hence, adepts' ideas and teachings varied greatly from place to place. In fact, most adepts met Huyên only briefly and received little training from him. For the most part, they just adopted his prophetic message and, perhaps, took refuge in him as a "living Buddha." Meanwhile, others could associate themselves with Huyên simply to yoke his charisma and perceived powers.

Therefore, Đoàn Minh Huyên's contribution to the movement(s) that he set in motion was to inspire religiously inclined adepts at a moment of crisis, particularly the cholera epidemic, rather than to train or indoctrinate them. Indeed, there was nothing new about Huyên's teachings. He did not so much invent, explain, or systematize the Dragon Flower prophecy as much as he gave it voice through the magic of his uncanny personality and spiritual prowess. As a result, each cloister that extended from his influence tended to reinvent Master Buddha's message with divergent thoughts and practices.

Initially, Đoàn Minh Huyên's message was peaceful, evasive, and inclusive, attracting a wide range of delta peoples, including Vietnamese, Khmer, Chinese, and, perhaps, even Cham and Malays. However, after the French seized control of the delta from 1859 to 1867, some of Master Buddha's "disciples" turned towards militancy and ethnic tribalism. For example, Trần Văn Thành (?–1873) claimed to succeed Master Buddha by producing a seal that was used to print talismans bearing the Sinographs "Bửu Sơn Kỳ Hương" (寶山奇香).[48] These talismans were probably borrowed from secret societies' initiation rituals and facilitated the organization of Thành's anti-colonial forces until his death in 1873.[49] Because of Thành's activities, the French associated the phrase "Bửu Sơn Kỳ Hương" and its epony-

---

47   Ho-Tai Hue-Tam, *Millenarianism and Peasant Politics in Vietnam*, 18, 33.
48   Several esoteric litanies are dedicated to elevating Trần Văn Thành as Đoàn Minh Huyên's successor. Nguyễn Hữu Hiệp, *Nhứt sư nhứt đệ tử* (Hà Nội: NXB Văn hóa Dân tộc, 2010), 191–210.
49   On the links between the Sinographs "Bửu Sơn Kỳ Hương" and the secret societies, see Đỗ Thiện, *Vietnamese Supernaturalism: Views from the Southern Region*, 196. For ideological similarities with the secret societies, see Ho-Tai Hue-Tam, *Millenarianism and Peasant Politics in Vietnam*, 31–33.

mous anti-colonial poem with Master Buddha, thereby providing the nomenclature by which Huyên's "sect" is known today.[50]

While some adepts adopted Đoàn Minh Huyên's prophetic message in opposition to colonial power, their movements remained ethnically inclusive and diverse throughout the nineteenth century. For example, Trần Văn Thành studied embodied talismanic techniques (*V. bùa gồng*) from the Khmer, enlisted them in his army, and made a Khmer his highest-ranking subordinate.[51] Later on, another Khmer known as "Chief Buddha," after apparently reviving from death, was said to become a living Buddha akin to Master Buddha.[52] Aside from these Khmer adepts, Ngô Lợi (1831–90), who also gained notoriety as an anti-colonial "living Buddha" with the title "Patriarch Master," was probably ethnically Hoa ("Chinese").[53] Although evidence about the degree to which Cham and Malays may have participated in such movements is scarce, cultural borrowings of Islamic forms of practice by traditions associated with Master Buddha suggest that Cham and Malays interacted with these traditions significantly, perhaps even as participants.[54]

---

50   It is clear from the Bửu Sơn Kỳ Hương poem that Đoàn Minh Huyên was not its author. The poem speaks of the rebirth of Emperor Minh Mạng (1791–1841), the military leadership of (a reincarnated?) Trạng Trình (Nguyễn Bỉnh Khiêm 1491–1586), and the restoration of "Việt Nam." However, Huyên died in 1856, before the French seized control of the delta. The cabalistic poem is described in Nguyễn Văn Hầu, *Nhận thức Phật giáo Hòa Hảo* (Hà Nội, NXB Tôn Giáo, 1968, 2017), 15–16.

51   Ho-Tai Hue-Tam, *Millenarianism and Peasant Politics in Vietnam*, 15.

52   *Phật Trùm* (?–1875) or "Chief Buddha," whose real name is unknown, hailed from Bokor (Tà Lơn) Mountain in modern Cambodia. He was known during his lifetime as Candle Adept (*Đạo Đèn*), because his thaumaturgical practices involved candles. He was later arrested and exiled by the French. Recluse (Trần Văn Nhựt) and Nguyễn Văn Hầu, *Thất Sơn mầu nhiệm*, 89–95.

53   "Patriarch Master" or *bổn sư* 本師 is a title of Śākyamuni Buddha and implies that Ngô Lợi was Maitreya, the initiator of a new *dharma* dispensation. He is said to have achieved enlightenment in 1870. The son of a carpenter, Ngô Lợi's ethnic origins are uncertain. However, his prolific writing in literary Sinitic suggests that he may have been Hoa or at least drew a congregation of Hoa followers. Đinh Văn Hạnh, *Đạo Tứ Ân Hiếu Nghĩa của người Việt Nam bộ, 1867–1975* (Tp. Hồ Chí Minh: NXB Trẻ, 1999), 58–68; Trần Văn Quế, *Tứ Ân Hiếu Nghĩa* (Sài Gòn: Tủ sách sưu khảo sử liệu Phật giáo Bửu Sơn Kỳ Hương, 1971), 15–18.

54   These cultural forms include worship spaces constructed like minarets, Hòa Hảo "reading and lecture halls" (*tòa đọc giảng*), and votive vermillion cloth (*trần điều*).

However, early in the twentieth century, some adepts who associated themselves with Master Buddha's teachings began to assume more nationalistic attitudes. In *circa* 1901–1902, a transvestite monk-nun and self-described madman/madwoman, who boated along the Vĩnh Tế Canal between Cambodia and southern Vietnam, linked the grievances that anticipate the Dragon Flower Assembly with the deposition of Emperor Hàm Nghi (r. 1884–5) and the conversion of delta peoples to the ways of the "heretical west" (*tà tây*).[55] Although he/she advocated absconding to the Seven Mountains like Đoàn Minh Huyên and never turned to violence, his/her rhetoric wed the Dragon Flower prophecy to the degraded Vietnamese monarchy and framed the destruction of the Buddhist religion as an affront by outside invaders. In other words, his/her exhortations could be skewed to rationalize a "just war" that would rescue Buddhism and the Vietnamese state from annihilation. Indeed, in 1913, a youth, who claimed to be a descendent of Emperor Hàm Nghi and a living Buddha, was caught in Saigon, the capital of French Cochinchina, plotting an attack armed with bombs and "Bửu Sơn Kỳ Hương" amulets after having trained in the Seven Mountains.[56]

Another adept who took after the mad monk-nun was Venerable Huỳnh Phú Sổ (1919–47?), founder of the profoundly consequential Sect of Hòa Hảo Village.[57] Ven. Huỳnh's major philosophical contribution to the body of thought that accrued around remembrances of Master Buddha and his teachings was to render the endemic tradition more cosmopolitan and conversant with intellectual circles, mainstream Buddhism, and secular politics. Moreover, in stark contrast to Đoàn Minh Huyên, he countenanced violence and wove a doctrine of social activism into the prophetic teachings of his predecessors.

Most striking was Ven. Huỳnh's reinterpretation of the teachings associated with Master Buddha and the Dragon Flower prophecy to ally with Imperial Japan's wartime ideology of "Zen at War."[58] Namely,

---

Đỗ Thiện, *Vietnamese Supernaturalism: Views from the Southern Region*, 196.
55   Sư vãi bán khoai, *Sấm giảng người đời* (Sài Gòn: Sen Vàng, 1949), 6, 36, 70.
56   Ho-Tai Hue-Tam, *Millenarianism and Peasant Politics in Vietnam*, 69–70.
57   Ibid., 119.
58   For the role of Zen traditions in Imperial Japan see Brian (Daizen) A. Victoria, *Zen at War* (New York: Weatherhill, 1997).

Ven. Huỳnh incorporated the Sixth Patriarch of the Meditation (Zen) Sect into his esoteric litanies, thereby highlighting the purportedly peasant and "Viet" origins of the Six Patriarch while situating his sect within the sphere of an internationalized Zen tradition.[59] Under Japanese aegis in the 1940s,[60] Huỳnh's (and especially his epigones') sectarian teachings not only became consonant with Zen's fascist iterations, they also found tangible expression as his sect developed its own militias, which, even after the Japanese surrender, retained their arms for the next decade.[61] Moreover, the epigones of Ven. Huỳnh crafted hagiographies of former adepts and "living Buddhas" that promoted distinctly "Vietnamese" nationalistic sentiments.[62]

But Đoàn Minh Huyên did not live to see any of this, as he passed away nearly a century before. According to a stele at his burial site, he died at noon on September 10, 1856.[63] In keeping with his "Intangible Way," before his death he forbade his followers to form a burial mound for his remains, although they did demarcate the place of his inhumation by erecting a low wall around it.[64] Because Western Peace

---

59 Đức Huỳnh giáo chủ (Huỳnh Phú Sổ), *Sấm giảng thi văn toàn bộ* (S.l.: Giáo hội Phật giáo Hòa Hảo, Ban Phổ thông giáo lý trung ương, 1966), 61, 99. The idea that the Six Patriarch Huineng was "Vietnamese" is a fringe theory based on the amorphous meaning of the Sinograph 粵, which can have widely divergent meanings depending on temporal and spatial context. See Thích Mãn Giác, *Was Hui-Neng Vietnamese?* (Los Angeles: CA: Vietnamese Buddhist Temple, L.A., 1990). For the meanings of "Viet" (粵/越) through history see Erica Brindley, *Ancient China and the Yue: Perceptions and Identities on the Southern Frontier, c. 400 BCE–50 CE* (Cambridge: Cambridge University Press, 2015).

60 Although Ven. Huỳnh Phú Sổ accepted Japanese entreaties, he was not necessarily pro-Japanese. He was primarily concerned with his sect's role in fostering a budding sense of anti-colonial nationalism. In fact, from early on he prophesized Japan's ultimate defeat. Francis R. Hill, "Millenarian Machines in South Vietnam," *Comparative Studies in Society and History*, 13, no. 3 (July 1971), 336.

61 Jessica M. Chapman, *Cauldron of Resistance: Ngo Dinh Diem, the United States, and 1950s Southern Vietnam* (Ithaca: Cornell University Press, 2013), 13–39; Ho-Tai Hue-Tam, *Millenarianism and Peasant Politics in Vietnam*, 124–136, 165.

62 Aside from legends about numerous anti-colonial freedom fighters, perhaps the most striking example of Hòa Hảo hagiographies' nationalistic character is the claim that *Phật Trùm*, the Khmer "Chief Buddha," essentially became Vietnamese after his resurrection and enlightenment. See Recluse (Trần Văn Nhựt) and Nguyễn Văn Hầu, *Thất Sơn mầu nhiệm*, 89.

63 That is, in the language of the stele, the *ngọ* hour on the 12th day of the 8th month of the Fire-Dragon (Bính Thìn) year.

64 Nguyễn Văn Hầu, *Sấm truyền Đức Phật Thầy Tây An*, 85–86.

Pagoda was the place where he was formally ordained, lived the later part of his life, and entrusted his remains, Huyên thereafter became known as the "Master Buddha of Western Peace," a name that both reflected the impact of his life for peoples at the Vietnamese frontier and evoked his bearing as a living Buddha akin to Amitābha, the Buddha in the west. Today, well over a million people in Vietnam and around the world follow Buddhist teachings that they trace back to Master Buddha. Many of them affiliate themselves with the large sects that enjoy official sanction under Vietnam's communist regime, namely Hòa Hảo, Tứ Ân Hiếu Nghĩa, and Bửu Sơn Kỳ Hương.[65] Meanwhile, many others participate in unregistered smaller lineages that also claim descent from Master Buddha. Overwhelmingly, these adepts' practices agree with Huyên's peaceful message, cultivating goodness according to the "Intangible Way" as the shallowed *dharma* fades into the offing of time.[66]

A Teaching

Đoàn Minh Huyên did not discuss his teachings discursively or embellish them with commentary, but rather dissipated them in "shallowed" form. The *dharma* sediment that filtered through

---

65 According to Vietnam's 2019 census, followers of Hòa Hảo account for about one percent of Vietnam's population or 96,200,000 people. The numbers of people who identify with Tứ Ân Hiếu Nghĩa (Four Debts of Gratitude, Filial Piety, and Righteousness) and Bửu Sơn Kỳ Hương (Marvelous Incense on the Mountain of the Jewels) were not revealed by the census, but they appear to be less than those for Hòa Hảo. General Statistics Office of Vietnam, "Phụ lục 3: Danh mục tôn giáo," in *Tổng điều tra dân số 01/04/2019*, online document, http://tongdieutradanso. vn/ket-qua-tong-dieu-tra-dan-so-va-nha-o-thoi-diem-0-gio-ngay-01-thang-4-nam-2019.html. The official religions Tịnh Độ Cư Sỹ (Pure Land Laypeople), Phật Đường Nam Tông Minh Sư Đạo (Way of the Enlightened Masters of the Buddha Hall Southern Sect), and Hiếu Nghĩa Tà Lơn (Bokor Mt. Filial Piety and Righteousness) may arguably be counted among sects associated with Master Buddha's teachings, but I exclude them since these connections are rather tenuous and, moreover, the sects themselves do not attribute their origins to Master Buddha.

66 Phạm Bích Hợp performed sociological surveys in 2007 that demonstrated ongoing belief in Master Buddha's core tenets like the Dragon Flower prophecy, aniconic worship, lay-orientation, and philanthropy well into the twenty-first century. Phạm Bích Hợp, *Người Nam bộ và tôn giáo bản địa* (Hanoi: NXB Tôn giáo, 2007), 315–361.

Huyên's decanting hermeneutic were ill-defined, provisional, and fluid.[67] Nevertheless, some characteristics of Huyên's teachings can be described. Three of these that found expression in lived practice are presented below: The Intangible Way, Four Debts of Gratitude, and Recollection of Buddha.

The Intangible Way—Đạo Vô Vi (道無爲)

Đoàn Minh Huyên expounded the Dragon Flower prophecy as the overarching conceptual canopy that sheltered a wide spectrum of divergent self-cultivation practices as well as their attendant this-worldly and supernatural abilities, thus accommodating an amorphous body of teachings that could follow along the fluid ethnic, geographic, and religious contours of the delta. But his was no doctrine of synthesis or hybridity, for the substance of Huyên's conceptual canopy was too diaphanous and airy. By embracing the prophecy, Huyên articulated a rarefication of *dharma* so extreme as to be virtually indistinct. During *dharma's* twilight, all that remained of Buddhism, Huyên taught, was *đạo vô vi*—the Intangible Way.

In this sense, Đoàn Minh Huyên's teachings agreed with preexisting, widely held Buddhist eschatological thought. According to *sūtra* and Buddhist tradition about *dharma's* cyclical degeneration and renewal, a Buddha's dispensation declines over three conceptual periods—true *dharma*, semblance *dharma*, and ending *dharma*—after which the next Buddha achieves enlightenment and begins a new dispensation.[68] As time passes and successive generations become further removed from the Buddha, *dharma* fades until it ultimately vanishes. Humankind's memory is tenuous, and, eventually, come the time of the "ending *dharma*" (V. *mạt pháp*, 末法), even the name of "Buddha" is forgotten. At that time, whatever specious recollec-

---

67   By contrast, Ngô Lợi (a.k.a. Đức Bổn Sư or "Venerable Patriarch Master") composed an astonishing twenty-four "*sūtra*" (*kinh*) in literary Sinitic that arranged the Dragon Flower prophecy and various aspects of Buddhist, Daoist, and Tantric thought into an elaborate synthesis. His epigones rendered many of these "*sūtra*" into vernacular forms. Đinh Văn Hạnh, *Đạo Tứ Ân Hiếu Nghĩa của người Việt Nam bộ, 1867–1975*, 78–85.

68   Jan Nattier, *Once upon a Future Time: Studies in a Buddhist Prophecy of Decline*, 90–118.

tion of Buddha, his teachings, and his body of devotees still lingers is obscure and confused. Concomitantly, distinctions between Buddha and demon, piety and sacrilege, enlightenment and insanity, devotee and heretic all disappear. The world spins vertiginously, drifting unmoored. This, Huyên described, saying, "Revolutions of time spin the mundane world of dust... Turning people, turning things, turning years, turning days..." (11, 161). Thus, in the twilight of Buddha's enlightenment, a confused world turns with uncertain trajectory through a transformation that denies absolutes, intractably unknowable and without bearing.

Đoàn Minh Huyên's articulation of the decline of *dharma* was precedented in Vietnamese Buddhism in 1740 with a ceremony performed before a "Dragon Flower platform" erected at Huế by Thích Liễu Quán (1667–1742), whom a eulogy inscribed six years after his death described as "a precious rarity" during the "*dharma's* withering."[69] However, whereas Liễu Quán's ceremony was intended to revive Buddhism in Vietnam by bestowing Buddhist precepts, which were grafted to Vietnam from the Chinese north, en masse, Huyên's evocation of the Dragon Flower prophecy dissolved them. Since Huyên believed that only the faintest echo remained of authentic *dharma* and its precepts, he was incredulous of their genuine forms. For him, the notion of "true" precepts was an intangible memory. Although Huyên acknowledged that following precepts was desirable, he felt that their practice was too tenuous to credit or prescribe. Therefore, he deemed himself a layman and taught his followers lay-oriented Buddhist devotion, as Huyên conveyed, "My lot is that of a devout layman, a teacher who teaches people to do good and cultivate" (96). Moreover, Huyên was too suspicious of expressing genuine *dharma* even to consider himself "Buddhist." Instead, he and his followers called their teachings "the good way" (*đạo lành*) and referred to themselves simply as "peo-

---

69   The 1748 stele said of Thích Liễu Quán, "Today, with our generation's teachings and withered *dharma*, none are able to perform the great task [of expounding authentic *dharma*], so [to have had] a monk like Liễu Quán is truly a precious rarity" (當今之世教衰法未能爲大事者故有如了觀和尚者實希矣). Trần Trung Hậu and Thích Hải Ấn, *Chư tôn Thiền Đức Cư sĩ hữu công Phật Giáo Thuận Hóa* (TpHCM: NXB Tổng Hợp TP. HCM, 2011), vol. 1, 121.

ple of the Way" (*người đạo*), a name that has sometimes led to their mischaracterization as Daoist.[70]

In his adaptation of Buddhist practices to lay contexts, Đoàn Minh Huyên bore similarities with members of Chinese lay Buddhist associations.[71] At the same time, he reflected parallel developments among some Buddhist traditions elsewhere in mainland Southeast Asia. For instance, Huyên's telling of the Dragon Flower prophecy was probably colored by its Khmer iterations.[72] In addition, Huyên's self-characterization as a lay devotee resembles the appearance of Burmese thaumaturges and Thai spirit-mediums, whose affiliation with Buddhism is ambiguous, but appeared especially at times when *dharma* was thought to be in decline.[73] As a lived tradition, Đoàn Minh Huyên's Intangible Way found expression through an iconic devotional practice. Since he believed that genuine forms of worship could no longer be determined, he taught his followers to do without traditional Buddhist paraphernalia, images and spaces—an aniconism that may have been inspired by Islamic practices associated with Cham and Malay communities.[74] Instead of worship at a temple with monks before an altar populated with votive statues and images, Huyên and his followers moved devotional practice into ordinary spaces, including the home. For observances, they simply offered water and incense before a vermillion cloth.

Another way Đoàn Minh Huyên practiced the Intangible Way was by vernacularizing Buddhist teachings. Although Huyên did support *sutra* recitation (142), he felt that the traditional Sinographic *sutra*, too, were suspect. Therefore, following the course of the *dharma's* receding, Huyên translated his teachings into intangible oracular

---

70   E.g., Đỗ Thiện's fifth chapter "Daoists from the Mountain" in his otherwise excellent *Vietnamese Supernaturalism: Views from the Southern Region*, 165–206.

71   Ho-Tai Hue-Tam, *Millenarianism and Peasant Politics in Vietnam*, 31–32.

72   Đỗ Thiện, *Vietnamese Supernaturalism: Views from the Southern Region*, 191; Philip Taylor, *The Khmer Lands of Vietnam: Environment, Cosmology, and Sovereignty* (Singapore: NUS Press and NIAS Press, Asian Studies Association of Australia, 2014), 1, 27–30.

73   Pattana Kitiarsa, *Mediums, Monks, and Amulets: Thai Popular Buddhism Today* (Chiang Mai: Silkworm Books, 2012), 16–18; Thomas Nathan Patton, *The Buddha's Wizards: Magic, Protection, and Healing in Burmese Buddhism* (New York: Columbia University Press, 2018), 12–37.

74   Đỗ Thiện, *Vietnamese Supernaturalism: Views from the Southern Region*, 196.

forms, effectively erasing the last "dregs of *dharma*" found in material texts. In addition, Huyên gave the symbolic transmission of his teachings new vernacular meaning by recreating the already immaterial bestowal of the "mind-seal" (*tâm ấn*, 心印) from teacher to disciple into the "bowels of the sect" (*lòng phái*), which consisted of cabalistic prayers intended to inscribe not just the mind of devotees, but also their physical, geomantic, and spirit-filled landscape.[75]

Finally, Đoàn Minh Huyên embodied the Intangible Way through eccentricity. Because of the intractable indeterminacy of true *dharma*, for Huyên the line between saintliness and insanity blurred. Instead of claiming authenticity as a teacher, Huyên embraced a maddening deferral of meaning that denied ultimate truth. His comportment was thus that of unmoored craziness "mobile, fluid, resilient—like reflections and shadows off the river waves."[76] Therefore, in defiance of traditional expectations, Huyên and several of his followers took to wandering, life at the margins, extreme frugality, and unconventional behavior.

Four Debts of Gratitude—Tứ Ân (四恩)

Although Đoàn Minh Huyên purportedly demonstrated his familiarity with *sūtra* literature to his detractors, he appears to have culled his teachings without recourse to material texts.[77] Indeed, the only source he referenced in *Esoteric Tradition* is an unidentified "good woman" (15). His ideas' indebtedness to scriptural study may be unclear, but aspects of his teaching certainly have canonical precedents. Specifically, concepts from the *Sūtra on the Contemplation of the Abode of Innate Heart-Mind*, namely the Four Debts of Gratitude (V. *tứ ân*, 四恩) and Four Wisdoms (V. *tứ trí*, 四智), appear in Huyên's *Esoteric Tradition*.[78] Whereas the Four Contemplations presumably

---

75   Ibid., 197.

76   Ibid., 204.

77   Ho-Tai Hue-Tam, *Millenarianism and Peasant Politics in Vietnam*, 11, 23; Nguyễn Văn Hầu, *Sấm truyền Đức Phật Thầy Tây An*, 49.

78   *Sūtra on the Contemplation of the Abode of Innate Heart-Mind* (V. *Bổn sanh tâm địa quán kinh*, 本生心地觀經) was purportedly translated into Sinographs in eight fascicles in Tang China in 740. (T.159.3.291–331).

applied to meditation practice (182), the Four Debts of Gratitude spoke to moral cultivation (88). In lived practice, the former emerged as the guiding tenets of Huyên's moral philosophy.[79] They were debts of gratitude to (1) father and mother, (2) the lands and waters, (3) Threefold Jewels, and (4) humankind.[80]

Đoàn Minh Huyên's Intangible Way prescribed an elemental life at the remote periphery, the starkness of which one of his disciples described as "treading here and there in grass sandals beneath the vast skies, donning tattered lotus robes amidst extensive mountains and rivers."[81] Despite Huyên's minimalist way of life, once agrarian communities began to form around his teachings, he needed to provide them unifying guidance. He accomplished this with the Four Debts of Gratitude.

Aside from identifying the family as the core social unit in the "fields," the first debt of gratitude to one's father and mother (*ơn cha mẹ*) addressed the question of continuity through the dispersion of Đoàn Minh Huyên's teachings without the benefit of institutional structures. Specifically, it established lineage as a model of transmission by making a child's filial duty to his parents the foremost moral imperative. This inviolable child-parent bond and concomitant sense of ancestry mirrored the teacher-disciple lineages that ramified from Master Buddha. Meanwhile, the second debt to the lands and waters (*ơn đất nước*) spoke to elemental life in the Seven

---

79 Much of the emphasis placed on the Four Debts of Gratitude in practice today among traditions that ramified from Đoàn Minh Huyên's teachings probably owes itself to Ngô Lợi's (a.k.a. Patriarch Buddha) systemization of teachings under the umbrella of the Dragon Flower prophecy according to the formula "study Buddha and cultivate humaneness" (*học Phật tu nhân*, 學佛修仁), which has generally been interpreted as a synthesis of Buddhist and Confucian moral principles. See Đinh Văn Hạnh, *Đạo Tứ Ân Hiếu Nghĩa của người Việt Nam bộ, 1867–1975*, 85–98.

80 This discussion of the Four Debts of Gratitude is indebted to Đinh Văn Hạnh, *Đạo Tứ Ân Hiếu Nghĩa của người Việt Nam bộ, 1867–1975*, 85–89; Đỗ Thiện, *Vietnamese Supernaturalism: Views from the Southern Region*, 193–195; Ho-Tai Hue-Tam, *Millenarianism and Peasant Politics in Vietnam*, 25; Nguyễn Văn Hầu, *Nhận thức Phật giáo Hòa Hảo*, 96–102; Recluse (Trần Văn Nhựt) and Nguyễn Văn Hầu, *Thất Sơn mầu nhiệm* 77–82; Trần Văn Quế, *Tứ Ân Hiếu Nghĩa*, 31–33; Vương Kim (Phạm Bá Cẩm), *Bửu Sơn Kỳ Hương* (Sài Gòn: BXB Long Hoa, 1966), 127–131; Vương Kim (Phạm Bá Cẩm) and Đào Hưng, *Đức Phật Thầy Tây An*, 83–92.

81 *Giày cỏ đến lui trời đất rộng; áo sen xài xạc núi sông dài.* Nguyễn Văn Hầu, *Sấm truyền Đức Phật Thầy Tây An*, 45.

Mountains. In the frontier, Huyên's followers took to transforming the sacred wilds, and so they beheld their natural surroundings and nature spirits with awe. Even today, some traditions in the Seven Mountains continue to venerate their natural landscape and its spirits by depicting nature images on the *trần điều*, the votive vermillion cloth. Embodied practices, too, reflected belief in the spirits of the land.[82] Thus, gratitude towards the lands and waters intimately bonded Huyên's followers with the liminal frontier at the "horizons of imagination."[83]

At the same time, indebtedness to the lands and waters implied gratitude to their dynastic as well as agrarian custodians.[84] Indeed, in *Esoteric Tradition*, Đoàn Minh Huyên mentions trustworthiness between subject and ruler (68, 75, 90). Generations later, some of Huyên's epigones took the second debt of gratitude to patriotic extremes, sometimes prefixed with modern neologisms like "fatherland." However, Huyên and most of his followers adopted an attitude of avoidance by cloistering in peripheral spaces rather than take political action.[85] Huyên was uninterested in statecraft; instead, he conveyed the eschatology of kingship. Like everything else about his teachings, Huyên understood the royal undertones of his teachings according to the Intangible Way. Specifically, during the *dharma's* receding, the symbiotic relationship between (often kingly) lay patrons and Buddhist monastics that marked so much of Buddhist history dissolved, effectively collapsing secular and religious spheres.[86] Hence, in place of a dynastic emperor, in *Esoteric Tradi-*

---

82   Jason Hoai Tran, "*Thần quyền*: An Introduction to Spirit Forms of Thất Sơn Vietnamese Martial Arts," *Journal of Asian Martial Arts* 13, no. 2 (2004): 70–71.

83   "Horizons of imagination" is my adaptation of Đỗ Thiện's "imagined horizon" in *Vietnamese Supernaturalism: Views from the Southern Region*, 177–8.

84   Ibid., 189–206.

85   Ibid., 189.

86   This collapsing of the ultimate secular and religious authorities through the Maitreya prophecy has a long history in Vietnamese Buddhism that can be traced at least to the fourteenth century, when stories were recorded about the Buddhist thaumaturge Từ Đạo Hạnh's (徐道行, 1072–1116) reincarnations as a Vietnamese king on earth and then as the *bodhisattva* who will become Maitreya in the Tuṣita Heaven. Nguyễn Tự Cường, *Zen in Medieval Vietnam: A Study and Translation of the* Thiền Uyển Tập Anh (Honolulu: University of Hawai'i Press, 1997), 180–1.

tion, Huyên's ruler is the so-called Lord of Enlightenment; that is Maitreya Buddha (200).[87]

As Đoàn Minh Huyên's presentation of the debt of gratitude to the lands and waters suggests, more than anything else Huyên's Four Debts of Gratitude carried soteriological meaning. This is even more evident in the last two debts of gratitude to the Threefold Jewels and humanity. With the former, Huyên beckoned his followers to take refuge in "Buddhism" as embodied in the threefold bodies of the religion: Buddha (V. *Phật*, 佛), his teachings (V. *pháp*, 佛; S. *dharma*), and their human vessels (V. *tang*, 僧; S. *sangha*). Nevertheless, his were attenuated Threefold Jewels, since, as discussed above, each was radically "shallowed" following the Intangible Way. As for the last debt of gratitude to humanity, Đoàn Minh Huyên taught universal compassion and altruism to his followers. Practicing these virtues entailed morality, reparation of character, and renunciation of wickedness, a message that likely resonated with Huyên's followers, many of whom were marginalize peoples, including criminals, vagabonds, outcasts, and defrocked monks.[88]

Taken as a whole, perhaps the most important aspect of Đoàn Minh Huyên's Four Debts of Gratitude was the idea of recollection and return imbedded in the language of indebtedness. Gratitude exists only as a product from a previous time, and so Huyên's emphasis on gratitude beckoned his followers to return to the past. This soteriological journey of return through memory constituted the essence of Huyên's teachings, to which we now turn.

---

87   Ho-Tai Hue-Tam, *Millenarianism and Peasant Politics in Vietnam*, 29. Some later traditions seem to have associated the "Lord of Enlightenment" with a reincarnation of Emperor Minh Mạng (1791–1841). See note on the Bửu Sơn Kỳ Hương poem above.

88   Ibid., 6–7, 23. That the intimate relationship between errant and fringe persons and religious specialists associated with Đoàn Minh Huyên's teachings perpetuated up through the twentieth is evidenced by contemporary anecdotal accounts. E.g., see the individual referred to as "Tiger" in Nguyễn Văn Quảng and Marjorie Pivar, *Fourth Uncle in the Mountain: A Memoir of a Barefoot Doctor in Vietnam*, 100–106, 309–313.

Recollection of Buddha—Niệm Phật (念佛)

Sunlit is the scene, shadowy the homeland;
  Shouldering blessings, one returns to the sights of old.
Possessing the karmic affinity, spirits and saints escort you,
  Because of your good recollection morning and night, time after time.
(196–197)

With these words in *Esoteric Tradition*, Đoàn Minh Huyên spoke of what must be considered the foremost practice of his teachings, *niệm Phật* or "Recollection of Buddha." Huyên felt that the potency of this practice was such that "with one utterance of correct recollection one is at peace" (8). Here, Huyên referred to the six-syllable incantation *Nam Mô A Di Đà Phật* ("refuge in Amitabha Buddha") associated with Pure Land Buddhism. At the same time, as the above quotation reveals, for Huyên "correct recollection" entailed a visionary journey. Thus, in Huyên's teachings, *niệm Phật* was as much about meditation and visualization as it was about vocal recitation of the mantra.

The movement of Đoàn Minh Huyên's visionary journey coursed through time and space. By recalling Buddha through recitation, practitioners summoned Buddha to the present. Simultaneously, by conjuring a memory they themselves journeyed back to the "fountainhead" of Buddhist time, Buddha's original disposition of pristine *dharma* likened in the excerpt above as the "homeland" among "sights of old." In this language of return through recollection, Huyên's teachings resemble those that have been practiced among Buddhists elsewhere in Southeast Asia to this day.[89]

At the same time, Đoàn Minh Huyên's visionary transformation through recollection evoked Māhayāna teachings about the relativity and non-duality of Amitābha's Pure Land "beyond-over-there" and Śākyamuni's seemingly defiled world in the here-and-now that are found in scriptures like the lay-oriented *Sūtra Spoken by Vimalakīrti*.[90] Huyên alluded to these teachings to add spatial depth to the temporal

---

89   Julia Cassaniti, *Remembering the Present: Mindfulness in Buddhist Asia* (Ithaca, New York: Cornell University Press, 2018), 27–28, 32–33.

90   *Duy Ma Cát sở thuyết kinh* 維摩詰所說經 (S. *Vimalakīrti nirdeśa sūtra*), T.475.14.538c9–12.

language of recollection. For instance, he said, "'Amitābha,' with the six words 'Nam Mô,' one transmigrates to be born in the Pure Land, coming and going at ease. Once you escape the sea of suffering, you cross over to take shelter from the cycle of mundane dust..." (94). Here, Huyên cast the Pure Land "over there" beyond the ordinary world. However, as we saw in the quote above, his journey beyond circled back to the familiar. Hence, the visionary path through cultivation led back to a "Pure Land" inherent in the immediate world of the present.

In essence, Đoàn Minh Huyên's pilgrimage through the delta water-scape and across the Bassac River, known to his devotees as "Jeweled River" (*Bảo Giang*), to the mountainous western periphery paralleled the *bodhisattva's* ferrying of sentient beings to the western Pure Land on the "other shore."[91] This journey through memory returned his followers to a pristine past, back to Buddha, while, simultaneously, his cultivation of *niệm Phật* recalled Buddha to the present, thereby conjuring a Pure Land in the here-and-now of the Seven Mountains. Ultimately, Huyên's flight to a remote past was a transformation of the local present. Through recollection of Buddha, he and his follow-ers transformed the world, cycling around to a renewed Fountain-head of *dharma* at Maitreya's Dragon Flower Assembly.

To understand the transformative power of Đoàn Minh Huyên's *niệm Phật* practice, it is helpful to see it through the imagery of pil-grimage. Even today, when one careens about remote Buddhist land-scapes in Vietnam, from an unseen distance, one senses the whiff of incense emanating from sparse hermitages and the faint murmurs of chanting bonzes (even if, nowadays, often replicated by the constant drum of audio systems). These synesthetic sensations texture the pil-grim's visionary trek through a transformative space. Meanwhile, the pilgrim's inner meditations resonate with the votive manifestations about them. The sacred landscape transforms the pilgrim, but, at the same time, it is the pilgrim's obeisance through journeying that engenders the scene's magic.

---

91   This journey across the "Jeweled River" to the Seven Mountains was expressed in a prophecy attributed to the sixteenth-century prognosticator Trạng Trình (Nguyễn Bỉnh Khiêm 1491–1586): *Bảo giang thiên tử xuất, thiên hạ kiến thái bình* 寶江天子出，天下見太平 ("At Jeweled River, the son of heaven will appear, and all under heaven will see absolute peace").

Similarly, Đoàn Minh Huyên sought to transform the frontier landscape through piety. Day after day, he and his followers made votive offerings of water and incense during matutinal and crepuscular observances in "recollection of Buddha." They cleared the land and inscribed it with talismans bearing the incantation *Bửu Sơn Kỳ Hương*—"marvelous incense pervades these jeweled mountains"— the same mantra with which they inscribed themselves with "the bowels of the sect" (*lòng phái*). Their inward and outward journeying was to take them back and beyond to a pristine "fountainhead" era that they summoned to the local present by virtue of their cultivation. Their chanting, incense, talismans, and visionary meditation permeated the land, inscribing it with prayers that recalled Buddha and transformed the world. Huyên articulated his ideas of journeying, return, and transformation in language reflective of his waterscape. For example, he used visionary imagery of ferrying through floods and storms that spoke to tangible exigences in the delta.[92] Through changing, fluid riverine places like his native islet, Huyên saw himself as a helmsman who would ferry his followers on their spiritual quest to the Seven Mountains (27, 29).

Besides imagery, by vernacularizing his message, Huyên made use of peculiarities in the Mekong Delta dialect(s) of Vietnamese to convey the visionary journeying of *niệm Phật* cultivation. For instance, since the Vietnamese word *thiền* (禪), meaning "meditation," can be pronounced *thuyền* like the word for "boat" (船) in the delta, Huyên was able to juxtapose boating and meditation to set cultivation practices in motion.[93] Thus, Huyên cast meditation as a journey with language like "At the Ship's Gate (at the gate of meditation), inspired, I concentrate on Amitābha in my bowels, relying on the Boat of Prajñā for peace (relying on *prajñā* meditation for peace)" (2–3) and "Whose boat (meditation) runs to Peach River? On the boat of Old Prajñā (through meditation of old Prajñā), Buddha enters to ferry the people" (47).

---

92 Đỗ Thiện, *Vietnamese Supernaturalism: Views from the Southern Region*, 192.

93 *Thiền* (禪) also refers to the Meditation Sect, a major Buddhist tradition in Vietnam that is related by lineage to Chinese Chán, Japanese Zen, and Korean Sŏn. In 1850 at Sam Mountain, Đoàn Minh Huyên was nominally ordained as a 38th generation bonze of the Lâm Tế (臨濟) lineage.

Similarly, Đoàn Minh Huyên took advantage of the multivalence of the word *trở* 翻 to creative effect in his vernacularized teachings. In Vietnamese *trở* can mean "turn," "return," "shift," and "transform." Thus, in *Esoteric Tradition*, Huyên utilized a concatenation of *trở* over several enjambed lines to convey his multifaceted message about reorientation, return, and transformation discussed above:

> Turning (*returning to/transforming*) people, turning things, turning years, turning days,
> Turning food and turning dress immediately,
>   Turning husbands, turning wives, turning lords and kings,
> Turning hills, turning mountains, turning gardens,
>   Turning buffalos, turning fields, turning roads that come and go,
> Turning time, turning seasons, and then,
>   Turning trees, turning fruits, turning flowers' timing,
> Turning intimates, turning friends and confidantes .... (161–165)

A Translation

Scholars of Sino-Vietnamese have sometimes described translation as shining a lamp or lighting a candle, an imperfect act that surrenders obscurities to darkness because of interpretive chooses made during translation.[94] But I am fond of shadow. Like Jun'ichirō Tanizaki (1886–1965), I find that it is the "magic of shadows" that engender mystery.[95] This is especially true for prophetic writers like Đoàn Minh Huyên, for whom "language, as an outdated convention, must be exploded by silence to communicate the idea of renewal" and so "necessarily cryptic."[96] Therefore, in this translation, I have made no effort to cast light through murk and instead let mystery dwell in the intractable dimness of language. Where obscurity dwelled in Huyên's prolific use of non sequitur, aposiopesis, rambling enjambement, and lexical arcana, I veered towards literal word-by-word translation and

---

94   E.g., Claudine Ang, *Poetic Transformations: Eighteenth-Century Cultural Projects on the Mekong Plains* (Cambridge, MA: Harvard University Asia Center, Harvard University Press, 2019), xii.

95   Jun'ichirō Tanizaki, *In Praise of Shadows*, trans. Thomas J. Harper and Edward G. Seidensticker (Stony Creek, CT: Leete's Island Books, 1977), 20.

96   Đỗ Thiện, *Vietnamese Supernaturalism: Views from the Southern Region*, 191.

retained word order with the hope of rendering in translation the distressed, disquieted, and disorienting sensations I encountered when reading the original. As for my commentarial thoughts about the text, I have banished them to the umbrage below the footer. After all, perhaps, Huyên liked shadow, too. At least, from what I can glean of him, he hoped that his words would lead us to an umbral place (196).

Aside from Đoàn Minh Huyên's mystical language, the difficulty of the script used in the text no doubt contributed to my confusion. *Esoteric Tradition* is written in *chữ nôm* or demotic Vietnamese Sinographs, the writing system that was used to represent Vietnamese vernaculars before they were gradually supplanted in the nineteenth century by *quốc ngữ*, the Vietnamese Latin-based alphabet that is used today. Whereas *quốc ngữ* was based on northern dialects of Vietnamese, the choice of phonetic components used in the text's *chữ nôm* reflect pronunciations of Vietnamese southern dialects. For example, speakers of southern Vietnamese dialects often conflate ending consonants, and so, in *Esoteric Tradition*, the word for "let be," which in conventional *quốc ngữ* is written "*mặc*," is rendered *mặt* (種). Similarly, the now standard *sang* ("go over") is *san* (訕), *màng* ("hope to") is *màn* (樠), and *bang* (realm) is *ban* (般). Initial consonants also reflect southern dialects such as the rendering of the northern "v" in *vật vờ* ("reeling") to the southern y-sounding "d" of *dật dờ* (逸暴). To appreciate Huyên's use of southern Vietnamese in *Esoteric Tradition*, I have consistently used non-standard *quốc ngữ* to approximate southern Vietnamese pronunciation (e.g., *nhân → nhơn*, *bảo → bửu*, *tính → tánh*, *hoàn → huờn*, etc.) and, where such distortions might be unintelligible to a reader of standard Vietnamese, I indicated conventional spellings parenthetically [*mặt(c)*, *màn(g)*, etc.].

Another feature of *Esoteric Tradition* that is difficult to render in translation is the poetry of Đoàn Minh Huyên's verse. Huyên's *Esoteric Tradition* consists of 201 lines of 6-8 verse, in which each of the 201 lines have an "upper" six-word segment followed by a "lower" eight-word segment. Although the extant text (see below) was written as a continuous string of Sinographs, traditionally, the first segments of each line would be written at the top of a page, while the second segments would be written at the bottom, creating a visual effect with all six-word segments at the upper portion of the page and the eight-word segments at the lower portion. In 6-8 verse, the sixth word of both segments rhymes with level (*bằng*, 平) tones, while the final level-toned word of the lower segment determines the rhyme of the next line. This arrangement can be visually represented as follows:

Thus, 6–8 verse allows for a continuous series of indeterminant lines linked by the final rhyme of one line with that of the sixth words of the segments in the following line. This rhyming structure facilitates memorization and oral transmission of the poem, often in fragments, as was probably the case with *Esoteric Tradition*. To help bring out the lyrical form of Huyền's writing and for ease of reference, in my translation and transliteration, each 6–8 line is numbered from 1 to 201.

This English translation and Vietnamese transliteration are based on a handwritten copy of *Esoteric Tradition* that was commissioned in 1973 by Nguyễn Văn Hầu (1922–95), to whom this study is immensely indebted. Hầu, a cultural historian of the Mekong Delta and himself a follower of the Hòa Hảo tradition, was presented an earlier 1909 copy of the text in 1973 during the course of his research. Upon further inquiry, Hầu learned from villagers of Tòng Sơn, Đoàn Minh Huyên's birthplace, that, when expelled from the village in 1849, Huyên left the text of *Esoteric Tradition* behind the community house, where he had been staying. After Huyên traveled to Trà Bư, his relatives tracked him there and beseeched him to return home. Huyên denied their wishes, but he did tell them about the text that he left at Tòng Sơn. Indeed, when his relatives got back to Tòng Sơn, they found *Esoteric Tradition*, which they circulated among the villagers both orally and by copying by hand. When not in use for study or reproduction, the original was placed on a votive altar in the village.[97]

Sixty years later, a copy of *Esoteric Tradition* was made by a certain "Disciple Trương." This would become the only surviving version of

97   Nguyễn Văn Hầu, *Sấm truyền Đức Phật Thầy Tây An*, 55.

Đoàn Minh Huyên's text. Due to the vicissitudes of twentieth century Vietnam, in the decades that followed, Đoàn Minh Huyên's text was thought to be lost. Eventually, in 1963, Tòng Sơn Village authorities rediscovered Disciple Trương's 1909 handwritten copy, which they entrusted to Nguyễn Văn Hầu in 1973. In that year, Hầu published his study and Vietnamese transliteration (*phiên âm*) of *Esoteric Tradition*. He intended to append a photocopy of the 1909 text to his study, but since its layout and condition were unsuitable for publication, he enlisted a scribe named Thái Văn Ý to recopy the text. In Hầu's testimony, Ý faithfully reproduced the text "as is" regardless of omissions, edits, additions, redundancies, and errors.[98] Ý's handwritten copy appended to Hầu's 1973 study is the version of the text used for this translation. Since the text is untitled, I have adopted Hầu's name for it, *Esoteric Tradition of Venerable Master Buddha of Western Peace* (*Sấm truyền Đức Phật Thầy Tây An*).

Although the villagers of Tòng Sơn found it meaningful to convey *Esoteric Tradition*'s origin as a single text handwritten by Đoàn Minh Huyên, the vagaries of its lost-again-found-again transmission through manuscript copying, fragmented oral recitation, and moot memorization should pique suspicion of its authenticity. Indeed, the appearance partway through the text of "sitting ruefully" (80), which was a stock phrase for beginning such prophecies, suggests interpolation in a layered text. Furthermore, in his study of about a dozen Sino-Vietnamese texts attributed to Huyên or his immediate followers, Hầu determined that at least half were apocryphal, while several others remained questionable.[99] Nevertheless, after studying the language and content of *Esoteric Tradition*, Hầu concluded that, if not brushed by Huyên himself, then it probably was by one of his contemporary ghostwriters.[100]

Here, I have followed Nguyễn Văn Hầu's assessment.[101] However, lingering doubts about *Esoteric Tradition*'s authenticity lead us to one

---

98   Ibid., 56–61, 91.
99   Ibid., 19–26, 50–52.
100   Ibid., 27.
101   I am, however, more skeptical of the other two *chữ nôm* texts that Nguyễn Văn Hầu deemed authentic, *Giác mê* (*Awakening from Delusion*) and *Thập thủ liên hườn thi* (*Ten Continuously Linking Poems*).

final consideration: genre. *Esoteric Tradition* is regarded as *sấm* (讖) or esoteric "weft" texts beyond *kinh* (經), conventional "warp" texts or "classics." Since at least the tenth century in Vietnam, Buddhists circulated *sấm* through texts, inscriptions, and oral songs. In the nineteenth century, the replication (transmission) of *sấm*, especially vernacular *sấm*, through manuscript and oracular culture was an intensely creative process across a wide swathe of participants. The transmission of *sấm* over time, therefore, was a collective process that accrued changing sentiments among people who found meaning in them.

Esoteric Tradition, then, even if apocryphal in part or in entirety, still conveys the prayers, sentiments, hopes, and fears of Mekong Delta inhabitants for whom Master Buddha's message resonated. Just as Śākyamuni Buddha's journey through countless past lives to Buddhahood suggests our own path to enlightenment, so too is Maitreya's story our own. In this sense, the Dragon Flower prophecy and the words of Master Buddha continue to perpetuate through generations "like the rhythms of a wooden fish."

ESOTERIC TRADITION OF VENERABLE MASTER BUDDHA OF WESTERN PEACE[1]

On the twenty-seventh day of the intercalary second month in the year Kỷ Dậu,[2] disciple Trương assisted in writing down a one fascicle litany.[3]

1   Upon Nhâm,[4] across to Hồ Cứ[5] I peregrinate;
       In the month of the boar,[6] I teach enlightenment to seek the
       way out.

2   Miraculous—I delight in the Đạo of Śākyamuni;[7]

---

1   The original text, which was composed by Đoàn Minh Huyên 段明暄 (1807–56) in *circa* 1842, is untitled.

2   April 17, 1909.

3   The original text is untitled. Disciple Trương referred to it only as *nhất quyển doãn* 一卷尹. The last Sinograph *doãn* appears nonsensical. Here, I follow Nguyễn Văn Hầu's (1973) transcription *giảng*, which means "lecture" or "litany."

4   Assuming that "Nhâm" refers to the "earthly branch" (*can*) of a given year, then most likely the year in question is Nhâm Dần or 1842, since Ven. Đoàn Minh Huyên was confined to Tây An Pagoda by 1851 before the next "Nhâm" year (1852). If so, then the text suggests that Master Buddha returned to or at least traveled through his native region, perhaps many times, several years before he revealed himself to his native villagers and family in 1849.

5   Hồ Cứ is now Mỹ Xương Village in Cao Lãnh District of Đồng Tháp Province. Hồ Cứ was a rival village across the Mekong River from Ven. Đoàn Minh Huyên's native village of Tòng Sơn, which is now Mỹ An Hưng Village in Lấp Vò District of Đồng Tháp Province. The words *bước sang*, "peregrinate across to" or "come over to" in the couplet may suggest that Master Buddha crossed over to the left bank of the Mekong River to Hồ Cứ from his native village during the early autumn of 1842.

6   The month of the boar is the tenth lunar month, approximately September.

7   Phật Thích Ca or "Śākyamuni Buddha" is the patriarch Buddha (*bổn sư*) of our present dispensation of the Dharma. Đạo 道, which means "way," is often used to describe various religious and philosophical traditions.

At the Ship's Gate,[8] inspired, I concentrate on Amitābha[9] in my bowels.[10]

3   Relying on the Boat of Prajñā[11] for peace,
    Entering the mountains of Five Entanglements,[12] I faithfully and sincerely cultivate with reverence.

4   Filial piety and trustworthiness, completely upholding these words,
    At the transcendents' shore and the cranes' spring,[13] I hold a hook and wait.[14]

---

8   The words *thuyền môn*, here translated "Ship's Gate," also means "Gate of Meditation." Since a Vietnamese word for "boat" 船 and transliteration of the Sanskrit *dhyāna* 禪 (meditation) are both pronounced *thuyền* in the Vietnamese Mekong Delta dialect, the Sinographs 禪門 simultaneously convey two meanings central to the Master Buddha's teachings, the vivid imagery and metaphor of ferrying through a water-bound world and the teachings of the Dhyāna (Meditation) Sect of Buddhism.

9   Phật Di Đà or Amitābha is a coterminous Buddha presiding over a Buddha Field to the west of Śākyamuni's. Amitābha's Buddha Field is also known as Tịnh thổ (S. Sukhāvatī) or "Pure Land."

10 In Vietnamese, bowels (V. *lòng*) are the site of visceral emotions, deep feelings, and penetrating cognition.

11 Prajñā (V. *bát nhã*) is wisdom abiding in emptiness (V. *không*, S. *śūnyatā*); it is one of the six *pāramitā* (V. *lục độ*) or Buddhist ideals to be perfected on the path to cross over to liberation from suffering. As with "Ship's Gate" above (note 6), "relying on the Boat of Prajñā" also means "relying on the wisdom (*prajñā*) from meditation (*dhyāna*)."

12 *Ngũ uẩn* or Five Entanglements (S. *pañca-skandha*) are constituents of the illusion of self: form (V. *sắc*, S. *rūpa*), sensation (*thụ, vedanā*), perception (*tưởng, saṃjñā*), impulse (*hành, saṃskāra*), and consciousness (*thức, vijñāna*). The Sanskrit version of the term seems to have meant something like aggregate heap or pile, but the Sinographic term used here, *uẩn* 蘊 implies something closer to intertwined bramble-wood or hempen knots. The image is that of a heterogenous knot of prickly twigs or bristly threads.

13 Transcendents or *tiên* 仙 are beings (usually former humans) who have achieved extreme longevity and attendant supramundane powers through various cultivation practices. Transcendents were thought to manifest as cranes as reflected in the depiction of transcendents' mystical transition from mortal life to immortality as "feathered transformation" (V. *vũ hóa*, 羽化) or sprouting wings to fly off as a white crane. Transcendents were sometimes thought to live on the periphery of the mundane world, as seems to be the case in these lines. They were also believed to inhabit heaven. In fact, elsewhere in the litany, transcendents seem to be conflated with the *sūtra* literature's *deva*, the heavenly beings of Buddhist cosmology.

14 This couplet puns on the word *câu*, which, in the upper line, means "words," while in the lower line means "hook" or "fishing hook."

5   I espy the masses' boat drifting in abandon,
     On the waves of the open sea, teetering on the rivers of
     delusion!

6   Take heed whoever conducts themselves gracelessly,
     Unconcerned about water and fire and thorns all around.

7   Because of themselves, everyone readily sees everyone,[15]
     Let themselves fall and bury themselves.

8   Transcendent Buddhas are utterly manifest and numinous;
     With one utterance of correct recollection one is at peace.[16]

9   Each and every one of us is amidst heaven;
     Humaneness and compassion must be upheld without
     deceitful speech.

10   Change in the world is sudden;
     The good endure, while the wicked perish, ordained by
     Heaven's Court.

11   Revolutions of time spin the mundane world of dust;
     Failing to understand, one conspires deeply towards others.[17]

12   Degenerate, one misses one's place with the heavenly Buddhas,
     As mountains split and land crumbles, drifting into the offing.

13   One must act as if heading out this very day;
     Young and old, please remember to uphold this with vigilance.

14   Years are like lightning, months like a shuttle;
     Rotations of time spin the world—cycles of karma are no
     game![18]

15   A good woman has transmitted these words:
     First, "the skyward path, the workings of heaven are vast."

---

15   Nguyễn Văn Hầu renders this line "Bởi mình ai dễ *mặc* ai," which means "For their
     own sake, everyone readily neglects everyone (else)."

16   Here *chánh niệm* 正念 (S. *samyak-smṛti*) refers to *niệm Phật*, the practice of focused
     recollection and constant mindfulness of Buddha(s), usually Amitābha Buddha.
     In practice, *chánh niệm* is usually accompanied by recitation of the Buddha's name,
     in Vietnamese *"Nam Mô A Di Đà Phật."* Master Buddha's use of *chánh niệm* sug-
     gests that he interpreted *chánh niệm*, the seventh practice of the Eightfold Path, as
     the recitation and mindfulness of Amitābha Buddha.

17   The phrase "conspire deeply towards others" may allude to the aphorism *mưu thâm
     họa diệc thâm* 謀深禍亦深 or "when one conspires deeply, the calamity is also pro-
     found."

18   *Luân hồi* 輪迴 (S. *saṃsāra*) or "cycles of karma" refers to cycles of suffering through
     karmic accretion that is associated with ongoing reincarnation.

16   Second, "the saints are responsive and bright;"
        Third, "the court draws together wavering families."[19]
17   Gazing towards the distance somehow seems close;[20]
        Near and far winds whisk dust clean away.
18   Black-haired children and hoary-headed men,
        People of the sunlit world, heed! —how can you not see our
        age?
19   The Đạo is depleted! The Đạo is depleted![21]
        Ancient places and old scenes will found an age of reparation.
20   Ruefully folding my arms, ruefully folding my arms,
        I see the forces of creation uncanny in their deft construction.[22]
21   In an age violent and cruel, few are filial and faithful;[23]
        Mouths are calculating, and bowels indulge in deep scheming.
22   The good encounter goodness, but become wicked in the end;
        Compounding karmic retribution amongst themselves, who
        will rescue them?
23   Forthrightly consider, straightforwardly take heed,
        A path leads to heaven—seek the way to go.
24   Why listen to speech of right and wrong?
        Blame corporeal eyes that fail to see.
25   Open your eyes widely;
        Waters stir and waves ripple thunderously by the ears.
26   How woeful, heed! How woeful, heed!
        Pity the world of dust! —I keep teaching, but none listen.

---

19   In these lines the Sinograph *vân* (雲), literally "cloud," is translated as a variant for
        the homophonous *vân* 云, which indicates the beginning of a statement or quote.
20   In Vietnamese, *xa gần*, translated "near and far" and "distant and close" can be
        understood both spatially and temporally.
21   Đạo means "way" or "path" (see note above). Here, the depleted Đạo means that
        the time of Śākyamuni's dispensation is running out.
22   Master Buddha's use of a qualifying word for animated objects, *con* (lit. child),
        in *con tạo* or "forces of creation" may suggest the personification of the Daoist
        inspired concept of *tạo hóa* (造化), which is usually understood as an impersonal
        force of creation and transformation akin to today's expression "laws of nature."
        However, it should be noted that in relatively rare cases *con* can also be applied to
        inanimate objects like knives (*con dao*) and spinning-tops (*con quay*).
23   There is an extraneous Sinograph in this line of the original text that does not
        agree with six-eight verse: "*Đời bạo ngược ít* người *hiếu trung*." Here, I am following
        Nguyễn Văn Hầu by deleting the word *người*, which does not significantly affect
        the meaning of the line.

27 As rising waters close in, and a gale moves the raft,
Hold the tiller and single-pointedly follow along.
28 The journey is precarious, the sights hazardous;
Alone it is all but impossible to punt and row through.
29 Why do you not examine what comes before and after?
If you disdain the helmsman, then who will help take you along?
30 People of our age are like a midday market,
Scattering and meeting, meeting and scattering so many times.
31 Crying unwanted cries and laughing unwitting laughter,
Feelings dissipate, oh dearests! —as our age dries up, what will be left?
32 Plaintive tears, plaintive tears,
Shall we pity those who harbor compassion in their bowels?[24]
33 Filter pure water! Filter pure water!
What is there to fear from the dissolution of ants and bees?
34 Restrain your mouth, and swallow your words;
Let be the affairs of the world and whomever scoffs.
35 Wholeheartedly pray with the words "Như Lai;"[25]

---

24 Here, Master Buddha like many Vietnamese Buddhists articulates Buddhist compassion in the canonical Buddhist idiom (*từ bi*, 慈悲), understood as a combination of kindness (V. *từ* 慈, S. *maitrī*) and pity (V. *bi* 悲, S. *karuṇā*), through the vernacular *thương*, which can simultaneously convey meanings of love and pity as well as hurtfulness, injury, and pain. Hence, Master Buddha voiced his understanding of compassion as that born from resonating with others' suffering as well as the universal suffering that is the inexorable condition of life. In this sense, Master Buddha's vernacularized understanding of compassion comes close to what Nāgārjuna is attributed with identifying as *sinh duyên từ bi* (生緣慈悲), "kindness and pity of the karmic threads of life" or just "compassion for living creatures" without denying the more refined compassion of Arhats and Buddhas marked by insight into reality through selflessness and nondiscrimination. See Nāgārjuna's (perhaps apocryphal) commentary on the "three compassions" or *tam bi* (三悲) in the *Treatise on Traversing Beyond with Great Wisdom* (V. *Đại trí độ luận*, 大智度論; S. *Mahāprajñāpāramitā-śāstra*), T.n1509.v25.p350b25–26.

25 Như Lai 如來 (S. *tathāgata*), "thus-come-one" or "as-is" is an epithet for Buddha(s). By speaking of "the words" *như lai*, Master Buddha may have been instructing his auditors to contemplate the literal meaning of the term as existential "thusness."

Brushing off the words "reputation" and "profit," letting be whomever vies to contest their skills.[26]

36   Scenes of natural calamities, places of natural disasters!
     With utmost effort forge iron to whet into a needle.

37   The scene is very severe! The scene is very severe!
     In the making of ten thousand autumns, how hard is it to find?

38   Withered with gloom, withered with gloom,
     This muddled era churns in an age of dreams.

39   The cat's cry resounds! The cat's cry resounds![27]
     Scaring snake and dragon to flee into the mountains and hide.[28]

40   Flags fluttering, drums rolling,
     People rise as others fall towards two disparate paths.[29]

41   Bowels writhing in pain, bowels writhing in pain!
     Transcendent Buddhas pity[30] them with a stomach withering from sorrow.

42   Exert yourself with the six words *nam mô*;[31]
     Amidst calamity, with luck a fish from a spring may come across a lotus lake.

43   Heavenly Buddhas, bowels rent with pity,
     Teach among the good to take refuge in the Dragon Flower.[32]

44   Wind stirs the tips of fluttering grasses,

---

26   In spoken vernacular, *tài* can mean both wealth and talent. The Sinograph in the text is 才 (talents, skills).

27   By alluding to the Vietnamese zodiac, the cat's cry suggests the year Quý Mão (1843), one year after Master Buddha delivered this litany in the year of the tiger, Nhâm Dần (1842).

28   The snake and dragon allude to the years Giáp Thìn (1844) and Ất Tỵ (1845).

29   That is rising towards higher rebirth (such as towards heaven) and falling towards lower rebirth (such as towards the hells).

30   *Thương*, here translated "pity," also means compassion, love, and hurt. See note above.

31   There is a superfluous Sinograph in this line: *gắng công* thường *lục tự nam mô*. Here, *thường* (constantly) is omitted from translation. The "six words *nam mô*" refer to recollection of Buddha through mindful recitation (see note above).

32   *Long Hoa* or Dragon Flower refers to the Dragon Flower Assembly (*hội Long Hoa*) where the future Buddha would establish a new dispensation of Dharma, rescue the suffering, and punish the wicked.

You shall see that the world is like a flag[33] under siege.
45 Reeling sights! Reeling sights!
Branches fall away toward a different age, transforming the
world.
46 Looking into the workings of creation—it's over;[34]
Teetering on the vast sea, falling away on the banks of a pond.
47 Whose boat runs to Peach River?[35]
On the boat of Old Prajñā, Buddha enters to ferry the
people.[36]
48 Exhorting people to cast away mundane dust,
He will lead them away from delusion's mooring, people
heed!
49 The likes of beasts and hungry ghosts,[37]
Are hopelessly lost, exiled to desolate plights.
50 Towards the west,[38] trek straight out in search,
For ten thousand eras seek recourse in precious pearls—what
is lacking?[39]
51 With sincerity I teach thoroughly,
Oh, young and old! Why do you not take care?

---

33 *Cờ* (flag) might alternatively refer to chess with possible translations like "the world is as if besieged in chess" or "the world is as if checked in chess."
34 In contrast to the earlier use of *con tạo* for the forces of creation, here, *máy tạo* suggest a more impersonal mechanism of creation.
35 The words *sông Đào* (滔陶), here translated "Peach River," can also mean "Đào's river," since the words *đào* is both a surname and a word for "peach." As such, *sông Đào* may allude to Tao Qian's 陶潛 (Đào Tiềm, 372?–427) *Record of Peach Blossom Spring* (桃花源記). The story narrates the journey of a fisherman who followed a secluded river to a hidden world of transcendents descended from men of a former era. If so, then "Peach River" evoked a transcendents' paradise.
36 Here, the personification of Buddhist wisdom, "Old Prajñā," is used as an epithet for Buddha. As noted above, "boat" (V. *thuyền*) can pun to mean "meditation" (V. *thiền*, S. *dhyāna*), while *prajñā* can be understood as the wisdom derived from meditation, namely that on impermanence and emptiness (S. *śūnyatā*).
37 *Ngạ quỷ* or "hungry ghosts" (S. *preta*) describe creatures born into one of the six paths of transmigration, where these unlucky beings suffer perpetual hunger, surviving like maggots on unsavory sustenance (excrement, rot, etc.). In Vietnam, they are often conflated with *cô hồn* or "forlorn ghosts," who lack descendants to provide for them with offerings.
38 The west is the direction where Amitābha's Buddha Field is thought to exist.
39 Seeking recourse in "precious pearls" refers to seeking refuge in the "Three Jewels" of Buddhism: Buddha, Dharma, and Saṃgha.

52 I now watch as suddenly in the world,
    Endless ghosts lead themselves along—who could shelter
    us?[40]

53 Here in the morning, lost by night in a life of hardships,
    Like a flash of lightning whose brilliance cannot endure.[41]

54 Spanning through the watches of the night, spanning through
    the watches of the night,
    Sighing and sighing, I worry for our generation,

55 As I mull over a world depleted;
    Suffering increases, adding to suffering in an age of affliction.

56 There! There! Ghosts and demons strike up chaos;
    Snakes afflict, and tigers bite at this thorny moment.

57 Some are besieged by bandits;
    Others starve, their lives now without peace.

58 Struggling through many upheavals,
    I am afraid that the state of the world is like a boat running
    away into the offing.

59 I am out of words! I am out of words!
    Admonishing and teaching people with the karmic affinity
    for goodness.[42]

---

40 If, instead of *bênh*, the Sinograph 兵 is read *binh* with the meaning "army" as did
    Nguyễn Văn Hầu, then the line means, "Endless ghosts lead an army of sorrow—
    how can we be alright?" In that case, the text's Sinographs for "army of sorrow"
    (埃兵) is a variation of 哀兵. It should be noted that *bênh* and *binh* are not clearly
    distinguished in spoken southern Vietnamese.

41 Likening the breadth of human life to a momentary thunderbolt is a common
    image for impermanence in canonical Buddhist literature such as the *Diamond
    Sūtra* (V. *Kim cương bát nhã ba la mật kinh*, 金剛般若波羅蜜經; S. *Vajracchedikā
    prajñāpāramitā sūtra*, T.235.08.752b28–29). In addition, in Vietnam, the image
    of lightning calls to mind a well-known *gāthā* poem by an eleventh-century monk
    named Vạn Hạnh, who began his poem, "Life is like a flash of lightning, com-
    ing into existence only to return to nothingness" (my translation). See *Thiền uyển
    tập anh* (禪苑集英), xylographic text in Nguyễn Tự Cường, *Zen in Medieval Viet-
    nam* (Honolulu, HI: University of Hawai'i Press, 1997), 53b, Nguyễn Tự Cường's
    translation on page 176.

42 *Thiện duyên* can be translated as both "karmic affinity for goodness" and "good
    karma," because of the cyclical nature of karmic causality. Those who meet a good
    teacher had the good karma for such a lucky encounter and, having learned good-
    ness from the teacher, cull through meritorious deeds the karmic seeds that mature
    later when they meet another good teacher in a future lifetime. C.f., this excerpt
    from Ven. Huỳnh Phú Sở's teachings, "With good karma you clearly get this Mad-

60 In my bowels, I reprove their abundant unscrupulousness;
     The sick and afflicted pray for relief in vain.
61 Perverted to deviant treachery,
     They destroy the monkhood, break observances, and scheme
     to harm people in their bowels.
62 Today's world has already shallowed,
     To open, transform, and establish the Fountainhead era.[43]
63 The wheel of heaven and earth revolves in cycles;[44]
     At this juncture, you will see fire burn ashen eyebrows.
64 Few show that they are able to fathom,
     As if holding a cup in the hand that sadly slips and shatters.
65 The old master's words of instruction said it all;
     Eating people, will people feast until nothing is left?

---

man/ just owing to a bit of good karma from a former life" (*Duyên lành rõ được Khùng Điên/ chẳng qua kiếp trước thiện duyên hữu phần*).

43 *Thượng ngươn* (上元), here translated Fountainhead, literally means something like "first prime" or "first of the first." For instance, in the Sinitic lunisolar calendar, the first full moon of the first month is called *thượng ngươn*, which is the Lantern Festival. In Sinitic numerology, astrology, and calendrical studies, *ngươn* 元 is understood as a unit of cyclical time generally calculated from smaller cycles like epoch (*hội*), revolution (*vận*), generation (*thế*), and solar year (*tuế*). Depending on the school of calculation, one *ngươn* cycle could consist of several thousand to over one-hundred thousand years. In Master Buddha's teachings, this numerological sense of cyclical time is conflated with Buddhist cyclical time in which one dispensation of the Dharma is divided into three eras from the moment a Buddha "turns the wheel of Dharma" with his first teaching until, eventually over many generations, his teachings are corrupted, forgotten, and lost. Thereafter, a new Buddha would appear to initiate a new dispensation. These three periods of dispensation are "True Dharma" (*chơn pháp*), "Semblance Dharma" (*giả pháp*), and Later Dharma (*mạt pháp*). Master Buddha articulated this canonical Buddhist periodization of cyclical time through the imagery of the watery landscape of his Mekong Delta homeland. Since, in Vietnamese, the word *ngươn* (cyclic era) is pronounced the same as a Sinitic word for "spring" or "fountain" (源), Master Buddha imagined through pun and metaphor a Buddhist cosmology in which the "Upper Spring" or "Fountainhead Era" originated in the Himalayas with the teachings of Śākyamuni, descended downstream along the Mekong River, and concluded at the "Lower Spring" or "Receiving Spring in Vietnam. Thus, Master Buddha saw Vietnam, specifically the Seven Mountains, as a site of shallowed waterscapes that mirrored the moral depravity and degeneration of Buddhism that he believed he had experienced. As such, it would also be the place of a new dispensation in a renewed era.

44 In Buddhism, turning of the wheel (of Dharma) is a canonical image for the dispensation of Buddhist teachings.

66 Grievances pile up with retribution,
    Greedy for wealth, they accumulate recklessly without re-
    flecting on themselves,[45]

67 Causing father and child to fight one another.
    If the father is not good and filially pious, then how could the
    child be good?

68 Loyalty to the ruler and the relationship between father and
    child come first,
    But betraying one's ruler and killing one's father, in what
    book's passage is that found?

69 Heaven renders a hundred beings to waste,
    Such that ferrying across is arduous with unspeakable toil.

70 Mountaintops float on water, and earth builds up,[46]
    Dragons lurk at the bottom of the sea as rivers constantly
    catch the dew.[47]

71 When of marvelous incense we partake,
    Longevity shall increase ten thousand years, and its fragrance
    shall linger enduringly.[48]

72 To live this life is insufferable, oh!
    Hundreds of thousands of miseries relentlessly pile up upon
    you.

73 Wealth will be no more! Poverty will be no more!

---

45 Here, *tích đại* (積大) is translated according to the vernacular so that *đại* means
    "recklessly" in "accumulate recklessly." Alternatively, Master Buddha may have had
    in mind *tứ đại* 四大 (S. *mahābhūta*) or "four elements," which, in Buddhist *sūtra*
    literature, refers to four elements (earth, fire, water, and wind) that aggregate to
    constitute physical existence.

46 The Sinographs for *phù thủy* (浮水) mean "afloat on water" or "drift on water."
    However, if they are taken for their pronunciation only, then they suggest geo-
    mancers' practice of manipulating the landscape by tapping "dragon veins" (V. *long
    mạch*, 龍脈) in the ground, building mounds, and planting talismanic flags in the
    earth, all of which were commonplace during Master Buddha's lifetime.

47 Lurking dragons implies geomantic dragon veins and dragon spirits, who were
    associated with rain and water.

48 In this line, Master Buddha relates the prophecy of the Seven Mountains or the
    "marvelous incense throughout the jeweled mountains" (V. *bửu sơn kỳ hương*, 寶
    山奇香). According to the prophecy, in the Seven Mountains, specifically Forbid-
    den Mountain (*núi Cấm*) a future Buddha would inaugurate a new dispensation
    as the landscape (and waterscape) physically transformed into a land of bejeweled
    mountains redolent with incense.

Lives will be lost as possessions dissipate, everyone just the same;

74 Causing wives to kill husbands,
And children to harm their mothers for lack of love.

75 When the common spirit among siblings split,
And ruler and subjects betray one another, then is the Receding Spring.[49]

76 Transforming the waters of the sea, shattering mountains,
Dispelling the realm of ghost and demons, righteousness and humaneness will inaugurate an era.

77 The Three Eras have already come around to be restored.[50]
Mulberry fields turn to blue seas, falling apart to spin in transformation.[51]

78 Tracing my fingers again and again, I calculate with my hands the nights and days;[52]
People of today seem to see that now is the time, and yet they do not.

---

49 "Receding Spring" or "Lower Spring" (*hạ ngươn*) is the dystopian end time of Śākyamuni's dispensation of Dharma. Master Buddha likened *dharma's* fading to a receding tide or river. See note on "Upper Spring" (*thượng ngươn*) above.

50 The "Three Eras" or "Three Springs" (*tam ngươn*) refer to the reoccurring periodization of a Buddha's dispensation into "true," "semblance," and "later" Dharma. See note above.

51 The image of mulberry fields turning into the sea and back again is a classical metaphor for epoch change. This allusion originated in the biography of Wang Yuan (王遠) in chapter seven of the *Biographies of Divine Transcendents* (神仙傳). In it, the transcendent Wang Yuan holds a feast in the human world and summons his subordinate Lady Ma (麻姑), whom he had not seen for five hundred years, to join him. After a short trip to Penglai, the mythical land of transcendents, Lady Ma appears before Wang Yuan and says, "Since I have waited upon you, [I] have seen the Eastern Sea three times become mulberry fields. Coming to Penglai, the water was shallower than in the past. When [I] came upon it, it was just about halfway [up]. How it shall once again revert back to land!" (my translation). For the full episode, see Robert Ford Campany, *To Live as Long as Heaven and Earth: Ge Hong's* Traditions of Divine Transcendents" (Berkeley: University of California Press, 2002), 259–264.

52 Master Buddha may have been referring to one of many methods of calculating auspicious and inauspicious times with the hands such as running the fingers over prayer beads or the *giáp độn* finger-counting technique.

79   It is written, "humans and beasts are alike;"[53]
     Yet whereas beasts know their nature, humans fail to show
     emotion.

80   Sitting ruefully, I sigh and reprove alone,
     Pitying that things of the world will suddenly be extinguished.

81   People compete amongst themselves haughtily with spirits and
     flesh,
     Cursing their own fathers and mothers everywhere upriver
     and downriver.

82   Transformation through rebirth, I see it all,
     A child who does not repent, at the end of life, will become a
     deviant ghost.

83   Marvelous is the way of Śākyamuni's boat![54]
     Quan Âm rescues from suffering, while Amitābha ferries
     away the living.[55]

84   In the Đoài mountains[56] uphold trustworthiness and sincerity
     in your belly,
     I, as teacher, will provide study for laymen who have yet to
     comprehend.

85   Brothers and sisters, whoever shall heed,
     Follow me and study the path—you must perk your ears and
     listen.

---

53   The textual origin of the Sinographic phrase "humans and beasts are alike" (人物與
     同) is obscure.

54   Here, Master Buddha takes advantage of the dual meaning of *thuyển*, which can
     mean both boat and meditation with the effect of juxtaposing the quest to ferry
     the world's creatures to salvation with Śākyamuni Buddha's way of meditation. See
     note above, too.

55   Amitābha is the Buddha of the Pure Land in the west (see above). Quan Âm (S.
     Avalokiteśvara) is an advanced bodhisattva (S. *mahābodhisattva*) associated with
     Amitābha's Buddha field. In Vietnam, the bodhisattva is imagined variously as a
     masculine yogin with one-thousand hand-eyes as well as various female emana-
     tions.

56   Đoài 兑 is one of the eight trigrams, ☱. It is associated with the west, and, in lit-
     erature, "mountains of Đoài" usually evokes sunset, since the sun sets in the west.
     Hence, "mountains of Đoài" (*non Đoài*), can be interpreted as the western moun-
     tains, where the Seven Mountains are located in the west of Vietnam's Mekong
     Delta, and evokes the literary allusion to "sunset mountains."

86   Buddha passed on how to plant the *bodhi* tree;[57]
     Uphold the words "illumined truthfulness," never dishonest.
87   Wanting to enter[58] the Sahā realm,[59]
     Through skill in means[60] and devotional charity,[61] store up
     fortune like the river's sands.[62]
88   Respect heaven. Respect earth and divine luminaries,
     At the ancestors' gate, venerate their shrines and fully uphold
     the Four Debts of Gratitude.[63]
89   We owe life to our parents, to whom we are foremost filial;
     For the task afterwards, earnestly act with propriety at dawn.[64]
90   Upholding loyalty to the ruler in the bowels without error,
     Polish the word "fidelity" displayed like vermillion on stone.
91   One who cultivates must teach one's children and grandchildren,
     So that Đạo will be passed on and inherited, and the gates of
     Buddha will long endure.

---

57   The *bodhi* tree or "tree of enlightenment" was a bo tree, under which Śākyamuni
     realized Buddhahood.
58   Nguyễn Văn Hầu amended the word *vào*, here translated as "enter," to *thoát*, mean-
     ing "escape," because he thought that from context, one should want to escape
     rather than enter the mundane world of suffering (Sahā realm). However, if Mas-
     ter Buddha was speaking from the perspective of a *bodhisattva*, who plunges into
     realms of suffering of their own volition to rescue others, then the line need not be
     corrected.
59   In Buddhism, the Sahā realm is the mundane "dusty" world marked by suffering.
60   "Skill-in-means" (V. *phương tiện*, S. *upāya*) is the Mahāyāna use of provisional,
     expedient means to lead creatures along the Buddhist path according to their rela-
     tive conditions and inclinations. See, for instance, the second chapter of the *Lotus
     Sūtra* (T.262.9.5b24).
61   "Devotional charity" (V. *bố thí*, 布施; S. *dāna*) is one the *pāramitā*, or qualities to
     master on the path towards Buddhahood.
62   In Buddhist *sūtra* literature, the expression "river's sands" usually alludes to the
     innumerable sands of the Ganges River.
63   Nowhere in his litany did Master Buddha explicitly delineate what he meant by
     "four debts of gratitude." However, the context of the lines about this expres-
     sion in the text seems to agree with tradition, according to which they are debts
     of gratitude to parents (*cha mẹ*), the land and waters (*đất nước*), Three Jewels of
     Buddhism (*tam bảo:* Buddha, Dharma, and Saṃgha), and humanity (*nhân loại*).
     This teaching about the "four debts of gratitude" has as its antecedent the *Great
     Vehicle Sūtra of Contemplation on the Mind's Ground of Original Life* 大乘本生心觀
     經 (T.159.3.297a12–13).
64   The "task afterwards" refers to posthumous rites associated with ancestor venera-
     tion, for which Master Buddha proscribed daily morning observance.

92 Śākyamuni, the thus-come ancestral Buddha,
     For six years suffered austerities regardless of travails.[65]
93 As this moment comes, divine dragons descend;
     We are as if on a little boat buffeted by the wind on the rivers
     and lakes.[66]
94 Amitābha, with the six words "Nam Mô,"[67]
     One transmigrates to be born in the Pure Land,[68] coming and
     going at ease.
95 Once you escape the sea of suffering, you cross over,
     To take shelter from the cycle of mundane dust and avoid the
     realm of life and death.
96 My lot is that of a devout layman,
     A teacher who teaches the people to do good and cultivate.
97 The Receding Spring in the world approaches,
     Awaken your heart, realize it for yourself earnestly and
     quickly.
98 It is not difficult to abide in cultivation;
     The words "devotional charity" should come first.
99 As benevolent spirits record on both sides,[69]
     Increase goodness and decrease evil—because of wickedness
     come these transmitted words.
100 In ancient times, Buddha taught but was not believed,
     People listened and abandoned him, saying that they were
     wise.
101 Greedy for wealth and cultivating a web of material things,
     In order to nourish their flesh, they did not heed a word.
102 Killing and injuring the living in disport,

---

65 Śākyamuni is said to have practiced severe asceticism and austerities for six years
     before achieving enlightenment.
66 Dragons are spirits related to bodies of water and rain-making.
67 See notes on recollecting the Buddha and Amitābha above.
68 The Pure Land is the realm of Amitābha. See note above.
69 *Thiện thần* 善神 or "benevolent spirits" are described in Buddhist literature like the
     Consecration Sūtra 灌頂經 as protective deities (V. *hộ pháp* 護法, S. *dharmapāla*,
     T.1331.21.497a21). Here, Master Buddha clearly has in mind the Vietnamese iter-
     ation of two such deities, Ông Thiện (Mr. Good) and Ông Ác (Mr. Evil), who are
     also called Khuyến Thiện (Encourage Good) and Trừng Ác (Punish Evil). These
     two spirits are said to record each individual's karmic merits and demerits accrued
     throughout life.

Deceitful husbands and prurient wives were rich in shameful speech.

103 Seeing this, I feel sorry for myself;
To speak of it is terrible, but to stay silent only compounds my sadness.

104 Flying high and running far cannot escape,
Being caught in the net and left exposed so pitifully.

105 Who knows that transcendent Buddhas will convene,
To save the living and ferry the dead everywhere in the realm of dust,

106 To teach and encourage the masses of the dusty world's numerous regions,
To uphold the words "forbearance and goodness" in bowels set on cultivation?

107 Abandon words and do not contend;
Bodhi[70]—one seed of a sincere heart can go beyond.

108 At the serene supreme assembly of the Dragon Flower,[71]
Come that time, whether morning or night, evil and good will eventually be known.

109 My lot is that of a layman who dares to expound,
The precepts, ceremonies, and disciplines that I demonstrate and explain.

110 At the Prime Fountainhead, Ven. Śākyamuni Buddha,
Descended to be born in the world at the time of the Dragon Flower Assembly.

111 Whence people with lives spanning a hundred years return,[72]
Their hundred years of longevity decrease, falling to depart in youth:

---

70 *Bodhi* means enlightenment or awakening in Buddhism.

71 The Dragon Flower Assembly is the convocation of a Buddha inaugurating a new dispensation of Dharma. The Dragon Flower Assembly was often conveyed with millenarian undertones. Belief in the imminence of this event was not unique to the Seven Mountains but was endemic throughout the Mekong Delta regions of Vietnam, and it is also a prominent feature, for instance, of Cao Đài theology.

72 In Vietnamese, "to return" is a euphemism for death that is used in expressions like "return to heaven" (*quy thiên, về trời*) and "return to the immortals and serve Buddha" (*quy tiên chầu Phật*). In Vietnam, one hundred years was considered human's natural life span.

112 Reduced all the way to thirty,
    People three *thước*[73] tall live a life of starvation.
113 With many periods of calamity and torment,
    To now be thus reduced is indeed without error.
114 People two *thước* tall do not last long;
    Disease and sickness incessantly bring hardship.
115 Reduced in age, just stepping over to ten.
    People one *thước* tall meet calamity—people, heed!
116 Truly, great changes are transpiring in the mundane world;
    Ten-thousand men and women trek right into the mountains.
117 What the books still record is not empty;
    A girl with a husband, in five months, forms a pair.
118 At the end of summer, customs are strained;
    At dawn and dusk, with the kingdom in chaos, people do not
    seem human.
119 Unjust punishment and imprisonment are everywhere;
    But right before the eyes a place awaits.
120 With death one returns through the six paths[74] and four births;[75]
    On the path of transcendents[76] and way of humans,
    fortunately one is at peace,
121 While the likes of *asura*[77] and *preta*,[78]
    Animals and the hell-born suffer many calamities and
    hardships.
122 The four births are delineated clearly:

---

73 The former *thước* was approximately half a meter, although Master Buddha's usage
    appears chiefly rhetorical as opposed to descriptive.
74 The "six paths" are six "walks of life" through which living beings transmigrate
    from one life to the next. They are the paths of the hell-born, hungry ghosts (V. *ngạ
    quỷ*, 餓鬼; S. *preta*), animals, *asura* (V. *tu la*, 修羅), humans, and deities.
75 The "four births" are four means of transfer from one path of transmigration to the
    next. They are (re)birth through eggs, the womb, moisture (i.e., creatures perceived
    to come into existence without eggs or womb like worms, etc.), and (immaculate)
    transformation (deities, *asura*, *preta*, hell-born).
76 From the explanatory passage that follows this line, it appears that Master Buddha
    associated the "path of transcendents" (V. *tiên đạo*, 仙道) with the "path of deities"
    (V. *thiên đạo*, 天道).
77 *Asura* are spirits distinct from heavenly deities and inclined towards violence
    (whether good or bad).
78 *Preta* are "hungry ghosts." See note above.

Eggs, fetus, moisture, and transformation are the realms of Saṃsāra.

123 Uphold fasting and the precept against killing[79]—people, heed!
　　　Above is the Pure Land, the place that awaits.

124 As a human, you can understand kindness;
　　　So with transmigration through life so tremendous, save all species of beings.

125 The saints and spirits are illumined, right, and good!
　　　But as for wickedly killing all creatures first and foremost,

126 The things living creatures do are full of upheavals,
　　　For they kill and harm the living without regard for heaven and earth.

127 Shiftily they indulge in killing for sport,
　　　Only to later return to hell, where their misdeeds are punished without mercy.

128 Murderousness, debauchery, vicious sins,
　　　Spiteful words, and treacherous speech—heaven will work to compound their punishment.

129 Brazen with duplicitous tongues and wicked mouths,
　　　Although people do not see it, people's sins are numerous.

130 Ever so greedy and devious,
　　　Hell awaits the time they cycle through Saṃsāra.

131 Unfilial, they go against their fathers' and mothers' words,
　　　Though their birth father and caring mother are sites of deep gratitude.

132 Only when shadow officers[80] come for them do they finally realize,

---

79　The precept against killing is one of five precepts for a Buddhist layman like Master Buddha was in *ca.* 1842 (monastics typically observed at least ten). *Trì trai* (持齋) or "fasting" was generally used in the *vinaya* (monastic disciplines) to refer to monastics' abstinence from food after noontime. However, Master Buddha associated the term with the precept of killing, suggesting that he meant vegetarianism. Indeed, the vernacular reading of the Sinograph for *trai* (齋) is *chay*, which means vegetarianism.

80　*Âm quan* (陰官) or "shadow officers" are beings who administer justice and punishment in the hells.

That punishment will be administered so that their lot will be
that of wailing day and night.[81]

133 Clearly irreverent towards the Three Jewels,
They disparage the Buddha Dharma in many places across a
great expanse.

134 As a human, be awakened and clear yourself;
The transcendent Buddhas cherish you, and heaven's court
has compassion, too.

135 Cultivate your heart, cultivate your nature, keep it up constantly;
Cultivate through *sūtra* teachings transmitted from Buddha's
hall,

136 Cultivate your nature, cultivate pleasant conduct,
Cultivate the six words of Amitābha—do not remiss.

137 Cultivate the two aspects of filial piety and righteousness;
Cultivate the relations, cultivate the disciplines, and strive for
fortitude of filial piety and loyalty;

138 Cultivate benevolence, cultivate virtue kept within your bowels;
Cultivate a body of polished jade, and you will be sullied with
mud—do not bear it;

139 Cultivate merit by restoring shrine mounds;[82]
Cultivate wealth for devotional charity, but without devious
practices;

140 Cultivate prayer for saintly longevity and heavenly spring,
For people's health and creature's care, for escape from
grievance, hunger, and cold;

---

81 The original text has the two Sinographs 分據 (*phận cứ*), here translated "[their] lot
will be." Nguyễn Văn Hầu interpreted the second character as an error for *xử* 處
(處), thus yielding *phân xử* (分處), which means "judge" or "arbitrate."

82 A *miễu* in the Mekong Delta region is a small shrine dedicated to local spirits. They
are usually built on quiet mounds, foothills, and embankments. Votive mounds
were created as sites of worship ceremonies. Nguyễn Văn Hầu interpreted the
Sinographs (廟垤), here transliterated *miễu đàn* and translated "shrine mounds"
as a variant of *miễu đường* (廟堂), which can be pronounced *miễu đàng* or *miễu
đàn* for some Vietnamese speakers in the Mekong Delta. *Miễu đường*, as Hầu
explained, refers to the ancestral temple of the royal family. That seems unlikely,
since, in 1842, the Nguyễn Dynasty's ancestral temple, called Temple of Generations of Ancestors (Thế Tổ Miếu, 世祖廟), was located in Huế far removed from
Master Buddha's homeland and known travels.

141 Cultivate prayer for the ten thousand seas and thousand
mountains,
  For the pristine rivers to flourish and the myriad islets[83] to be
  at absolute peace.

142 Dawn and dusk prostrate to Buddha and recite *sūtra;*
  Supplicate the Master to become virtuous and reborn on the
  marvelous path.[84]

143 Fish that swim deep in a river cannot be seen;
  Hawks in the vast, expansive sky fly stratospherically.

144 Enlightened, one enjoys the celestial peach;
  The deluded, hell—whence shall one be reborn?

145 One's hands bind oneself tight;
  Seeing this with one's own eyes, one holds one's silence, mute.

146 One bustles upon hearing about sin and fortune;
  When in pain one thinks of Buddha, but once it's gone then
  no more.

147 Find words of empathy and move your lips;
  But not of praise and scorn, say "enough!" without designs.

148 Cases of errancy will be clearly stated,
  So that, in Yama's court, such sins' retribution through
  Saṃsāra will be hard to fathom.

149 What the *sūtra* say and Buddhas teach are parched of words;
  The enlightened see this, but the deluded do not.

150 Some places are joyful, others miserable and compounded by
  sorrow;
  The mired and the pure, two paths—with which way will you
  be concerned?

151 With the right karma you enjoy high authority.
  Without it you encounter an impoverished later life.

---

83 Nguyễn Văn Hầu treated the Sinographs 萬般 as a variant for the phonetically
similar 萬邦 (*vạn bang*), which means "ten thousand states." However, considering
these lines' succession of geographic terms (seas, mountains, rivers), the Sinograph
般 is here read *bơn*, meaning an islet on a river.

84 Here, prostrating before the Buddha/Master with the resolve to become virtuous and reborn (in the Pure Land) reflects the practice of *phát nguyện* 發願 (S.
praṇidhāna) or "profession of the vow" to assume the *bodhisattva's* path towards
the enlightenment of a Buddha and rebirth in Amitābha's Pure Land. See *Amitābha
Sūtra Spoken by Buddha* 佛説阿彌陀經 (T. 366.12.347b7).

152 Gilded words inscribed for a thousand neighbors,
    Do not dither—people, heed!

153 The rivers and mountains already flooded,[85]
    How could you not see that you have rashly lost your chance
    for Dharma?

154 Muddled through many drifting currents,
    Your spirits take to flight, fluttering like reeling threads.

155 Darting past like an arrow,
    To a different homeland, a different place, a region apart from
    beast and fowl.

156 Day and night obscured in darkness,
    Only once your ethereal spirits scatter, and your corporeal
    ones are lost does the cycle of Saṃsāra transpire.[86]

157 Inaugurating the turning and founding of an era,
    With different kinds of beasts, different humans, and new
    people.

158 People, Buddhas, saints, transcendents, and spirits shall endure;
    What ghost or sprite could disrupt the world of dust?

159 Embracing the world like a gourd,
    The heavenly Buddhas will settle absolute peace everywhere.

160 Now as you meet a Buddha who will descend to the living,
    The hundred clans are advised to do good and cultivate
    themselves.

161 I see the affairs of the world drawing near:
    Turning people, turning things, turning years, turning days,

162 Turning food and turning dress immediately,
    Turning husbands, turning wives, turning lords and kings,

---

85 Nguyễn Văn Hầu thought that the Sinograph for *lụt* (潦), meaning "flooded," was
    an error for *cạn* (泔), meaning "dried up" or "parched." Hầu's reading thus agreed
    with language elsewhere in the litany such as "parched of words," "age dries up," etc.
    Here, the Sinograph is translated "flooded" in consideration of the imagery of *nổi
    dặt dờ*, which means "drifting currents."

86 Here, Master Buddha conveys the belief that humans possess an aggregate "soul"
    composed of ethereal and corporeal spirits known as *hồn* and *vía*, respectively.
    After death, the ethereal spirits ascend towards the heavens, while the corporeal
    spirits descend to stay on earth, often remaining with the corpse. Humans are
    thought to have three ethereal spirits, but while men have seven corporeal spirits,
    women possess nine.

163 Turning hills, turning mountains, turning gardens,
    Turning buffalos, turning fields, turning roads that come and
    go,
164 Turning time, turning seasons, and then,
    Turning trees, turning fruits, turning flowers' timing,
165 Turning intimates, turning friends and confidantes,
    With speech and voice different from the past;
166 Turning bowels intent on slippery speech,
    Turning sickness, turning disease—how could the medicines
    of old treat them?
167 In the world at present, ghosts and demons run amok;
    Dharma spirits and talismans—can they save us?
168 As a human, do not rely on your ability;
    What you see in the morning, by evening where is it to be
    found?
169 For a time, you breathe in and out,
    But once your breath ceases, how can you fathom the scope of
    where you will end up?
170 One does not know how it was before birth;
    With death one returns to the shadow realm, and the spirit
    enters the gates of hell.
171 Three times a day the aggrieved spirit is beaten,
    Such profound, cruel grievance—who do you suppose would
    come to the rescue?
172 It is right before your eyes! Why are you ignorantly unconcerned?
    When the river has no bridge, whose ferry will you call upon
    to carry you?
173 Left parched passed noon,
    How could it do to go on toiling to dig a well?
174 When still of unmatched vitality,
    Why not cultivate and practice, for once old, what will you
    know?
175 When born in the past, one's nature was originally good;
    As one matures and accumulates wickedness, one frets that
    one has harmed oneself.
176 By nature, at birth, humans possess a spiritual quality;

It is because of oneself that one is deluded by dust and
confusion—who else is there to blame?

177 That sins amass in a jumble is not in error;
   I beseech you to repent and whet your spiritual nature,

178 So as to restrain yourself;
   With wife bound and children tethered, teetering adrift you
   shall not fall.

179 Sahā is an idyllic realm,[87]
   If you delight in seeking *prajñā* as you approach the open
   mahā[88] sea.

180 If hungry, then find recourse in Śākyamuni's field;
   If thirsty, then rely on the Lady Buddha's water for
   nourishment.[89]

181 The teacher's words, in times past, explicated;
   Take refuge in the words "tranquility" to trace the way
   through the clouds.

182 Sunlight is falling aslant through the trees,[90]
   Polish the words "four wisdoms"[91] and resolve to always study
   prudently.

---

87 Here, Master Buddha evokes the relativity of purity and defilement found in a
   number of *prajñāpāramitā sūtra*, which teach that the messy mundane world is
   essentially pure and, therefore, through personal cultivation and reparation, one's
   mundane existence can become the site of perfect enlightenment to pure Buddhahood. For example, in a passage in chapter one of *Sūtra Spoken by Vimalakīrti*
   (V. *Duy Ma Cát sở thuyết kinh*, 維摩詰所說經; S. *Vimalakīrti nirdeśa sūtra*),
   Vimalakītri, an advanced *bodhisattva* posing as a sick laymen, explains to Śāriputra,
   Śākyamuni's muddled student who suspects that his teacher's enlightenment is
   imperfect, because the world he inhabits is full of misery: "Could it be that because
   the sun and moon are impure, the blind cannot see them...? ... All living creatures
   sin, so they cannot see that Thus Come's (Śākyamuni's) Buddha realm is marvelous
   and pure. That is not the fault of Thus Come. Śāriputra, it is not that this land of
   ours is impure. You just cannot see." (T.475.14.538c09–12).

88 Here, mahā, a Sanskrit term meaning "great," is transliterated in Vietnamese as *ma ha*.

89 The Lady Buddha (V. Phật bà) is Quan Âm (S. Avalokiteśvara) in her female manifestation. Here, Master Buddha appears to allude to her depiction wearing white
   robes and holding a vase of dulcet nectar that soothes living creatures' suffering.

90 The image of slanted sunlight implies that the day is nearing its end; in other
   words, time is almost up.

91 It is unclear what Master Buddha meant by "four wisdoms," since the term has
   different meanings across many canonical texts and traditions, and nowhere in the
   litany did he explicate. He may have had in mind the four kinds of cognition theo-

183 Cultivation does not distinguish rich and poor;
> Dawn and dusk, observe the incense censer and bowl of water.[92]

184 With empathy, heaven and the Buddhas will see;
> Why desire for quantity? One should not crave like a pig.

185 Two spirits hold the registers on both sides,
> Recording sins and fortune to submit on humans' behalves.

186 With jade right at home, why not polish it?
> What dust is there to speak of?—smile and pass it on.

187 Without seeing ahead, without looking back,
> People today seem as if dreaming—how could their vision be steady?

188 A phoenix mirror illuminates above and below;
> A ruddy horse takes off, galloping up and down both ways.

189 Flashing by like a flitter of moonlight,
> Sometimes full, sometimes crescent, it ever so brightens and fades.

190 Flowers fall—in just a moment, spring passes;
> If you do not cultivate in youth, then once old what will you know?

191 With loose words, speaking irreverently,
> What do you know of rules and ritual?

192 Birth in this life is so miserable,
> That spiraling downward, in what lifetime can you live again?

193 I advise you to reform your evils and do good;
> Devotedly cultivate the Three Jewels and study for penetrating clarity.

194 The snake that is able to cultivate can become a dragon;
> As a human, why not look within yourself,

195 Such that your body suffers adrift,
> With calamity here and disasters there, transforming to be reborn in every way?

---

rized by Yogācāra masters that like the "four debts of gratitude" are found in the *Great Vehicle Sūtra of Contemplation on the Mind's Ground of Original Life.* They are the mind's cognition of rounded reflection, equanimity, marvelous observation, and actualization. (T.159.3.298c10–25).

92 Incense and water are the votive staples of Master Buddha's spartan tradition.

196 Sunlit is the scene, shadowy the homeland;
       Shouldering blessings, one returns to the sights of old.[93]

197 Possessing the karmic affinity, spirits and saints escort you,
       Because of your good recollection morning and night, time
       after time.[94]

198 My words spoken short and long have dried up,[95]
       Prostrate to Teacher,[96] go back and return to your original
       home.

199 Mouth chanting the recollection of Amitābha,
       Hands tracing the prayer beads, I keep vigil over my bowels.[97]

200 Reverently make offerings to the Lord of Enlightenment[98] for
     prosperity,
       For people's health and creatures' care, for a heavenly spring
       of absolute peace,

201 For kind fathers and pious children, for loyalty and fidelity,
       For pristine rivers and pacific seas, for peace and stability
       inside and out.

*Handwritten by Thái Văn Ý, who served as scribe, on the twenty-fifth day of
the eighth month in mid-autumn of the year Quý Sửu.*[99]

---

93   The world of living is described as the "sunlight word," while the realm of the dead
     is depicted as the "shadow realm." Here, Master Buddha returns to the idea that the
     transition at death is to return.

94   Here, the Sinograph *trưa* 晬, which normally means "noontime," may be a mistake
     for the graphicly similar *đêm* 眈, which means "night." In any case, the expres-
     sion *sớm trưa* means "morning and night" rather than "morning and noontime,"
     since the former is the phrase's meaning in classical usage as in the folk-expression,
     ở người dãi gió dầm mưa/màn trời chiếu đất sớm trưa nhọc nhằn ("Oh, you!—
     exposed to the wind and seeped in rain/ with sky for your mosquito net and the
     earth as your mat, you are weary morning and night."). This interpretation "morn-
     ing and night" agrees with Master Buddha's instructions elsewhere in the litany
     for morning and evening recollection practice (i.e., recitation and mindfulness of
     Buddha. See note on *chánh niệm* above).

95   Here, Master Buddha is referring to the 6–8 verse in which he composed *Esoteric
     Tradition*.

96   Here, Master Buddha's use of *thầy* or "Teacher" probably referred to Buddha as an
     epithet rather than himself as a first-person pronoun.

97   Here, Master Buddha describes the practice of "recollecting Buddha" (*niệm Phật*)
     by focusing the mind and reciting the name of Amitābha with a beaded rosary.

98   "Lord of Enlightenment" was an epithet for the imminent Buddha (Maitreya).

99   September 21, 1973.

SẤM TRUYỀN ĐỨC PHẬT THẦY TÂY AN

[1a]*Tuế thứ Kỷ Dậu niên, nhuận nhị ngoạt nhị thập thất nhựt,*
Trò¹ Trương trợ bút, nhứt quyển giảng.

1	Thừa Nhâm hồ cứ bước sang,	ngoạt trư² giáo giác kiếm đường chạy ra.
2	Nhiệm mầu vui đạo Thích Ca,	Thuyền môn hứng chí Di Đà lòng chuyên.
3	Nương thuyền bát nhã cho yên,	vào non ngũ uẩn tín thành sùng tu.
4	Hiếu trung trọn giữ một câu,	bãi tiên suối hạc cầm câu đợi chờ.
5	Liếc xem thuyền bá bơ vơ,	sóng khơi biển thảm³ dật dờ sông mê!
6	Bớ ai ăn ở vụng về,	không lo nước lửa nhiều bề chông gai.
7	Bởi mình ai dễ thấy⁴ ai,	để cho sa sảy mình chôn lấy mình.
8	Phật tiên chí hiển chí linh,	một câu chánh niệm thời mình thảnh thơi.
9	Ai ai cũng ở trong trời,	nhơn từ phải giữ đừng lời trớ trinh.
10	Biến dời cuộc thế thình lình,	thiện tồn ác thất thiên đình số phân.
11	Vẫn xoay⁵ thế giái phàm trần,	sự mình không biết mưu [1b]thâm ở người.

---

1   Nguyễn Văn Hầu: *Đồ*. This and further comparisons of my rendition with Nguyễn Văn Hầu's transliteration come from Hầu's *Sấm truyền Đức Phật Thầy Tây An* (Tòng Sơn: Ban Quản tự Tòng Sơn cổ tự, Ban Chẩn tế Giáo hội Phật giáo Hòa Hảo, 1973).

2   Hầu: *tháng heo*
3   Hầu: *thảm*
4   Hầu: *mặc*
5   Hầu: *xây*.

12 Hư nên nhờ phận Phật trời, non băng đất lở giữa vời linh đinh.

13 Phải làm như bốn nhựt trình, trẻ già xin nhớ giữ gìn mà coi.

14 Niên như điễn ngoạt như thoi, vần xoay[6] thế giái luân hồi chẳng chơi!

15 Có người thiện nữ truyền lời, Nhứt Vân thiên lộ máy trời thinh thinh.

16 Nhị Vân thánh ứng quang minh, Tam Vân triều hội gia đình phả vân.

17 Ngó xa xem cũng thấy gần, xa gần gió tạc(t) bụi trần sạch không.

18 Hắc đầu tử bạch đầu ông, bớ người dương thế sao không coi đời?

19 Đạo vơi vơi đạo vơi vơi, đàng xưa cảnh cũ lập đời sửa xây.
20 Buồn khoanh tay buồn khoanh tay, thấy trong con tạo khéo xây lạ lùng.

21 Đời bạo ngược ít[7] hiếu trung, miệng thời toan tín(h) lòng dùng mưu sâu.

22 Thiện phùng thiện ác đáo đầu, oan oan tương báo ai hầu[8] cứu cho?

23 Thẳng mà tín(h) thẳng mà lo, thiên đàng hữu lộ phải dò nẻo đi.
24 Nghe chi những tiếng thị phi, trách con mắc(t) [2a]thịt vậy thì chẳng coi.

25 Mở hai con mắc(t) thôi lối, nước xao sóng dợn ầm ầm bên tai.
26 Cực bớ ai cực bớ ai, cám thương trần thế dạy hoài không nghe.

27 Nước gần lớn gió đưa bè, giữ cầm lèo lái một bề thuận theo.
28 Dặm cheo leo cảnh cheo leo, một mình khó nổi chống chèo đặng đâu!

29 Làm sao chẳng xét trước sau? khinh khi chú lái ai hầu rước đưa?
30 Người đời như buổi chợ trưa, tan rồi lại hiệp hiệp tan mấy hồi.
31 Khóc lỡ khóc cười lỡ cười, tình tan(g) hời bậu cạn đời còn chi.

32 Lệ lâm li lụy lâm li, thương chăng thương kẻ từ bi giữ lòng.

33 Lọc nước trong lọc nước trong, sợ chi lũ kiến chòm ong chơi bời.
34 Ăn nhịn miệng nói nhịn lời, mặt(c) tình thế sự chê cười mặt(c) ai.

35 Dốc câu đặng chữ Như Lai, phủi câu danh lợi mặt(c) ai tranh tài.

36 Cảnh thiên thai chốn thiên thai, chí công luyện sắt giồi mài nên kim.

---

6 Hầu: *xây.*
7 This segment has an extra Sinograph: *đời bạo ngược ít* người *hiếu trung.*
8 Hầu: *hầy.*

37 Cảnh rất nghiêm cảnh rất nghiêm,   muôn thu xây dựng⁹ khó tìm đặng đầu.

38 Buồn dàu dàu buồn dàu dàu,   hỗn ngươn xoay lại [2b]đời nay mơ màn(g).

39 Mèo kêu vang mèo kêu vang,   rắn rồng sợ chạy vào ngàn ẩn thân.

40 Ngọn cờ phất trống thùng tan,   kẻ lên người xuống hai đàng khác nhau.

41 Quặn ruột đau quặn ruột đau,   Phật tiên thương chúng dạ sầu héo khô.

42 Gắng công lục tự nam mô,¹⁰   vạ may cá suối gặp hồ liên hoa.

43 Phật trời lòng lại xót xa,   giáo trong thiện chúng Long Hoa mà nhờ.

44 Gió đưa ngọn cỏ phất phơ,   sẽ coi cuộc thế như cờ bị vây.

45 Cảnh đã xoay cảnh đã xoay,¹¹   nhành rơi¹² đời khác đổi thay cuộc đời.

46 Xem trong máy tạo hết rồi,   ngửa nghiêng biến thẳm rã rời bờ ao!

47 Thuyền ai chạy tới sông Đào?   thuyền ông Bát nhã Phật vào độ dân.

48 Khuyên người sớm xả bụi trần,   dắt cho khỏi chốn mê tân bớ người.

49 Súc sanh ngạ quỷ là loài,   màng chi những chốn lạc loài đọa thân.

50 Tây phương thẳng bước chơn lần,   hưởng nhờ muôn thuở bửu châu thiếu gì?

51 Tín thành truyền dạy vân vi,   bớ người lớn nhỏ sao không giữ gìn?

52 Nay xem cảnh thế thình lình,   vô thường quỷ dẫn ai bênh¹³ đặng nào.

53 Sớm còn tối [3a]mất lao đao,   ví¹⁴ như trời chớp sáng nào đặng lâu.

54 Dặm canh thâu dặm canh thâu,   thở than than thở lo âu cho đời.

55 Nghĩ trong cuộc thế vơi vơi,   khổ tăng gia khổ trong đời gian nan.

56 Kìa kìa quỷ mị khởi loàn,   xà thương hổ giảo đa đoan hội nầy.

57 Phần thời giặc giã phủ vây,   phần thời đói khát thân rày chẳng yên.

---

9   Here, I take 朵 as a variant of 孕.
10 This segment has en extra Sinograph: *gắng công* thường *lục tự Nam mô*.
11 Hậu: *cảnh đã xây*.
12 Hậu: *nhành lai*.
13 Hậu: *binh*.
14 Hậu: *tỷ*.

58 Lăng xăng nhiều cuộc đảo điên,   sợ trong thế sự như thuyền chạy khơi.

59 Đã hết lời đã hết lời!   khuyên răn dạy biểu cho người thiện duyên.

60 Trách lòng nhiều sự chẳng kiêng, ốm đau cầu giảm an thuyên chẳng màn(g).

61 Biến sanh những sự tà gian,   hủy tăng phá giới lòng toan hại người.

62 Thế nay cạn sự đã rồi!   mở mang dời đổi lập đời thượng ngươn.

63 Chuyển luân thiên địa tuần hườn,   hội này thấy lửa tàm lam cháy mày.
64 Ít ai tỏ biết đặng hay,   ví như cầm chén rủi tay bể rồi!
65 Thấy xưa lời dặn hẳn hòi,   thực nhơn nhơn thực đến hồi chẳng không.

66 Oan oan tương báo chập chồng,   tham tài tích đại mình không xét mình.

67 Khiến xui phụ tử tương tranh,   cha không lành thảo con lành đặng đâu?

68 Trung quân phụ tử làm đầu,   phản quân sát phụ hãy[15] câu sách nào?

69 [3b]Trời xui trăm vật trăm hao, để cho đồ khó[16] xiết bao nhọc nhằn.

70 Ngọn phù thủy cuộc đất xây,   rồng nằm đáy biển sông hằng hứng sương.

71 Bao giờ hưởng thọ kỳ hương,   tuế tăng vạn tuế lưu[17] phương lâu dài.

72 Sanh thân này khổ bớ ai   trăm ngàn việc khổ chất hoài vô thân.

73 Phú hết phú bần hết bần,   than vong tài tán quan dân cũng đồng.

74 Khiến xui vợ lại giết chồng,   con mà hại mẹ tình không yêu vì.
75 Anh em đồng khí tương ly,   quân thần phản nghịch thế thì hạ ngươn.

76 Đổi dời hải thủy băng sơn,   tiêu đường quỷ mị nghĩa nhơn lập đời.

77 Tam ngươn quy dựng[18] lại rồi,   tang điền thương hải rã rời đổi xoay.

78 Lẫn lẫn tay tính tối ngày,   người nay như thể thấy rày lại không.

79 Chữ rằng nhơn vật dữ đồng,   vật còn biết tánh người không tỏ tình.

---

15 Hầu: *hồi*.
16 Hầu: *đồ khổ*.
17 Here, I take 晉 as a variant of 留.
18 Like above, I take 朶 as a variant of 孕.

80 Ngồi buồn than trách một mình,
thương trong thế sự thình lình tiêu tan.

81 Đua nhau rượu thịt nghinh ngang,
chửi cha mắng mẹ nhiều đàng ngược xuôi.

82 Biến sanh thấy sự hẳn hòi,
tử nhi vô hối hết đời tà ma.

83 Nhiệm mầu thuyền đạo Thích Ca,
Quan Âm cứu khổ Di Đà [4a]độ¹⁹ sanh.

84 Non đoài giữ dạ tín thành,
thấy cho cư sĩ học hành chưa thông.

85 Anh em ai có phục tòng,
theo tôi học đạo phải dùng tai nghe.

86 Phật truyền trồng thọ bồ đề,
giữ câu minh chánh chớ hề sai ngoa.

87 Muốn cho vào²⁰ chốn ta bà,
phương tiện bố thí hà sa phước dành.²¹

88 Kính trời kính đất thân minh,
tông môn phụng tự giữ toàn Tứ ân.

89 Sanh tại tiên hiếu song thân,
việc²² hậu vi nghĩa ân cần sớm mai.

90 Trung quân lòng giữ chẳng sai,
giới câu tiết chánh tỏ bày bia son.

91 Mình tu phải dạy cháu con,
đạo truyền kế đạo Phật môn lâu dài.

92 Thích Ca Phật tổ Như Lai,
lục niên tân khổ chẳng nài nhọc công.

93 Đến nay về hạ thần long,
ví²³ như thuyền nhỏ bị phong giang hồ.

94 Di Đà lục tự Nam mô,
vãng sanh Tịnh thổ²⁴ ra vô thanh nhàn.

95 Thoát nơi khổ hải mới san(g),
lánh vòng trần tục khỏi đàng tử sanh.

96 Phận tôi cư sĩ tín thành,
thấy truyền dạy chúng làm lành tu thân.

97 Hạ ngươn cuộc thế cũng gần,
tĩnh tâm tự giác ân cần cho mau.

98 Chuyện²⁵ tu chẳng khó ở đâu,
lấy câu bố thí làm đầu rất nên.

99 Thiện thần [4b]biên chép đôi bên,
thiện tăng ác giảm hư nên lời truyền.

100 Thuở xưa Phật dạy chẳng tin,
kẻ nghe người bỏ nói mình khôn ngoan.

---

19 I take ± as a variant of 渡.
20 Nguyễn Văn Hầu amended *vào* in this segment to *thoát*.
21 Hầu: *gìn*.
22 Hầu: *một*.
23 Hầu: *ti*.
24 Hầu: *độ*.
25 The Sinographic text has a tone indicator to distinguish this Sinograph's reading as *chuyện* from *truyện* and *truyền*.

101 Tham tài dưỡng vật đa đoan,   để nuôi thân thịt không toan nghe lời.

102 Sát sanh hại vật ăn chơi,   gian phu dâm phụ nhiều lời trở trinh.

103 Thấy rồi mình lại tủi mình,   nói ra thời tệ làm thinh thêm sầu.
104 Cao bay xa chạy khỏi đâu,   mắt(c) trong lưới nhặt dãi dầu khá thương.

105 Phật tiên tương hội ai tường,   cứu sanh độ tử mọi[26] đàng trần gian.

106 Giáo khuyên trần chúng nhiều phang,   giữ câu nhãn thiện lòng toan tu hành.

107 Chừa[27] lời đừng có đua tranh,   bỏ để một hột tâm thành đặng siêu.

108 Long Hoa thẳng hội tiêu diêu,   dữ lành đến đó mai chiều sẽ hay.
109 Phận mình cư sĩ dám bày,   luật nghi phép tắc diễn bày tỏ ra.
110 Nhứt ngươn đức Phật Thích Ca,   giáng sanh cõi thế Long Hoa hội kỳ.

111 Người sanh bá tuế sở quy,   bá niên giảm thọ hạ dời[28] thiếu thời.

112 Giảm chí tam thập đến nơi,   người cao ba thước là đời cơ nguy.
113 Tai ương khổ não nhiều kỳ,   giảm chí vậy thời nay thiệt chẳng sai.

114 Người cao hai thước chẳng dài,   ôn hoàng tật [5a]bịnh liên lai khốn nàn.

115 Giảm chí thập tuế bước san(g),   người cao một thước tai nàn bớ dần.

116 Thiệt là đại biến phàm trần,   vạn nhơn nam nữ thẳng lần sơn trung.

117 Sách còn ghi nói chẳng không,   con gái có chồng ngũ ngoạt thành song.

118 Mạt hạ phong tục long đong,   thần hôn quốc loạn người không y người.

119 Oan hình lao ngục khắp nơi,   nhãn tiền tựu thị là nơi để dành.
120 Thác về lục đạo tứ sanh,   tiên đạo nhơn đạo phước mình thành thơi.

121 Tu la ngạ quỷ là loài,   súc sanh địa ngục nhiều tai khốn nàn.

122 Tứ sanh phân nói rõ ràng,   noãn thai thấp hóa là phang luân hồi.

123 Trì trai giái sát bớ người,   cảnh trên Tịnh thổ[29] là nơi để dành.

---

26   Hậu: *mỗi.*
27   Hậu: *chử.*
28   Hậu: *di.*
29   Hậu: *độ.*

124 Làm người cho biết hiền lành,   vãng sanh vi đại cứu chư các loài.

125 Thánh thần minh chánh thiện tai,   ác sát mỗi vật đầu bài vi tiên.

126 Chúng sanh nhiều việc đảo điên,   sát sanh hại mạng không kiêng đất trời.

127 Đối thừa sát hại ăn chơi,   sau về địa ngục tội hành không dung.

128 Sát hại tà dâm tội hung,   vọng ngôn trá ngữ thiên công gia hình.

129 Lưỡng thiệt ác khẩu trở trinh,   người tuy chẳng thấy tội mình nhiều thay.

130 Tham lam gian giảo vậy vay,   ngục hình dành để đợi khi luân hồi.

131 Bất hiếu phụ mẫu nghịch [5b]lời,   cha sanh mẹ dưỡng là nơi ơn dày.

132 Âm quan về đến mới hay,   hành hình phận cứ[30] đêm ngày khóc than.

133 Bất kính Tam Bửu rõ ràng,   khinh khi Phật pháp nhiều đàng thinh thinh.

134 Làm người tự giác tự minh,   Phật tiền mến tưởng thiên đình cũng thương.

135 Tu tâm tu tánh giữ thường,   tu trong kinh giáo Phật đường truyền ra.

136 Tu tánh tu hạnh nết na,   tu câu lục tự Di Đà đừng quên.

137 Tu hành hiếu nghĩa đôi bên,   tu cang tu kỷ gắng bền hiếu trung.

138 Tu nhơn tu đức để lòng,   tu trau vóc ngọc lắm bùn đừng mang.

139 Tu công bồi đắp miểu đàn,[31]   tu tài bố thí việc gian thì đừng.

140 Tu cầu thánh thọ thiên xuân,   dân khương vật phụ khỏi oan cơ hàn.

141 Tu cầu vạn hải thiên san,[32]   hà thanh hưng vượng vạn bơn[33] thái bình.

142 Thìn hôn vái[34] Phật đọc kinh,   lạy thầy đức hóa tái sanh đạo mẫu.

143 Sông sâu cá lội thấy đâu,   mênh[35] mông trời rộng chim hâu[36] bay cao.

144 Giác thời đặng hưởng thiên đào,   mê thời địa ngục ngày nào đặng sanh?

---

30 The original text has the two Sinographs 分攄 (*phận cứ*). Nguyễn Văn Hầu interpreted the second character as an error for *xử* 處 (處), thus yielding *phận xử* 分處, which means "judge" or "arbitrate."

31 Hầu: *miểu đàng* (*miểu đường*).

32 Here the word *sơn* is pronounced askew (*đọc chệch*) with literary license as *san* to preserve the rhyme.

33 Hầu: *bang.*

34 Hầu: *lạy.*

35 Hầu: *minh.*

36 Hầu: *hâu.*

145 Tay mình lại chặt lấy mình,   mắt thời thấy đó làm thinh không
                                                    rằng.
146 Tai nghe tội phước lăng xăng,   đau thời tưởng Phật hết rằng thời
                                                    thôi.
147 Kiếm lời dễ cảm khua môi,   khen chê phải [6a]chẳng nói thôi chi
                                                    màn(g).
148 Dị đoan án nói[37] rõ ràng,   Diêm đình tội để khó toan luân
                                                    hồi.
149 Kinh rằng Phật dạy cạn lời,   giác[38] thời đặng thấy mê thời thấy
                                                    đâu.
150 Chốn vui chốn khổ thêm sầu,   đục trong hai ngả toan âu nẻo nào?
151 Hữu duyên đặng hưởng quyền cao,   vô duyên lại gặp thân sau cơ bản.
152 Lời vàng tạc để thiên lân,   có đâu trẻ nải quá chừng dân ôi.
153 Nước non nay đã lụt[39] rồi,   nào hay vội lỡ một hồi pháp cơ.
154 Mê man nhiều nỗi dật dờ,   hồn bay phưởng phất như tơ lộn
                                                    cuốn.
155 Thoát qua như ngọn tên bay,   khác quê khác xứ khác nơi[40] thú
                                                    cầm.
156 Đêm ngày mù mịt tối tăm,   hồn sa phách lạc mới nên luân hồi.
157 Mở mang xoay lại lập đời,   khác loài thú vật khác người tân
                                                    dân.
158 Còn người Phật thánh tiên thần,   yêu ma nào có loạn trần đặng đâu.
159 Tóm thâu thế giái một bầu,   Phật trời phân định đâu đâu thái
                                                    bình.
160 Nay đã gặp Phật giáng sanh,   khá khuyên bá tánh làm lành tu
                                                    thân.
161 Sự đời xem thấy cũng gần,   trở người trở vật trở năm trở ngày.
162 Trở ăn trở mặc bằng nay,   trở chồng trở vợ trở vì quân
                                                    vương.
163 Trở non trở núi trở vườn,   trở trâu trở ruộng trở đường [6b]vào
                                                    ra.
164 Trở thời trở tiết những là,   trở cây trở trái bông hoa trở kỳ.
165 Trở bậu trở bạn cố tri,   lời ăn tiếng nói vậy thời khác xưa.
166 Trở lòng ăn nói đẩy đưa,   trở căn trở bịnh thuốc xưa trị nào.
167 Đời nay ma quỷ loạn vào,   pháp linh phù thủy cứu nào đặng
                                                    chăng?
168 Làm người chớ cậy tài năng,   mai thời thấy đó tối rằng thấy đâu?
169 Có khi hơi thở ra vô,   đứt hơi nào biết quy mô chốn nào?
170 Sanh tiền mình chẳng biết sao,   tử về âm cảnh hồn vào ngục môn.
171 Nhứt nhựt tam đả oan hồn,   oan thâm nghiệt trọng ai hiểm cứu
                                                    cho?

---

37   Hầu: *nội*.
38   There is a redundant Sinograph here for *giác* 覺.
39   Hầu: *cạn*.
40   Hầu: *nay*.

172 Nhãn tiền sao chẳng biết lo,

sông không cầu bắc mướn đò ai đưa?

173 Để cho khát nước quá trưa,

ra công đào giếng cù cưa đặng nào?

174 Thuở còn trai tráng dường bao,

sao không tu tập già nào biết đâu?

175 Xưa sanh tánh thiện làm đầu,

lớn khôn tích ác mình âu hại mình.

176 Thiên sanh nhơn hữu tánh linh,

mê trần mê lẫn tại mình trách ai.

177 Tội làm một mẽ⁴¹ chẳng sai,

xin người tự hối giồi mài tánh linh.

178 Để cho mình buộc lấy mình,

thề thằng tử phược linh đinh không rời.

179 Ta bà là chốn thành thơi,

vui cầu bát nhã gần vời ma ha.

180 ⁽⁷ᵃ⁾Đói thời nhờ ruộng Thích Ca,

khát thời nhờ nước Phật bà dưỡng thân.

181 Lời thầy xưa có tỏ⁴² phân,

nương câu thanh tịnh dõi lần đường mây.

182 Mặt trời chênh⁴³ xế bóng cây,

giồi câu tử trí tánh hằng học khôn.

183 Tu hành chi luận giàu nghèo,

vùa hương bát nước mai chiều giữ coi.

184 Hữu tình trời Phật xét soi,

màng chi nhiều ít heo đòi không nên.

185 Lưỡng thần cầm sổ đôi bên,

chép ghi tội phước tâu lên cho người.

186 Ngọc nhà⁴⁴ sao chẳng trau giồi,

sá chi phấn thổ vui cười tay trao.

187 Chẳng coi trước chẳng nhắm sau,

người nay như mộng thấy đâu cho bền?

188 Gương loan sáng tỏ dưới trên,

ngựa hồng cất chạy xuống lên hai đường.

189 Phất qua như bóng nguyệt quang,

khi tròn khi khuyết nở tàn dường bao.

190 Hoa rụng⁴⁵ hồi lại xuân qua,

trẻ không tu tập thời già biết chi?

191 Buông lời nói chẳng kính vì,

biết đâu phép tắc lễ nghi chuyện nào?

192 Sanh thân này khổ biết sao,

để cho sa sẩy kiếp nào đặng sanh?

193 Khá khuyên cải dữ làm lành,

sùng tu Tam Bửu học hành cho thông.

194 Rắn còn tu đặng đặng thành rồng,

làm người sao chẳng xét trong thân mình?

---

41 Hầu: *tôi làm một mảy.*
42 Hầu: *cạn.*
43 Hầu: *chinh.*
44 Hầu: *lành.*
45 Hầu: *đong.*

195 Để cho thân chịu linh đinh,

tai kia họa [7b]nọ biến sanh mọi bề.

196 Dương là cảnh âm là quê,

phước mình gánh vác đặng về cảnh xưa.

197 Hữu duyên thần thánh tiếp đưa,

vì mình thiện niệm sớm trưa lấn hồi.

198 Văn dài lời nói cạn rồi,

lạy thầy trở lại phản hồi bổn gia.

199 Lầm rầm miệng niệm Di Đà,

tay lần chuỗi hột lòng ta giữ lòng.

200 Kính dưng minh chúa hưng long,

dân khương vật phụ thiên xuân thái bình.

201 Phù từ tử hiếu trung trinh,

hà thanh hải yên an ninh trong ngoài.

*Tuế thứ Quý Sửu niên bát nguyệt nhị thập ngũ nhật Trọng Thu
Thái Văn Ý phụng tả thủ bút*

歲次己酉年閏貳月二十柒日，徒張助筆畫卷尹

承壬虎拒跳郎、月猪教覺鈀唐趄州、丹牟盂道

釋迦、禪門興志弥蛇蠢專、姹禅般若朱安臥兼

五蘊信誠崇修、孝忠全俜爻句、墨仙濟鶴拎馴

化除倒祐船百巳為濤淵浚摻逸蒙淹迷、峪埃

婆拎用米、空卢諾焗鈗度蔡美、軸鲐埃駆慌底

妹沙雛鲐埓祁鲐、伏仙至显至灵、爻句正念時命浚

台埃巳捥冲美、仁慈師鎮付度派貞、变報后世辰

今、善存票夬天躜分。蓬境世界尼塵、事命坐別謀

[1a]

深於仏、盡乎迦尒伏夫、柬崩坦坧钟渴灵丁邶々如
本日呈祉藉嗔迦停仃房槐、平如电月如罐、蓮塔世
界逾迴庄刪、古仆善女伴疫、一雲天路損吳声也、
二雲聖應光明、三雲朝會家廷紛纭、祚賒袑拱償
斯賒斯迤鉴培塵泟空、黑頭子白頭翁咟仆晹吔𡩋空
槐㥍道鴻々道鴻々、唐智景前立他使墙、愴頙殟憸
頙稇㑌冲見造窖墢迤迄暴虐𠃊仆孝忠、呪时羑
信吞用謀淺、善途善恶别頭、寬々相報埦候救寁崎麻
信崎麻尸、天唐有路沛跳亀䠶雍之仍喈是水、賣兒耝

誤資刀、此如矢霧則荷功數、聽更改戰更改收、咀嘆嘆咽戶歐朱堡。

揚沖勾世滿々、苦增加苦沖危浪難、箋々鬼魅起亂蛇偽亮哎受

端會尼、分時賊假荷巾、分時消身劇庄安、叐稱統局倒顛哎

沖世事如耕趣湖危歇廁危歇廁、勅術代表朱州善緣責悉誰

事庄坐、癢病求減安疫庄幔、變生仍事那呀、髮僧破戒惹散宮

仆、世於近事色未、嗚若援對立區上元、轉輪天地循環、會尼覓焰

蠶藍煙眉凸埃訴別巧哈、吾如拎識啼插破未祭習劇咻哞咀食

人々食典回庄坐、冤々相報慨盡貪財積大命坐祭**命**、退哎父子

相爭、咤坐令討見令巧虎、忠君父子々頌、反君察**父**喊勾冊节、

[3a]

吴吹萬物萬耗、底朱徒苦爭色辱烟、荒淨水局坦堪蟾蝁躯底

滩怪樂霜、色除享為奇香、歲增萬歲晋方數魏、生身尼苦咱

埃、萬新役苦贸帳等身、富歇富贫歇贫、身亡財散定民拱同、

遠吹醬吏折種、兒兩害娱情空天為、英施同气相僑君臣反逆

世財下元、咐彼海水冰山、消唐鬼魅美仁立姚、三元通朵束来、

桑田滄海沼涞树送、踏々稱信最尋、仆齡如休覓尉束空、

字浪人拘與同拘伴別性仆空訴情、魅盆嘆責文命、傷冲也事

辰冷消散都凭醋盼迎逸、吐咤啼娱纸唐套吹、變生覓事

哗咽、死而每悔歇他邪魔舟年禪道釋迦、親音救苦弥陀

[3b]

土生、蒙先侍胞信誠、紫朱居士李行諸通、心藥姪埃古優從、

跣砰奇道師用聰駝、佛付種樹善挭、持勺明正渚分差沘、問

朱釙才娑婆、方便布施河沙福仔、敦矣敬坦神明、崇門奉祀仔

全四恩生在先孝雙親、段後為差戀勲嚴埋、忠若惡得庄

差硃勺筭正沂碑、碑龕、令修師吡招景、道付絡道侍門欸賤、

釋迦侍祖如來六年辛苦庄柰辱功、真齡米下神竜吡如船

乳被風江湖弥砣六字南無、往生淨土哷螕清閒覘尼苦海買訕、另

妄坐俗塊唐宛生、分砰居士信誠、紫傳吡众夕參修桑、下元局也

拱斯醒心自覺戀勲朱毛、付修庄善扲芄、祕勺布施夕頭吡識善神

編創姓边、善增惡減、虚半廚伴、諜碧佛吡症信心、仆補吶爺沖

禎、貪財养物及端底骏身酪空养髒廁、殺生害物嗦喇奸夫滋

婦銃廚詠员、偺乖命吏咿咻吋蔽溫声涤熱高懸睬

趣塊虎、貂呻狸狙觪油奇佟、伏仙相会塊祥、教生度死每唐

坐间、教勅坐众彭方、行勺恶善恶罪修行、谙廁仃古都茣善

提文吃心減仃起、龍华勝會遊邅、佑仝大媼旡朝化哈、分命屠士

溫拼律侵法則浂挑评叶、一无術帘搔潑除生塲世龍华會期、

仆生百岁所遁百半减为下稀少时减至三十义尾、仆高凹楚升色饿

危災狹苦惱铳期减至至时矜溇庄羔、仆高战楚聪溫瘅疾、

[4b]

病患困難、減至十歲、躯仙、得高父焚炎、姓咽民（笑州）大變凡坐、萬人
男女跑路山中、卅群詭明庄空冤妇古烟五月庵、末夏尼俗竜冬晨香
国亂仆空依仆、庭形勞獄至尼眼前就是廿尼底仆、托米六道四生、仙
道人道福仆清台、偕羅餓鬼卅類、畜生地獄魑灾困推四生分呐
缯娜卵胎濕化羿方輪迴、持齋戒殺陌仆境迷凈土羿尼底仆、少
仆朱別覽發、牲生為大救諸谷額、霎神明正善哉、惡殺每物亞排
為先、眾生彭搜倒顏殺生害命空堅坦矣、咄承殺害嗼制勒半地
獄眾仃空容、投害非漢罪文妄言誅語天功加形、而否惡口誅貞仆岙
庄覽眾仃靜台、貧益卅唉至羿、獄形仃底待數輪迴、不孝父母逆

[5a]

剧吒生撰養罪尼恩贻、滏安米天買嘹、衔形分據店、爭喫没、不敬

三室赠嫩、輕軟怖法鮇唐声、漂仦自覺自明、佛仙覺想天庭

脩傷、脩心惰性脩常、脩冲経教佛堂付㗻、脩性脩行涅郍、脩句六

字弥羌仃消、脩行孝美堆边、脩綱脩紀动忤孝忠、脩仁脩德底慈

脩掳胁王琮嫭仃芟、脩功墦垃庙垴、脩財布施役忤忤仃、脩永聖考天春民

康物阜塊定亂寒、脩永萬海千山、河清梁旺萬般太平、晨昏拝佛誦経、

袍崇德化再生道年、滥婆鲔源债瑰、溟濛美睈占侯悲萬覺忤

卯享天桃、迷忤地獄母帝卲生弤躺吏賀祂爺、輯忤倪妬夕声空

浪愿眶眾福凌孫、痲忤想佛駸浪忤帯鈎剥易感咕嗽唎唉神

庄呐芊之模、異端案内燈燃、倒庭眾苦菩輪迴、経浪佛代沸倜覺

覺財邛儅迷財儅覓、隻盃準苦淥愁、燭凄战我弄政臬節有緣

邛享權高、無緣吏喂身數飢貧、剧廣鑒底干新、古觉礼乃过澄

民喂諾策餘包澕未、帝咍唔埝文问法虬、迷老薪娑際魂悲

方弗如綵喻汪挽戈如厐瓷悲、榕圭魏榕脍獸禽、店导宠沒最

心諉沙魄落買戠輪迴、嗎芒撬吏立鎏、榕顙獸物榕小新民、群小

佛聖仙神、天魔帝古乱麈邝瓷、秘攷世界文飘、佛美分足瓷、太平

餘它喂佛降生、奇勒百姓少爸修身、事世怙儅拱斯、阻小阻物阻诫阻

吳祖唉祖壽永餘、祖壹祖媠祖位君王、祖柬祖尚祖梱、祖對祖吮祖唐

[6a]

[6b]

付村如曠釋迦、遏肘如諾庆妃养乐、前桼婴去许分、狼勾清淨唯

騒唐运、太吴征燼俸揆、砵勾四智性恒李坤修行之論颥甄行

未、鉢诺理朝俘槐、有情美庆策媈、慢方魁益攥限室鐵、而神

拎数堆边刾摸罷福奏迏未作、土如寧庄捂揍、託之移土盂呉婤

塲、庄視暑庄性年、作龄如贵愭鴆未作、翻鶱川许迀止駄紅

拮趁厭迕钺唐、佛戈如俸月光软驗軟头委残荒色、花冬闰更春冬

祉空修習肘皃别文、嗓厕吶庄敦為别龍法則礼俊傳亦生杲

尼苦别年、底未沙唯翻帚印生、奇勒改共夕令崇修三室李行乘

通塔伴修印成蜂夕四宝庄察冲身命、服未身貏昊迀災箕衬

[7a]

奴父生每反、陽廿境、陰廿主、福爺梗角㸌來境、哲、有緣神聖接

遠為齡善念最非踞悶、呵覷府呀淋素、袒紮俎爽反必奉豪、嘛

嘐晚念弥陀、枂珞緯纪悉此价憑、敏让明王興隆民康物阜千

春太平、父慈子孝中貞、河清海晏安寧沖外、

歲次癸丑年八月二十五日仲秋　蔡父意　奉　瀉手筆

[7b]

References

Ang, Claudine. *Poetic Transformations: Eighteenth-Century Cultural Projects on the Mekong Plains*. Cambridge, MA: Harvard University Asia Center, Harvard University Press, 2019.

Brindley, Erica. *Ancient China and the Yue: Perceptions and Identities on the Southern Frontier, c. 400 BCE–50 CE*. Cambridge, United Kingdom: Cambridge University Press, 2015.

Cassaniti, Julia. *Remembering the Present: Mindfulness in Buddhist Asia*. Ithaca, New York: Cornell University Press, 2018.

Chapman, Jessica M. *Cauldron of Resistance: Ngo Dinh Diem, the United States, and 1950s Southern Vietnam*. Ithaca: Cornell University Press, 2013.

Dật Sĩ ("Recluse," Trần Văn Nhựt) and Nguyễn Văn Hầu. *Thất Sơn mầu nhiệm*. S.l.: NXB Từ Tâm, 1955, 1972.

Di Lặc chơn kinh diễn am 彌勒真經演音 (*Vernacular Exposition of the True Sūtra about Maitreya*), xylographic text, Hanoi, National Library of Vietnam, accession no. R.1800.

Đinh Văn Hạnh. *Đạo Tứ Ân Hiếu Nghĩa của người Việt Nam bộ, 1867–1975*. Tp. Hồ Chí Minh: NXB Trẻ, 1999.

Đỗ Thiện. *Vietnamese Supernaturalism: Views from the Southern Region*. London: RoutledgeCurzon, 2003.

Đức Huỳnh giáo chủ (Huỳnh Phú Sổ). *Sấm giảng thi văn toàn bộ*. S.l.: Giáo hội Phật giáo Hòa Hảo, Ban Phổ thông giáo lý trung ương, 1966.

General Statistics Office of Vietnam. "Phụ lục 3: Danh mục tôn giáo." In *Tổng điều tra dân số 01/04/2019*. Online document. http://tongdieutradanso.vn/uploads/data/6/files/files/Danh%20muc%20ton%20giao%20TDT%202019_update.docx.

Hill, Francis R. Hill. "Millenarian Machines in South Vietnam." *Comparative Studies in Society and History*. 13, no. 3 (July 1971): 325–250.

Ho-tai, Hue-Tam. *Millenarianism and Peasant Politics in Vietnam*. Cambridge, MA: Harvard University Press, 1983.

_____. "Perfect World and Perfect Time: Maitreya in Vietnam." In *Maitreya, the Future Buddha*. Edited by Alan Sponberg and Helen Hardacre, 154–170. Cambridge: Cambridge University Press, 1988.

Kitiara, Pattana. *Mediums, Monks, and Amulets: Thai Popular Buddhism Today*. Chiang Mai: Silkworm Books, 2012.

Kulp, S.A. and B.H. Strauss. "New Elevation Data Triple Estimates of Global Vulnerability to Sea-level Rise and Coastal Flooding." *Nature Communications*. 10, no. 4844 (2019). https://doi.org/10.1038/s41467-019-12808-z.

Li, Tana. "Epidemics in Late Pre-modern Vietnam and Their Links with Her Neighbours." Conference paper presented at Imperial China and Its Southern Neighbours. Institute of Southeast Asian Studies, Singapore, 28–29 June, 2012.

_____. "The Water Frontier: An Introduction." In *Water Frontier: Commerce and the Chinese in the Lower Mekong Region, 1750–1880*. Edited by Nola Cooke and LI Tana, 1–17. New York: Rowman and Littlefield, 2004.

Lu, Dennis and Christopher Flavelle. "Rising Seas Will Erase More Cities by 2050, New Research Shows." *New York Times*, October 29, 2019. https://www.nytimes.com/interactive/2019/10/29/climate/coastal-cities-underwater.html.

Nattier, Jan. *Once upon a Future Time: Studies in a Buddhist Prophecy of Decline*. Berkeley, CA: Asian Humanities Press, 1991.

Nguyễn Bá Thanh Long. *Cổ Vật Hải Phòng*. Hải Phòng: Hội cổ vật Hải Phòng, Bảo tàng Hải Phòng, 2009.

Nguyễn Hữu Hiệp. *Nhứt sự nhứt dệ tử*. Hà Nội: NXB Văn hóa Dân tộc, 2010.

Nguyễn Long Thành Nam. *Phật giáo Hòa Hảo trong dòng lịch sử dân tộc*. Sante Fe Springs, CA: Tập san Đuốc Từ Bi, 1991.

Nguyễn Tự Cường, *Zen in Medieval Vietnam: A Study and Translation of the* Thiền Uyển Tập Anh (Honolulu: University of Hawai'i Press, 1997.

Nguyễn Văn Hầu. *Nhận thức Phật giáo Hòa Hảo*. Hà Nội, NXB Tôn Giáo, 1968, 2017.

_____. *Sấm truyền Đức Phật Thầy Tây An*. Tòng Sơn: Ban Quản tự Tòng Sơn cổ tự, Ban Chẩn tế Giáo hội Phật giáo Hòa Hảo, 1973, 1990.

Nguyễn Văn Quảng and Marjorie Pivar. *Fourth Uncle in the Mountain: A Memoir of a Barefoot Doctor in Vietnam*. New York: St. Martin's Press, 2004.

Patton, Thomas Nathan. *The Buddha's Wizards: Magic, Protection, and Healing in Burmese Buddhism*. New York: Columbia University Press, 2018.

Phạm Bích Hợp. *Người Nam bộ và tôn giáo bản địa*. Hanoi: NXB Tôn giáo, 2007.

Quốc sử quán triều Nguyễn. *Đại Nam nhất thống chí*. Edited by Đào Duy Anh. Translated by PHẠM Trọng Điểm. 5 vols. Viện Sử học, NXB Thuận Hóa–Huế, 2006.

Strong, John S. "A Family Quest: The Buddha, Yaśodhara, and Rāhula in the Mūlasarvāstivāda Vinaya." In *Sacred Biography in the Buddhist Traditions of South and Southeast Asia*. Edited by Juliane Schober, 113–128. Honolulu: University of Hawai'i Press, 1997.

_____. *The Buddha: A Short Biography*. Oxford: Oneworld Publications, 2001.

Sư vãi bán khoai. *Sấm giảng người đời*. Sài Gòn: Sen Vàng, 1949.

Tanizaki, Jun'ichirō. *In Praise of Shadows*. Translated by Thomas J. Harper and Edward G. Seidensticker. Stony Creek, CT: Leete's Island Books, 1977.

Taylor, Philip. *The Khmer Lands of Vietnam: Environment, Cosmology, and Sovereignty*. Singapore: NUS Press and NIAS Press, Asian Studies Association of Australia, 2014.

Thích Mãn Giác. *Was Hui-Neng Vietnamese?* Los Angeles: CA: Vietnamese Buddhist Temple, L.A., 1990.

Thích Quảng Huyền. *Dharma Mountain Buddhism and Martial Yoga*. Temple publication. Frederick, MD: Chùa Xá Lợi, 2007.

Trần, Jason Hoài. "*Thần quyền:* An Introduction to Spirit Forms of Thất Sơn Vietnamese Martial Arts." *Journal of Asian Martial Arts*. 13, no. 2 (2004): 64–79.

Trần Trung Hậu and Thích Hải Ấn. *Chư tôn Thiền Đức Cư sĩ hữu công Phật Giáo Thuận Hóa*. 2 vols. TpHCM: NXB Tổng Hợp TP. HCM, 2011.

Trần Văn Quế. *Từ Ấn Hiếu Nghĩa*. Sài Gòn: Tủ sách sưu khảo sử liệu Phật giáo Bửu Sơn Kỳ Hương, 1971.

Trịnh Hoài Đức 鄭懷德 (1765–1825). *Gia Định thành thông chí* 嘉定城通志 (c.1820). Sinographic text in *Gia Định thành thông chí*. Edited by Đào Duy Anh. Translated by Đỗ Mộng Khương and Nguyễn Ngọc Tỉnh. Tp. Hồ Chí Minh: NXB Giáo dục, 1999.

Upatissa. *The Stream of Deathless Nectar: The Short Recension of the Amatarasadhārā of the Elder Upatissa: a Commentary on the Chronicle of the Future Buddha Metteyya, with a Historical Introduction*. Translated with introduction by Daniel Malinowski Stuart. Bangkok, Thailand: Fragile Palm Leaves Foundation, 2017.

Victoria, Brian (Daizen) A. *Zen at War*. New York: Weatherhill, 1997.

Vũ Đức Liêm. "Rama III, Minh Mạng and Power Paradigm in Early Nineteenth Century Mekong Valley." *Rian Thai : International Journal of Thai Studies* 5 (2012), 293–326.

_____. "Vietnam at the Khmer Frontier: Boundary Politics, 1802–1847." *Cross-Currents: East Asian History and Culture Review* 5, no. 2 (2016): 534–564.

Vương Kim (Phạm Bá Cẩm). *Bửu Sơn Kỳ Hương*. Sài Gòn: BXB Long Hoa, 1966.

_____. *Đời hạ ngươn*. Sài Gòn: NXB Long Hoa, 1960.

Vương Kim (Phạm Bá Cẩm) and Đào Hưng. *Đức Phật Thầy Tây An*. Second edition. Sài Gòn: NXB Long Hoa, 1954.

Walters, Jonathan S. "Story, Stūpa, and Empire: Construction of the Buddha Biography in Early Post-Aśokan India." In *Sacred Biography in the Buddhist Traditions of South and Southeast Asia*. Edited by Juliane Schober, 160–192. Honolulu: University of Hawai'i Press, 1997.

Weber, Nicolas. "Securing and Developing the Southwestern Region: The Role of the Cham and Malay Colonies in Vietnam (18th–19th Centuries)." *Journal of the Economic and Social History of the Orient* 54, no. 5 (2011): 739–772.

Richard Stone (Hokkaidō University)

LOOKING FOR ONE'S SELF
IN THE OPPOSITE SEX

Introduction from the Translator

As a general truism, Nishida Kitarō has largely been accepted as Japan's first original philosopher. While the accuracy of this point may be debatable, it is at least not without good reason that Nishida has been so widely accepted in this role. Nishida's philosophy, particular his first major work, *An Inquiry into the Good*, sparked major interest in philosophy and Japan, and has served as one of the central pillars of twentieth century Japanese thought. However, even assuming that Nishida was indeed the first original philosopher in the history of Japan, we should note that the impact his work made on Japanese society was not immediate. In fact, upon its initial release in 1911, Nishida's all-important *An Inquiry into the Good* sold a mere 750 copies.[1] A respectable number, certainly, but hardly enough for Nishida to become a recognizable or revolutionary name. The fact of the matter seems to be that, in the years immediately after its release, both *An Inquiry into the Good* and the articles that lead up to its publication were sufficient for Nishida to be recognized in philosophical circles as an author of great talent, but hardly enough for him to be known as the representative philosopher of the Japanese people.

The key to Nishida's work finally becoming a best-seller, and unquestionably being recognized for his position in Japanese thought has typically been understood as the publication of Kurata Hyakuzō's (1891–1943) *Departing with Love and Knowledge (Ai to Ninshiki to*

---

1   Yusa Michiko, *Zen and Philosophy: An Intellectual Biography of Nishida Kitarō* (Honolulu: University of Hawai'i Press, 2002), 130.

no Shuppatsu).[2] While, certainly, there were young students like Nish-
itani Keiji and Miki Kiyoshi who had discovered Nishida's thought
before the publication of Kurata's work in 1921, they were not necessarily common. Indeed, as Miki himself states, he was one of the few
who had managed to do so before Kurata managed to make Nishida
into a public figure:

> In that year, I enrolled in Kyoto University's philosophy department, and was
> thus able to learn about Professor Nishida directly. My decision to study in
> Kyoto came about only after I had encountered *An Inquiry into the Good*. At
> that time, the Iwanami edition had still yet to come out and the book was out of
> print, so I had to find a used copy. Professor Nishida was as of yet still not widely
> known, although I had been told that he was something of a peculiarity in the
> world of Japanese philosophy. The reason that Professor Nishida would become
> widely known later on is, as I recall, the introduction given to his book in Mr.
> Kurata Hyakuzo's *Departing with Love and Knowledge*, which was quite popular
> with the young men of that time.[3]

As the story goes, Kurata's youthful and passionate confessions—
and the important role that his fated meeting with Nishida's text had
in facing them—struck a chord with the Japanese youth of the pre-
war era. The immense popularity was enough to bring *An Inquiry*

---

2   A note on the title is in order here. First, the Japanese title is 愛と認識との出発.
    We should first begin by recognizing that the meaning that Kurata intends is not
    entirely clear, even in Japanese. Typical attempts to translate the title have under-
    stood Kurata to mean that Love (愛) and (と) Knowledge (認識) will be depart-
    ing, beginning, or originating (出発). Thus, we have examples such as J. Thomas
    Rimer's ("Kurata Hyakuzo and *The Origins of Love and Understanding*" in *Culture
    and Identity: Japanese Intellectuals during the Interwar Years*, Princeton University
    Press, 1990) choice of *The Origin of Love and Knowledge* or Michiko Yusa's (2002)
    choice of *The Departing Point of Love and Cognition*. The inclusion of two "to"s in
    this title present us with another possible interpretation. Rather, from my under-
    standing, it would make much more sense to look at these as "with" in English (in
    the same way that it would be translated as "with" if it were written only as *ai to no
    shuppatsu* or *ninshiki to no shuppatsu*). If my understanding is correct, then Kurata
    would be the one setting off, and he would be doing so with both love and knowl-
    edge. While there is undeniable ambiguity in the title, I believe that my decision
    to render the title as *Departing with Love and Knowledge* matches well with the
    original Japanese and also makes sense in the context of the work itself.

3   Miki Kiyoshi, "Nishida Sensei no Kotodomo," in *Pascal·Shinran*, ed., Omine Akira
    (Kyoto: Toeisha, 2001), 270.

into the Good into the limelight, and introduce a generation of young readers to Nishida's work.

The source of Nishida's fame, Kurata Hyakuzō was born in 1891 to a relatively well-to-do family in the Hiroshima prefecture. Up until his time in middle-school, Kurata had proven himself to be a capable student who worked hard, consistently performing admirably in his studies. Around the time of his graduation from middle school, Kurata set his sights on the elite First High School in Tokyo, where he desired to study philosophy. However, due to practical concerns related to future employment prospects, Kurata faced opposition from his family (specifically, from his father, who wanted him to study law). Although he was able to eventually enter the school successfully in 1912, a series of disagreements with his father concerning his future (compounded with several pathologically intrusive existential quandaries) provided the young Kurata with a severely stressful situation, wherein he was left unsure of the nature of his own life and what value had has as an individual. It is on this note that, during the following 10 years leading up to the publication of *Departing with Love and Knowledge*, Kurata would experience a whirlwind of existential dread, philosophical break-throughs, romance, and his first big-success as a writer, *The Priest and his Disciples*.

Departing with Love and Knowledge itself was a collection of essays written from 1912 to 1921, as a reflection on his youth. In spite of the fact that the book was one of the most commercially successful and popular books of the Taisho period (1912–26), it has been long-forgotten by both academics and laypersons alike. The book has no over-arching story or narrative. Rather, it is composed of a series of seventeen essays written by Kurata at various parts of his youth. All of the essays published in the book serve to highlight a certain aspect of Kurata's growth from an uncertain high-schooler to a critically-acclaimed playwright, with all of them providing an introspective look into the theoretical and philosophical worries that haunted him. The most remarkable and unique feature of the text is the ostensibly confessional manner in which it is written. While confession was one prominent theme in early twentieth-century Japanese literature, Kurata's writings vary in tone to the similarly confessional or semi-fictionalized novels being written by some of his contemporaries.

Instead of being written as either a fictional narrative or as a strictly philosophical work, Kurata's essays instead appear much closer to a diary of sorts. All of the essays contained within *Departing with Love and Knowledge* offer a personal glimpse into the "inner-life" (内部生活) of Kurata himself. The language Kurata invokes in this text to transmit his existential problems was often bombastic, and helped give an added sense of dramatic flair to the worries with which he was facing. Complementing this bombastic form of writing was an odd form of synesthesia, with colors often used to describe the inner-life of both Kurata himself and others (Nishida's inner-life, for what it is worth, is described as a profound shade of blue).[4]

Of these seventeen essays, two of them deal extensively with the philosophy of Nishida Kitarō. In "The Epistemic Efforts of Life," while Kurata gives a relatively extensive, schematic interpretation of Nishida's work, it is likely the following essay, "Looking for One's Self in the Opposite Sex," that is of more importance to those interested in the history of Japanese philosophy. In this essay, Kurata gives a much more personal account of his meeting with Nishida's philosophy and the spiritual and ethical benefits that it offered for him. Or, rather, to be more specific, Kurata outlines the way in which Nishida's philosophy helped him overcome his solipsistic tendencies that had come about during a highly stressful period of his high-school life. This essay, which concerned precisely the most turbulent point of Kurata's struggle with his father to avoiding transferring to the law department, highlights an important moment in his philosophical life: the realization of his own self. According to Kurata himself, the episode was largely due to a philosophical epiphany or awakening to the fact that he is, in fact, an individual self, separate from his father or anyone else in the world. Yet, entailed within this realization was the lonely fact that, although his own existence as an individual was certain, the same could not be said of other minds. The compound pressure that came from both his epistemological concerns and tension in his personal life took an indubitable toll upon Kurata, as he describes in detail in this essay. The "solipsism" he experienced, i.e.,

---

4   Kurata, Hyakuzō, "The Epistemic Efforts of Life," in *Departing with Love and Knowledge*, (Tokyo: Iwanami Shoten, 2016), 51.

the uncertainty of the existence of others, drove him to chase away his closest friend and falter in his studies.

It was within this context that Kurata discovered what was (at that point in time) Nishida's little known philosophy. Quoting Nishida's famous edict that "it is not that experience exists because there is an individual, but that an individual exists because there is experience,"[5] Kurata describes vividly his feelings while reading, for the first time, the work of a philosopher capable of shaking the indubitable fact that he can intuit only his own existence as causing a "single tear to flow down his cheek." More importantly, though, it led Kurata to the conclusion that individuated selfhood is a secondary and unnatural way of being, and that he had to return to primal state described by Nishida in pure experience. The union between self and other, the most originary state of being, could only be found in love. This, Kurata believed, was the great lesson that Nishida's philosophy had taught him. In the rest of the essay (including the here untranslated second part), Kurata outlines his quest to achieve this originary state of being through the consummation of his existence with the opposite gender.

The essay is, in at least one sense, a possible clue for understanding both the intellectual concerns of the youth in the Taisho and early Showa periods as well as a means to get a grasp on how Nishida was able to become so influential within Japanese society. Kurata's attempts to make sense of the conflicts between his sense of self, his familial duties, and the influx of Western though (all the white living in Tokyo, separated from his friends and family) likely spoke to many young men in the 1920's and 1930's. Moreover, the (problematic) manner in which Kurata approaches relations with the opposite sex as a means to realize his personality may also be symptomatic of a larger problem. Keeping all of this in mind, a careful reading of Kurata's text could offer a great deal of information for those interested in the history of Japanese literature, thought, and philosophy.

---

5   Nishida Kitarō, *An Inquiry into the Good* (New Haven, CT: Yale University Press, 1990), xxx.

"Looking for One's Self in the Opposite Sex" Part 1

Similarly to a bright white flower blooming in the middle of a large field for the first time, when we first escape from our old habits and beliefs and open our eyes, everything around us seems to shine brightly. Our eyes are opened to the wonders all around us. At this time, dawn finally breaks after the long night that we had been living in. From this point [of awakening] onward, we become able to start living in earnest. We stand tall and begin to let our minds play. We thus bravely march along the frontlines and attempt to lead a rigorous life. I had never been as aware of my own existence as I was when I first experienced this awakening.

Yet, if we take a look around ourselves after this awakening, we will be shocked by the existence of grass, trees, bugs, and beasts that live by bathing in the same sunlight and breathing the same air that we do. We will thus be even more surprised by the existence of our fellow companions (*Mitmensch*), who are navigating the same kind of agonizing lives as ourselves. For those of us who have awakened to the "self" that lies at the bottom of our life, discovering other living beings always comes to us as both an alarming surprise and an important event. This problem of the connection between one life and another, the consciousness of one soul interacting with another, brings us to think of our inner-life. The more *freundlich* or *moralisch* of a demeanor one has, the more important this problem will appear to be. If one does not manage to take care of this issue, then it will become almost impossible to develop one's inner-life in a new direction. I believe this problem lies at the center of our inner-turmoil, and is probably responsible for a great deal of our suffering. In my case, at least, I have thought about this problem to the point that I lost weight. I, who had become painfully aware of my own self, have been unable to rid myself of these thoughts ever since I came into contact with the life of something other than myself. This problem was always bearing down on me, pressuring me. I believed that if I could not thoroughly work out this problem, I would not able to lead an earnest life. I could not take a powerful, fully-personal stance on this issue. [I was so caught up in these concerns that] my conduct became vague and stale. My actions all wavered between affirmation and negation.

This half-hearted way of life became torturous. I had to do something about this problem.

I was convinced that this [problem of] the interaction between one life and another—between one soul and another—was one of the great and solemn facts of the universe. As I attempted to get down to the very bottom of this problem, I became convinced that I could come into contact with a value great enough to move my very being in its entirety.

At this time, I became unable to separate philosophy from my daily life. I wanted to construct an unshakable foundation for living. Thus, I had to consider the interactions and relations between the life of the self and the life of the other from a philosophical standpoint.

I am alive. I believed there to be no fact more certain than this. One can immediately intuit the existence of their own self from within. I thus could not doubt this belief. Yet, how could the existence of others ever be certain to me? Although this metaphysical problem exceeded my own [philosophical] capacities, I still needed to gather my thoughts on the matter somehow. While I do not wish to write out my complicated epistemological theory here, it should suffice to say that—at that time—I was enthralled with Idealism. No matter how I thought of it, I could not admit the existence of others as anything other than a representation (*Vorstellung*) of the subject. For me, the existence of others was something faint like a shadow. It was not even comparable to something as powerful as the certainty of my own existence. I had high expectations for Personal Idealism and began to research it, but I was unable to accept the process in which it established the existence of other selves. Whenever I was thorough in taking Idealism to its intended conclusions, I always ended up falling into solipsism.

I was haunted by my awareness of the fact that I might be "the only person in the world." I was restless due to the loneliness of my cold [and solitary] existence. At the same time I was also enthralled with an unspeakably grave sense of authority and value for extreme self-affirmation. The self was solitary and it was everything. It sat at the center of the universe, lording over its every corner. Individualism is the path that is inevitably taken by those who awaken to the self. [Yet] even for such an awakened individual, there are still various external

pressures in one's daily life. For me, who was both faced with such
pressures and was pre-disposed towards individualism, the decision
to take such an epistemology as my foundation led to an extreme form
of individualism. When individualism conforms to the demands of
the self, it will necessarily fall into egoism. As long as I was earnest
in my attempt to provide a foundation for my inner-life in reality, I
was bound to become an egoist. Around that time, I had been drawn
into Schopenhauer's philosophy and was utterly moved by it. This
deeply pained, ironic, and utterly mad philosopher's thought proved
to have a disturbing affinity with my egoism and inevitably ended up
being a sad, pessimistic influence on my own thinking. I couldn't help
but become conscious of the blind violence at the core of the inner-
life that tried to assert (主張する) itself. I became fully aware of the
random, disharmonious assertions of a will trying to live. In my case,
considering the noticeably strong and rampant sexual desires I had at
the time, it was even easier to feel the brunt of this blind force. What
a wild and incomprehensible life I was living! As I watched over this
painful life carefully. I was still forced to live as though I was merely
being dragged along [by something]. At this point in my life, there
was no greater delusion than love. Moreover, there was no greater
mistake one could make in their life than sacrifice. I could not understand either of these two things at all. I tried listening to a Christian
tell me about love. I also tried fishing around for information about
theories concerning sacrifice in books as well. Yet, no matter what
explanations I received, they all lacked the fundamental capacity to
sway me. The reason for this being that my egoism was deeply rooted
in epistemology. My process of moving from solipsism to egoism was
a matter of necessity. The only thing that could bring me to part with
my egoism would be an epistemological theory that could fundamentally shake my solipsism.

Yet, sadly, I was not able to approach any books that discussed love
and sacrifice from a metaphysical standpoint. Nothing I found was
anything more than a vague and uncritical sham [of an explanation].
There was nothing as deep as the awakening to the existence of my self
nor was I able to obtain any kind of awareness that could penetrate to
the bottom of the other's soul. I [thus] found the vague claims concerning the importance of love and sacrifice to be mysterious. In this

way, I came to doubt the power, warmth, and light that love produces from the very bottom of life. Mr. Nishida is a passionate "philosopher of love (愛の哲学者)." Mr. Nishida furthermore states in his theory of religion—which comprises the core of love—that "a mutual relation between those with different natures cannot be established without an element of selfishness."[6] I believed that when an individual who had awakened to the reality of the self's existence came to thoroughly affirm the existence of others then a truly powerful love is borne. However, how could I possibly affirm the existence of others? How could I ever certainly, clearly, and vividly be sure of the existence of others in the same way that I can affirm the existence of my own self? And how could I ever admit an essential relation between the lives of the self and the other? I was perplexed. I could only reach the conclusion that such things were an impossible dream so long as I took solipsism as the foundation [for my thought]. At this point, I attempted to consider every question and critique of solipsism that I could think of. However, I could not come up with any other end point for Idealism than solipsism. Whenever I tried to look at the problem of interpersonal relations from this perspective, I could only end up passing through individualism to an extreme egoism.

Now that I think back on that time, my way of life was merely intellectualistic. I also don't think that my way of thinking—which was conceptual and did not greatly value emotions—was correct. However, my demand to understand the life of the self outgoing from "reality" was the only conscience that I—with my metaphysical inclinations—had in my life. For me, it was merely enough to fulfill my needs and continue living. I wonder just how uncertain I felt when I tried to go about my actual life after I had become trapped by this huge problem with such poor and undeveloped thought. I had attempted to follow the path left by those who had come before me and had only been able to *nachdenken* without ever proceeding on my own with *vordenken*. I wondered why it was that I felt as though I had to keep thinking in order to live even despite my limited intellect. I thought I wouldn't be able to accomplish this goal. Yet even still, whenever I thought that something might be needed for the sake of living, I wasn't able to just

---

6   Nishida 1990, 154

sit still. From my childhood I had decided that I wanted to be the type of person who could think about things [for myself]. I believed that thinking (*denken*) was necessary for living (*leben*).

The problem of the contact between one life and another is a solemn and important fact in this universe. I wanted to be faithful to [the nuances of] this problem. I did not want to take a vague and hollow attitude towards it. Although I was young, I had decided to pursue the path that I believed to be the truth.

In this way, I became an extreme egoist. Moreover, the lingering bad influence from Schopenhauer's philosophy brought me to become a rather combative egoist. From the beginning, I was a desperate egoist steeling myself against the pain and disharmony of life. I wanted to fight as much as I could, taste everything in life that any egoist must taste, and then die. I cannot forget the strange tension that I had felt during that time. My life had been dyed in the color of blood. I began to swell with overflowing desire. I possessed sexual desire that I had no hope to satisfy and walked around town like a beast. Doing so made me think of the afternoon rape incidents in Luoyang of yore. As I looked upon the foolish masses [during these walks], I started to believe that I could easily oppress them if I only had an army. The faces of Napoleon, Dong Zhuo, and Masakado all flashed before my eyes. I wanted to be strong. This was my only wish. I transferred into the law department [during this time]. I thought seriously about how I wanted the power to fulfill all of my desires. Power! Power was what occupied my thoughts. Power and desire! These two things are what made my heart beat. For me at this time, love and sacrifice were utterly mistaken. Instead of these, Hobbes' concept of the natural state of man, the state in which we find the war of all against all, resonated much more strongly in my mind. [The sound of] Schopenhauer's words, *Alles Leben Leiden*, rang constantly in my ears.

Yet, as my thought began to turn towards egoism, I came across that which would make me feel the most direct and harrowing thing of all. That was the presence of my irreplaceable friend "S." If I may say as much myself, the two of us had a friendship so earnest that we would shed tears for one another. I was proud of the detailed understanding we had of each other and the real (実在的) friendship that we had. I have vivid memories of the two of us sitting together at our desks [at school] in our youth. An almost inseparable bond existed between the two of us. Yet I was unable to confirm the existence of this very friend of mine. I wanted to affirm his existence from the perspective of reality but I wasn't able to. I wanted to touch the secrets of his soul but I wasn't able to. I wanted to cry from happiness after quivering from the tight embrace between one life and another but I wasn't able to. Even as I cried, I had to take the existence of my friend to be something faint like a shadow. I had to deny any real (実在的) interaction between us and keep all of our interactions to the economical level. For me, this was a terribly sad, anguishing, lonely, and tearful event. I was genuinely distraught. I remember one section of a letter I wrote to my friend.

> My friend. Between us there is now and forever a grey curtain descending from the sky that separates we two. The two of us remain caught on opposite sides of this curtain, listening faintly to the anguished breathing of the other. I can no longer look into your misty eyes with my own. I can no longer embrace you. Oh, what are we to do?

Yet, according to my intellectual way of life at the time, the only thing I could do was to abandon my friend. This was because I could not accept leaving any soul-less, empty interactions between us.

I admired the earnestness of my friend's attitude at that time. His kind disposition was enough to make me cry.

> You say you will separate from me. But I do not wish to let you go. If you want to separate from me, then I will only want to slowly embrace you so that my warm breath meets your chest all the more. My friend, if you leaving me now causes you pain, then return to me.

He wrote this for me. He furthermore warned me against running recklessly towards a transfer to the Law Department and wrote,

> Oh, my friend. Here on this cold dawn, I insist that you that you try and lay this mercury upon the palm of your hand. Its sharp chill will certainly be enough to make even your very soul shudder. At this time, I believe that your thought will be elevated by a greater power.[7]

---

7   While there is likely not enough context to make sense of this letter on its own, one possible understanding could go as follows: Kurata, as a solipsist, had lost sense

My friend wrote as such. Leaving behind such a loyal and dear friend was so agonizing that I truly felt I wanted to start crying. Now that I had separated from my friend, I was truly alone. Everything but the recurring gray shadow raging in my chest was gone. I took my position within the loneliness of my solitude. I did not even have the energy to quietly gaze at things or be impressed upon by nature. Even the very color of this solitude was a disquieted, unstable, and urgent thing. Even still, my inner-life was just as violent and tense as it had been in the beginning. Even as my inner-life took on such a ghastly color, it continued to burn [in this way]. It had become red like burning ashes.

After a while I once again began to doubt myself. I doubted whether or not the principles I was living my life by were actually fine. On the whole, I was an unashamed romanticist. From the time of my youth I had grown up being surrounded with warmth and love. I understood the happiness and joy in things from a young age. I was also quick to be moved to tears. I had never so much as fought with my friends. To be a combative egoist was entirely out of line with my personality. I wonder why, in spite of this fact, I still had to be an egoist. Life must be a unity of the intellect, emotions and the will. Is it not a mere plain fact that I loved my friend? As a psychological fact, knowledge and passions are identical and neither can be [considered] superior to the other. So why did I only follow along with only my intellect and ignore the indubitable facts of my own emotions? This is something that deserves to be questioned. Yet, it is also an indubitable fact that I could not affirm the reality of my friend's life. Thus, it would appear that this was due to me not taking life as something organic. My life was not a unified whole. It was torn asunder. My knowledge and my emotions were at odds with each other. There was a rupture. There was a vivid cut. As I looked on at that cut, I realized there was nothing I could do. For me and my metaphysical inclinations, the fact that these contradicting facts were opposing each other inside of one life was a truly agonizing event.

---

of the "reality" of the world. Yet, by experiencing the reality of the cold mercury upon his hands, Kurata could come into contact with something greater than his own abstract epistemological solipsism, and thus open his mind to an even greater source of philosophical inspiration.

I was truly suffering. I had no idea how I should live. I was like a frog wandering lost after escaping from his well. My internal strife prevented me from going to school. I would often wander around the neighborhood, leaving the destination to my feet, walking in random directions before coming home. That was the easiest way for me to live. Naturally, I couldn't study.

One day, while I was out for a walk, I stopped at a bookstore on my way home. I bought a single book with a dark blue cover. I had never heard of the author, but the book's title pulled me in.

It was *An Inquiry into the Good*. I started to read the book without thinking about anything in particular. After a while, my eyes were taken in by the following words.

Look!

> Over time I came to realize that it is not that experience exists because there is an individual, but that an individual exists because there is experience. I thus arrived at the idea that experience is more fundamental than individual differences, and in this way I was able to avoid solipsism.[8]

It was written right there. He managed to avoid solipsism!? The impression of these few words were burnt onto my retina.

I thought my heart had stopped. What I felt wasn't quite happiness or sadness so much as a quiet tension in my chest. I wasn't able to keep on reading. I closed the book and sat quietly at my desk. A single tear rolled down my cheek.

I put the book in my bag and left my dormitory. It was a quiet evening with a rare lack of wind. I was holding onto a certain indescribable feeling as I walked about the town. That night, I used a candle in place of a lamp in order to read this book that was full of surprises. I read through the book once, quick as a flash. It seemed difficult and I didn't quite grasp it, but I was charmed by this original and intuitive philosophy. The epistemology in this work was able to overthrow my own philosophy. I believed that this book was able to lead me to a bright new field. At this time I was surrounded by a quiet and metaphysical air. I felt myself melting away. I immediately wrote a letter to my friend and returned to the philosophy department. I told him

---

8   Nishida 1990, xxx.

that as long as we could renew our friendship, we would be able to withstand any hardship. My friend sent me a telegraph telling me to come now. I put down everything else and went to O-town so that I could be embraced by my friend.

We were able to shack up for the winter in a small house facing a quiet field at the base of Mt. So. This house is where I continuously read *An Inquiry into the Good*. This book fundamentally changed my epistemology. It instilled in me a metaphysical philosophy of love and religion. A deep, distant, esoteric, philosophy reminiscent of a summer dawn poured into my chest like light or rain. It was then integrated [into me] as though it had been absorbed into my [very] essence.

It is impossible to find love by looking at the fundamental movements between one spatio-temporally distinct human and another, as we would try to do from the perspective of the theory of evolution. If we try to start from such a position, interpersonal relations will end at mere egoism. However, what we can do is to draw out love from the most profound source of our life of the other. We can directly contact the essence of love. Love is a fundamental and real demand of life. Its source is the most profound and critical demand of life that stems from the distant origins of reality.

I never doubted that the notion that the individual consciousness of my [own] self was the most fundamental and absolute reality. I believed that, first, my self existed and only after that could various experiences take place after this. Yet, this epistemology was utterly mistaken. All of my turmoil, anguish, and the pathologies borne from them were contained in this mistake. The most primitive state of reality was not individual consciousness. That is one independent and complete natural phenomena. It is a unitary *Sein* with no such consciousness of self or other. It is the only reality. It is the only background. It is the spontaneous self-development of a singular experience. It is neither subjective nor objective, but is rather one absolute. Individual consciousness is not only something which is developed outgoing from the most primitive state of reality, its existence presupposes other selves to stand opposed to it as a necessary condition. For there is no subject that exists on its own without an object.

Hence, individual consciousness is not what is fundamental to life. The form of its existence is something which has distanced itself from life's most primitive state. It is a secondary and unnatural existence. It is not capable of existing independently and in its completion by itself. This is a defect that is held from individual consciousness from the beginning.

Thus, love and knowledge are not two separate spiritual/mental acts. The ultimate goal of knowledge is immediately the final goal of love. We must know in order to love, and love in order to learn. We can never escape from the law of identity. To know the form of the flower is to know the soul of the flower. A botanist who knows the truth of a flower must in turn be a flower. In other words, they must allow for their own self to enter into and become one with the flower. This mind in which there is no differentiation between self and other is precisely love.

> ... love is the power by which we grasp ultimate reality. Love is the deepest knowledge of things. Analytical, inferential knowledge is a superficial knowledge and it cannot grasp reality. We can reach reality only through love. Love is the culmination of knowledge.[9]

In this way, such epistemic love is the most crucial effort of life to support itself. Leaving behind our transient individual consciousness to find the most primitive, natural, and eternal form of true life is the most rigorous demand of religion. In this sense, love is, in and of itself, something religious. That is, love is the source of life's warmth, force, and light.

My thought changed as I was shacked up for the winter in O-town. The tension in my heart, as a selfish, combative killer, was loosened. I could feel a nostalgic love flowing through my heart. I had been waiting for my mind to calm as does the spring after a storm. And this spring had indeed come. I [thus] went back to Tokyo.

Yet, this calm, easy state of mind did not last long. I began to feel considerable instability from the bottom of my soul. It was an unspeakable feeling of anxiety. It felt as though my mind had lost its center and was fluctuating from left to right. I could not find any

---

9   Nishida 1990, 175

mental stability. It felt as though my soul was preening, looking for something. I was taken aback by a dreadful loneliness. I could not help but feel the cold, dangerous feeling that comes with being an existence who cannot stand to be alone. I couldn't find anything to grasp on to. I was left only to live while holding on to the chaos, loneliness, and yearning strong enough to make me think the center of my consciousness had moved.

I don't even know how many hysteria-fueled letters I must have sent to my friend in O-town. Loneliness and fear compelled me to take up my pen and write. A rainy and humid June had come. Day after day, depressing rain fell to the point that it seemed as though everything would erode. The muggy, depressing, and warm weather only served to bring an irritating sense of insecurity to bear down upon me. I was forced to live my life while being threatened by this ungraspable sense of insecurity in this humid climate, under the gloomy and cloudy sky with this heat.

Because it was rather anguishing to merely live vaguely without being able to actually discuss anything with my friend who was busy studying for tests, I went on a journey to Mt. Tsukuba. It was a lonely and sad trip. Mt. Tsukuba was quiet, surrounded by a pure white mist. I thought intently about how indifferent nature is as I hobbled along the mountain path. I quietly and coldly thought that nature, which had entrusted me with this lonely self, had nothing to do with me and I had nothing to do with it. There was no way that nature would do anything for me. Even if I were to beg while onto the bark of a grand tree or cry into the rain-muddied earth, there was no hope [of having nature acknowledge me].

I believed that I wouldn't be able to do anything if I did not have another soul to embrace. I believed that I could not go on without another life to let the fire of my own life alight. I wanted to experience the embrace between two souls, their kiss, their sobbing, and their weeping. I wanted to find my self within such an embrace.

I wrote the following on an old notebook left for those who had climbed the mountain in a teashop at the peak before beginning my lonely descent back down:

I came to the mountains searching for something. Yet, what I was looking for wasn't to be found in nature. It was other people. It was love. Even if some transcendent God existed it would mean nothing to me. Oh, is there no personal, immanent God? Is there no woman who will embrace me, in both spirit and flesh?

I had become even lonelier after I returned from the mountain. I became even more concerned as well. Still, I was able to give a clear form to the insecurity and disorder in my mind. It was because I could not give myself the object of my life's yearning. While the object of that yearning was not distinctly determined, I knew that it had to be something personal. I was seeking another personality. I was pining for the life of another. I could not stand to live by myself alone. I wanted to establish the ultimate foundation of my life in the absolute, found through embracing another life. It was this transformation in my inner-life that caused my mind's insecurity and chaos. I believed that it had to be this longing for life that [caused] the loneliness in my mind.

As all of this was happening, summer break eventually arrived and I returned to my hometown. My longing for life continued to deepen at this time. Moreover, day after day, I began to worry more. This shows both my religious enthusiasm and deprivation. As I led this overbearing life, my mind found no respite, regardless of whether I was standing, sitting, or sleeping.

I read nothing. I wrote nothing. I merely lazed about my house, only meandering about the mountains once I had become unable to bear just sitting around. [It was as though] my life was holding its breath and staring at something.

Around this time, my life started to become rather different than before. The fervent turmoil in my interiority would not allow me to lead a merely intellectual lifestyle. The chaos of my interiority was urged on by the demands of my emotions and I became able to meditate on them. How could one possibly gain a truly powerful life from a [following a] system made up of [mere] concepts? I began to think that a fulfilling life must be one in which its value can be intuited from the interior.

In my head, my thoughts cycled from my friend to God to women. I thought seriously about God. I laid my frail body upon dry grass and thought hard about God as I looked upon the bright blue sky. Yet, no matter what I did, I was unable to get any vivid feeling of God's love. I could not help but believe in the existence of an immanent and personal God in the sense that Nishida described it. Yet, this [sense of the word God] is none other than a different name for the originary state of reality. It is none other than the one reality, the one scene, *Sein*. There was no way that love could exist in such a complete and independent being. Through love, we can reach God. But from whence is God's love born? Rather than God's existence, I failed to understand God's love. Even if I read *An Inquiry into the Good*, I was still unable to understand this point. I could not appeal to any god, nor was there any god appealing to me. I never got the feeling that I was loved. There was nothing here that I could depend upon.

I searched for the object of my longing in my friend. [After all,] did I not have a friend in the flesh who understood me well and held affection for me? Yet, I was unable to find satisfaction here as well. My friend lacked flesh.[10] This caused me to despair at the very least. At this time, I highly valued that which we call "flesh." Flesh is the symbolic existence of life. Life is the one-ness (一如) which exists as an indivisible unity between spirit and flesh. When looked at from the inside, life is spirit. When looked at from the outside, it is flesh. Spirit and flesh cannot be thought of separately from one another. The spirit does not exist alone without the flesh.

As I longed for something personal, I began to want to long for spirit and flesh as well. Insofar as I desired an interpenetrating embrace between one life and another, I hoped for a living union of spirit and flesh. Because of this desire, I needed to find a woman. My longing for something personal took me to God, then to my friend, and finally led me to women. I then began to feel as though the object of my longing had been clearly determined. The entirety of my life began to look upon women while overflowing with feelings of religious reverence. In the corner of my soul, there had long been hidden a helpless longing for the opposite sex. This feeling had once been

---

10   Trans. Note: The contradiction between Kurata having a friend "in the flesh (肉づけられたる)" and "lacking flesh (肉が欠けている)" is both apparent in the Japanese and likely done on purpose here to emphasize non-platonic inter-sexual relations and his platonic relation with his friend.

put into motion as a lonely desire for sex and been completely dyed in the color of my lifestyle as a combative egoist. Yet, after having awakened from that savage way of living and returning to a more profound, quiet, and earnest religious feeling, this feeling also became more profound, kinder, and more sincere. Toward the opposite sex, I felt generous, honest, and magnanimous. As soon as I came to thinking about the problem of sex, my chest began to flutter. Thus was the extent of the solemn expectations I held for this problem. There was no mistake: the capacity to bring out my natural talents and allow me to grow [as a human being] was hidden within the opposite sex. Moreover, there was no mistake that within women lied the secret to making light shine through their contact with men. I wanted to be able to come into contact with that secret. I truly believed that in the contact between the two sexes, the embrace between the two sexes, a value and significance [profound enough to] leave us paralyzed would burst forth as a golden light. I believed that when I, who had the flesh and spirit of a man, united directly with the flesh and spirit of a woman, I would find the most sublime religion. True religion was to be found in sex. Oh, was there no woman who could make my male soul affirm [even] death? Oh, women! I anxiously pursued the venerable, primitive [existence known as] women.

The shadows of various women passed by side. I was surprised first by the conventionality of women. I had become sick of their cowardice. I was disappointed by their smallness [i.e., the small-mindedness of women], unable to accept men's grand desires for personality. I did not want the kind of one-sided and naive love that you find between an older sister and her little brother. I wanted an embrace strong enough to cause one life and another to wail together. Whenever I would charge in, they [i.e., women] would run away. I couldn't help but wonder if my grave, serious efforts would not be reduced to mere play as I pursued women. I began to wonder if perhaps maidens would not be of any use [in my quest]. Between alcohol, flesh, and addiction, we find tears of passion. I believed that amidst these things, there might be a woman capable of making me fully aware of life. I thus threw away common-sense and went to the right light district to pursue such a personal love from women. Here, I did not go searching for the flesh [of a woman]. I was still a virgin and, for certain reasons, my genitalia had been rendered dysfunctional due to disease. Still, I went to seek out a woman who would be willing to accept my entire life, not only my flesh or my soul. Yet, this ended in disappointment. I couldn't help but find it mysterious how the beautiful bodies of these women, with such glossy black hair and graceful white skin, could house such inferior souls. It got to the point that I felt as I though I wanted to merely take from them their corporeal beauty. Why were women so horrible? It wasn't so much the case that I was angry. [Rather] it was more the case that I was sad. I came to believe that my only option was to eradicate women, and leave behind only their flesh.

Those who have strong desires towards women may very well not be able to satisfy those desires through women [alone]. Women living in the real world may all be shallow and conventional. There may not be a woman willing to accept a man like me, who if looked at from the standpoint of social conventions, is not healthy. Oh, is there no woman who can make a man affirm [even] death? Is this nothing more than the empty wish of an idealist?[11] I could only let out a grand sigh as I entertained such thoughts.

Looking back, I had come this far by racking my brain, thinking about interpersonal relations. This was not a proud memory. If I could not search for fulfillment through women, then where could I find it? Turning back now after all this work would have been a shame. I couldn't bring myself to do such a thing. I wanted to clash. I needed to clash. I wanted to clash with the crisis of a life with great value and meaning. I wanted to find a total affirmation or negation of life in its entirety.

This is what I thought. Thus, I started to look for women as though I were a starving man looking for food. Lo and behold, I found one.

End Part 1.

---

11   Trans. Note: Here, idealist is written in Katakana. It's likely that this signals an idealistic view of life, rather than Idealism as a philosophical position.

References

Kurata, Hyakuzō. *Departing with Love and Knowledge*. Tokyo: Iwanami Shoten, 2016.

Miki, Kiyoshi. "Nishida Sensei no Kotodomo," in *Pascal·Shinran*, ed., Omine Akira, 69–82. Kyoto: Toeisha, 1999

Nishida Kitarō, *An Inquiry into the Good*. New Haven, CT: Yale University Press, 1990.

Rimer, J. Thomas. "Kurata Hyakuzo and *The Origins of Love and Understanding*" in *Culture and Identity: Japanese Intellectuals during the Interwar Years*, 22–36. Princeton: Princeton University Press, 1990.

Yusa Michiko. *Zen and Philosophy: An Intellectual Biography of Nishida Kitarō*. Honolulu: University of Hawai'i Press, 2002.

Tanabe Hajime

REQUESTING THE GUIDANCE OF PROFESSOR NISHIDA[1]

Translated by Richard Stone and Takeshi Morisato

There is no need for me to once again state that Professor Nishida's masterpiece, *The Self-Aware System of Universals* (一般者の自覚的体系, hereafter *SASU*) is a stupendous monument that shows the heights and depths of the philosophical thinking of the Japanese people. We can only look up in amazement when we are faced with the endeavor to think of the formulation of this system of self-awareness with superhuman energy and persistence, to deepen the base to further depths, to seek further heights by improving upon his own improvements, and to create an awe-inspiring system which can only be compared to a Gothic Cathedral. The intellectual jewels, which adorn the entirety of his system, come bursting forth from his profound experiences. We can only give thanks to Professor Nishida and allow ourselves to be raised by these teachings.

Yet, Professor Nishida's profound thought is probably something which can only be understood completely only through long efforts, such as his own academic lifestyle. For an inexperienced junior like myself, there are certainly more than a few areas that I have difficulty understanding. I have already troubled him with the questions that go beyond my own understanding whenever each of the articles contained in *The SASU* were published in journals and have personally received his instruction. Yet regardless of this, whenever I read through this book, I still agonize over the difficult questions I have, just as before. To ask Professor Nishida personally for guidance about this, and to be able to familiarize myself with his teachings through conversation has always been a part of my blessed happiness. Perhaps

---

1   [While the title has historically been translated as "Looking up to the Teachings of Professor Nishida," I feel the idiomatic phrase 教えを仰ぐ should be translated more faithfully to its Japanese meaning.]

we may say that there is no one else as obstinate and unmovable as myself. However, even if this is true, there might still be someone who has questions similar to my own but is not fortunate enough to be able to personally ask Professor Nishida about his teachings. Now, rather than lament my own shallow foolishness, I have decided to continue on for the sake of people like this as well, and publish my questions so that I may receive the guidance of the professor. I will also be able to organize my own understanding still more precisely by submitting my questions in writing. I would like to ask for Professor Nishida's forgiveness in advance, for being so rude as to bother him because of my own foolishness, and presenting these erroneous questions due to my own shallow mistakes. If he should kindly choose not to withhold his esteemed teachings, perhaps I will not be the only one who once again renews his gratitude to him.

1

The starting point of *The SASU* is the "expressive universal" (表現的一般者). From his previous work, *From the Actor to the Seer* (働くものから見るものへ), to the first half of *The SASU*, the so called "judicative universal" (判断的一般者) acted as the starting point of Professor Nishida's system. However, in the latter half of this book, the expressive universal gradually proceeds to the forefront, and finally, takes the position of the starting point of the whole system, while the judicative universal recedes to a subordinate position as the noematic determination of the expressive universal.[2] We cannot be conscious of expression as the self-determination of the self-aware universal, rather it gives the noetic determination, or the noema, that transcends this self-determination. It is the noematic content in the noetic determination of the self that sees itself as it becomes nothing. We can call its noetic direction as "acting" in the broad sense. Acting or expression is not a reflection of content which we are conscious of, it is the intui-

---

2   589–590. [The editors of the *Tanabe Hajime Zenshū* gives this reference. However, no version of the SASU corresponds to this pagination. We are aware that these missing references would have to be reformulated and updated when the translations are compiled into a critical edition in the future.]

tion of that which has transcended consciousness. The contents of the self are not seen, rather the content which has transcended the self appears before us by means of the self becoming nothing (自己が無になる). What lies at the bottom of this noetic determination is the flow of internal life. If this is transcended, the religious experience known as the self-awareness of absolute nothingness exists as the ultimate. Yet, this absolutely undetermined position exists outside of the realm of philosophy, which cannot allow for a complete lack of conceptual determination. Philosophy takes the most concrete noetic determination, the flow of internal life, as its ultimate. Still, even the flow of internal life cannot enter the scope of philosophy as it is. Philosophy, in so far as it is the self-awareness of reason, must also reflect the flow of internal life on its determined aspect (限定面). This [reflection of internal life] is noetically identified as the acting universal in the broad sense, and noematically as the expressive universal. Furthermore, when the determination of this universal limits the significance of the self that sees itself as it becomes nothing and moves towards the determination of self-awareness, the acting universal in the narrow sense and the universal of intellectual intuition are established in noetic and noematic directions, respectively. Each of them only constitutes one side of what is called the "intelligible universal" (叡知的一般者). In this sense, we can noetically see the act of will as the self-determination of the intelligible universal and noematically the content of "consciousness-in-general" as the intellectual and intelligible self.[3] The judicative universal means that the significance of the noematic determination of such intellectual, intelligible self takes a leading role (while its noetic significance reaches its minimum); and contrariwise, the self-aware universal constitutes the noetic determination [of the self] that determines itself out of its self-love in accord with the bodily determination. The existence of the conscious self cannot be anything other than the noetic determination of the self-love that loves itself in accordance with its corporeal matter. Moreover, for the self to truly love itself, it must return to the concrete self from the abstract self and finally be led to see its own self by making itself into nothingness. Thus, self-love means transcending bodily

---

3   Nishida is referencing Kant's Consciousness in General here.

determination, proceeding on to the self-awareness of the intellectual self, and ultimately approaching the self-awareness of absolute nothingness, which sees [itself] as being nothing.

If the simplistic account of the main parts of the self-aware system of universal I have just provided is without any grave errors, then the following issue stands out to me first. Professor Nishida has taken self-awareness to be the essence of consciousness, and further argues that self-awareness gives self's self-determination inside the self. In this context, we can think that the true meaning of self-awareness is accomplished as the self becomes nothing and sees [itself]. To lose the self, then, is actually to truly gain the self, and return to the natural state (本然) of the self that becomes nothing and sees is taken to be self-love. These profound teachings which have given an account of self-love, or the existence of the self, are an expression of Prof. Nishida's unique experiences. These are incomparable, high level, and profound thoughts, at which I can only marvel. However, can philosophy really systematize this kind of religious self-awareness? A system presupposes the final concrete entity, the absolute whole, not simply as something to be sought after, but as something given. If this final entity is not taken as the substratum of this system, then it cannot have a principle at the end. Of course, Professor Nishida has strictly distinguished the position of religious experience itself from the position of philosophical reflection and thereby specifies that the final self-awareness of absolute nothingness belongs to the former and not to the latter. Then he takes the noetic determination of the self-awareness of absolute nothingness, which holds the experience of internal life, to be the final entity in philosophy. However, according to Professor Nishida, this experience must be substantiated by, and reflect, the "self-awareness of absolute nothingness." Therefore, it is appropriate to think that the place of absolute nothingness directly determines itself. As long as this is the case, in his system of self-awareness, the final universal exists not only as that which is sought after, but also as the given. I have one basic question regarding this point. Professor Nishida has, since his last work, searched for the essence of consciousness using the structure of the judicative universal as a guide. [In this investigation he claims that] by the transcendence of the predicate, he has simultaneously sought the individual subject's place and interpreted consciousness as the self-determination of this transcendent place. As an unprecedented insight, I have nothing but great respect for these profound thoughts. The fact that Professor Nishida regards the interpretation of self-awareness given by German idealists from Kant onward to be incomplete, and that he adds a determination of place to the self based on the condition that the self sees itself in a unity of subject and object, provides an invaluable revision to these idealist philosophies, particularly the later work of Schelling and Hegel. Yet, as far as I can see, place is not that which spontaneously determines the self. It is the opposite, in that only through determination can it first appear as a place. Of course, we can say that "place" in essence precedes determination while the former appears to us as such through the latter in the sense that what precedes us is that which comes after us in essence and what follows us precedes us in essence. Yet regardless of this, what precedes the determination of a place at that time is its *Dasein*, not its *Sosein*. In so far as *Sosein* is concerned, a place first becomes a place through determination. What becomes a problem when we take self-awareness, in which a place determines itself, as a philosophical principle is undoubtedly the place's *Sosein*, not its simple *Dasein*. Should this be the case, a place will first become a place by being determined, so we cannot think of a place as something that is independent of any determinations and instead determines them as that which precedes any of them. We cannot say that a place makes determinations spontaneously by a principle of determination, which is included within the place itself. Put in others words, a place indicates the idea (in the same sense found in Kant's critique of reason) that reflects upon determinations or seeks for a reflection of them, and is not anything given to determine determinations. On the other hand, perhaps the place that Professor Nishida describes is a place of nothingness, and not a place of being. As such, we could say that there is no need to look for *Sosein* outside of *Dasein*. In actual religious experience, such a final universal likely appears as an omnipresent "I" as the "holder" [of all experience] (主). In accord with the particular noema of the natural beauty (such as what we understand in the Zen expression "red blossoms, green willows" (柳緑花紅), the "I" of absolute nothingness becomes active and subsumes this particular noema, thus turning all that is into the "I."

Yet, the final universal experienced here (as is the case in Dongshan's (洞山) three threads of hemp (麻三斤) or Zhaozhou's (趙州) oak tree (柏樹子) is only symbolically expressed through the particular noema; it is not what we are chorologically self-aware of as the final universal which subsumes noema and transcends noesis, the universal that philosophy demands. It only gives the appearance of the great effect that has transcended reflection. Nevertheless, when we take a philosophical standpoint and speculate on the place of self-awareness pertaining to absolute nothingness, in the same way that we understand undetermined existence as that which has less concreteness than this place and has been subsumed by it, as the place's self-aware determination based on itself, we are theorizing this place to be the final entity. As such an entity, this must have *Sosein*. In other words, the various universals at steps below the acting and the expressive universal in the broad sense as substantiated by internal life and the existence in them must be comprehended based on the necessary internal order of the final entity through its self-determination as the final transcendent noesis and further by its abstract determination. Is this not precisely the same as how Plotinus conceives of three hypostases coming successively from the One? They differ from one another only in that there is a strong noematic tendency present in the whole of Plotinus' philosophy, while in Professor Nishida's work, the transcendence of noesis, which is his unique and profound thought, acts as its basis. However, if we take this noetic transcendence as the place of self-awareness pertaining to absolute nothingness and think of the universals at various steps and the being within them as its self-determination, then this falls into one type of emanative constitution, and we must therefore say that it follows the same path as the philosophy of Plotinus. Still, even if I say as much, I would never want to disparage the philosophy of Plotinus or Brentano as a whole. Much less should I even consider myself to be someone who would ignore the characteristics of Professor Nishida's noetically deepened thought. What I doubt is only whether or not philosophy as a religious philosophy (in the sense that Plotinus' philosophy was religious philosophy) might lead us to abandon philosophy, insofar as we are constructing a final inaccessible universal and interpreting actual existence through its own self-determination. I wonder if such a posi-

tion would perhaps rather (mis-)take philosophy as a layered structure of the universal that contains the various stages of its development, the stages pre-rendered through self-awareness, instead of
basing itself in reality, and while maintaining that living ground, seeking a differential and thematic noeticicization, spirtization, subjectifi-
cation, or otherwise [what we mean by the term] self-awareness. From
the beginning, Professor Nishida doesn't intend to provide an emanative construction, nor does he believe that philosophy's possibilities
fail to go beyond an idealist interpretation. It is the opposite; he pays
special attention to the irrationality of reality, and stresses the primitive nature of willful acting, which constantly creates our reality. Yet,
regardless of this, along with the beings at the various steps that are
subsumptively gathered by transcendental noesis, [this] irrational
reality becomes nothing more than a shadow existence, and acting as
well cannot avoid turning into idealist production. Yet, regardless of
this, the beings at the various steps are subsumed by transcendental
noesis, irrational reality becomes nothing more than shadow-being,
and acting as well cannot avoid turning into idealist production.
Thus, what is manifest is nothing other than a detached observation
(諦観) of all that is. I cannot help but believe that turning philosophy
into religion leads to this problematic point. Hegel's system is one
conspicuous example of this. Professor Nishida's philosophy has, by
his self-awareness of place, become far more noetically refined than
Hegel's. Even so, by taking the self-awareness of place in absolute
nothingness as the ultimate, and attempting to systematize all the
universals by its self-determination, I wonder if he has now become
unable to avoid the same tendencies [as Hegel]. In the event that philosophy takes religious truth as its own content, it is no longer *philosophia* (love of wisdom/knowledge 愛知). Instead, it becomes *sophia*
(wisdom/knowledge).[4] This is already the destruction of philosophy
as *philosophia*. Of course, *philosophia* presupposes *sophia*. Yet, just as
the professor stated when he cited Augustine on the relationship
between self-knowledge and self-love, love of knowledge must simultaneously define the contents of knowledge. When we discuss love of

---

4   Note in Japanese, 愛知 could denote both love of wisdom and knowledge. This
     ambivalence helps Tanabe talks about knowledge/noesis in contrast with *sophia* in
     the following passages.

knowledge, we cannot assume knowledge to only be the path to progress sought after by our love of knowledge. Love of knowledge already contains knowledge in itself as infinitesimal knowledge. Knowledge does not exist independently of love of knowledge, [rather] it can only be realized by our love of knowledge. Love of knowledge is defined by knowledge, while knowledge is simultaneously defined by love of knowledge. This relationship must be mutually transformative. As is taught to us by the most profound aspect of Professor Nishida's philosophy, self-awareness is the self's becoming nothing. To truly live must be to die. Furthermore, if we think about this from the opposite side, we must live in order to die, and there must first have been a self for the self to become nothing. Still, at the same time, to live is to die, and the self's becoming what it is must mean that it becomes nothing. That which is self-denying, or in other words dialectical, lying at the bottom of this existence is what makes the entirety of our reflective self-awareness dialectical; and due to this [dialectical foundation of existence], the determination of this reflection must be mutually transformative. Hence, religious self-awareness is established where we can recognize the absolute sublation of the dialectical. This is living while dying, and having a self while having no self. Nay, it is because we are completely dead that we are completely alive. It is because the self is nothingness that we reach the state where all that *is* (すべての有) is the self. Here, there is no room to introduce something like mutually transformative determination. This is because it gives the position of absolute unity where there is neither that which defines nor that which is defined. While I may be horribly unqualified to even speak of the position of religion, I cannot help but wonder if it is not something akin to this. [At least], I do still think that what Professor Nishida has called the self-awareness of absolute nothingness is something like this. If this is the case, we must say that philosophy and religion, in virtue of their [very] natures, should not be united. This is because, as opposed to religion as the absolute stillness that subsumes all *dunamis*, philosophy must persistently remain as the dynamic movement that seeks stillness. The former holds the standpoint where quieting all movement, while on the contrary, the latter makes any stillness tentative, thereby constantly turning it into movement. If we speak from the perspective of *Dasein*, the same stillness found in religion is also presupposed in philosophy. However, in religion, this stillness appears, once and for all and absolutely, from the perspective of *Sosein* as well. On the other hand in relation to *Sosein* in philosophy, this stillness is always made into a temporary state and must remain only as a moment in the unlimited development of movement. In other words, religious experience is trans-historical, while philosophical reflection is both historical and relative. Of course, that which is historical is established on that which is trans-historical, and that which is relative presupposes that which is absolute. However, the absolute that appears as a moment can only appear as a differential point, and its whole is nothing more than what we can seek through this point as mediation. The trans-historical, which is presupposed as the basis of the historical, can only be a differential point included in the direction of the historical and hence, it is no more than an idea that we can eternally seek after through the latter. Nevertheless, turning philosophy into religion leads to eliminating this distinction, taking the trans-historical absolute to be the principium of the system—not as a mere direction of a differential point, but as an integral whole—and giving order to and organizing [as into a system] the historical and relative. This is the point where I hold my fundamental questions towards Professor Nishida's philosophy.

2

Some would argue that the doubts I have expressed in this essay stem from my inability to fully realize the true meaning of Professor Nishida's "noetic self-awareness of place" and mistaking it for the ancient noematic determination of emanative metaphysics. Even I have long been aware that my questions arise due to the fact that my intellect is inexperienced and that I am unable to follow his profound thoughts. However, I intend to understand noesis as that which subsumes noema, place as that which envelopes objects. A noetic ad chorological determination is certainly not something that espouses Emanation in the sense of a noematic and objective determination. I do know that, at this point, Nishidian philosophy stands beyond even Hegel. I have no intention to disregard the characteristics of Professor Nishida's self-awareness of, not being, but [rather] nothingness. However, regardless of all this, I cannot help but think that when the universal at all levels and all that is emplaced should be noetically turned into the self by means of the self-awareness of absolute nothingness, everything changes into the shadow of existence and is only surrounded by the light of quiet and detached seeing (静観諦観); in this case, lived reality as it is or action ends up completely losing its original meaning. Certainly, I can somewhat understand the idealist argument that that which is with shape is the shadow of that which is with no shape. Particularly, the Eastern religious self-awareness as "becoming nothing and seeing" is, for me, an ideology in a high ground that I cannot reach but sincerely long for. Yet, however I think about it, such a self-awareness of absolute nothingness can only be approved of as a religious experience that can appear at every point in reality, and must not be understood as the principle of a philosophical system which organizes reality's various standpoints as a whole. As the differential principle that provides meaning to reality at all its points, the standpoint of philosophy must also acknowledge this kind of religious self-awareness. Yet, at the same time, we must not allow it to be the integral principle of philosophical self-awareness. As I stated previously, as religious self-awareness follows the noema of reality, the final universal appears therein. In this case, there is no opposition between particular and general or distinction between noema and noesis between [religious self-awareness and the ultimate universal]. Nevertheless, philosophy must always hold a reflective standpoint of such opposition or distinction. Furthermore, if, based on the opposition or distinction, we take a religious self-awareness—which annihilates these distinctions—to be the most concrete and, hence, the final, and [also] if, in accordance with the gradual increase in distance between these distinctions and the development of the conspicuousness in the opposition, we establish the various stages of the universal as the abstract determination of the ultimate, then such a philosophical system would necessarily take religious self-awareness as the transcendent model for philosophical self-awareness and demand the conceptualization of religious self-awareness where it cannot reach this [demand] due to its limitation as reflective thinking, shall thus become nothing other than a merely incomplete version of religious self-awareness. The process of turning philosophy into religion grants a peculiar and independent function to philosophy but cannot in turn escape a propensity to make philosophy into a merely incomplete imitation of religious self-awareness. Intrinsically philosophy aims to have a "non-standpoint" (無立場) that remains free towards all other standpoints. Religion is also one of those standpoints, which is precisely why it should be transcended. However, if we take religious self-awareness as the unachievable, transcendent model that philosophy attempts to achieve and [furthermore] take it to be the final standpoint of self-awareness, then religion is no longer a standpoint that should be transcended by philosophy. Instead, it represents another standpoint that serves as the transcendent archetype of philosophy itself. Perhaps if we say that the standpoint philosophy should take is the standpoint of standpoints, then in this case religion is not only one standpoint [amongst others], but is the very standpoint of standpoints. From the beginning Professor Nishida's understanding of religion does not indicate (as is the case in the major religion of the West, Christianity) the faith in noematic God's creation of the world or control over reality, but refers to an Eastern self-awareness of nothing as its standpoint. Thus it is not one standpoint, but it is a standpoint without a standpoint (立場なき立場). Hence if we take this to be the standpoint of philosophy that serves as the standpoint of standpoints, we could say that this philosophy does not imply any kind of emanative philosophy. Yet, even what we can call the standpoint without a standpoint—that is, the self-awareness of absolute nothingness—as a religion, when it plays the role of the standpoint that gives the final principle to a philosophical system, becomes a single standpoint that guides us to understand the lower determinate and abstract standpoints as its determinations, thereby failing to remain as the "standpoint without a standpoint." Philosophy must rather be released from this and with this as the most extreme point, must be something that freely floats above this. If philosophy were to take this religious standpoint as its own standpoint, then it would be destined to meet with its own abolition. As we observe in set theory's paradox, "the set of all sets," the contradiction that the absolutization of the self necessarily relativizes the self shows its face here. Just as axiom theory must give way to intuitionism here, philosophy must also concede some points to relativism over absolutism. Of course, in its essence, philosophy also cannot adopt the position of a so-called "relativism" which, in some sense, attempts to deny any absolute whatsoever. This would be an obvious denial of philosophy. However, putting the absolute at the most extreme point as something merely sought after is quite different from setting forth an absolute as something given and making it the ground of this [philosophical] system. Here lies the reason why philosophy exists as the knowledge-loving movement that seeks the absolute while constantly following the relative. It is the same as the way in which the intuitionalism of set theory neither gives the finitism (*Finitismus*) that completely denies any unlimited set nor takes the absolute world-view of axiom theory but tries to stop at the always incomplete, open process of negation that pertains to *frei werdende Wahlfolge*. If we compare continuity to the concrete standpoint of religion, then religionized philosophy corresponds to axiomatic constitution of continuity, and what I view as the correct standpoint of philosophy would be precisely put in contrast with the standpoint of free becoming in the intuitionalism. Although mathematical intuition is noematic, the content of this noema is, as Professor Nishida's profound interpretation shows, the noetic determination itself.[5] Hence, we should be able to describe philosophy (or the formal structure of self-reflection on thinking life) as the self-awareness of the act of thinking.[6] The foundations of today's mathematics must be able to shed some light on the formal structure of philosophy. Then is it not a matter of course that those, who can admit the difficulties of axiom theory and [instead] agree with intuitionalism in mathematics, should cast doubt upon religious philosophy in the field of philosophy? It is not that I have used mathematical foundationalism as a clue to think of a philosophical standpoint, but that I think it is possible to more clearly state my doubts towards the latter by means of the former. I believe my fundamental doubts towards Professor Nishida's philosophy have more or less been made clear by the above.

---

5   335–6.
6   545.

If we take a look at my doubts towards the previously stated philosophical standpoint, some of us might claim that it is nothing more than a formal argument with no correlation to the concrete content of philosophy, thereby representing a superficial and uninvolved struggle of a critic who lacks imagination. Yet, I do not believe that this is the case. To the contrary, all my questions about the concrete content of Professor Nishida's philosophy, in my case, exclusively derive from my doubts against this fundamental position. I would like to to state this more clearly here.

According to professor, similarly to what Plotinus claimed, acting is a detour to seeing. The ultimate significance of our existence lies in seeing. To see is to turn the self into nothing and thereby engaged in [the act of] seeing. By the seeing self's becoming nothing, the true self can be seen. When the self becomes nothing, everything, at once becomes the self. In such a self-awareness of absolute nothingness, everything external becomes internal. Our existence completes its meaning within such religious self-awareness. The various standpoints, which do not reach this, are all understood as its determinations. As I have previously stated, it is based on this idea that Professor Nishida formulates the self-aware system of the universal—extending from the self-awareness of absolute nothingness to the judicative universal. However, if we were to take a standpoint like this, the irrationality or valuelessness of reality all stems from the abstraction of self-awareness, or in other words, from the fact that the seeing self has not yet reached absolute nothingness. If one were to achieve the self-awareness of absolute nothingness, the seeing self would be brought to nothing, by which all becomes the self. Hence, this would leave no that which is exterior or alterior to it, or in other words, there should be none of what we call the irrational as that which we cannot see. Much less should there be any grounds for the existence of that which would be seen as of anti-value insofar as the joy of the true seer is realized through the completion of self-awareness. In actuality, what we call "religious experience" is established in trans-rational and trans-valued self-awareness where the irrational is rationalized and the anti-value is valued. But when philosophy goes beyond accepting religious experience as one standpoint and further determines it as its ground in its process of completing itself as the standpoint of standpoints, all the irrational would be interpreted as the hypothetical manifestation of the rational and the acting that rationalizes the irrational becomes a shadow of the world as the detour to seeing. Does this not bring us back to Hegel's attack against quietism in philosophy? I find it particularly difficult to let go of the questions I have on this point about Professor Nishida's view of history and interpretation of the anti-value.

Professor Nishida greatly appreciates the irrationality of history and, in going against the rationalist philosophy of history, emphasizes that historical content is that which transcends the determination of idea(s).[7] According to him, historical content is noetically based on the self-determination of the self that sees itself as nothing. However, noematically, it is an incomplete self-determination, which is incapable of fully expressing this content. The self that is incapable of giving a complete expression of itself—or in other words, the self that cannot reach a noematic determination of itself in this sense—is the historical self. In this way, "existence and content in history are never joined. Existence cannot determine content and content cannot determine existence." What I cannot understand is this: under what circumstances does this detachment between content and existence occur? Of course, to ask "why" of the existence of irrational reality, or the existence of history as the incomplete noema of the self where it cannot fully achieve its true content is definitely going beyond the bounds of philosophy. Still, not asking "why" but "how" and seeking the constitutive principle of this existence is certainly philosophy's duty. However, we cannot give this [principle] only through the principle of self-awareness. This is because self-awareness indicates the universal's determining its own self within itself, and a sort of self-determination where the principle of determination lies within the universal. How can the noematic content of history fail to completely express this [self-awareness] when it is substantiated by a standpoint of becoming/seeing as absolute nothingness while taking internal life (which is its final self-determination) as its substratum? It is here that noema can never be made to reach noesis, and thus there must be a principle to explain the incompleteness of noematic content. This

---

7   518 ff.

principle is obviously within self-awareness and, furthermore, must oppose self-awareness. If self-awareness is taken as the principle of light, then if there is no principle of darkness that rebels against it, the irrationality of history cannot be understood. From the beginning, darkness is subordinate to light. The latter is the active affirmation to the former as the passive negation. However, while negation is subordinate to affirmation, it is a separate force that opposes it. Even if we say that it is merely the principle of passive degradation, that which works as the restrictive force of degrading must be a force in and of itself. This power is subordinate to the power of active affirmation and is not something capable of becoming independent from it. However, the force of active affirmation is always accompanied by the power to negate its own self in one side of itself. It works as the enemy of self and always holds the force to destroy itself inside. If internal life, which is the content of the self-aware determination of absolute nothingness as the ultimate were really to hold this kind of self-negation within itself, would this really allow for a self-awareness of absolute nothingness? A [so-called] self-awareness that leaves behind anything that cannot be made into the self can hardly be called absolute self-awareness. If the self-awareness that becomes, and sees as, nothing were to also transcend Hegel's concept and take the awareness of place, which has completely wiped out any noematic residue, as its essence, then it can only be practiced in accord with the noematically determined content. Only in this is it possible to escape from the dogmatism of emanative logic. If this is the case, self-awareness must always be mediated by self-negation, and although we say "self-awareness of absolute nothingness," it can only be done through the mediation of negative determinations. However, this robs self-awareness of its absoluteness and makes it an incomplete and relative self-awareness. If we take seeing the noematic content of internal life, which has been determined by negation as acting (行為), then acting, or in other words working (働くこと), is not only a detour to seeing from the standpoint of the self-awareness of absolute nothingness. This detour must also be an inescapable and necessary mediation. In order for seeing [to be possible], acting is absolutely necessary. However, can seeing, which is only possible with the mediation of acting, really see absolutely? To act means that the seer transitions from the stage in which it becomes invisible through determining itself to the stage in which it is seen. In other words, this is not seeing absolutely; it is making the invisible visible by means of this roundabout route. Perhaps it is not at the stage in which we become nothing and see, but only at the stage in which we see as being we can establish "working." Professor Nishida also clearly admits that "the acting self includes such a contradiction."[8] We must say that insofar as the [acting self] is acting, it is not visible absolutely. Yet, insofar as it is visible, there is no acting in it. Professor Nishida further argues that,

> Given the essence of noesis as the self-aware determination that subsumes noema, there must be that which is infinitely profound that transcends [even] artistic intuition at the bottom of the acting self. The determination of such an acting self can be considered to be historical.

By the term, "that which is infinitely profound," he must mean that which serves as the foundation of active seeing, the seeing that cannot be exhaustively seen through the mediation of acting. Such a thing could likely ground the irrationality of history. If this were truly the case, then the irrational principle, which lies in the foundation of history and is the originary ground of action, must always be a principle of negation vis-à-vis the self-awareness of absolute nothingness. We thus face a difficult point in that, so long as the self-awareness of absolute nothingness subsumes history with the mediation of the acting, it is not actually an absolute self-awareness and if it is to be the true absolute self-awareness, then it cannot subsume history or acting. As soon as we accept a principle of negation in the self-awareness of absolute nothingness, it loses its absoluteness in the domain of philosophy, thereby failing to give the constitutive principle of the whole, and remains merely as a limit principle of reflection that we can only seek after. The fact that Fichte—who in his early philosophy faced suspicions of atheism as a result of using activity and acting as the fundamental principle of his thought—found it necessary to develop a new epistemology that examines existence prior to consciousness in order to transition to the religious standpoint of his later work—which accounts for the religious joy of the true seer—should suffice

---

8   583.

as one historical example that proves my point. If this really does happen to be the case, then Nishidian philosophy—which takes the self-awareness of absolute nothingness (the noetic self-awareness that subsumes all visible noema and leaves no object external to itself) as its final principle and, by the determination [of this principle], attempts to formulate everything into the system of self-awareness, regardless of its emphasis on the irrationality of history—seems to have tremendous difficulties in accommodating the very irrationality of history into its system. That which is infinitely profound at the base of irrational, historical existence, must be the invisible origin of acting. Seeing is first undertaken through the mediation of the principle of negation standing in opposition to its own self; hence, religious self-awareness is only established in the free overturning of its standpoint that is in accord with irrational reality while taking the determination of historical noema as its mediation. Hence, it is not something to be taken as the final principle of philosophy that represents the standpoint that integrally subsumes history as a whole. Can we truly combine the self-awareness as the principle of philosophy and another as the absoluteness requisite for religion by the concept of "self-awareness of absolute nothingness"? I cannot let go of my question regarding this point.

That which is infinitely profound and serves as the ground for acting, i.e., that which I have described above, cannot enter into self-awareness. It is the principle of negation that eternally opposes the seer. Moreover, it is by means of this principle that the irrationality of history, or absolute contingency, is established. If this is the case, then the origin of anti-value should further be sought in resistance against the acting universal in the narrow sense of the negation principle or otherwise, the intelligible universal. The irrationality of history may merely be the opposition of the acting in general (the acting universal in the broad sense represents this) against seeing, but anti-value is born from the opposition between acting and the force that tries to negate this within itself. I also think this is what Professor Nishida means when he takes the will of self-negation as be the origin of evil.[9] However, can we ever really give an account of the self-negating will from

---

9   492.

the standpoint where we merely take the self-awareness of absolute nothingness as the final principle and organize the various universals and everything emplaced in them into a system? I think that if self-negation is the very nature of the will, by means of this the freedom of the will is formed, and also if we take the will as the concrete form of self-aware determination, then we can likely respond that accounting for the self-negation of the will as the origin of evil in a system of self-awareness is not at all problematic. However, I rather believe that the very move to take will as the concrete standpoint of self-awareness is contradictory to the demand to subsume the entire system with the self-awareness that turns itself into absolute nothingness and sees itself. The absolute free will, which is capable of infinitely negating itself, is probably a more profound existence than a mere "intelligible self" in the sense, precisely as Professor Nishida argues, that "a self in error is more profound than a correct self."[10] Yet, if, as he claims, the self-awareness of absolute nothingness is something "we can achieve by going through the bottom of the intelligible self,"[11] then can it truly be the ultimate place (最後の場所)? Professor Nishida furthermore takes it as "that which is substantiated by the self-awareness of absolute nothingness, and that which holds the significance of negating the determination of the intelligible self," and explains things such as anti-value will or negative will.[12] But how can the self-awareness of absolute nothingness oppose seeing and become the place of negative will, which tries to hold the standpoint of seeing as being (rather than as nothing). If we were to conceive of such a negative will as its direct and chorological determination, then the self-awareness of absolute nothingness is not the self-awareness of absolute nothingness itself. It would only be a stage in its process towards this [self-awareness], and so, I wonder, there would be no true self-awareness of absolute nothingness aside from the limit [concept] that contains this process and its accompanying negativity. It is here that we find an incompatibility between absolute nothingness and negative will. Is it really possible for the principle of anti-value as self-negation to be included in the

---

10   513.
11   513.
12   515.

self-aware system of the universal which takes the self-awareness of absolute nothingness as its final principle?

If my doubts truly have any basis, then I believe I may be forgiven for further submitting the following question. Professor Nishida has attempted to formulate Eastern religious experience in accord with the methodology of thinking available in western philosophy, developed his new and unique predicate logic of place by raising Aristotle's individualistic logic of subject to the extreme, and thus tied mystical experience with logical construction: this project has provided a truly revolutionary and original viewpoint. However can this be so easily connected with the philosophy of will, the idealistic analysis of will that first appeared in Christianity and later brought to completion by German Idealism in modern period? I cannot help but question if Professor Nishida, who was sympathetic to Fichte's similar idealist notion of the will, is not betrayed by this same thought [of Fichte] in his current standpoint of choratic self-awareness. The true standpoint of absolute seeing and the standpoint of willful action which can only have any meaning as the realization process of the invisible, cannot be constitutively joined with each other within the bounds of any conceptual knowledge in philosophy. I believe that philosophy does not have any such capability. It can only take the standpoint of reflective judgment where we can only relate one with another as a limit [concept]. Even with Professor Nishida's grand efforts, I still suspect that the standpoint of seeing and the standpoint of acting have not yet been joined together. I believe that this is a limit of philosophy itself. It is here that we see Augustine's difficulty in joining Neo-Platonic philosophy and Christianity.

3

Speaking from the standpoint that I have adopted above, I have several questions regarding Professor Nishida's comparative critique of phenomenology and Kant's philosophy.

Husserl's Phenomenology, he argues, refines the conscious self as the content of the self-aware universal from the determination of its internal perception and continues to the willful determination of the intelligible universal. It further abstracts the will's noetic content and takes a merely formal standpoint. By doing this, it comes to take intentionality and its effect as the essence of consciousness. Its so-called "pure ego" is also not anything that has achieved the standpoint of the "intellectual self-awareness of internal life" (内的生命の知的自覚), it is merely a purification of the internal and perceptive self. Therefore, the pure consciousness of such a pure ego gives a consciousness that we are conscious of, and not a consciousness that is conscious. This Nishidian criticism of phenomenology has acutely shown the limits of Husserl's position and offers us a great deal to learn from it. It is obvious that phenomenology cannot be taken as the [one and] only philosophy as Husserl believes [it should be]. I have absolutely no intention to defend Husserl on this point. However, if, the consciousness which is actively conscious (that Professor Nishida emphasizes in his criticism of Husserl), or the consciousness that embraces all objects and intuitively recognizes all content as its own self-determination (i.e., self-consciousness), can only be realized at the standpoint of religious self-awareness, and if we can only demand a limit relation to it from the standpoint of philosophy, that is to say, an adaptation of this [religious self-awareness] as the ultimate principle that constitutively organizes various standpoints really does lead to the problems I have mentioned in the previous section, then can we not say that Husserl, who called for a "rigorous science," had no choice but to stop at a contemplation on the essence of intentional consciousness? The fact that intentionality is nothing more than the essence of presentational consciousness, and loses the concrete content of willful, intelligible self-awareness is precisely what Professor Nishida has pointed out in his criticism. We can also say that Husserl's phenomenology is, in the end, nothing other than the reflection of mere intellectual consciousness. Yet, we should consider what Husserl has achieved within the bounds [of this reflection] to be a great exploration in previously untrodden territory [in the field of philosophy]. We cannot ignore the enduring significance of its results and only acknowledge the limits of this standpoint. If an "object" in Husserl's epistemology only means the limit of noematic determination, then we can say that there is no consideration of the noetic universal that subsumes even this. Still, we must acknowledge that this is a valid restriction in reference to Husserl's position, which avoids falling victim to the problem of "mystical intuition." Rather, the shortcoming of his position that we should denounce is that it constitutes a kind of intellectualism that does not ever go beyond an abstraction of intellectual consciousness, while taking this abstraction to express the concrete structure of consciousness as a whole. The fact that this problem betrays the intrinsic inclination of phenomenology to demand complete concreteness is a weak point that we cannot defend on any grounds. Heidegger's procession from Husserl's phenomenology of consciousness to a phenomenology of existence, and his shifting the basis of phenomenology to hermeneutics of expressions that always transcend consciousness, clearly aim to compensate for this weakness. That the expressive universal in Professor Nishida's self-aware system, which is more concrete than (and thus transcends) Husserl's position of the abstract and formal noesis of the intelligible universal given to pure consciousness, is often compared to Heidegger's standpoint proves this relationship [between Husserl's and Heidegger's phenomenology]. Nevertheless, Professor Nishida has pointed out that, even if we can claim that Heidegger's philosophy escapes from Husserl's standpoint of an internal consciousness where we simply "see" and approaches the standpoint of the self-determination of the intelligible self by taking the position of hermeneutic consciousness, because Heidegger still takes an abstract standpoint which eliminates the self-aware content of the self itself just as before, he cannot escape the limits of phenomenology, nor can he establish objective truth through the content of an intelligible noema.[13] I as well will not hesitate to admit that Heidegger's phenomenological ontology is unable to escape from such an important restriction or inappropriate abstractions.

The existence placed at the ground of Heidegger's phenomenology is an individual existence that negotiates with things as tools and achieves autonomy in resoluteness towards death. This [interpretation of existence] goes against the orientation of his ontology and causes us to lose our path to truly interpreting social existence. Because it

---

13   459.

lacks any negotiation with the world, which should be experienced religiously as the unity in which all that is shares the same life without any obstructions (instead of the negotiation with them as tools), the finite existence of the single individual floats atomically in space. I believe this is the fundamental flaw in Heidegger's ontology [which is otherwise] rich in creative thought. However, this is due to the fact that hermeneutical phenomenology, from its outset, was inadequate in following its intrinsic tendency to seek the most concrete phenomenon. If Heidegger had taken an already hermeneutical position in the beginning, I believe his philosophy could have escaped the abstractness that I have previously charged Husserlian phenomenology with. This is because that which is interpreted is not limited merely to abstract linguistic expressions. The interpreted can be an expression as the direct determination of internal life. Heidegger's existence made as the object of self-interpretation could not achieve this and this is the shortcoming of his philosophy; but it is not a defect of either hermeneutics or phenomenology proper. If we were to start from the self-interpretation of a communal existence that negotiates [existence] in the unity of world and life, then wouldn't hermeneutical phenomenology be able to reach the standpoint of the "self-awareness of internal life"? I, similarly to Professor Nishida's understanding, think that the existence which interprets itself in hermeneutical phenomenology is not only that which has meaning within itself and clarifies this meaning by itself [alone]. [If this is all there is to the notion of existence, then] the anticipation of the possibility of freed act in self, given to Heidegger's central concept of understanding will completely lose its meaning. Heidegger's "interpretation" indicates an interpretation of expression in the noematic direction corresponding to Professor Nishida's "active universal" in the broad sense. Could such an interpretation of expression be in principle roughly the same as Professor Nishida's "self-awareness of internal life"? I wonder if it may be possible for hermeneutical phenomenology to avoid many of the faults that Professor Nishida has pointed out in relation to phenomenology. However, the one point at which Professor Nishida's demand and hermeneutical phenomenology will never agree upon is that, as opposed to his self-awareness of absolute nothingness, where all is included within the choratic determination of the universal and nothing remains outside of self-aware determination, the self-aware-ness of being in hermeneutical phenomenology can never escape a so-called givenness (負課性) and always leaves something outside of itself, thus that the self cannot completely subsume [in itself] and thereby, the complete internalization of transcendence rooted in this [givenness] is no more than an idea. Considering this from the standpoint I have stated previously, it is rather phenomenology that more appropriately upholds the general boundaries of philosophy. To internalize all transcendental objects through the self-awareness of absolute nothingness and to subsume all that is in the universal as the self-aware determination lies in the domain of religious experience that transcends philosophy. Philosophy should not constitute itself with this as the final principle but only be capable of holding a limit relation (極限的関係) to it. As I have already stated my questions regarding this point, there should be no need to repeat myself here.

What Professor Nishida finds to be a running problem in general phenomenology is that, because its noetic determination does not hold the meaning of seeing the content of its own self, thus being abstract, it cannot establish objective truth, and that in order to escape from this, he argues, one must take a position in which noesis includes noema and that this [inclusion of noesis in noema] must derive from the self-awareness of the internal life of the pure self which subsumes intelligible noema. Kantian philosophy's "consciousness-in-general" regards this kind of intelligible noema as the essence of self-awareness. From this, we can establish the feature of critical philosophy, the subject that constitutes the object. We can say that a lack of such a principle of objective constitution is a serious weak point of phenomenology. The standpoint of phenomenology, even in Heidegger's work, does not actually go beyond the standpoint that focuses on the self-awareness of individual consciousness, and precisely as I have stated previously, does not follow the spirit of the discipline that is supposed to take the most concrete position. Due to this, it is a fact that Heideggerian phenom-enology does not include any relation to that which is most concrete which should ground the negotiation between the world and the self as the trans-individual unity of life. We cannot deny that both Hus-serl and Heidegger suffer from the flaws that Professor Nishida has pointed out and his criticism includes many important suggestions for phenomenologists. However, I cannot help but think that there is an important restrictive condition on this interpretation, namely the argument that the shortcoming of phenomenology is seemingly juxtaposed to the strong point of Kantian philosophy and the latter is shown to offer the constitutive principle that Professor Nishida demands. According to my own understanding, what Professor Nishida calls the intelligible self is roughly the following. In the self-aware system of the universal, internal life as the final concrete existence is what determines the individual universal itself, but it is not determined as the universal. Its self-awareness is only what we should call the self-awareness of absolute nothingness, and it cannot be the self-awareness determined as the universal. As its noematic determination, the active universal and the expressive universal first appear in the noetic and the noematic direction of this determination respectively. Because the active self has the significance of the noetic self-determination where it becomes nothing and sees, we cannot at all claim as long as the active self is seen, it is not seeing as being nothing: hence, it suffers from the contradiction that it is not the true active self. Therefore, we cannot say that it noematically determine its content without end. This active universal in the broad sense is divided into two: that which is in accord with the noesis side and that which is in accord with the noema side. While the former is the expressive universal, the latter is the acting universal in the narrow sense. The self-determination of the acting universal cannot be established in the sense of seeing all content of expression as the determination of its own self. Yet, only insofar as the self-determination that sees its own content is established, can acting have the meaning of self-expression. At this point, the seen noematic content can only be what is, in other words, the content of the noetic determination of the self-itself. This is the intelligible self as that which sees ideas, and what noematically becomes an idea must noetically be the acting. The intelligible self is, in other words, the acting self in the narrow sense. Hence, through the split between acting in the narrow sense and expression deriving from the contradictory nature of acting universal, the restoration of the unity between both gives the intelligible universal. Because of this, it sees the content of its own self as an idea and within the bounds of its determination, reflects the final self-awareness of absolute nothingness. Kant's consciousness-in-general represents the pure formalized version of the acting self-awareness of such an intelligible self without [paying attention to] its content. It is possible to regard this as the intellectual/intelligible self (知的叡智的自己) in the sense that it is something downgraded in the noematic direction of the intelligible self. However, because it is characterized as the projection of absolute nothingness that sees the content of its own self, as opposed to conscious self determined by internal perception, it has the significance of being the standard for the objective constitution of objects. As long as consciousness of reality realizes the intelligible self of the consciousness-in-general, it can know the objective world of objects as the content of self-awareness. Knowledge can only be established as self-awareness.

If there are no serious errors in the understanding I have provided above, then, we can see that consciousness-in-general, as the intelligible self, signifies the objective constitution of objects because, while being the acting universal in the narrow sense, it sees the content of its own self, and thereby the idea as seen noema gives the content of self-determination as noesis. In other words, insofar as it reflects the self-awareness of absolute nothingness, where the self becomes nothing and sees its own content, the acting universal becomes the consciousness-in-general. However, the acting self shows the contradictory nature that, when it is seen as the acting self, it cannot be considered to be the self that becomes nothing and sees. We can say that it is that which regards the self-awareness of absolute nothingness as the limit (case) and keeps an infinite distance from it. The irrationality of history that I described in the previous section corresponds to this distance. The irrationality of history derives from the principle of negation that resists against the point that the self-awareness of absolute nothingness subsumes all that is within itself as the final universal. In this manner, furthermore, this principle of negation serves as the ground for the contradictory nature of acting. If this is really the case, the formation of consciousness-in-general must be completely under the historical condition. The acting universal reflects the self-awareness of absolute nothingness in order for [the consciousness-in-general] to be established so long as the principle of negation that lies in the foundation of the latter is subsumed by within the former, that is to say, so long as history is rationalized. Consciousness-in-general can be established within the bounds of the understanding that the history can be rationalized, and we can describe it as the reflective range or categories that express historical rationality in the realm of knowledge. This [consciousness-in-general] and the final self-awareness of absolute nothingness are separated by an infinite rift and in this rift governs the principle of negation. This point precisely corresponds to the fact that Kant has determined the epistemic world of objects constituted by consciousness-in-general as the phenomenal world while, in contrast to it, determined the noumenal world of things-in-themselves as the objective, and yet unknowable, realm of objects that always transcends knowledge. Knowledge of transcendental objects is only plausible for intellectual intuition as creative reason. In relation to it, all existence will for the first time become internal. Because Kant mainly thinks about the phenomenality and the transcendental intentionality of knowledge from the direction of the sensible givenness as the matter for knowledge, he did not give any account of the historical condition of consciousness-in-general. Yet, if we look at the sensible receptivity as the origin of transcendental intentionality from the side of absolute contingency or irrationality, it would necessarily bring us to pay attention to the historical condition of consciousness-in-general. Opposed to this, creative reason can only subsume and internalize all that is as the trans-historical, absolute epistemic subject. However, because such an absolute epistemic subject and consciousness-in-general are separated by this gulf of absolute contingency and historical irrationality, consciousness-in-general can only be the limit vis-à-vis the infinite process of scholarly consciousness (学的意識) which develops infinitely towards the idea of absolute truth. Furthermore, what we call "limit" here is not a single extreme showing the direction of a series. Similar to limit elements of continuity, it signifies the principle that differentially rationalizes history at its each point. Consciousness-in-general corresponds to the limit of the infinite series that we should seek after as such a differential point. The idea as its content exists independently of, and without any relation to, history and yet it does not stop at being something more abstract than history in the sense that we cannot exhaustively pile history onto it. In accord with history, which always transcends it, the idea must bear the significance of the principle that differentially rationalizes history at each point. In this sense, we can talk about the historicity of the idea. The idea has is truly capable of conditioning reality by such a historicity. If the idea were devoid of such limit, it would have to be separated from reality. Therefore, the intelligible self which sees the idea, or consciousness-in-general as its intellectual side, must always be relative to history, and unable to escape from historical conditions. It is most certainly not what sees the content of self as the subject that trans-historically and absolutely constitutes the objective knowledge or the world of the truth-goodness-beauty. It is only the limit point that tries to reflect such a self-awareness of absolute nothingness under historical conditions. Nevertheless, Professor Nishida's system thinks of consciousness-in-general or its intellectual mode as the intelligible self as the absolute that generally sees the idea and does not seem to recognize its status as being historically conditioned. It is not a coincidence that Professor Nishida calls the intelligible universal the universal of intellectual intuition in the first half of this book. It is taken to be that which absolutely reflects the final self-awareness of absolute nothingness from the standpoint of the intellectual intuition in creative reason. The historical conditions that arise due to the separation made by the rift between the absolute nothingness and irrationality are not at all discussed as problems. He only claims that history is one level more concrete than the idea, that the former cannot be loaded on to the latter, and that history is not to be understood merely as the determination of the intelligible universal, but rather as something that transcends it. Yet, he does not give any account of how the intelligible universal is conditioned by history. If the historicity of the idea is ignored only by claiming the irrationality of history, will the idea have no choice but to become something completely divorced from reality? The idea conditioning history is only possible when history, in turn, conditions the idea. The idea must be both trans-historical and historical. Its historicity must always be the differential that remains in consonance with history. It cannot be that which covers everything with all finite values and sublates historicity. Nevertheless, in Professor Nishida's system of self-awareness, because the self-awareness of absolute nothingness constitutes the final universal that subsumes the whole, the idea also becomes absolute as that which reflects this [self-awareness], and thereby tends to trans-historically constitute the intelligi-

ble world of objective truth, goodness, and beauty. In this way, as I
stated in the beginning of this article, [this system] cannot actively
ground the irrationality of history and even though it claims that acting contains a contradictory nature, it does not sufficiently clarify
how this is the case. As a result, the living reality is changed into the
shadowy existence, acting becomes a mere roundabout path to seeing, and the standpoint in which all becomes the self by turning the
self into nothingness becomes the ultimate. Even I myself have respect
for such a profound religious experience, but I wonder that this philosophy gives us reason to fear the espousal of contemplative detachment from reality if it does not only take such a position [of absolute
self-awareness] as its limit [case] and move towards this relations, but
also actively takes it as the ground of its system. Is it not philosophy
that which defends an incomplete standpoint, only dwelling in the
infinite movement reflected upon within the limit relation to an
absolute, and precisely because it has the unbridgeable gap, holds the
power of life lying in reality through acting? That "acting" exhaustively absorbs "seeing" violates the essential significance of philosophy. I cannot help but being skeptical about the process of turning
philosophy into religion. My doubts regarding the interpretation of
Kant's consciousness-in-general also arrives at the same conclusion.

　　To this point, I have expressed my fundamental questions regarding Professor Nishida's philosophy with the utmost frankness. I would
like to apologize here for my bluntness. I humbly beg his pardon and
generosity.

NOTES ON CONTRIBUTORS

MARGARET CHU (The Royal Commonwealth Society in Hong Kong) has taught variously in Germany, Hong Kong, Macau, the Mainland, and the UK. She has worked for think-tanks, free-lanced for the South China Morning Post, and served as executive council members of the English-Speaking Union in HK and Peace International. She was also a member of the Royal Over-Seas League, London. Her research interests include the relationship between history and philosophy, philosophy and education, politics and philosophy, Confucianism & Neo-Confucianism, people's movements and revolutions.

MAITREYEE DATTA is currently associate professor of Philosophy at Jadavpur University, Kolkata, India. Her previous publications include, "Does a Philosophical Probe into Our Experience of Temporal Passage determine Its Status?" *Axiomathes* (March 2019), "Is Tense Real: A Nyāya Buddhist Controversy," *Mind and Cognition: An Interdisciplinary Sharing*, A Festschrift Volume on Amita Chatterjee, eds., Kuntala Bhattacharya, Madhucchanda Sen, and Smita Sirker (New Delhi: D. K. Printworld, 2019). Her research interests are philosophy of time, metaphysics, and Buddhism.

QUẢNG HUYỀN 廣玄, secular name TRẦN KHẢI HOÀI 陳啓懷, is an ordained Buddhist monk of Đạo Sơn Pagoda (renamed Xá Lợi Pagoda 2005) in Frederick, Maryland. His previous work includes his temple's publication of *Dharma Mountain Buddhism and Martial Yoga* (Chùa Xá Lợi, 2007). He is currently pursuing a doctorate in Sino-Vietnamese Studies (Hán Nôm Học) at Cornell University. His dissertation explores the sixteenth-century prophet Nguyễn

Bỉnh Khiêm (1491–1586), his literary legacy, and his remembrance through storytelling, religion, and prophecy.

ADRIAN KREUTZ (University of Amsterdam) researches analytic philosophy and political theory. He has published original articles and review essays on Buddhist logic and ethics in *Comparative Philosophy* and *Philosophy East & West*. He is especially interested in comparative analysis between Madhyamaka, Zen, and paraconsistent logic. Besides that, he is working on normative issues in political theory.

TAKESHI MORISATO (Sun Yat-Sen University) currently serves as the editor of the *European Journal of Japanese Philosophy* (EJJP), the book series, "Studies in Japanese Philosophy" (Nagoya: Chisokudō Publications) and "Asian Philosophical Texts" (Milan: Mimesis International). Additionally, he works as the regional editor of the "Bloomsbury Introduction to World Philosophies" (London: Bloomsbury) and the associate editor of the *Journal of East Asian Philosophy* (New York: Springer). His previous publications include, *Faith and Reason in Continental and Japanese Philosophy* (London: Bloomsbury, 2019), and his research interests are in metaphysics, philosophy of religion, the Kyoto School, metaxology, and world philosophies.

ROMAN PAŞCA is assistant professor at the Department of Japanese Philosophy at Kyoto University's Graduate School of Letters. He currently serves as vice-president of the European Network of Japanese Philosophy (ENOJP). His research focuses on the development of the concept of "nature" in premodern Japanese philosophy, especially in the works of Edo period philosophers like Andō Shōeki, Yamagata Bantō, Ishida Baigan, Ninomiya Sontoku, etc. He is also working on the relation between nature and self within the frame of environmental ethics. His publications include *Nature, Self and Language: the Philosophy of Andō Shōeki* (forthcoming 2020).

NA SONG (University of Göttingen) is currently working on her doctoral thesis under the title of "The Transformation of Guanxue Holism in the Late Qing and early Republican period through a case study of the Yanxia School (煙霞學派)." Her research interests are Chinese intellectual history, Confucianism, modernity, and Conservatism.

CODY STATON (Sun Yat-Sen University) holds a PhD in philosophy from KU Leuven (Belgium). He has been a Visiting Scholar at The Hong Kong University of Science and Technology and is currently affiliated with Sun Yat-Sen University (Zhuhai, China) as a Research Associate. He is a founding member of the European Network of Japanese Philosophy and serves as a review editor for numerous publishers. His research and publications focus mostly on Kant, topics dealing with the imagination, aesthetics, Japanese philosophy, and intercultural approaches to philosophy.

RICHARD STONE (Hokkaidō University) is currently working on a doctoral thesis disclosing the historical background and formative process of Nishida's early philosophy. His research interests include modern intellectual Japanese history and Kyoto School philosophy.

YIJING ZHANG (Sun Yat-Sen University) received her PhD in philosophy from Sorbonne University in 2016. Her publications include (English, French, and Chinese) articles on the translation and the reception of European philosophy in China and of Chinese philosophy in Europe, with an emphasis on the relationship between language and thought. She has translated Gaston Bachelard's *La Poétique de l'espace* into Chinese and now she is preparing a French commentary on the first Chinese translation of Aristotle's *Categories* made by Jesuits in the seventeenth century. She is a member of the editorial board of the collection "Studies in French philosophy" (Shanghai: Shanghai Renmin Publications). Her research interests are Greek-Chinese comparative philosophy, French philosophy, and the history of western Sinology.

Printed by
Geca Industrie Grafiche – San Giuliano Milanese (MI)
February 2020